P9-EFH-112

Yale Historical Publications, Miscellany, 106

The Downfall of the Anti-Semitic Political Parties in Imperial Germany

Richard S. Levy

New Haven and London   Yale University Press

1975

Designed by John O.C. McCrillis
and set in Baskerville type.
Printed in the United States of America by
The Murray Printing Co., Forge Village, Mass.

Published in Great Britain, Europe, and Africa by
Yale University Press, Ltd., London.
Distributed in Latin America by Kaiman & Polon,
Inc., New York City; in Australasia and Southeast
Asia by John Wiley & Sons Australasia Pty. Ltd.,
Sydney; in India by UBS Publishers' Distributors Pvt.,
Ltd., Delhi; in Japan by John Weatherhill, Inc., Tokyo.

For My Father

Acknowledgments

This book began as a dissertation directed by Henry A. Turner of Yale University. His sympathetic understanding and intellectual rigor were what I needed most in the early stages of this work. My special thanks go to him. My thanks also to Hans Gatzke and the late Hajo Holborn who encouraged me to investigate the problem of German anti-Semitism, read the manuscript, and aided me with sound advice. For forcing me to rethink and expand my conception of this work I am grateful to the late John Snell of the University of North Carolina and Werner T. Angress of the State University of New York, Stony Brook. Many others have helped me along the way, and I should like to mention a few of them: David Jordan of the University of Illinois at Chicago Circle, whose friendship and intelligence helped me through several dark moments; the staffs of the Wiener Library, London, and the Jewish Reading Room of the New York Public Library for their courteous assistance; the University of Massachusetts department of History, for releasing me from teaching duties in the winter and spring of 1970 in order to do further research and begin revision; George L. Mosse of the University of Wisconsin and Peter G. J. Pulzer of Oxford University, for helping me locate valuable source material; and Therese Weiss of the University of Illinois at Chicago Circle, for her careful preparation of the manuscript.

My debt to these and many others is great, and it is a pleasure to acknowledge them here. Of course, for what follows the final responsibility is solely mine.

Chicago
May 1974   R.S.L.

vii

Contents

Introduction

The history of the anti-Semitic political parties of the German Empire is a history of failure. By 1914 these parties were thirty years old and not one of their declared or undeclared objectives was realized. They had been unable to pass a single indisputably anti-Jewish measure through the Reichstag. In twenty-seven years of parliamentary activity, anti-Semitic politicians managed to bring only seven anti-Jewish bills to the stage of plenum debate. On the eve of the First World War the signs of dissolution were clear. Leaders were dead or out of touch with the new generation. The party faithful had dwindled. Their organizations and publications collapsed and folded. Prominent anti-Semites were disgraced by scandal, derided for their demagogy, and pitied for their ignorance. Parliamentary anti-Semitism had failed on its own terms and on those of its friends and enemies. This verdict was general.

The near destruction of European Jews has so overshadowed this early defeat of German anti-Semitism that historians have been persuaded to see in this period the "origins of totalitarianism" or a "rehearsal for destruction." Historians interested in the genesis of Nazism find in late nineteenth-century anti-Semitism examples of the "Nazi personality" and prototypes of National Socialist organization and technique. They study the careers of early anti-Semitic politicians only in so far as they foreshadow those of later activists in the Weimar Republic and Third Reich. Unfortunately, this search for parallels and prototypes distorts the history of the nineteenth century. Categories and analyses that work for Nazi Germany work less well when imposed upon Wilhelminian Germany. The forms, the leaders, the theory of political anti-Semitism in the nineteenth century have been reduced to a symbolic importance. To establish a presupposed link between anti-Semitism in the empire of Bismarck and the Reich of Hitler, the most significant fact of the earlier phenomenon, its failure, has been ignored or denied. All the recent

1

works on imperial anti-Semitism, no matter how much they vary in value, share this basic assumption of continuity.

This study questions the assumption and the fact of continuity, yet owes much to previous interpretations of German anti-Semitism. The work of Paul W. Massing, *Rehearsal for Destruction: A Study of Political Anti-Semitism in Imperial Germany* (New York, 1949), deserves special mention. Massing's analysis of Wilhelminian social forces and his description of anti-Semitism in the political context of the empire are of lasting value. Sensitive psychological portraits of anti-Semites, judicious assessment of the limited sources at his disposal, and frank discussion of the significant questions concerning anti-Semitism are among Massing's many virtues. My debt to him is considerable, but we disagree on many points of interpretation and emphasis. The most basic difference is announced in our titles. Massing sees a direct link between imperial and Nazi anti-Semitism. The failure of parliamentary anti-Semitism in the *Kaiserreich* was not definitive. It was an unsuccessful dry run that paved the way for the Nazis. The early movement did not win sufficient response from Germans because the time was not yet ripe; or, to continue his metaphor, neither the theater nor the audience was ready. In contrast, I see imperial anti-Semitism as qualitatively different from the Nazi variety. Its program was far more limited, and it failed through human actions, not historical providence.

A more recent full-scale treatment of the subject is Peter G. J. Pulzer's *The Rise of Political Anti-Semitism in Germany and Austria* (New York, 1964). Pulzer's extensive rather than intensive approach and his extremely broad conception of "political" have produced a wide-ranging survey of all aspects of imperial anti-Semitism. The book rests, however, on the unspoken assumption that the anti-Semitism of the empire is important only as far as it adumbrates Nazi anti-Semitism. His main interest is in the "forerunners of Nazism," in organizations and individuals that I consider to be of peripheral importance. Those anti-Semites who struck an "unpolitical" pose and railed against parliament were acting out a different sort of politics, as Pulzer points out. But to emphasize them because their behavior seems Nazi-like distorts the picture. In imperial Germany the most prevalent variety of anti-Semitism was deliberately parliamentary. The parliamentary anti-Semites held center stage, and their agitation was uppermost in the minds of contemporary Germans. They were of two kinds: 1) those whose primary purpose was to enact anti-Jewish legislation, and 2) those who were willing to foster and use anti-Semitism in order to marshal support for other aims not directly touching upon Jewish life. Both kinds of parliamentary anti-Semitism are closely studied in what follows, but the central focus is on the first, the parties which proclaimed anti-Semitism an end in itself.

Hans-Jürgen Puhle examines the second kind of parliamentary anti-Semitism in his *Agrarische Interessenpolitik und preussischer Konservatismus im wilhelminischen Reich, 1893-1914* (Hanover, 1966). Puhle details the exploitation of anti-Semitism by the Agrarian League and German Conservative party but touches only briefly on the anti-Semitic political parties themselves. He denies both the failure of political anti-Semitism in the *Kaiserreich* and the slackening of its tempo in the decade before the war, a development which almost every other historian accepts. The decline of the anti-Semitic political parties, Puhle argues, was matched by the steady growth of the empire's most powerful pressure group, the Agrarian League. He asserts that the league created, diffused, and passed on a potent blend of anti-Semitic racism, nationalism, and imperialism, first to the German Conservative party and then to the Nazis. The league, therefore, is the link between the empire, the Third Reich, and Auschwitz. The Agrarian League was indeed one of the most powerful right-wing groups disseminating anti-Semitism. But the all-embracing importance attributed to it by Puhle is, at least as far as anti-Semitism is concerned, not warranted by the facts. There is evidence to suggest that the league lost some of its credibility by 1914, not only with the German public, but even with parts of the Conservative party. This is especially true of the league's anti-Semitism. In 1913 and 1914 the Conservatives showed intentions of turning away from use of outworn and thoroughly discredited anti-Semitic techniques first popularized by the anti-Semitic political parties.

Yet Puhle performs a valuable service by calling attention to a type of anti-Semitism which, while clearly political, did not exercise its greatest influence in the German parliaments. For a number of powerful right-wing organizations anti-Semitism became an overt or covert part of the defense of social and economic privileges. The anti-Semitism of pressure groups and vested interests had political effects that often reinforced but sometimes ran counter to the goals of the parliamentary anti-Semites. The failure of the anti-Semitic parties cannot be correctly assessed without reference to this more broadly defined political anti-Semitism. However, a useful distinction between the anti-Semitism of the parties and that of the pressure groups like the Agrarian League can be made at the outset. The anti-Semitism of the Agrarians, as poisonous as any other, was strictly subordinated to the economic and political interests of large-scale agriculture. This cynicism always struck the anti-Semitic parties as demagogic: the use of their sacred cause for ulterior and selfish motives. They suspected, and rightly so, that neither the Conservatives nor the Agrarians fully appreciated the Jewish danger or cared much about solving the Jewish question. Such anti-Semitism by itself was not likely to lead to the kind of anti-Jewish actions desired by the "sincere" anti-Semites or the more violent ones actually carried out by the Nazis. One of the greatest failings of the anti-Semitic parties of the empire was their inability to recruit the German right to their own brand of "sincere" anti-Semitism.

H. Schleier and G. Seeber, "Zur Entwicklung und Rolle des Antisemitismus in Deutschland von 1871–1914," *Zeitschrift für Geschichtswissenschaft* 9 (1961), make a strong case for the underlying economic causes of parliamentary anti-Semitism. Its growth and decline as a mass movement was directly related to the condition of the German economy. The crash of 1873 and the uneven recovery of the next twenty years were reflected in the birth and growth of the parties. The economic upsurge of the mid-1890's initiated their decline. Schlaier and Seeber see parliamentary anti-Semitism as a protest movement of the economically endangered—and, I would add, politically neglected—classes of German society. But despite these truths, an exclusively economic theory of causation is sometimes misleading. In the differing contexts of Hessian, Prussian, and Saxon anti-Semitism, economics played a large role. But the economic interests and fears of anti-Semites varied greatly from one part of Germany to another. A serious weakness of the anti-Semitic parties was that they could not attract backers with recognized, common economic interests. Moreover, economic causes alone do not clarify the form or content of anti-Semitism. Political anti-Semitism appealed to the Protestant but not the Catholic peasants of Hesse, though both suffered from exactly the same economic problems. Some areas of Germany continued to respond favorably to anti-Semitism long after the economic situation improved. Finally, economic considerations shed little light on the religious and cultural roots of Jew hatred in Germany or on the symbolic roles Jews were forced into by anti-Semitic propaganda.

The sudden appearance of political anti-Semitism not only in Germany but all over Europe at the end of the nineteenth century has set Hannah Arendt, *The Origins of Totalitarianism* (2nd ed., New York, 1958) looking for a European, not simply a German, explanation of the phenomenon. She dispenses with the traditional theories that stress religious bigotry, scapegoatism, or extreme nationalism in favor of a more modern development—the decline of the nation-state. The Jew helped create the modern state, played a key role in the functioning of the state system, and then became identified with state authority. With the decline of the nation-state in the "age of imperialism," Jews lost their mediating function, the justification for their apparent wealth and supposed power. In response to the crisis of industrialization in the last half of the nineteenth century, several social classes came into conflict with the state and hence with the Jews, who were most closely and completely identified with the state. Arendt's is a brilliant thesis even if many of its particulars are both vague and moot. But the universal explanation does not stand up well for Germany. Those groups with the clearest grievances against the Wilhelminian state, the workers and the Catholics, proved the least vulnerable to parliamentary anti-Semitism. Furthermore, with the Nazis clearly in mind, Arendt exaggerates the "internationalism" of German anti-Semitism, overemphasizes the oppositional nature of the anti-Semitic political parties, and attributes to them revolutionary intentions they did not have.

Arendt's attempt at a synthesis is important. This book, however, is more limited in its aims. The origins of the twentieth-century catastrophe lie in the German past, but before we can synthesize we must work through the evidence of political anti-Semitism in the German Empire. Only after this has been done can we deal with the problem of continuity. This history of parliamentary anti-Semitism in Wilhelminian Germany is a contribution, however modest, toward an ultimate synthesis.

Why did parliamentary anti-Semitism fail in the German Empire?

What was the significance of that failure for later disaster? These are the questions I want to answer. I concentrate on the major anti-Semitic political parties in the context of their times and accept their activities as a genuine response to contemporary needs and views. I discuss the goals, methods, and personalities of anti-Semitic politicians and tell the story of the growth, transformation, and dissolution of parliamentary anti-Semitism in the *Kaiserreich*. In addition, an investigation of the resistance to (and, in some cases, complicity with) anti-Semitism on the part of Jews and non-Jews, Reich and state governments, political parties and private individuals is of major importance. In the conclusion to this study I attempt to assess the state of German political anti-Semitism, in its broadest terms, on the eve of the war. I raise but certainly do not answer the question of continuity, the relationship of imperial to Nazi anti-Semitism.

Finally, some words of caution. The definition of "anti-Semitism" I use is not without its shortcomings, but it is sufficient for the task I have set myself. I distinguish between anti-Jewish sentiment, fairly widespread throughout much of European history, and the organization and utilization of that sentiment to some end. The anti-Semites who appear here are men who wanted to act, and move the state to act, on their sentiments. I say also little about the psyche of the individual anti-Semite and anti-Semitism as an emotional disorder.

The reader will not find in these pages either a general history of the German Empire or of the Jewish people in Germany. Episodes from both histories are discussed only when relevant to the activities of the anti-Semites. In particular, it may strike some readers that I am not sufficiently interested in the Jewish response to anti-Semitism or the crisis of Jewish identity which it provoked. It is not for want of sympathy with those struggles that I concentrate on other things. It is because my subjects, the anti-Semites, cared little about the reaction of their victims. Finally, I cannot pause to expose and destroy centuries of infamous anti-Semitic lies. Suffice it to say that I do not subscribe to the still popular "grain of truth" theory. Wrongdoing by individual Jews does not explain anti-Semitism. At most such wrongdoing feeds the hatred of the already ill willed. There was indeed a complex problem caused by the self-conscious adaptation of Jews to German life. This "Jewish question," recognized by Germans and Jews of goodwill, was not beyond a reasonable and peaceful solution.

But the "Jewish question" as formulated by the anti-Semites was no question at all. It was a passionate denial of the possibility of German-Jewish community, resting on prejudice, distortion, and untruth. It would be idle to suggest that the charges of anti-Semites have been refuted by time and tragedy, or that they no longer trouble the world. At issue here, however, is not the "truth" of anti-Semitism, but its frightening ability to move men.

CHAPTER 1

Setting the Pattern, 1878–1887

> Struggle is part of all historical movements. It is unavoidable.
> But that struggle can be waged in an honorable way, on the
> basis of our law and our morality.
>
> Paul Förster (1888)

"Just as surely as the mouse never eats the cat, the Jew can never become a true Christian." An unknown artist inscribed this popular sentiment on the Freising cathedral in Bavaria. It stood beneath a picture of a sow giving suck to piglets and a Jew, the repulsive *Judensau*, found also in Wittenberg, Magdeburg, Regensburg, Kehlheim, Heilbronn, Wimpfen, Heiligenstadt, and on many other German churches. The slurs on Jewish character as expressed in the symbol and the saying—cunning, treachery, perversity, filthiness, and inferiority—have proved as durable as the granite of the cathedrals. Throughout the centuries they recur constantly in literature, song, and caricature. The emotion charged connotations of the *Judensau* are never very far from the surface of more "refined" attacks by successors of the unknown artist. Not the oldest piece of evidence, or confined only to Germany, the *Judensau* is a striking example of the long tradition of Jew hatred among the Germans.

Upon this tradition the anti-Semites of the German Empire built their movement. They drew heavily on the past to formulate and corroborate their indictments, to gain easier acceptance for their claims, and to give their cause a degree of historical respectability. In order to gather "proof" for their polemics against Jews, anti-Semites went beyond the folk wisdom of the Freising cathedral. They raided the German classics and distorted the views of world-famous poets, historians, and philosophers. Lessing, Goethe, Herder, Humboldt, and Hegel had written on Jewish-German relations, that is, on what came to be called "the Jewish question," in a relatively

8

impartial way. With unscrupulous editing and quoting out of context, anti-Semites managed to use the words of these great and humane men to convey their own hatreds. But even without this distortion, the anti-Semitic politicians and publicists of the *Kaiserreich* could draw from a large body of older anti-Jewish literature. Anti-Semitic tracts from the early eighteenth century, for example, established the standard misinterpretations of the Talmud and Schulcan Aruch that were employed in the imperial era.[1] Even Jewish writers contributed unwittingly to the arsenal of the anti-Semites. For with the gradual disappearance of the ghetto and the rapid weakening of traditional Jewish ties in the early nineteenth century, men like Ludwig Börne, Gabriel Riesser, and Heinrich Heine had made their self-conscious entries into German life. Through their own writings and those of their enemies, the private crises of these individuals had become public concerns.

The ideas of anti-Semitic politicians were also strongly influenced by the century-long discussion of Jewish emancipation. The debate over the first attempts to free the Jews of Prussia from widely varying legal restraints, for example, had produced a considerable and, at times, violently anti-Semitic corpus of writings.[2] From the last quarter of the eighteenth century, projects designed to remold the ethnic characteristics of Jews, forcing them by law to be "good Germans," had become common. Such plans reflected a widely held belief that Jews had to fulfill certain preconditions before being freed from ancient legal oppression.[3] Even those favorably inclined toward Jews, men of enlightenment like Lessing and Wilhelm von Humboldt, subscribed to this "contractual" idea of emancipation; they thought that some "improvements" were needed. Their undoubted goodwill consisted in believing that Jews would be more likely to assimilate and to make the changes deemed necessary, if first granted equality.[4]

The contractual interpretation of Jewish emancipation had still been much in evidence at the Prussian United Diet, convened by Friedrich Wilhelm IV in 1847. The delegates to this consultative assembly spent nearly two weeks deliberating on a uniform law to replace the eighteen different codes bearing on Jewish status in Prussia. The Diet debated whether Jews had made enough moral progress to merit an increase in political liberty, or whether they ought to be excluded from equal participation in a "Christian state."

In the assembly Jews found eloquent defenders and detractors; among the latter was the young Otto von Bismarck, whose anti-Semitic speech was frequently quoted by later anti-Semites. But none of the speakers suggested that Jews deserved complete equality as an inalienable human right. Not until the revolutionary year of 1848, when the Frankfurt National Assembly included complete civil equality among the fundamental rights of all Germans, was this possibility considered. Although every state except Bavaria gave Jews equal rights within the following year, this brief period of full freedom on the basis of the rights of man came to an abrupt end. The failure of the revolution and the resulting reaction allowed most German states either to rescind or to curtail Jewish rights and to reassert the idea of a contractual basis for emancipation.

In spite of renewed legal obstacles during the 1850's, Jews generally became more active in German life, adopting the German language in preference to Yiddish or Polish, taking part in municipal government, and holding honorary offices.[5] Individual Jews had played conspicuous roles in the revolution of 1848 and in the movement toward German unification of the next years. In both cases they drew favorable and unfavorable comment. The suddenly perceived presence of a number of Jews in political movements, cultural endeavors, or business enterprises occasionally produced a strong reaction from some segments of German society. These activities, the actual amount of Jewish participation notwithstanding, came to be labeled derisively as "Jewish monopolies." Thus, the conservative *Neue Preussische Zeitung* (*Kreuzzeitung*) referred to the *Deutscher Nationalverein*, an association which promoted German unity in the 1860's, as "Young Israel," although only thirteen of its one hundred and ninety founders were Jews.[6] Not only the Prussian nobility, but the middle classes too gave occasional expression to anti-Jewish bias in these years. Novels by Wilhelm Raabe (1831–1910) and Gustav Freytag (1816–1895) pitted the crafty, ambitious Jew against the honest, hardworking German. Both authors, favorites of later anti-Semites, portrayed sinister Jews engaged in petty trades as the most typical "Semites."[7] The less articulate artisans and peasant masses have left little evidence about their feelings toward Jews in the 1850's and 1860's. During the revolution of 1848, however, elements from both classes had been active against Jews, the peasants by resorting to violence and the hard-pressed craftsmen by launching petitions that called for government restrictions on unfair Jewish competition.[8]

Generally speaking, however, acts of violence and open expressions of anti-Jewish feeling were rare in the 1860's, a period of economic prosperity and rising expectations. The traditional antipathy of German for Jew remained submerged, rising to the surface of public life only briefly and then failing to strike a responsive chord in most Germans. Outwardly, ancient conceptions of the Jew seemed to be losing ground to more liberal ideas of human dignity and equality. With deceptive ease the Jews of Baden (1862) and Württemberg (1864) achieved full citizenship. On 3 July 1869, the Emancipation Law of the North German Confederation freed Jews from all limitations arising from religious affiliation. Upon the adherence of Bavaria to the German Empire in 1871, Jews all over Germany were granted *de jure* equality.

But once again, the period of unhampered enjoyment of civil rights proved short. In 1873 a great financial crisis swept Germany and, in the long run, did as much psychological as purely economic damage. The *Krach*, depression, and agonizingly slow recovery of the next twenty years put an end to the rosy optimism and the "live and let live" attitude which marked the early days of the new empire. Before a backdrop of persistent economic and psychological disorientation, latent hatred of Jews burst into the open.[9]

On the eve of that outburst, the Jews had never in their fifteen-hundred-year presence on German soil constituted a less cohesive group. What the anti-Semites called "Jewry" was in fact numerous, often hostile factions: orthodox and reformed, baptized, agnostic, and atheistic, East European immigrant and long-settled German, Yiddish and German speaking, the rich and well-to-do of Germany's commercial cities and the impoverished, who had become Germans after the partitions of Poland in the eighteenth century. As a group, the Jews of Germany stood ill prepared to face a concerted attack upon their well-being.

In the two decades prior to the *Krach* of 1873, Jews made use of greater economic freedom and, in some states, expanded civil rights to enter new occupations. The liberal professions beckoned especially to them, the more so because conservatively oriented state administrations remained closed or demanded conversion as the price of entry. Jews therefore came to be concentrated in the already highly competitive fields of law and medicine. By the 1870's liberal journalism became largely the province of Jewish reporters, editors, and publishers, particularly in the national capital of Berlin.[10] Although the various branches of commerce remained their main occupation, individuals undertook industrial enterprises that flourished in the late 1850's and 1860's. However, Jews took relatively little part in those industries that would undergo vast expansion in the last quarter of the century. The small-scale family firm, by which several Jewish entrepreneurs rose to momentary prominence, was about to be relegated to a minor position in the German economy. Similarly, the age of the Jewish banker was coming to an end. In the 1870's the numerous Jewish-owned banks with small capital were absorbed by more sizable Jewish banking houses, but the capital of these larger banks scarcely increased, while the powerful non-Jewish enterprises far outstripped them.[11] These economic developments, added to centuries of discrimination, produced a Jewish social structure markedly different from that of non-Jewish Germans. Except in Posen, few Jews were artisans or factory workers. Still fewer tilled the soil. Seeking better economic and educational opportunities, they participated in a general shift of population from the countryside to the city, but in proportionally much greater numbers than the population as a whole. They also attended public schools and universities in numbers out of proportion to their approximately one percent of the total population.[12]

By the date of legal emancipation, Jews had become conspicuous not only because of their position in the economy and visible concentration in urban areas but because of their politics as well. The political orientation of German Jews very nearly corresponded to the monolithic Jewry described by their anti-Semitic enemies. Since midcentury they had associated themselves with the liberal causes that bettered their lives and championed equality for all. The great majority of the Jewish electorate, perhaps as much as eighty-five percent in the 1870's, voted for one of the liberal parties.[13] As a result of their political affiliation, many prominent Jewish leaders were to be found in the camp of "free trade." For example, Eduard Lasker and Ludwig Bamberger, leaders of the National Liberal party, diligently promoted laissez-faire legislation in the Reichstag. The doctrine of free trade, however, was not a Jewish invention as the anti-Semites later claimed, but an article of faith for most liberals. Nonetheless, the disillusionment with liberal economics which followed hard upon the *Krach* of 1873 often took on a decidedly anti-Jewish emphasis. Some who speculated on the origins of the disaster stressed "Jewish responsibility." The fabled traits of Jews suddenly found embodiment in insolvent promoters with Jewish names. Although the business ethics of Jews and non-Jews probably differed little during the boom years 1867–1873, the number of "Jewish bankruptcies" appeared to many contemporaries as a serious misuse of recently won political and economic rights.

To those who lost heavily in the crash and to those who wished to use it as a prime example of dangerous defects in the new German Empire, any judicious assessment of "Jewish responsibility" proved unsatisfying. Several circumstances fed their suspicions and made it an easy matter for them to portray the *Krach* as a product of Jewish mendacity. The crisis had begun with the collapse of the Austrian *Creditanstalt,* a Rothschild banking concern. Lasker and Bamberger had sponsored the *Aktiennovelle* of 1870, liberalizing the formation of corporations with limited liability and leading to a massive increase in joint stock companies, many founded on flimsy capital and with clearly fraudulent intentions.[14] It made no difference that Lasker had courageously warned against widely prevalent financial abuses, accusing many high-ranking noblemen and government officials of misusing their powers and engaging in shady speculations.[15] In spite of his public stand, there was widespread willingness to believe in Jewish guilt and to ferret out Jewish-sounding names from the list of bankrupts. Otto Glagau, soon to become one of the leaders of the parliamentary anti-Semites, found immediate acceptance for his unfounded contention that ninety percent of the fraudulent bankrupts were Jews. In 1875 the journalist Joseph Cremer claimed on the scantiest evidence that Jews had launched the *Kulturkampf* to cover up their economic swindling. Articles later attributed to Cremer, which appeared anonymously in the right-wing Catholic newspaper *Germania,* demonstrated the usefulness of anti-Jewish sentiment for applying political pressure.[16] In the same year, the lesson was driven home again by the *Kreuzzeitung,* ultrarightist organ of the

German Conservative party, which featured a series of anti-Semitic articles by F. F. Perrot. Perrot attacked Bismarck, calling him a pawn of the Jews; his personal financial adviser, Gerson Bleichröder, was dubbed the "ruling banker."[17]

The *Germania* and *Kreuzzeitung* articles exploited the considerable anti-Jewish feeling occasioned by the *Krach* in order to criticize Bismarck's reliance on the liberal "Jew party," his laissez-faire economic policies, and the anti-Catholic legislation of the *Kultur-kampf*. However sincerely anti-Semitic the authors of these attacks were, their anti-Semitism was used to achieve ends not exclusively associated with the Jewish question. This "demagogic" brand of anti-Semitism rarely lasted longer than the political grievances which led to its adoption. With the gradual liquidation of the *Kulturkampf*, and after 1879 when Bismarck ceased relying on the liberal parties in the Reichstag and Prussian parliament, anti-Semitism as a political weapon disappeared from the official policy of the Catholic party. The Conservatives made only sporadic use of it in the next decades, primarily while in opposition to the government of the Reich during the 1890's.

Otto Glagau's commitment to anti-Semitism was of a different kind, neither expedient in nature nor of temporary duration. His was the "sincerity" of the fanatic. Until his death in 1892, he dedicated himself to organizing action against Jews. Through his pamphlets and his periodical, *Der Kulturkämpfer* (1880–1888), he kept up a drum-fire of charges against "the Jewish hydra." It was Glagau who first made the distinction between "demagogic" anti-Semitism as practiced by the Conservatives and the "sincere" anti-Semitism which he advocated.[18] The existence of "demagogic" anti-Semitism posed one of the most serious problems for the parliamentary anti-Semites of the *Kaiserreich*. Their relations with powerful groups which exploited them as well as their cause was to become a constant source of strife.

Whether demagogic or sincere, the anti-Semitic writings of the 1870's were remarkably similar in style and content. None of the polemics bothered much with proof, not even the specious statistical variety that later dominated the genre. Apparently, anti-Semitic writers did not need much hard evidence to convince an audience which shared many of their suspicions or required little persuasion in order to accept an indictment of Jews. The need for creativity was also minimal. Readily accepting the old charges against Jews—their conspiratorial ambitions, unshakeable solidarity, abhorrence of honest labor, and hatred of gentiles—the anti-Semites merely adapted and applied them to the contemporary world. In their all-embracing condemnations of Jews, their verbal violence, and their totally unreasonable response to the supposed misdeeds of some Jews, the writings of the 1870's fixed the pattern for all future agitation. The Jewish stereotype soon became rigid; elements could be added, but none deleted. For example, the myths of the all-powerful Jewish banker and the "Jewish press" long outlived their links with reality, surviving the *Kaiserreich* and the Weimar Republic despite the facts.

Saddling Jews with responsibility for the economic crisis of 1873 served merely as a point of departure for the anti-Semitic publications of the 1870's. At first accused of a financial swindle, the Jews were quickly identified as the primary cause of all the evils of German national life. They appeared as the crafty enemy, an alien force with international connections and bent on conquest. One of the most forceful statements of this expanded view of Jewish guilt was offered by Glagau:

> Actually, they dominate us. They possess a dangerous superiority of power and exert the unhealthiest influence. Once again as in centuries past, an alien tribe, so small in number, rules a truly great nation. All of world history has no comparable example of a homeless people—a physically and psychically degenerate race—commanding the globe by means of mere cunning and slyness, usury and shoddy dealings.[19]

True, Glagau argued, in mere numbers they were weak, but they controlled the commanding heights of the economy. In their hands the stock exchange, banking, and the press had become the means of conquering Germany and the whole non-Jewish world. Another extremely popular anti-Semitic pamphlet by Wilhelm Marr (1819–1904), *The Victory of Jewry over Germandom*, also displayed little doubt about the cause of Germany's troubles. Posing as the "dispassionate chronicler" of German disaster, the author described the "eighteen-hundred-year war" consciously and successfully waged by Jews against Germans. Marr, a Hamburg publicist and inventor of the term "anti-Semite,"[20] blamed the Jews for all the ills and weaknesses of the nation. There had been a time when German intellectual as well as physical resistance could have prevented the imminent disaster, but, alas, that time had passed. All-conquering "Jewish realism" had nearly achieved the total "Jewification" (*Verjudung*) of Germany and the world.[21]

For the anti-Semites of the 1870's, the Jewish problem had taken on greater dimensions than ever before. In addition, three other factors differentiated their literary outpourings from most earlier writings on the Jewish question. First, they reached a far greater audience than formerly. Glagau's exposés appeared serially in the *Gartenlaube*, a middlebrow periodical with approximately 270,000 subscribers.[22] Marr's *Victory of Jewry* was reprinted thirteen times in its first year. Both the *Germania* and *Kreuzzeitung* were widely read journals. Along with the best sellers of Marr and Glagau, hundreds of lesser known anti-Semites helped disseminate the Jewish stereotype in cheap, easily obtainable pamphlets and newspapers.

Second, whereas even the enemies of the Jews had previously felt compelled to mention the possibility of Jewish assimilation, if only to reject it, from the 1870's on, the notion that Jews might become good Germans became less obligatory for anti-Semites even to discuss.[23] Partially responsible for this growing certainty of "Semitic otherness" were the racial theories of the Renaissance scholar and French diplomat, Count Joseph Arthur de Gobineau (1816–1882), popularized in Germany by Richard Wagner and Ludwig Schemann.[24] Later, the extension of Darwin's biological discoveries to the realm of social problems reinforced the anti-Semites' conception of a bitter struggle for survival between the races, a war ordained by nature itself.[25] There were important exceptions among the anti-Semites who, like Adolf Stoecker and Heinrich von Treitschke (discussed below), refused to disqualify Jews from membership in Germandom solely because of race. But for most, concern was with the harmful potentialities and immediate dangers of the Jewish presence.

Third, although many of the anti-Semitic authors of the 1870's described the process of Jewification as irreversible or already far advanced, all the "sincere" anti-Semites nevertheless called for resistance to the Jewish onslaught, recommending measures aimed directly or indirectly at Jews. Such was the explicit aim of new anti-Semitic organizations, the first of which was founded by Wilhelm Marr in 1879. On the last page of his *Victory of Jewry* (sixth edition), Marr announced the formation of the *Antisemiten-Liga* to rescue Germandom from the Jewish peril and "secure for the children of Teutons their full rights to office and dignity in the German fatherland." The league's statutes pledged members to the use of "lawful means" but was otherwise silent about how the task could be accomplished. Marr revealed in his next pamphlet, *Elect No Jews! The Way to Victory of Germandom over Jewry*, that he intended taking the struggle into the political arena. His *Antisemiten-Liga* sprouted branches in Berlin and Hamburg. In the pages of *Die Deutsche Wacht*, official organ of the league, Marr demanded a "parliamentarization of the Jewish question" and an end to the "abstract idealism which insists upon the equality of all men."[26] But the league did not prosper, and its founder left Berlin.

The first sustained attempts to utilize anti-Semitism as a political weapon took place in the national capital. The so-called Berlin movement started there in late 1878 and was closely connected to Chancellor Bismarck's "change of course." After passage of the Anti-socialist Laws in 1878, Bismarck ended his reliance upon the National Liberal party and the less frequent aid of the left-liberal *Fortschritts-partei*. The end of liberal predominance in national politics was marked by adoption of protective tariffs and reorganization of the civil service, from which unreliable liberal elements were purged, and by introduction of a socioeconomic reform program, to which the Conservatives and Centrists gave support. Under these new political conditions erstwhile allies became the new enemies of the day. Anti-liberal agitation emanating from the chancellor's office provided the climate in which the Berlin movement briefly flourished.

The central figure in the movement was Fourth Court Chaplain Adolf Stoecker (1835–1909). A graduate of Halle University, Stoecker had come to the attention of Kaiser Wilhelm I during the Franco-Prussian War because of his stirring "national" sermons on the battlefield near Metz. Throughout a thirty-year political career, Stoecker's oratorical ability remained his greatest asset, compelling the rapt attention of even his most ardent and skeptical enemies.[27] In 1877 he took over leadership of the Berlin city mission, which performed charitable works among the penurious masses of the capital. He quickly saw that the alienated workers could not be effectively ministered to unless their desperate economic situation were relieved. Early in 1878, therefore, he founded the Christian Social Workers' party (*Christlichsoziale Arbeiterpartei*) with the intention of bettering the lot of labor and, at the same time, winning back the souls of German workers from the atheistic, antinational Socialist Workers' party (renamed the Social Democratic party of Germany in 1890). The court chaplain espoused several of the Socialists' demands, notably those calling for direct taxation on income and inheritance and a normalization of hours in certain industries. From the Center party program he lifted a plank demanding abolition of work on Sundays and factory labor for married women or children.[28] However, Stoecker never freed himself from the suspicion that he was acting as a tool of throne and altar. He too obviously treasured his relations with the imperial court and high-ranking Junkers. The advocacy of labor legislation could not in itself overcome the implacable distrust of the workingman, as was clearly demonstrated by the Reichstag elections of 1878: in the three Berlin electoral districts where the Christian Socials ran candidates, the party received only 1,421 votes out of a total 53,718.[29]

Even before his disappointment at the polls, however, Stoecker had come to identify liberal "Manchesterite Jews" as the chief opponents of his economic reforms. Exasperated, he responded in September 1879 to a steady stream of criticism from the left-liberal press by branding it as a typical and regrettable outgrowth of modern Jewry's arrogance. His speech of 19 September, entitled "What We Demand of Modern Jewry," met with an enthusiastic response, and in the following months whenever he spoke on the Jewish question great crowds gathered to hear his flaming denunciations.[30] But the court chaplain now addressed an audience different from the one he had first tried to reach with his Christian socialism. Although "Workers" did not officially disappear from the party name until 1881, Stoecker's anti-Semitic speeches appealed primarily to the discontented *Mittelstand*. His new audience and the membership of the later anti-Semitic parties consisted of small shopkeepers, clerks, self-employed artisans, technicians, petty civil servants, primary and secondary school teachers, and the less successful or wealthy practitioners of law, journalism, and medicine.

The term *Mittelstand* is difficult to render into English because in German its meaning is imprecise. It designates no particular social class, if by class is meant a group with fairly uniform economic interests. Definitions usually excluded noblemen, proletarians, the upper middle class, and, less often, the peasantry, leaving a great middle stratum of German society as the *Mittelstand*.[31] In the late nineteenth and early twentieth centuries, the term masqueraded as sociological, but its real significance was ideological. Its literal meaning of "middle estate" recalled preindustrial society. The *Mittelstand*, according to Marxist prognosis and much contemporary non-Marxist opinion, was living on borrowed time: the steady progress of capitalism would soon crush it. Ever larger and more competitive units were about to displace the small businesses of *Mittelständler*. Similarly, their skills would become either obsolete or subject to the control of organized capital. The majority would soon fall helplessly into the ranks of the proletariat. Although the prediction erred in most respects, the fears of lost status and threatened livelihood resulted in powerful discontent. Formerly the bulwark of left liberalism, sections of the *Mittelstand* turned against liberalism and toward anti-Semitism during the 1870's.

An early example of this *Mittelstand* shift to the right can be traced in the career of Wilhelm Marr. An avowed apostle of progress, Marr was expelled from Switzerland in 1845 because of his "communist" agitation among artisans in the canton of Vaud. Back in his native Hamburg during the revolution of 1848, he edited a much-feared satirical journal and was one of the acknowledged leaders of the radical democrats. He later maintained that it was his experience during the revolution that made him an anti-Semite. Jews had conned well-meaning but naive radicals like himself into working for Jewish emancipation. When the emancipation proved to be one of the few measures to survive the failure of the revolution, Marr became suspicious. As a left-liberal member of the Hamburg legislature in the 1850's, he tried to alert his colleagues to the "Jewish swindle," but succeeded only in isolating himself completely.[32] "Semitic vindictiveness," according to his own pathos-filled account, soon made it impossible for him to earn a living as a journalist. Cut loose from his left-liberal friends, he wandered through North and Central America, from which he returned a convinced racist. In need of employment, he began to eke out a perilous living as a pamphleteer. One of his first works was a generally ignored anti-Semitic tract entitled *Der Judenspiegel* (Hamburg, 1862), in which he warned Germany to beware the kind of exploitation he had experienced at the hands of an "alien essence."[33]

For others, too, seeing the Jew as a personal nemesis rested on painful experience. In the early 1870's, Otto Glagau followed the path to the right marked out by Marr in the previous decade. As a reporter for the liberal *National-Zeitung*, Glagau had invested in shares of the Jewish-owned *Lindenbauverein* and lost heavily after the fraudulent concern folded. He turned to the writing of anti-Semitic plays and pamphlets and finally to the organization of an anti-Semitic political movement.[34]

Not all *Mittelständler* had such vivid experiences with "Jewish villains," nor was their break with liberalism so abrupt as that of Marr and Glagau. But many such "little men" were pushed to the wall by the crash of 1873. In the preceding boom years, they had speculated with small savings in a desperate attempt to sustain a well-defined social status. They invested in the riskiest ventures, which promised high returns and delivered bankruptcy instead.[35] Unable or unwilling to see their economic plight as the result of impersonal economic forces, many *Mittelständler* began lashing out at the laissez-faire policies of the "Jew-ridden" liberal parties. Whether personal losses and misfortunes or merely mounting insecurity were the causes, the *Mittelstand* clearly became the prime recruiting grounds for anti-Semitic organizations in the 1870's. From this group were to come the leaders of the anti-Semitic political parties as well as the great majority of the rank-and-file membership. Among the forty-four anti-Semitic Reichstag deputies elected between 1887 and 1912 were two nobles, one peasant, and not a single factory worker. All the others were of the *Mittelstand*, a striking confirmation of the vulnerability of this group to anti-Semitism.

In the autumn of 1879, Stoecker discovered and began cultivating his true constituency among the *Mittelständler* of Berlin. Although the Christian Socials did not formally write anti-Semitism into their program until 1896, the court chaplain's agitation became decidedly anti-Semitic as soon as he turned from the conversion of the proletariat to the winning of *Mittelstand* voters. With his first anti-Semitic speech in September 1879, he launched a new crusade aimed at breaking the near-monopoly of elective offices exercised by the left liberals in the national capital. For the struggle "to lay Berlin at the feet of the Hohenzollerns," anti-Semitism was a natural, but not an exclusive weapon of the Christian Socials. In the wake of Stoecker's turbulent agitation, but beyond his direct control, a new anti-Semitic enterprise was undertaken.

During the summer and autumn of 1880, an Anti-Semites' Petition circulated throughout Germany.[36] Its long preamble addressed to the Reich chancellor set forth the standard indictment of Jews. Through economic exploitation of "national labor," through conquest of power positions, this "alien tribe" verged on complete domination over the Aryan race. Prefaced by a clear allusion to the possibility of violence on the part of the masses, the petition urged upon the chancellor four measures to safeguard the nation: the prohibition or limitation of Jewish immigration, a special census of Jews living in Germany, exclusion of Jews from positions of governmental authority, and an end to the employment of Jews as teachers in public schools *(Volksschule)*. With only slight variations, these four points remained the basic program of all future anti-Semitic political parties for the duration of the German Empire.

The driving force behind the petition was Bernhard Förster (1843–1889), a teacher at the Friedrich preparatory school in Berlin, a lecturer at the Royal Academy of Art, and, later, the much-despised brother-in-law of Friedrich Nietzsche. In 1880 the erratic Förster got involved in a brawl with a Jewish businessman. Anticipating disciplinary proceedings which were certain to have resulted in his dismissal, he resigned his teaching position and began to take active part in the anti-Semitic agitation in Berlin.[37] While attending one of Richard Wagner's early Bayreuth festivals in the summer of 1880, he conceived of organizing a petition that would constitute "a plebiscite of the German people on the Jewish question." To carry out the project, Förster enlisted his brother Paul, an ex-army officer named Max Liebermann von Sonnenberg, and another school teacher, Ernst Henrici, all of whom were to become key figures in the development of parliamentary anti-Semitism. Within three months' time, eager volunteers solicited the signatures of 225,000 adult German males. By October 1880, 265,000 signed the document. Well over half the signatures came from Prussia; Berlin alone contributed twelve thousand.[38]

An implementation of the petition demands, the anti-Semites fully realized, would necessitate revocation of Jewish emancipation. But in their opinion, Jews had been granted citizenship on a conditional basis, that is, in exchange for the implied promise of total assimilation. According to Paul Förster, liberals had foolishly given equality to Jews in 1869 with no guarantee that they would give up their Jewishness.[39] Characteristically, the Jews had taken advantage of humane legislation without living up to their part of the bargain. "Emancipation in the true sense of the word," an anti-Semite later explained, "means full assimilation into the foreign body politic. Have the Jews really done this? Have they changed from Jews into Germans?"[40] The answer to these rhetorical questions was, of course, no. Anti-Semites were not the only Germans to believe that emancipation had been a contractual agreement. Nor were they alone in believing that Jews had failed to fulfill their part of the bargain.[41] But only the anti-Semites, with a few exceptions, insisted that the Jews were by nature incapable of honoring the contract, of becoming good Germans. The petition of 1880, like much of the anti-Semitic literature of the 1870's, adamantly denied the possibility of Jewish assimilation. Instead, the petition announced that it was time to strive "for emancipation of the German nation from a kind of alien domination which it cannot long tolerate."

Before the excitement engendered by the petition died down, a new anti-Semitic organization got its start in student circles around the universities of Leipzig and Berlin. The *Verein Deutscher Studenten* (Union of German Students), a breeding ground for activists in the cause of extreme nationalism, developed during the 1880's into the youth wing of the anti-Semitic political parties. According to one of its official histories, the *Verein* "arose and became great by means of the anti-Semitic movement of the 1880's . . . ." Stoecker and Liebermann von Sonnenberg maintained close relations with the student group, addressing annual conventions and cultivating its promising young leaders, like Friedrich Naumann and Hellmut von Gerlach.[42]

This forceful entry of anti-Semitism into German university life owed a measure of its success to the historian Heinrich von Treitschke, professor at the University of Berlin and editor of the *Preussische Jahrbücher*. In a series of articles appearing in the *Jahrbücher* for 1879 and 1880, Treitschke justified anti-Semitism as "a natural reaction of Germanic national feeling against an alien element. . . ."[43] His influence in making anti-Semitism at home in the university is beyond doubt, for such was his prestige and popularity among students that his utterances on the Jewish question possessed an authoritative character. His phrase, "the Jews are our misfortune," appeared on rubber stamps, at the head of many later anti-Semitic newspapers, and eventually became a favorite motto of the Nazis. Although he condemned exaggerated pictures of Jewish conspiracy and the unhistorical thinking involved in blaming Jews for all German woes, the professor occasionally campaigned for anti-Semitic candidates in the Berlin movement. For the educated he was a most effective demagogue.[44]

With the backing of the court chaplain and a famous German historian, anti-Semitism gained in respectability. But the greatest asset of the movement in its formative years was the apparent youth and energy of its adherents. In late 1880, the appeal of anti-Semitism for the young was once again demonstrated by the establishment in Berlin of the Social Reich party *(Soziale Reichspartei)*, the first openly anti-Semitic political party. Ernst Henrici, then only twenty-seven, established the new party on the strength of the petition agitation. Like Glagau, he began his political career in the camp of left liberalism, a speaker at meetings of the *Fortschrittspartei*. Dissatisfied by the laissez-faire aspects of the left-liberal position, he turned to the works of Ferdinand Lassalle, claiming later that they had had a great effect upon his party program.[45] Henrici set forth that program in a series of triumphal mass meetings beginning on 17 December 1880. The Social Reich party pledged loyalty to kaiser, Reich, and, especially, to the German people. It adopted the four demands of the Anti-Semites' Petition as the main objective for "any truly national party."[46] As was to be the case with every succeeding anti-Semitic political party, Henrici's advocated socioeconomic reforms to complement the anti-Semitic planks. In most respects this part of the program resembled that of the Christian Socials, that is, a collection of ideas from several different political competitors. However, unlike the Christian Socials, the Social Reich party stressed the need for greater concentration of powers in a centralized national administration. It also called for the creation of a national economic council *(Reichswirtschaftsrat)* and was the first German political party to urge the acquisition of overseas colonies.[47]

Another of the pioneering anti-Semitic political organizations spawned by the Anti-Semites' Petition was the *Deutscher Volksverein,* founded by Liebermann von Sonnenberg and Paul Förster in March 1881. This group's only programmatic innovation was to demand revocation of Jewish citizenship in clear terms. In its statement of purpose, the four petition demands became part of a projected aliens law which was to govern Jews after abolition of the Emancipation Law of 1869.[48] Like so many other anti-Semitic organizations during the imperial period, the *Volksverein* lived but a short time. Its only real importance was as a vehicle for the personality of Max Hugo Liebermann von Sonnenberg.

Born in West Prussia in 1848 of a landless Junker family, Liebermann followed in the footsteps of his father and uncle. At the age of eighteen he entered the Prussian Army just in time to miss the Austro-Prussian War of 1866, a great tragedy for this ardent patriot. He got his chance, however, during the Franco-Prussian War (1870–1871) in which he served bravely. Twice wounded and awarded the Iron Cross, he never forgot the glory of the war. In 1911, the year of his death, he confessed to never having recovered the sense of significance experienced in battle.[49] His political life was in a sense anticlimactic. Following the war, a promising career in the *Kriegsakademie* was cut short under less than honorable circumstances. Unable to make good on some personal notes, Liebermann, in his own words, "fell under the stranglehold of the usurers" while trying to get out of debt. He left the army in 1880 as a first lieutenant with a small pension. "This most German of men" took his military mannerisms, a love of giving orders and being obeyed, an intense nationalism, and a speaking style second only to Stoecker's in forcefulness into the political battleground of Berlin.[50] More than any other individual, Liebermann was able to stamp his own character upon parliamentary anti-Semitism during the imperial era. He presented the war against Jews as a struggle for the fatherland in the most noble tradition of true patriotism. He presented himself, in a poem which became his epitaph, as a knight in armor:

> What I know is right and good
> For that I'll stand and fight
> Honorably, and with visor open,
> My sword for the right.[51]

But Liebermann was too coarse and unchivalrous, too remorselessly witty, to be mistaken for some helpless Don Quixote. His sword whetted in Berlin, he went on to become one of the anti-Semites' ablest politicians.

In 1881 Liebermann and Henrici joined with Stoecker in the Berlin movement, which had become a loose coalition of parties and groups dedicated to freeing Berlin from left-liberal domination. The movement, enjoying covert government support, ran common candidates against the *Fortschrittler* in the Reichstag, Prussian state parliament, and Berlin municipal elections.[52] In April 1881, the coalition created a much-needed directing agency, the Conservative Central Committee, made up of representatives from the Conservative party, Christian Social party, advocates of a reformed guild system for artisans, renegades from the Center party, and the anti-Semites led by Henrici and Liebermann. The latter found it expedient to call themselves "independent anti-Semites" in order not to be confused with Stoecker and the Christian Socials.[53] Only common enmity toward liberalism tied the various factions of the central committee together. The individual objectives of the partners, on the other hand, conflicted with one another. The Conservatives sought a political foothold in Berlin. Stoecker, a member of the Conservative party group in the Prussian parliament for Minden (Westphalia) since 1879,[54] also maintained close relations with the state socialist, Adolf Wagner, who pressed for a more thorough program of social welfare legislation than the Conservatives could support. The main objective of the independent anti-Semites was revocation of Jewish emancipation, a goal never publicly endorsed by any member of the central committee.[55]

The Berlin movement marked the first attempt at cooperation between anti-Semites and other right-wing groups. Like all such attempts during the German Empire, this one too failed to please either the anti-Semites or their would-be allies. The alliance became strained almost immediately, when, in April 1881, the newly formed central committee issued an election manifesto devoid of overt anti-Semitism. Clearly appealing to the *Mittelstand,* the program could and did lend itself to the anti-Semitic interpretation placed upon it by most of the Berlin movement candidates for the Reichstag elections of 1881.[56] But Henrici and his followers objected to the timidity of the movement's official statement and to the Conservatives' "demagogic" manipulation of anti-Semitism. The most flamboyant of the independents, Henrici ignored the official guidelines of the central committee, repeatedly attacking his supposed allies in the Conservative party. He conducted a kind of "instinctive propaganda," availing himself of the anti-Jewish sentiment present in the capital and trying to intensify it. He proved particularly adept in outdoing Stoecker's essentially moderate anti-Semitic statements. For example, Stoecker as a Christian minister was bound to admit Jews to full participation in German life, after their "heartfelt" conversion to Christianity. But Henrici, like all the independents, was under no such compulsion. For him, the Jews were an alien race. Neither the baptismal font nor mixed marriage could transform them into Germans. In raucous public gatherings he made it clear that his party sought "permanent improvements" in the Jewish problem, not merely temporary advantages such as the removal of the left liberals from Berlin.[57]

For his allies in the Berlin movement and his more conservative colleague Liebermann, Henrici became a liability. In July 1881, his appearance in Neustettin (Pomerania) was followed by the burning of the local synagogue, the entry of Prussian troops, and the imposition of martial law. Although this kind of violence was rare in imperial Germany, Henrici's questionable tactics and ideas offered a convenient means of discrediting the whole Berlin agitation as rowdy, dangerous, and generally unrespectable.[58] The hard-pressed left liberals of Berlin took advantage of the opportunity to strike back at their enemies, labeling the Social Reich party "the worst of a gang of extremists."[59] After the bloody Russian pogroms of 1881, the liberals accused the anti-Semites of trying to introduce the same type of barbarism in Germany. The Conservative Central Committee, in response to adverse publicity, expelled Henrici in August 1881. But the young man, confident of his personal following, continued his candidacy for the Reichstag in the third electoral district of Berlin. In a defeat that was decisive for the Berlin movement, Henrici received the fewest votes of all, 843 to his opponents' 12,846. Of the official candidates for the movement, Liebermann made the strongest showing. Nevertheless, the *Fortschrittspartei,* led by its luminaries Eugen Richter and Rudolf Virchow, returned to the Reichstag in complete control of the capital.[60]

After the poor showing in the Reichstag elections of 1881, the anti-Semitic character of the Berlin movement and the role played by independent anti-Semites were much diminished. In the municipal elections of 1883, the Conservative Central Committee replaced the anti-Semitic organizations with citizens' leagues *(Bürgervereine)*. In spite of the "improved tone" of the movement, the central committee's candidates did no better at the polls. Until the mid-1890's, combined Conservative-Christian Social-anti-Semitic candidates succeeded in winning a few seats in the Berlin municipal council, but here, too, they exerted only negligible influence upon the overwhelming left-liberal majority.[61]

For the independent anti-Semites, the Berlin movement provided valuable political experience despite the poor election results. In the struggle for *Mittelstand* voters they imitated the left liberals and Socialists, their main competitors. They borrowed the election meeting, a method for insuring popular participation in the selection of party candidates developed by the left liberals in the revolution of 1848. Under anti-Semitic auspices this democratic political institution soon degenerated into a carefully rigged show of public support for a candidate chosen by a very few party leaders.[62] From the Socialist Workers' party the anti-Semites appropriated the mass meeting and developed it into a fine art. Liebermann and Henrici became acknowledged masters at staging these grandiose affairs. Typically, they began with patriotic songs and cheers for the kaiser. Then followed the introduction of notables, and a debate, lecture, or campaign speech, usually lasting two hours or more. When Socialists, armed with their own speakers and penny whistles, infiltrated a rally, the gathering devolved into an insult match or a singing contest in which *"Deutschland über Alles"* was pitted against familiar proletarian anthems. Anti-Semitic mass meetings in Berlin drew audiences ranging from a few hundred to two or three thousand. Eventually, the rally technique was employed all over Germany as a tool of anti-Semitic indoctrination, fund raising, and year-round electoral campaigning, as well as for occasional dramatic protest demonstrations.[63]

During the Berlin movement, the benefits of new political techniques were offset by the appearance of a serious weakness which was to plague all succeeding anti-Semitic enterprises—the lack of regular or adequate financing. The movement had no organized contribution system with which to meet the costs of free beer, meeting halls, and

election publicity. Individual donors, like the department store owner
Rudolf Hertzog, helped defray some of the expenses,[64] but the exact
sources of finance for the movement, as well as for the later anti-
Semitic political parties, remained unverifiable, producing many
unsubstantiated accusations discussed at length later in this study.
Wherever the money for agitation came from, it is certain that the
independent anti-Semites contributed little. The popular base of the
Social Reich party and Liebermann's *Deutscher Volksverein* was
restricted to the *Mittelständler* of the capital, who were not very
wealthy. Until the anti-Semites succeeded in increasing the number
of their *Mittelstand* followers—to make up collectively for what
individuals alone could not render—they remained dependent upon
the Conservative Central Committee for the requisite funds. As
long as they depended on the committee, however, the anti-Semites
were "independent" in name only.

The unsuccessful Berlin movement taught the anti-Semites involved at least one significant lesson about decorum. In casting about
for the cause of their failure, dignified anti-Semites like Paul Förster,
Stoecker, Glagau, and Liebermann seized upon Henrici's rowdyism.
Stoecker scolded him for the violence of his public remarks and his
name-calling, which impeded serious discussion of the Jewish question. Liebermann too took pains to disassociate himself from Henrici's extremism. *Radauantisemitismus* (rowdy anti-Semitism), these
gentlemen maintained, had alienated the respectable *Mittelstand*
voters and simply could not be tolerated now or in the future.[65]
Clearly, the respectable anti-Semites greatly outnumbered the rowdies, for, in a process which later assumed a ritual character, they
drove Henrici out of the anti-Semitic organizations. He lost control
of the Social Reich party in 1882. After several years' absence, first
in Togoland, then in America, where he married a woman of "mixed
blood," Henrici was unable to reenter anti-Semitic politics in Germany. Although some anti-Semites had referred to him, while safely
absent, as the "true father of anti-Semitism," none of the parties or
groups found room for him.[66]

In addition to norms of acceptable behavior, there came out of the
disintegrating Berlin movement two distinct types of anti-Semites.
A few individuals, emboldened by the failure of the movement,
began to speak out against dragging the Jewish question through the

mire of German politics. For men like Paul de Lagarde, Theodor Fritsch, Eugen Dühring, and Friedrich Lange, the power of the Jews over German life was symptomatic of a grave disease. Before eliminating Jewish influence, they argued, serious preparations had to be undertaken to rid Germany of the excrescences of modernity, of which the Jews were only one significant example. An inner revolution of the spirit would have to precede the reordering of the external world. Although these individuals were pronouncedly anti-democratic and harked back to a romantic, preindustrial ideal, they were not conservatives. They yearned for political power with which to rearrange their world in drastic fashion. They were, in fact, revolutionaries and will be referred to as such in this study. Most of the revolutionary anti-Semites were nonviolent, content to spend their lives in preparation for the revolution and prophesying, at least for the present, to an unreceptive audience. Common to all of them was the belief that Germany had to undergo purification and a long period of education before the implementation of sweeping changes. German culture had to be led back to "more moral forms," and only then would the "Jewish race be dealt with in a final way."[67] For the revolutionaries, the immediate need and emphasis was on regeneration of the German people, paving the way for a revolution which would see true Germanic values conquer all the evils of the modern age.[68]

Bernhard Förster, the chief organizer of the Anti-Semites' Petition, became in many ways typical of the "nonpolitical," revolutionary anti-Semite. After the petition failed to elicit a response from the chancellor, Förster rejected all ordinary political experiments as hopeless. His pessimism led to a total rejection of modern German life. He no longer felt at home in Germany, even among his anti-Semitic associates. Reforming the Bismarckian state was out of the question. An entirely new beginning had to be made. The degradation of the German people had gone so far that any effort to counteract it on German soil was bound to be fruitless. Thus, with some financial aid from the Paraguayan government and after two years of exploration (1883–1885), Förster established the colony *Neu-Germanien* on the La Plata River.[69] In the promotional literature for the experiment, he set forth the reasons for his despair in the "old" Germany:

The "old world" has in fact become old. It shows the clearest symptoms of decrepitude, of senile impotence, of incipient dissolution. . . . What is flawed and rotten in our modern society is just what society calls "educated, liberal, and humane"; the voter and the newspaper reader are products of our schools and our taverns. Our people are healthy only in so far as they are "uneducated." . . . They vote for some little Jew or lawyer or professor for "parliament." . . . They read long newspapers, smoke tobacco, drink beer, wear glasses and use canes they have no need of, and prefer the stale air of taverns and coffee houses. . . . Here in the classic land of "education," falsehoods, and corruption every honorable prophet will remain in the wilderness. No, the subtropic zone of the southern hemisphere is the land of our hope.[70]

Neu-Germanien, however, did not attract the necessary saving remnant of the German race, those unspoiled artisans and peasants, who, after a period of hardship and struggle, were to effect the redemption of Germandom. Internal dissension, climatic difficulties, Förster's vegetarianism, his overbearing spouse, and a loss of financial credit led to the disintegration of the colony and to its unhappy founder's suicide in 1889.[71]

Revolutionaries like Förster remained without lasting influence on the great majority of active anti-Semites in imperial Germany. Although elements of the revolutionary outlook began to make headway among anti-Semites after 1900, revolutionaries were unable to set the tone of the movement until just before World War I. Sometimes publicly honored and frequently quoted, they nevertheless either withdrew voluntarily or were pushed aside as the great majority of anti-Semites gravitated toward a parliamentary political solution to the Jewish question, a solution to be achieved within the legal framework of the German state. Men of this second type did not indulge in wholesale condemnations of modern culture. They believed in the new Germany and were generally at peace with recent German history. After all, in their youth they had experienced the realization of the dream of unity and creation of a strong state. They recognized certain faults and flaws in German life, but these were directly traceable to Jewish machinations, a certain amount of treachery or stupidity on the part of some highly placed Germans, and a lack of awareness in the overly good-natured, yet basically sound, German public. This second type of anti-Semite was far from revolutionary, and the revolutionaries in his midst, who shared his anti-Semitism, constantly embarrassed him.

Paul Förster, the brother of Bernhard but of altogether different temperament, longed for a solution to the Jewish question that would not sacrifice the respect of his contemporaries. A veteran of the Franco-Prussian War, he remained first and foremost a zealous nationalist, a man much more in tune with his times than Bernhard. Paul also held opinions about the origins of Germany's troubles that were far more typical of Wilhelminian anti-Semites than were those of his brother. "Surveying German history," he once said, "gains for one the conviction that all evil has come from the foreigner." The power of the Jews was no mere symptom or just one aspect of a graver German problem as the revolutionaries maintained, but the cause, the prime mover behind Germany's difficulties. "Jewish levellers," according to Paul Förster, were using un-German doctrines such as liberalism and socialism to "spread dissolution and to alienate the people from itself."[72] Although hatred and fear of Jews probably ran as deep in him as in the revolutionaries, Förster tried to clothe his anti-Semitism in contemporary fashions.

For men of Paul Förster's persuasion, a *Weltanschauung* resting on a sincere belief in Jewish conspiracy answered all doubts and fears about Germany's future. These conventional, as opposed to revolutionary, anti-Semites trusted in the kaiser, his chancellor, and the bulk of the German public. Although they, like many other of their fellow Germans, worried about incipient demoralization, the growing radicalism of exploited workers, and the disintegration of German cultural values, the conventional anti-Semites sought, or were open to, simple causes and simple remedies. To those in search of easy solutions for complex problems, the conception of the Jew as the root of all evil was eminently appealing. For the conventional anti-Semites, the aphorism of Otto Glagau became an all-embracing rationale and an abiding faith: "The social question is the Jewish question." What could be simpler or more comforting to those who believed in Germany? By directing efforts at the Jews, by reforming abuses which allowed them to flourish, these anti-Semites could save the nation while leaving it virtually intact. Very little had to be changed: some social and economic reforms, but no thoroughgoing revolution; exclusion of Jews from public schools, but no fundamental reorganization of national education; laws curbing Jewish power, but no radical restructuring of the Bismarckian state. Moreover, the job could be tackled soon, without waiting for the creation of new institutions or an inner revolution of the spirit.

The distinction between conventional and revolutionary anti-Semite is essential to the understanding of anti-Semitism in the German Empire. Nazi writers and most recent historians have imposed upon Wilhelminian anti-Semitism an artificial dichotomy between racists and nonracists. They have delineated a continuous growth of "racial consciousness" leading directly from the *Kaiserreich* to the Nuremberg Laws and beyond.[73] Nonetheless, the important distinction among anti-Semites of imperial Germany was not one of racial ideology. Almost all anti-Semitic publicists were racists from the beginning. Even the exceptions like Stoecker and Paul de Lagarde also made frequent use of the endemic racist terminology. Stoecker's Christian Social followers, though they adhered to the court chaplain's formula in the matter of "heartfelt" conversion and Jewish assimilation, worked from principles and arrived at conclusions indistinguishable from those of outright racists.[74]

The really significant division among anti-Semites in the imperial era came not on the issue of racism but rather on the question of strategy. A revolutionary minority willingly or unwillingly separated itself from those who sought a parliamentary solution which accepted and worked within the legally sanctioned institutions of the German state. Both revolutionary and conventional anti-Semites believed that the Jews were a separate, unassimilable, and dangerous race. But they had different expectations regarding the swiftness of victory over the Jewish enemy and different opinions about the sole importance of the Jewish problem.

The two types of anti-Semites were very much aware of their differences, although they did not often employ the designations used here. The revolutionaries observed the efforts of the optimistic, conventional anti-Semites with disdain, regarding them as just another sad indication of German degeneration. As much concerned with anti-Semitism's "good name" as the conventional anti-Semites, the revolutionaries constantly scolded them for attracting "racketeers" and rowdies like Henrici, who "squandered the moral wholesomeness of the movement."[75] The conventional parliamentarians, for their part, looked upon the revolutionaries as hopelessly utopian, however good their intentions. The less generous among them referred to the revolutionaries as "masked ball anti-Semites" because of their unrealistic politics. In newspaper articles and public appearances, conventional anti-Semites strove again and again to distinguish themselves from the unsettling revolutionaries.[76] During the imperial era, the revolutionaries were largely ignored by their German contemporaries. Like Bernhard Förster, they frequently felt the need to leave an inhospitable Germany which was not yet ready for or interested in their prophecies. It was the conventional anti-Semites who determined the character of political anti-Semitism in the *Kaiserreich*. Their essentially orthodox political ambitions first aroused anger, then fear, and finally resistance from many elements of German society.

In the decade of the 1880's, the idea that the Jewish question ought to be solved in the German parliaments by means of an anti-Semitic party gradually gained acceptance among the conventional anti-Semites over the opposition of the revolutionaries. However, the drift toward political organization was slow. The piecemeal failure of the Berlin movement and the experiments associated with it between 1882 and 1885 impeded the immediate formation of an independent, broadly based, and nationwide anti-Semitic political party. The uncertainty and hesitancy of these years were well illustrated by the rise and personal development of Liebermann von Sonnenberg. With the fizzling of his *Deutscher Volksverein,* Liebermann came to occupy a middle position between the "nonpolitical" revolutionaries and the less articulate majority of conventional anti-Semites. At first, he doubted the efficacy of parliamentary politics or the need for a separate anti-Semitic party. Yet, in spite of his doubts, he laid plans for just such a party, outlining some preliminary steps: "moderation, restraint, economy, good housekeeping, and a strong family sense" would break the hold of the Jews. Boycotts of Jewish businesses and a refusal to subscribe to the "Jewish press" were further measures urged by Liebermann to enable the creation of an anti-Semitic political party.[77] Until this preliminary program took effect, he held to the hope that existing political parties could be harnessed to the anti-Semitic cause. According to his analysis of the political situation in 1882, the left liberals, Socialists, and most National Liberals were already thoroughly Jewified. No help in the struggle against Jewry could be expected from them. But the situation was more promising with the healthy elements of the National Liberal party, the Center, and both conservative parties. In time, these could be invested with anti-Semitic content and thus be won over to an implementation of the demands contained in the Anti-Semites' Petition.[78]

Part of Liebermann's reluctance to form an independent political party stemmed from his ambivalent feelings about the German Reichstag. In one respect the institution was sacred, created and sanctioned by his two heroes, Otto von Bismarck and Kaiser Wilhelm I. On the other hand, he participated in a heated protest meeting in 1884 which urged the chancellor "to find a more representative institution" than the Reichstag, which had refused to vote the necessary funds for a new position in the foreign office.[79] Liebermann showed temporary interest in creating a new legislative body based on occupational and class divisions rather than universal suffrage. Throughout the 1890's and again after 1912, antiparliamentary, corporatist projects such as Liebermann's were advocated by elements of heavy industry, large-scale agriculture, and the bureaucracy and were usually accompanied by plans for a forcible revision of the franchise.[80] But Liebermann never developed his plan for the "social reorientation" of the state beyond a few vague generalities. Moreover, his doubts about the worthiness of the Reichstag gradually weakened. Eventually he, like most parliamentary anti-Semites, treated the German Reichstag with respect as long as it offered hope of success, and even long after that hope had lost all justification. Although often accused of being antiparliamentary, the conventional anti-Semites were far less so than the German Conservatives or Kaiser Wilhelm II, who on occasion referred to Reichstag deputies as "a band of apes" or "blockheads and dumbbells."[81] Liebermann was one of those who remained within the parliamentary framework, and, by the end of his twenty years as a Reichstag deputy, he was being considered as a possible vice-president of the parliament.[82]

In the 1880's, Liebermann's soldierly disposition prompted him to action rather than to a cautious weighing of the pros and cons of political organization. He thought of himself as a practical man, ill-suited for "pen pushing" or theorizing. From the first he shunned ideology in favor of practical organization and agitation. His avoidance of "unfruitful academic squabbles" separated him from his revolutionary friends. Thus, he remained in the background during the Dresden International Anti-Semitic Congress of September 1882, which was given over to a long-winded debate of eight theses presented by Adolf Stoecker. Bernhard Förster and Ernst Henrici took the lead in attempting to persuade the court chaplain to include more of the racist vocabulary and to muffle the religious overtones of his propositions.[83] The congress, attended by delegates from Russia, Austria-Hungary, France, and the Balkans as well as Germany, disbanded with only one concrete achievement to its credit, the creation of a steering committee grandly called the Universal Alliance for the Combating of Jewry. By means of the universal alliance, a second international congress was called for April 1883, to be held in Chemnitz.[84]

Before the second congress met, Bernhard Förster and Henrici left Germany. Stoecker, after the browbeating he received in the previous year at Dresden, boycotted the Chemnitz gathering, which only forty delegates took the trouble to attend. Into this leadership vacuum stepped Liebermann von Sonnenberg, the advocate of "reasonable anti-Semitism" and practical action. "The universal alliance," he announced, "must concern itself only with tasks and goals, the solution and attainment of which appear possible with the means and powers at hand."[85] The most serious opposition to Liebermann's "reasonable anti-Semitism" came from a Berlin contingent led by Dr. Ammann, a substitute for Henrici. Ammann obstinately advocated the adoption of Eugen Dühring's writings on the Jewish question as the ideological basis for the whole anti-Semitic movement. Dühring (1833–1921), a lecturer in economics and philosophy at the University of Berlin until his dismissal in 1877, had written *The Jewish Question as a Question of Race, Morals, and Civilization with a World-Historical Answer*.[86] He had a few followers in the anti-Semitic clubs of Berlin and Westphalia. But his hotheadedness, arrogance, and left-wing views made most conventional anti-Semites suspicious. At Chemnitz the delegates did not object to Dühring's convoluted racial theories. But his "practical" program, which included the "mediatization of Jewish money princes," came dangerously close to socialism. Even more distressing to the conventional anti-Semites were the antichristian strictures in Dühring's latest book, *The Replacement of Religion by Something More Complete*. In its pages, he rejected Christianity as nothing more than degenerate Judaism. The Old Testament, for him, was clever Jewish propaganda, the spirit of which had been smuggled into Christianity in its present form.[87] Typically, however, the conventional anti-Semites dealt more cautiously with the problem of Jewish influence on German-Christian culture. "Christianity" was written into the program of the *Deutscher Volksverein* and, of course, the Christian Social party. Talk in these circles about "positive," that is, purged Christianity was rare. Liebermann spoke for the majority when he asserted: "Anti-Semites are not antichristian or irreligious. It is not necessary to discuss the religious factor at all."[88]

Liebermann regarded the adherents of Dühring as an obstacle to effective action as well as unnecessarily heretical. With some justice, he maintained that the number of anti-Semites who read and actually understood Dühring was deservedly small. Dr. Ammann, however, persisted, making the familiar revolutionary arguments against politicalization of the Jewish question and closing with a formal resolution for the acceptance of Dühring's writings. The assembled delegates backed Liebermann, voting down the proposal 38 to 2. After this defeat, the followers of Dühring never again attempted to penetrate the ranks of the conventional anti-Semites.[89]

Liebermann's victory at the Chemnitz congress was a significant step forward in his personal career. Yet that career appeared doomed, for in spite of his official optimism, strongly supported by the congress chairman, Otto Glagau, the movement seemed to be in its death agonies. By the spring of 1883 the tenuous international connections established at Dresden had already begun to wither. Until the end of the empire, German anti-Semites maintained only very casual contact with their Hungarian and Austrian counterparts. The stark anti-Germanism of the French and Russian anti-Semites made any collaboration with them impossible for nationalists like Paul Förster and Liebermann. In 1884 the universal alliance perished. Its members were unwilling to put Germany's problems in the forefront or to follow "the leading power as a model for future activity," as Liebermann insisted.[90] Meanwhile in Berlin, Liebermann's *Volksverein* and his newspaper were failing because of a lack of interest. In 1885 both finally collapsed, and he announced his imminent departure for Paraguay to join Bernhard Förster. But instead of the subtropics, Liebermann went to Leipzig, where Theodor Fritsch offered him employment on the staff of a new anti-Semitic newspaper, the *Antisemitische-Korrespondenz*.

Theodor Fritsch was one of very few anti-Semites of imperial Germany who played an active role in the Weimar Republic. He seems to have undergone no period of uncertainty, no development; he maintained the same position and said the same things in 1883 and 1933. Born of peasant parents in Wiesenau (Prussian Saxony) in 1852, he became a milling engineer and in 1879 began printing a small anti-Semitic newspaper from Leipzig especially for millers.[91] According to the Nazis, who honored him as the "Old Master," his main contribution to the solution of the Jewish question was the *Handbuch der Judenfrage* (*Antisemiten-Katechismus* until 1893), a compendium of misinformation and anti-Jewish quotations from the classics of world literature, which by 1943 had gone through forty-eight editions. Fritsch was a thoroughgoing revolutionary. He portrayed himself as the underdog, the prophet unheard, for all his half-century of intense activity. He held several of Dühring's opinions on the Jewification of Christianity, but was cautious enough at first to avoid airing them in public.[92] A deep-dyed pessimist, he remained severely critical of the German Empire and its institutions. But in the mid-1880's, Fritsch found himself in the company of more conventional men. With the help of Liebermann and the lure of his financially successful publishing house, he exerted some influence over the anti-Semitic clubs or *Reformvereine,* which were coming to life in Westphalia, the Kingdom of Saxony, and Silesia.[93]

Unlike Bernhard Förster or Eugen Dühring, Fritsch made a conscious attempt to win the conventional anti-Semites over to his point of view. He tried his best to keep the movement out of what he termed "the party swindle." "Slogans in political speeches and newspapers" would not, he declared, "suffice to carry through a great movement of the intellect." Instead, he advocated the steady dissemination of anti-Semitism in all areas of German life, especially the schools.

After long years of preparation, the proper course of action would create a "consensus of the fatherland," above any party and free of the parliamentary "faction jobbery."[94] To gain adherents for this conception of the solution to the Jewish question, Fritsch established his own *Reformverein* in Leipzig during the spring of 1886. But he labored under a severe handicap, the inability to speak in public, a serious deficiency in an age which prized oratorical skill. Therefore, in public debate the defense of his position was left to Liebermann, an able speaker but an uncertain champion of his employer's ideas.

Under the pseudonym Thomas Frey,[95] Fritsch presented his own views through the medium of his newspaper. Late in 1885 he opened the monthly *Antisemitische-Korrespondenz* to a discussion of the apparent failure of anti-Semitism. In its "forum for inner party matters" the paper gave anti-Semites a chance to express their opinions on what ought to be done next. Few of the suggestions designed to halt further degeneration corresponded to Fritsch's own. Wilhelm Marr, for example, demanded a purge of rowdy, unworthy elements. Heinrich Nordmann, author of two early anti-Semitic pamphlets, was the only one to call for the creation of a separate anti-Semitic political party. The forum represented all shades of opinion, but most contributors showed the same hesitancy and ambivalence as Liebermann: political action should take the form of preliminary economic boycott, the building of an anti-Semitic press, and greater reliance on the "most anti-Semitic" of the regular parties, the German Conservative party. Everyone agreed that even though organized anti-Semitic agitation was failing, anti-Semitic sentiment was flourishing all over Germany.[96]

The open forum led directly to a congress at Kassel in June 1886, attended by representatives of forty *Reformvereine* as well as interested well-wishers. Fritsch pushed for the creation of a unified organization to conduct massive propaganda on a nationwide basis and to distribute his anti-Semitic publications. He remained silent on the subject of parliamentary politics. Liebermann, however, advanced a different idea. Heartened by the spread of anti-Semitic *Reformvereine*, he urged the congress to form an alliance which was to "prepare the ground for a great national German reform party."[97] Fritsch had no choice but to accept formation of the German Anti-Semitic Alliance *(Deutsche Antisemitische Vereinigung)*, but he made clear his wish that the organization wait to see if it could rally sufficient support to warrant becoming a political party.

However, the pressures working toward the conversion of the alliance into a full-fledged political party were growing irresistible. A serious new rival to the leadership of the anti-Semites exercised by Liebermann and, behind the scenes, Fritsch, appeared in west central Germany. There Otto Böckel, a librarian at the University of Marburg but soon to become the "peasant king," seceded almost immediately from the alliance and formed a separate, specifically anti-Semitic political party. His powerful agitation among the Hessian peasants showed what might be achieved with independent political activity. The promise of immediate successes greatly influenced the members of the anti-Semitic alliance, few of whom possessed Fritsch's ability to think in terms of long-range effectiveness and ultimate goals.

In addition to Böckel's exciting example, another development outside the anti-Semitic movement helped transform the alliance into a political party. The Reichstag had slowly been gathering prestige in the eyes of the German public. It had passed laws of great significance for everyday life during the 1870's and 1880's. It had approved pioneering welfare legislation, instituted protective tariffs, and taken measures against the socialist danger. In domestic affairs at least, the Reichstag had become the arena in which the national destiny seemed to be working itself out. An increasing number of German newspapers sent their own reporters to cover the debates and often reprinted them word for word. Visitors to the Reichstag building were willing to pay scalper's prices for a ticket to the gallery in order to see Bismarck, Stoecker, Richter, and the elder Liebknecht in person. In the eyes of many anti-Semites, the Reichstag assumed the character of a proper vehicle for the realization of their goal, the exclusion of the Jews from German national life.[98] Certainly, the grudging acceptance of the Reichstag by the conventional anti-Semites did not spring from an appreciation of the democratic process. This was and always remained foreign to their thinking. But the Chinese Exclusion Law of the United States (1882) and the aliens bill debate in the English Parliament provided persuasive examples of how legislative bodies in other countries sought to close their borders against what they considered a national menace. In the recent past the Reichstag itself had passed exceptional laws against Roman Catholics, Socialists, and Poles—why not Jews as well?[99]

The attempt to achieve the goals of the Anti-Semites' Petition through the Reichstag was a fateful step in the history of German anti-Semitism. The Emancipation Law of 1869 had been incorporated into the German Constitution (Article 191b). Thus, the complete petition program envisioned nothing less than a change in the constitution. Winning a majority in the Reichstag was only one great obstacle in the way of constitutional revision. The Bismarckian state gave the *Bundesrat*, whose members were chosen by the individual state governments, a veto over legislation proposed by the Reichstag (Article 78). While in the Reichstag a simple majority was required, only fourteen *Bundesrat* delegates were needed to block constitutional amendments. The *Bundesrat* possessed greater powers than the Reichstag. Furthermore, it met in secret and therefore escaped public notice, a fact which incidentally fostered the illusion of Reichstag potency.[100] By placing their hopes in a political party, the anti-Semites set themselves the task of enlisting 199 of the 397 Reichstag deputies and most of the individual German state governments in the cause of revoking Jewish emancipation.

It is uncertain whether any of the parliamentary anti-Semites appreciated the enormous difficulty of this task. Later events certainly revealed their almost bottomless optimism and political obtuseness. In the 1880's, despite the reverses of the Berlin movement, many thought that anti-Semitism was the wave of the future, and that it would rapidly surge over the whole German people. The aim of anti-Semites, according to Otto Böckel, ought to be the election of a "Reichstag faction, the exclusive purpose of which is the struggle against Jewry. . . ." Eventually, a purely anti-Semitic majority would effect a change in the constitution, giving due recognition to the racial differences between Jews and Germans, between "the guest people and the host people." Until the turn of the century at any rate, an anti-Semitic Reichstag majority in the not-too-distant future seemed a possibility worth discussing and planning for in anti-Semitic circles.[101]

For the time being, in 1886, Liebermann set his sights lower. A friendly state administration could enact some of the petition demands, and a simple majority in the Reichstag—perhaps a coalition of anti-Semitically inclined parties—could pass others. Although the anti-Semites could not look forward to an immediate parliamentary majority, the rest of the legislators, Liebermann reasoned, would not be able to ignore a powerful, unified anti-Semitic faction.[102] He, at least, was ready to lead the German Anti-Semitic Alliance into the political fray. In the autumn of 1886, under its banner, he ran unsuccessfully in several by-elections.

In the national elections of 1887, Otto Böckel won a sensational victory in Marburg. Liebermann too made a strong showing in nearby Fritzlar but failed to gain a seat. This evidence of popular appeal swept aside all remaining opposition to the conversion of the anti-Semitic alliance into a political party. Böckel's victory revitalized the anti-Semites. In 1888, the *Antisemitische-Korrespondenz* suddenly found enough readers to appear as a fortnightly instead of a monthly. A new spate of organization on the grass-roots level took place. Between 1885 and 1890 the number of *Reformvereine* tripled, rising to 136.[103] This network of local anti-Semitic clubs provided the potential means for national political campaigning and propaganda work. Toward the end of 1888, the *Antisemitische-Korrespondenz* began to speak of the alliance as a political party. Almost imperceptibly, it had in fact become one. Fritsch continued to fight a losing battle against parliamentarizing the Jewish question. Gradually, however, he began to withdraw in order to concentrate on his publishing enterprises. He reemerged only after the crushing defeat of the parliamentary anti-Semites in 1912.

At the end of the decade 1878–1887, German anti-Semites had completed the formative stage of their development. Over these stormy years the content of their program, the stereotyped image of the Jew, and the techniques of agitation had become firmly fixed. Leaders who conformed to the spoken and unspoken ideals of their followers had come to the head of the movement; others who did not had been expelled. Finally, a great number of anti-Semites in Germany had become committed to a parliamentary solution of the Jewish problem, to the formation of an independent political party, and to the achievement of anti-Semitic legislation in the Reichstag.

All that remains to be told of parliamentary anti-Semitism in imperial Germany is the slow discovery by the anti-Semites that a satisfactory parliamentary solution was impossible.

CHAPTER 2

The Outsiders: Anti-Semitism in Hessenland, 1883–1890[1]

> It was in autumn 1883 when I came to learn of a particu-
> larly striking case of the misery brought upon our people by the
> Jews. A formerly prosperous peasant had been completely
> impoverished by a Jew. A few days after the public auctioning
> of the peasant's farm, the Jew was found murdered. The
> peasant came before the court in Marburg and was acquitted.
> But the proceedings exposed a hideous picture of Jewish
> usury. I followed the trial with great tension; the day on which
> judgment was pronounced found me among the impatient
> mob. Never shall I forget the moment when the acquitted
> victim of the Jew stepped through the doors of the courthouse.
> Hundred-voiced bravos convulsed the air. The masses of
> people were beside themselves with joy. In that stirring hour
> I pledged to myself: "You must combat with all your power
> the machinations of the Jews. The people yearn for an eman-
> cipator!" From that hour forth I have been an anti-Semitic
> agitator. The image of the peasant robbed by the Jew drives
> me onward.
>
> Otto Böckel, *Die Juden*

With these melodramatic words the extraordinary Otto Böckel
described his entry into anti-Semitic politics. As sole candidate of the
"Böckelite party," he won election to the Reichstag in 1887 and thereby
succeeded in vastly strengthening the self-confidence of conventional
anti-Semites and erasing their last doubts about the wisdom of political organization. Before he left his Hessian peasants seven years
later, he had made Hessenland into "the cradle of political anti-
Semitism," the only sure source of anti-Semitic strength until 1919.

Böckel was born in Frankfurt am Main in July 1859. His father, a
dour man and stern disciplinarian, owned a small construction

business and was able to send Otto to a preparatory school in Frankfurt. At school he became the favorite of the philologist Tycho Mommsen, brother of Theodor Mommsen, and showed great facility in the study of modern language. He mastered English, French, Italian, and, according to the claims of an uncritical biographer, thirteen other European languages. The elder Böckel sent his son to the universities at Giessen and Heidelberg to prepare for a law career, but the young man's interest lay elsewhere. Interrupting his law studies, he spent several semesters at the universities of Leipzig and Marburg taking courses in modern languages. He also developed a passionate interest in European folksongs, legends, and adages. A fine student with a promising academic career, he received his doctorate in 1882. He did his one year of military service and then went back to Marburg where he found employment as an assistant librarian at the university. With opportunity to continue his studies and leisure to pursue his hobby, Böckel, perhaps with Goethe as inspiration, made frequent expeditions into the Hessian countryside. He collected and saved from the oral tradition numerous songs and stories.[2] At the same time, he came to know the troubles of the agricultural population in a period of rapid industrial development. Böckel naturally drew a comparison between the idyllic past, which he discovered in folklore, and the woeful present. Eventually this comparison led him into anti-Semitic politics.

Although he became an effective and popular polemicist, Böckel showed little originality in dealing with the Jewish question. His pamphlets and speeches contained few new ideas and treated the old allegations against the Jews uncreatively, merely rehashing much of the popular literature of the Berlin movement. A fair example of his methods and anti-Semitic views can be found in his most popular pamphlet, *Die Juden, die Könige unserer Zeit* ("The Jews, Kings of Our Time"), which went through 123 editions by 1909. In its pages Böckel used statistical evidence with a complete lack of scruple. For example, he applied figures on the increase of the Jewish population in urban centers to Germany as a whole, thus "proving" that Jews would outnumber Germans by 1980 or "a little later." Like Wilhelm Marr, he too emphatically denied religious prejudice as a motive for his anti-Semitism. He was a convinced racist who looked upon the Jews as a "stubborn, old, and thoroughly alien race."

They were urban, rootless, unproductive, and inimical to German well-being. Most important, they were the exploiters and tormentors of Böckel's beloved country folk.[3]

Böckel differed from most of his anti-Semitic colleagues in that he had a clear idea of the world he wanted to save from corrosive Jewish influence. His peasant populism inspired several scholarly works on folklore and some less successful attempts at the novel and the lyric. Literary value aside, his poetry is worth examining for the light it throws on his attitude toward German history and the peasant's central role in it:

Auf freiem Grund ein freier Mann
Bleib, Bauer, allezeit,
Du hast aus schwerer Frohnden Zwang
Dich und Dein Volk befreit.
. . . .
So lang Du auf der Scholle stehst
Hat Deutschland keine Not,
So lang Du Deine Saaten säst,
Hat unser Volk sein Brot.
. . . .
In Sturmesdrohn und Wettersnot;
Du Deutschlands erster Stand,
Halt aus, als letztes Aufgebot
Ruft dich das Vaterland.

On free land a free man,
Stay, peasant, evermore;
From hard bondage art thou thy own
Thine nation's emancipator.
. . . .
So long as thou on the soil standeth
Germany knows not want's dread;
So long as thou the seed soweth
Our nation has its bread.
. . . .
In threat of storm and seas so heavy
Thou, the first in German land,
Hold ready for the last great levy
Summoned forth by the fatherland.[4]

In war and peace, in past and future, Germany's most valuable resource had been and would remain her peasant class. Böckel's novel about the War of Emancipation (1813–1814), *Die Napoleoner,* bore the same message; simple but intrepid men of the soil had redeemed Germany from French tyranny. Rural Germany and its people were, for Böckel, the most important source of moral and economic well-being, the nation's repository of courage, steadfastness, and common sense. In his idealization of rural life, the peasants were "a Germanic tribe *(Volksstamm)* sedentary for almost two millenia, tilling the soil of their fathers, great in their humble works, and holding honorably to the way of their ancestors."[5]

Böckel owed much of his populist thinking to the prolific Wilhelm Heinrich Riehl (1823–1897), whom he frequently quoted. Riehl, a scholar-poet, professor at Munich University, and confidant of King Maximilian II of Bavaria, played a seminal role in the formation of *völkisch*[6] thought. Riehl, like Böckel, had set off the rootedness of the peasant against the restless frivolity of the urban dweller; the countryside for Riehl and Böckel was the locus of abiding folk virtues. Both men felt that only the peasantry could halt Germany's moral degeneration. But what Böckel rejected in Riehl's outlook was a veneration for the medieval relationship between peasant and lord.[7] When he entered politics, he did so with the slogan, "Against Jews and Junkers."

On his expeditions from Marburg, Böckel discovered the peasant way of life, or rather his romantic vision of it, to be in a state of decay. Already in the 1880's, he fretted, "the best songs had been lost; they lay in the graveyard." The old songs were no longer being sung in the authentic way.[8] This forgetting of "the ways of the fathers" symbolized a great danger not only for the peasantry but for the future of Germany as well. Böckel ominously warned: ". . . even the peasant class is slowly perishing and changing its essential character. This course of development is very regrettable. It signifies the beginning of the end—the end of more than just German folklore."[9] Though filled with foreboding, he, at least in his early years, had little in common with the revolutionary proponents of cultural discontent such as Bernhard Förster, Dühring, or Fritsch. His yearning for the "days of quiet glory" did not find an outlet in reactionary politics, in schemes to save the "Germanic type," or in long treatises on Germany's inevitable doom. He remained an optimistic activist until the grounds for his optimism crumbled. His hero was the conventional anti-Semite, Otto Glagau, whom he later eulogized as the "true father of the anti-Semitic movement."[10] Ambition, pragmatism, and organizational ability counterbalanced Böckel's romantic imagination and kept him an effective force in anti-Semitic politics for several years.

Like most of his anti-Semitic colleagues, Glagau included, Böckel understood little of economics. He thought in terms of individual and group heroes, collective villains, and dark conspiracy. Perhaps he stood too near the events to realize that the effects of industrialization, the changeover to capitalistic farming, and the rapid growth of urban centers had finally overtaken Hessenland. Yet the marked acceleration in economic development and disruption of traditional life which accompanied the Prussian annexation of Electoral Hesse could not have escaped his notice. Hessians of all classes came to recognize the year 1866 as a dividing line between the old and the new life. The larger economic forces behind this dramatic line of demarcation, however, remained obscured. To understand how Böckel marshaled the support of Hessenland peasants, these larger forces must be analyzed.

The period 1850–1875 was a flourishing era for German agriculture. In the late 1840's, the manorial system of open-field farming came to an end in Hessenland. The change from manorialism to the capitalistic exploitation of agriculture began later and took longer to complete in western Germany than in the lands east of the Elbe River.[11] But by 1871 Hessenland, like most of the rest of the German Empire, was an area of independent farmers. The transformation of Hessian agriculture was carried out in conjunction with and as a result of the first period of railroad building. Construction of the two main railroad lines between 1845 and 1852 opened up urban markets for Hessian agricultural produce. Particularly in this matter Prussian annexation made a profound difference, for only after the laying down of several branch lines under Prussian guidance did improved communications take their full effect. The subsidiary tracks connected the Hessian interior with Frankfurt am Main and the great cities of the North.[12]

Increasing demand for agricultural products, better means of transportation to carry them to market, and German population growth increased the value of agricultural land remarkably.[13] In Hessenland where the usual farm was from five to twelve and one-half acres, a great number of transactions in which land changed hands took place during the 1870's. Many who had found safety in the communal farming of the open field system were unequal to the demands of capitalistic agriculture; others prospered and rented or bought more land. The city of Marburg, Böckel's eventual political headquarters, provides an excellent illustration of the radical change apprehended with fear by some, with great hope by others. Between 1852 and 1861, the population of the town actually fell almost ten percent. After the Prussian annexation of 1866, the population in Marburg increased at a faster rate than in Germany as a whole; by 1895, twice as many people lived there as in 1852. Aside from weaving and pottery, all Marburg's industry took root after the arrival of the Prussians.[14]

A Jewish lawyer from Berlin, J. Rülf, returning to his birthplace near Marburg in 1882, was amazed and gratified by the drastic alterations he saw. Signs of prosperity were everywhere. New business establishments, straight streets newly laid, and fresh coats of paint had made the once sleepy village almost unrecognizable. Sons returning from city garrison duty with the Prussian army had modernized and redecorated the interiors of parental homes. Girls paraded the streets dressed in what they thought were the latest city fashions. But not all the effects of annexation were as pleasing as these to the visitor. The townspeople constantly grumbled about rising household expenses, military conscription, which robbed them of the valuable manpower represented by their sons, heavy taxes—three times those of the neighboring Grand Duchy of Hesse—costlier credit, and higher workers' wages. Everyone seemed to be in uniform. All these things Rülf's old friends and neighbors regarded as "Prussian" and foreign.[15]

This kind of change, taking place nearly everywhere in Germany, happened too quickly for most Hessians. What appeared clear to Böckel and his contemporaries was that this whole upsetting development had come from outside Hessenland. In fact, the stagnant, patriarchal government of Electoral Hesse had suddenly given way to the most efficient, rationally directed administration in Europe, that of the Prussian state. The Prussian financial, commercial, military, and railroad systems had almost immediate effect upon the old routine way of life.[16] The unification of Germany, an unloved native dynasty, and economic prosperity made it possible for the majority of Hessians to accept these changes without overt hostility. A wary apprehensiveness characteristic of the predominantly peasant population prevailed as long as the times were good. But they were not good for long.

The steadily rising agricultural prices of the period 1850–1875 gave way to fluctuating and sharply lower prices in the last quarter of the nineteenth century. Railroads built in more fertile areas of the world where both land and labor were cheap combined with lessening costs of overseas shipping to bring serious competition to German markets. The expanding domestic market in Germany only partially offset the trend of lower prices. Agricultural indebtedness began to increase extraordinarily. Almost half of the "little peasants" in all parts of Prussia, including Prussian Hesse, had mortgaged from thirty to over sixty percent of the value of their lands by 1883. Rents based on long-term leases, signed in the period of high land values, became burdensome. Loans floated in times of plenty had to be repaid with lower returns for farm products. Even in German agriculture's flourishing period, profit yields had not, according to one expert, been great enough to justify the purchase of more land.[17] Now depressed prices accentuated the financial troubles of the peasant population.

Hessenland's main agricultural pursuit, livestock raising, suffered only a slight drop in prices (1887–1889) compared to the heavy and prolonged losses in the grain market. Intermittently severe shortages of fodder, however, often forced the sale of unfattened animals at lower prices. In 1892 and 1899 hoof-and-mouth disease hit Hessenland especially hard, killing off livestock before it came to market. Even the well-to-do peasant employer of seasonal labor had problems. The increased flow of the landless to the cities diminished the supply of available laborers and consequently increased the wages of those who stayed behind. Moreover, a backward technology kept the Hessian peasantry uncompetitive and in a perpetually hazardous situation. Thus, acceptable prices for livestock were no true indication of peasant well-being.[18] The tax burden in the Prussian parts of Hessenland, always a source of discontent, grew even more onerous during the years of agricultural depression. Where debts did not result in foreclosure or the division of farms for sale, they produced a confusing welter of short-term credit devices almost always disadvantageous to the peasant debtor. The anti-Semitic parties later exploited the discontent arising from heavy taxation and a confusing credit system. Their radical remedies, though unoriginal, became staples in all subsequent anti-Semitic party programs.

The desperation of the peasants begged for a leader who could channel it into effective political protest. The worsening economic situation and a tendency to identify most public and private grievances with the coming of the Prussians were two conditions which Böckel exploited to achieve power in Hessenland. Interestingly, he suffered none of the supposed ill effects of either condition. Unlike several leading anti-Semites he was not yet deeply in debt; his income was modest, but his way of life unextravagant. At the same time he saw Germany's destiny tied to that of the Prussian state and welcomed this circumstance. Very early in his career, he established relations with the anti-Semites of Berlin and seemed always at home there; after his semiretirement he chose to live in Brandenburg. He was a German nationalist, a *"Bismarckianer"* in his own words, and shared none of the peasant's anti-Prussianism.[19] Thus, he remained the outsider, an educated city dweller, possessing none of the motives of those who came to worship him as "the second Luther."

In the early 1880's Böckel set out to become the *Volksbefreier*, to emancipate the German people from Jewish oppression. He brought to this task intelligence, energy, and good looks.[20] His personal role in the creation of an anti-Semitic movement in Hessenland ought not to be underestimated. On the other hand, to overemphasize Böckel's personality leaves several important questions about the origins of Hessian anti-Semitism unasked. The presence of a capable demagogue, the effects of industrialization, and animosities toward Prussia do not alone explain why protest in Hessenland adopted an anti-Semitic form. All these factors were present elsewhere in Germany and yet did not result in a viable anti-Semitic movement. It was not Böckel's charisma but conditions peculiar to Hessenland that gave him the opportunity of translating his personal beliefs into an effective anti-Semitic movement. Prime among these conditions was the situation of Hessenland's Jewish population.

Hessian Jews were not highly regarded in imperial Germany. Most of Böckel's contemporaries readily assumed that Hessian anti-Semitism, in particular, was a response to serious economic exploitation of the peasantry by the Jewish population. When the young Bismarck spoke to the United Diet in 1847 about areas where usurious Jews held the peasantry in virtual bondage, the anti-Semites of the next generation claimed that he had had Hessenland specifically in mind.[21] The *Verein für Sozialpolitik*, which counted many famous scholars and state socialists among its members, concluded a survey of usury in Hessenland (1887) with the assertion that "usurious exploitation is predominantly carried on by Jews."[22] No matter how economically and historically determined a role the Jews were forced to play in Hessenland, no matter how little their business ethics differed from those of Christian competitors, they themselves bore the largest measure of responsibility for the success of Böckel's anti-Semitism. Thus ran the interpretations of many by no means hostile observers.[23]

There were those who denied this explanation. Chief Rabbi Munk, a constant defender of Hessian Jews, refused to accept this simple and apparently reasonable interpretation of the rise of anti-Semitism in Hessenland. He concluded his statistical analysis of the criminality of Hessian versus Prussian Jews with the rebuke that "the alleged connection between the anti-Semitic movement and the moral conduct of Jews is nothing but a convenient lie."[24] The study actually showed a proportionally smaller rate of lawbreaking among the Jews of Hessenland. No matter what contemporaries thought, it was not "excessive Jewish criminality" that kindled anti-Semitism in Hessenland.

In Hessenland, unlike the rest of Germany, the Jewish population was just beginning to resettle in larger towns and great cities at the time of Böckel's appearance. In the last quarter of the nineteenth century more than half still resided in small towns and villages where the only contact with Hessian peasants was in the business sphere. In all of Hessenland in 1890, seventy thousand Jews lived dispersed among 2,800,000 Christians.[25] No "rootless" newcomers, Jews had lived in the area since the thirteenth century, in Marburg and Giessen since the early fourteenth century. Historically, relations between Jews and peasants had usually been peaceful although not based on any mutual respect or sympathy. The anti-Semitic riots of

1819 had taken place almost exclusively in larger towns and had not spread to the countryside. Anti-Semitic violence had flared up in rural areas during the early stages of the revolution of 1848, but died down quickly.[26]

Legal emancipation for the Jews of what became Prussian Hesse followed the temporary incorporation of the state in the Napoleonic Kingdom of Westphalia (1808). But after the defeat of the French, Jews retrogressed into a protected status with special taxation and stringently limited economic freedoms. In 1833 the Electoral Hessian government once again promulgated the *de jure* emancipation of Jews. Civil equality, however, did not include petty traders or wandering peddlers; even with bribery, obtaining licenses for branches of business included in the emancipation edict became virtually impossible for Jews. In the period of reaction following the revolution of 1848, theoretical equality also disappeared. Civil service positions were closed to Jews; they suffered from arbitrary police power and the tyranny of petty bureaucrats. Squeezed into viciously competitive marginal businesses and trades, the Jews of Hessenland and of Prussian Hesse in particular were among the poorest in Germany.[27]

Well over half the Jews in the Grand Duchy lived off retail trade. In 1895, two hundred Jews acted as cattle dealers, ninety-six as moneylenders. In absolute numbers, therefore, they were far from the monopoly Böckel claimed for them in these two businesses.[28] There were locales where Jews did exercise a monopoly over the middleman functions in agricultural goods, but these were not always the same places that Böckel's movement did especially well. Certainly, no statistics can adequately describe the personal hatred, the reciprocal distrust on the part of mutually dependent peasants and Jews, or how these tensions mounted in a time of economic stress. But as important as the objective economic role played by Hessian Jews in the growth of anti-Semitism was the way they were portrayed to Hessian peasants by Otto Böckel.

Although overdrawn and exaggerated, Böckel's accusations against the Jewish population, like those of Otto Glagau in the 1870's, found a ready response in Prussian Hesse and then in the Grand Duchy of Hesse as well. Even if Böckel's charges of Jewish exploitation were widely believed, many questions about the immediate origins of Hessian anti-Semitism still need answering. Why, for example, did no significant anti-Semitic movement take root in Baden, Bavaria, or the Rhineland, where Jews conducted as large a part of the trade in agricultural products as they did in Hessenland?[29] Why did the anti-Semitic parties maintain considerable strength in Hessenland even after the peasants' economic situation improved? The intensity and constancy of Hessian anti-Semitism remain inexplicable unless the symbolic significance of Hessian Jews is considered. That symbolic role was not primarily economic in its origins.

In 1866 the Jewish population openly welcomed the annexation of Electoral Hesse by Prussia. To Jews, the coming of enlightened Prussian administration meant the end of arbitrary rule and the beginning of complete occupational freedom. The rapid changes which startled the peasants and town dwellers were cause for rejoicing in the Jewish population. Within a decade after annexation, the stimulating presence of Prussia resulted in a visibly improved economic position for Jews. Entrance into the liberal professions, better educational opportunities, and freedom of movement contributed to their material advance. A sizeable shift in Jewish population from the Grand Duchy to Prussian Hesse took place in the 1870's, reflecting the generally more favorable conditions.[30]

As things got better for Jews and worse for the peasants, previously obscured "connections" between the Prussian masters and those who benefited from their mastery, the Jews, were discovered. In Hanover, Holstein, and southern Germany resentment against the haughty Prussians was general before and after 1866. But nowhere did Prussian presence so obviously improve the position of the Jews as in the annexed portions of Hessenland. In Hanover, where anti-Prussian feeling remained strongest, the forced adoption of the Prussian constitution of 1850 brought no improvement in the legal position of Jews.[31] With real equality of status since 1848, the Jews in Hanover pursued varied occupations. The sudden coming of the Prussians, therefore, did not result in dramatic material advancement for them. Furthermore, it was difficult to identify Jews as allies of either the Prussians or the anti-Prussians. They were prominent in the National Liberal party, which welcomed annexation, and the Guelph or Hanover separatist party, which continued to fight against Prussia in the Reichstag.[32] Only in Prussian Hesse and in the neighboring Grand

Duchy, for reasons discussed below, could the "connection" between Prussians and Jews assume a sinister meaning.

Gradually, the symbolic relationship between Jews and Prussians began to alter. Instead of remaining the mere beneficiary, the Jews became, thanks to anti-Semitic agitation, the silent partner, the real instigator of Prussian domination. Böckel succeeded in making over the popular image of Jews. Instead of passive parasites, they became the sole, active agents responsible for all the troubles of the peasant. The observant lawyer, Rülf, described the perverted logic of this transformation:

> It was indeed apparent that all affliction, all dissatisfaction, all regression, all the multifarious disadvantages which fell upon the rural population since 1866 had worked directly to the advantage of the Jews; consequently, the Jew must bear all guilt. This reasoning—always at hand—was zealously awakened and cultivated by agitators.[33]

Whether Böckel was conscious of what he had accomplished is difficult to substantiate. Certainly, portraying Hessian Jewry as a wing of the Jewish conspiracy endangering Germany and as the agent of a soulless modernity conformed well to the beliefs expressed in his writings and those of other conventional anti-Semites.

Whether conscious or instinctive, shifting the focus of political attack from mighty Prussia to the Jewish population of Hessenland proved a good stratagem. To large numbers of the Hessian middle class, especially those aligned with the powerful National Liberal party, Prussia represented positive virtues. The diehard *Hessische Rechtspartei*, which campaigned for "redress of the injustice of 1866" in the 1890's, found relatively little support in Hessenland.[34] Many outside the peasant class had come to regard annexation as the price of unification and Germany's rise to power. A purely anti-Prussian party could not hope for great success, especially when it based its appeal on unalluring legal arguments. The Jews of Hessenland, however, constituted an identifiable group by both religion and economic position. For all but a few of their fellow citizens, they possessed no positive virtues. Böckel built his success upon the substitution of the Jewish for the Prussian enemy. He readily abandoned the hopeless struggle against Prussia in favor of a political program aimed at a group of relatively weak outsiders in contact with his electorate on the local and individual level.

Böckel did not have to start from scratch in acquainting Hessians with the Jewish danger. In 1880 and 1881, Ernst Henrici, Bernhard Förster, and Liebermann von Sonnenberg had occasionally visited the major towns of Hessenland. They had recognized the possibilities for agitation but left them unexploited.[35] In 1882, Ludwig Werner (1855–1935), later an anti-Semitic Reichstag deputy and an active figure throughout the Wilhelminian period, founded an anti-Semitic *Reformverein* in Kassel and took over the publication of a newspaper. Böckel used both of these institutions as stepping-stones in his political rise. Under the pseudonym Dr. Capistrano, a fifteenth-century Franciscan famous for delivering Jews to the pyre, Böckel contributed lively articles to Werner's newspaper. As Capistrano, he addressed anti-Semitic organizations in Berlin where he met Glagau and Dühring. He joined the Kassel *Reformverein* and began urging the formation of a new political party. For three years he worked within the existing framework of anti-Semitic organization, gaining the reputation of an up-and-coming anti-Semite. In 1886, however, he began to carve out an independent position. He won over the Kassel *Reformverein* to his plans and founded another in Marburg (August 1886). With the support of these two groups, he announced his candidacy for the 1887 Reichstag election in the Marburg-Kirchain district.[36]

Thus far, the anti-Semitic politicians of Berlin had appealed without success to the urban *Mittelstand* exclusively. Now Böckel consciously chose Marburg for his first campaign. To win this Reichstag seat, a safe Conservative party mandate since 1871, he and his supporters had to direct their agitation toward the peasantry, which comprised three-quarters of the district. Success depended on their ability to rouse the heretofore apathetic, nonvoting peasant masses. With none of the specialized forms of organization which later gave Hessian anti-Semitism its special character, Böckel relied upon ceaseless activity. His well-liked opponent *Justizrat* Carl Grimm appeared three weeks before the election to address influential merchants, teachers, and professionals. After his confidently expected victory, he would disappear for another three years. Böckel, in contrast, worked the district. Speaking at open air mass meetings, presiding at peasant fairs, everywhere demonstrating his impressive knowledge of peasant lore, he devoted his full energy to the task. After the 1887 campaign, it was never again possible to win a Hessenland Reichstag seat in the old casual manner. Böckel forced his opponents to modify their election strategy completely.[37] In 1887, his victory in Marburg changed the face of Hessian politics and earned him national notoriety. Receiving 7,411 votes to his rival's 4,314, he gave indisputable proof of his personal appeal.[38] At twenty-seven he was the youngest man in the Reichstag.

Immediately after the election Böckel began to consolidate the victory and to strengthen his hold upon the peasants. He purchased his own press organ, the *Reichsherold*, which appeared from Marburg twice weekly until 1894 and thereafter sporadically, with Böckel as editor, publisher, and main contributor. During its brief heyday, the *Reichsherold* reached fifteen thousand subscribers, many of whom had probably not been newspaper readers before.[39] The paper's success finally alerted government officials to the growing movement. Their repressive measures, however, came too late to stifle Böckel and may have even played into his hands.

In Prussia, strict laws regulated all forms of political agitation. Rigorously enforced against the Socialists, after 1887 the laws were invoked more frequently against the anti-Semites too. In the politically volatile areas of Prussian Hesse, the very mention of the word "Jew" at a public meeting often led to a dispersal order from the police. Böckel once spoke at great length and with customary forcefulness about Jewish evil without uttering the fatal word. Coming to the end of his speech, he cast a glance at the police overseer and then concluded with: "And he who has brought this upon us is . . . the Jew!" He had already left the podium before the policeman could end the proceedings.[40] When refused admittance to a public hall by the local government official, he spoke from the window of a peasant hut or resorted to open air meetings. When officials prohibited the use of marching bands, Böckel substituted torchlight processions which marched from village to village singing Lutheran hymns and patriotic songs. Mounted peasant youths guarded his wagon while hosts of followers, all wearing the blue cornflower as an identifying party badge, trailed along behind. With tactics such as these he appealed to the rough-and-ready nature of his peasant adherents.

The pomp and pageantry he introduced into Hessian politics increased his popularity.

Until 1890, Böckel confined his agitation to Prussian Hesse. Then the *Reichsherold* and a number of new organizations facilitated anti-Semitic penetration of the Grand Duchy of Hesse.[41] He felt strong enough to take advantage of the significant legal differences between the Grand Duchy and Prussian Hesse. In the Grand Duchy, for example, it was not necessary to make prior announcement of a meeting; thus, Hessian anti-Semites were able to take hostile town officials by surprise. In addition, greater laxity in the police supervision of meetings during the first crucial months of his efforts allowed Böckel to gain a strong foothold there.[42] In the Grand Duchy of Hesse, Böckel's anti-Semitism continued to thrive on the same conditions that had given it birth: agricultural depression, the unsettling changes accompanying German industrialization, and the alleged responsibility of the Jews for the time of trouble. Here, too, he found it possible to exploit native anti-Prussian feeling.

In 1866, although the Grand Duchy had escaped annexation, it suffered the same loss of political sovereignty as the neighboring Baden, Württemberg, and Bavaria.[43] Unlike its neighbors, however, the Grand Duchy came under more than just the political influence of Prussia. After the annexation of Frankfurt am Main, Electoral Hesse, and Nassau, one of the Grand Duchy's provinces, Oberhessen, suddenly became an island surrounded by Prussian territory and directly subject to Prussian economic pressures.[44] Long after the Prussian-German state had been accepted by the rest of the population in the Grand Duchy, the peasants of Oberhessen continued to resent the intruders. The peasant protegé of Böckel, Philipp Köhler, considered himself the champion of the residents of Oberhessen. Late into the 1890's, as a member of the Hessian state parliament, he expressed views about the Prussians which were more typical than those of his master:

> Prussia has practiced all manner of chicanery on us. . . . We are not treated like German *brothers*, but according to the old Prussian principle, . . . "we all wish to be good Germans, but first we must become pure Prussian!"[45]

Köhler accused the Grand Ducal government of introducing Prus-

sian militarism and "that Prussian spirit which flatters those above
and browbeats those below." He was especially angry about the willingness of the Grand Duchy to bow to the demands of Prussia in
economic matters, such as the disadvantageous railroad treaties,
which "deliberately sacrificed the interests of the peasants" to those
of the East Elban landowners.[46]

Böckel's often quoted slogan, *"gegen Junker und Juden"* (against
Junkers and Jews), must be seen in the light of his constituents'
anti-Prussianism. It has been interpreted exclusively as proof of his
radicalism and his politically motivated animosity toward the German Conservative party.[47] But the slogan also expressed the anti-
Prussian resentments of his followers. Moreover, it provided a neat
formula by which Prussians and Jews were tied together in the consciousness of the electorate. Böckel emphasized this connection in
other ways. He cleverly singled out Ludwig Bamberger (1823–1899)
for special attack. From 1874 until 1890 Bamberger represented the
Grand Ducal district of Bingen in the Reichstag. As a National Liberal,
he had worked zealously for German unification. In the Grand
Duchy, the National Liberal party had acted as a "fifth column"
during the early 1860's, pushing for strong Prussian leadership in the
teeth of the anti-Prussian majority.[48] Böckel used Bamberger in the
same way the Austrian anti-Semites used the Rothschilds, as a per-
sonification of the Jewish conspiracy. Bamberger had been a revolutionary in 1848. He still possessed international financial connections with the *Banque des Pays Bas* and affiliation with the left of the
liberal movement. Moreover, he played an active and conspicuous
part in German national life. According to Böckel, Bamberger had
been one of those most responsible for the liberal measures "pernicious to peasant well-being," the creation of the *Reichsbank* and use
of the gold standard for German currency. He and his kind, Böckel
stated in his declaration of war, were at the root of the troubles
plaguing Germany and Hessenland.[49]

In Prussian Hesse, Böckel had relied on the students of Marburg
and Giessen universities to carry on the agitation. Many were from
the North, where the anti-Semitism of Court Chaplain Stoecker and
Heinrich von Treitschke remained intellectually fashionable in spite
of the Berlin movement's lack of political success. By 1886 Marburg
had its branch of the anti-Semitic *Verein Deutscher Studenten,* whose

members proved valuable, energetic, and capable agitators in Böckel's cause.[50] Many received their first political training in his campaigns of 1887 and 1890. Among the Giessen volunteers was Heinrich Class, who later became the leader of the Pan-German League (1908) and converted that organization into an openly anti-Semitic one.[51] But with the expansion of his movement into the Grand Duchy of Hesse, Böckel needed a more constant source of support than the ever-changing student bodies of these universities. He took two measures to this end: the recruitment of "foreign" agitators, refugees from the Berlin movement like the merchant, Wilhelm Pickenbach; and the creation of a peasant political organization, the Central German Peasant Association *(Mitteldeutscher Bauernverein)*.

Böckel's first measure eventually caused his downfall in Hessenland. These strange Prussians in their frock coats and stovepipe hats alienated his peasant followers.[52] The peasant association, on the other hand, was an instant success. While Böckel remained in control, this organization provided a secure basis for his political party. From its local chapters, future peasant leaders were to receive their schooling in *völkisch* thought and practical politics. Its purpose, in Böckel's words, was

> to combine the peasant farmers into a great cooperative with the closest possible connection to the party; to work for the party in parliamentary elections on all levels; and to create thereby a free peasant class.[53]

Membership in the peasant association reached ten thousand in its first year. By mid-1892, it counted fifteen thousand members, organized in four hundred local chapters. For one mark per year the member became eligible for all services and received the *Reichsherold* without extra charge. Special bureaus provided legal assistance, arbitration services, agricultural information, and cheap insurance against cattle diseases, hail and fire damage. By becoming a member of the association, a peasant could participate in consumer cooperatives and savings and loan banks, thereby "eliminating the Jewish middleman."[54]

Böckel used the *Reichsherold* and the peasant group with great skill. The newspaper served simultaneously as the official voice of the party and the association. The columns of the paper carried stories of

Jewish evil right next to price reports from the Frankfurt market, tips on what and when to buy, and numerous accounts of peasant activities all over Hessenland. Böckel envisioned a complete network of organizations to tie the rural population to his anti-Semitic party. By means of the *Reichsherold* he first created a desire for a youth wing of the peasant association and then the illusion of widespread local groups waiting only to be united before embarking on great tasks. He then offered to place himself at the head of such a group. In this manner was born the Central German Youth League (*Mitteldeutscher Jugendbund*), a valuable training ground for a second generation of anti-Semitic peasants. In similar fashion, Böckel used the reciprocal support of the association and the *Reichsherold* to promote peasant solidarity. When the Jewish cattle dealers of Allendorf and Langgöns boycotted the local market in retaliation for anti-Semitic agitation, Böckel revived and developed the "Jew-free" markets of the Middle Ages. The *Reichsherold* devoted constant attention to them and spoke in glowing terms about their effectiveness. By 1893, ten "Jew-free" markets were operating in Hessenland.[55]

According to a government survey completed in March 1891, Böckel's party was making alarming progress in the Grand Duchy of Hesse. From Darmstadt along the radial railroad lines, the agitation and organization spread into the province of Starkenburg. The district officials of the province of Oberhessen showed dismay at the movement's obvious success. Anti-Semites coming over the border from Prussian Hesse, the officials claimed, had achieved anti-Semitic majorities in twenty-three of the villages around Büdingen alone; they were on the rise in the administrative districts of Friedberg, Giessen, Lauterbach, and Schotten. In January 1892, the party calendar reported the founding of peasant association branches outside Hessenland in neighboring Westphalia. The movement reached its zenith in the winter of 1892–1893 and suffered its first setback. The *Mitteldeutscher Handwerkerverein*, designed to complement the peasant organization and to gain a foothold in the cities of Hessenland, failed to win support from the urban *Mittelstand*. In Hessenland Böckel's movement remained strictly rural, but nonetheless impressive, in its impact.[56]

Böckel's success among the Hessian peasants puzzled many of his contemporaries. Most of his ideas were not new. Cooperatives of all kinds, state credit facilities, and free agricultural schools had been attempted before and gradually began competing successfully with his.[57] According to the press organ of a special anti-anti-Semitic organization, which watched Böckel carefully in these years, the "positive measures" of the peasant association often proved unbeneficial. Recommended insurance companies folded. Consumer co-ops managed by incompetents fell immediately into debt. The sluggish "Jew-free" markets often allowed Jews to participate after all.[58] Despite these failings, Böckel alone succeeded in conquering the heretofore invincible suspicion of the Hessian peasants. Neither failure nor personal scandal shook their faith in him. He made his followers believe in his and their own special mission. The peasants, perhaps for the first time, felt themselves part of a great movement, a movement which would first of all improve their perilous economic position and, secondly, save all Germany from the Jewish danger. Right up until the elections for the National Assembly in 1919, the Hessians kept on responding to the anti-Semitic parties, providing them over the years with thirty-five Reichstag seats.

The problems which Böckel faced and overcame with his electorate were of the most elementary kind. Peasants were not only wary of the state but extremely suspicious and jealous of one another. Since the end of manorialism in the 1840's, they had been unable and unwilling to band together to improve their condition. Peasants dealt with Jewish cattle dealers because they were neutral outsiders. Many of the transactions could have taken place without them had the peasants trusted one another.[59] The *Reichsherold* made constant pleas for cooperation and "open-handed frankness" among its readers. Using biblical language, the "Ten Commandments for the Livestock Jobber" enjoined peasants, first of all, to be good anti-Semites. The other nine commandments, however, revealed basic peasant problems: narrowness of view, technical backwardness, dishonesty, and laziness.[60]

Political ignorance and apathy, too, prevailed among the peasants. The horizon of the Hessian peasant rarely extended beyond his own village or the local marketing center. Participation in Reichstag elections had customarily fallen below seventy-five percent and, until Böckel's coming, even lower in the rural areas of Hessenland.[61] But Böckel overcame the primitive nature of his electorate brilliantly.

Personal contact replaced lengthy manifestoes and abstract principles for party action. He and his colleagues visited the towns and villages continuously. In the first four months of 1890, he held sixty-three rallies. For most of 1892–1894 his party conducted an average of twenty-five to thirty "major political gatherings" a month.[62] Many of these meetings were devoted to election agitation, which usually began a full year in advance. Mass meetings featured lectures, discussions, and entertainment, all of which aimed at "enlightening" the peasant about the Jewish question and the possibilities for economic improvement.

As a peasant leader, Böckel found it necessary to modify and simplify his pronouncements regarding the Jews. The relatively sophisticated racist terminology directed at the educated *Mittelstand* yielded to "common sense" explanations of Jewish evil. When speaking to an educated audience, he made numerous distinctions which would have been meaningless to his peasant followers or even offensive to their religious piety. In the *Reichsherold* the pseudoscientific jargon of anti-Semitic congresses gave way to a pseudoreligious style, more in line with peasant values.[63]

Böckel also developed the community sense of the peasantry by playing subtly and effectively on their feelings of inferiority and animosity toward the city and city ways. The loss of piety, a wasting away of the Germanic sense of honor, a veneer of "civilization" which masked brutal exploitation of the countryside—all these, he preached, were city vices. At the same time, he tried to convey something of his own hopes for the peasant's central role in Germany's future. Again answering the needs of his electorate, he let fall the poetic romanticism of his nonpolitical works and substituted a militancy which shocked his more conservative anti-Semitic colleagues:

> There is still a class that can rescue us; that class is the long-scorned peasantry. The peasant who has stood aside for decades —he now is summoned to step forth. Now or never the time of the peasant is come. . . . Thus, we call, "Peasants, form the battalions for the nation's defense: assemble ye round the banner of the Central German Peasant Association and then—Forward! Forward!"[64]

A large measure of his success came from his unparalleled ability to tailor the content of the anti-Semitic program to the peculiar requirements of the Hessian peasants. None of his anti-Semitic colleagues in other parts of Germany ever matched the harmony achieved between Böckel and his constituents; none could ever succeed in building as powerful a base of popular support.

Nevertheless, Böckel's standing within anti-Semitic circles was no true reflection of his strength in Hessenland. His methods, like Henrici's before him, called forth immediate and sustained criticism from Stoecker and Liebermann. Occasionally Böckel's attacks on capitalism failed to distinguish between "good" and "bad" varieties, between capital and "Jewish capital," exploitation and "Jewish exploitation."[65] For Stoecker, he was little better than the Socialists. Böckel's anti-Conservative stands and sensationalism, according to the court chaplain, constituted a danger to the preservation of the state second only to the Jews in magnitude. In fact, as long as he was in the Reichstag (1887–1903) Böckel remained the most egalitarian of the anti-Semites. Although more skeptical than Liebermann or Stoecker about how much of Germany could be saved intact, Böckel was not a revolutionary. His voting record in parliament revealed no coherent political program or philosophy. Much of his reputed radicalism derived from his enemies of the moment, Stoecker, Liebermann, the German Conservatives, and, later, the Agarian League. He was in this respect, as in many others, a sheer opportunist.

In the early years of his activity, however, Böckel pursued one aim with consistency. He sought to gain a clear and independent identity for the anti-Semitic movement and for himself. If, as he hoped, a national anti-Semitic party were to be formed, it had to represent the whole nation. If it were to be successful, such a party had to stay free of those who wished to use it for "demagogic" instead of "sincere" anti-Semitism, for selfish political ends instead of as a means of solving the Jewish question.[66] In his opinion, the German Conservative party presented the greatest danger to anti-Semitic independence. Thus, calling for an end to Junker privilege not only satisfied the anti-Prussian sentiments of his Hessian followers, but served notice to a wider German public that "anti-Semitism is not just the plaything of the Conservative demagogues." He attacked Stoecker because he saw in him a man fettered to the church, the imperial court, and the Conservative party, not the free and unhampered individual destined to lead the independent anti-Semitic party. Böckel pointedly refused to join the Conservative faction in the Reichstag after his election in 1887. He preferred to stand alone.[67] Between Liebermann and Böckel, on the other hand, there was only one significant difference. Liebermann's desire to ally anti-Semitism to older, stronger groups conflicted with Böckel's intentions. Quickly they became bitter rivals, whose differing ideas about tactics prevented the formation of a united party.

In 1887, riding high after his election victory, Böckel made an unsuccessful bid for leadership of a united party of anti-Semites. The election victory of 1887 should have, in his opinion, vindicated his methods and gained not only acceptance for a parliamentary solution to the Jewish question, but a prime position for its foremost protagonist, Otto Böckel. Yet to dislodge the "old fighters," who gathered around Liebermann von Sonnenberg, proved beyond Böckel's powers. Paul Förster and Liebermann had long years of anti-Semitic activity behind them. They typified even at this early date what had become the "tradition of the movement." More patriotic and, at the same time, more respectable than Böckel, they represented the values of a whole generation of anti-Semitic followers. Furthermore, Böckel's conduct in the Reichstag soon offended the extreme nationalists among the anti-Semites. Like the left liberals and Social Democrats, he objected to the increased taxes attendant upon army reform, the greatest part of which would fall upon the poor. By opposing the government's military bill of 1887 and "associating with the left," Böckel did injury to what the anti-Semites considered one of their major assets, an unimpeachable nationalism.[68] Moreover, Böckel's successes as the "peasant king" did not carry much weight in *Reformvereine* made up of urban *Mittelständler*. The special demands of peasant agitation, egalitarianism, and strident populism made him a dubious character to the majority of the anti-Semitic *Mittelstand*.

In the bid for power, Böckel also underestimated the strength of his rivals. Liebermann enjoyed prestigious connections with German Conservatives and commanded respect outside anti-Semitic circles. He had never completely renounced the efficacy of a parliamentary solution to the Jewish question. His own brand of "reasonable anti-Semitism" was not far different from Böckel's. Liebermann also had the help of his employer, Theodor Fritsch, who had taken an immediate dislike to the impudent young man. He allowed only one article by Capistrano-Böckel to appear in his *Antisemitische-Korrespondenz*. He used the newspaper's "forum for inner party matters" as a weapon against Böckel, attacking his "rowdiness" as an example of the dangers of politicalization.[69] When Fritsch's paper appeared in the spring of 1888 with a new subtitle, "central organ of the anti-Semitic movement," Böckel rebelled.

Partly from thwarted ambition, partly from a sense of injustice, he singlehandedly impeded the political unification of the various anti-Semitic organizations which were springing to life all over Germany in the late 1880's. While the unification congress of Bochum, Westphalia (10–11 June 1889) was still in the planning stages, he correctly interpreted it as a plot to deny him political leadership of the new party. He failed, however, to gain support for a boycott of the congress and had to attend it himself in order to avoid complete isolation.[70] At Bochum he objected vehemently to the lack of organization for fund raising and the inordinately long party program, which no voter would read. When the Berlin and Leipzig contingents tried to delete the word "anti-Semitic" from the new party name, Böckel led a walkout which included his Hessian delegation and that of a growing anti-Semitic group from the Kingdom of Saxony.[71]

Instead of a unified party, two separate anti-Semitic political parties came into existence as a result of the congress. Liebermann formed the German Social party *(Deutschsoziale Partei)* out of those who remained behind at Bochum. Böckel chose to call his followers the Anti-Semitic Peoples' party *(Antisemitische Volkspartei)* until 1893, when he and Oswald Zimmermann, leader of the Saxon anti-Semites, joined together under the name, German Reform party *(Deutsche Reformpartei)*. Meanwhile, for the Reichstag elections of 1890, a truce with Liebermann's German Socials made for fairly harmonious cooperation. The three leaders agreed not to compete against one another.

The results of the election appeared to justify Böckel's obstinacy. All the anti-Semitic victories came in Hessenland, his own realm. His followers and Zimmermann won four of the five anti-Semitic seats. The fifth seat, in Fritzlar, went to Liebermann. In the first balloting the anti-Semites got 30,467 votes; in the second balloting, required when no candidate gained an absolute majority, their total rose to 47,536.[72] Böckel, Oswald Zimmermann, Wilhelm Pickenbach, and Ludwig Werner entered the Reichstag as the *"Fraktion" der Antisemiten*. Liebermann refused to join the group and remained an independent. The task before these men seemed clear and feasible in 1890: campaign incessantly, gather strength quickly, put the anti-Semitic program into effect. Just how to accomplish this formula, however, continued to be a major divisive issue among anti-Semites. For the next few years, they were "many armies, but with a single enemy and a single bulwark to storm."[73]

CHAPTER 3

Anti-Semites and Conservatives:
Cooperation Becomes Competition, 1890–1893

The electoral successes of 1890 confirmed the parliamentary anti-Semites in their decision to seek a political solution to the Jewish question. The lingering doubts that survived the 1880's now vanished, and until the turn of the century an uncritical optimism was to hold sway among the anti-Semitic parties. At the Leipzig congress of the German Social party in the spring of 1891, one speaker after another revealed the new confidence and high hopes prevailing in the anti-Semitic camp. Even the customarily gloomy Theodor Fritsch felt called upon to make a few cheerful predictions. In a halting speech he attempted for the last time to win over the conventional anti-Semites to his revolutionary views. He cautioned the delegates to see anti-Semitism as nothing more than a point of departure for the total reformation of Germanic life. Parliamentary anti-Semitism could not by itself accomplish this overwhelming task, although it had made a good start in the right direction.[1] But victory at the polls made the conventional anti-Semites less receptive than ever to Fritsch's ideas. They listened politely and then simply re-dedicated the party to the program of 1889, which placed the "Jewish question in the forefront of its strivings" and assumed that legal parliamentary activity could do all that had to be done.[2]

Although the optimism of the anti-Semites was excessive, grounds for cautious hopefulness were abundant. The election victory itself, the proliferation of *Reformvereine*, the spread of Böckel's movement into the Grand Duchy of Hesse, the acquisition there by Philipp Köhler of the first anti-Semitic seat in a state parliament, all helped demonstrate the drawing power of anti-Semitic agitation to German politicians. These signs of increasing popularity filled the opponents

67

of anti-Semitism with anxious concern. The belief that the German Socials and Reformers would soon disappear became harder to support, the more so after the daily press began devoting considerable attention to them. Now the parties and phenomenon of anti-Semitism were found important enough to be included in general political surveys and to merit the attention of independent analysts like Hans Delbrück, who was neither pro-Jewish nor anti-Semitic.[3]

A promising beginning on the road to political significance had been made which only public indifference could endanger. The anti-Semitic politicians avoided this hazard in the next few years through a variety of actions, some planned and others improvised. Although extremely embarrassing to the conventional anti-Semites, violence and disorder helped keep them in the public eye. In March 1891, the army had to be called out to restore peace in Hanau (Prussian Hesse) after a crowd stoned one of Böckel's gatherings and threatened him with lynching. Filled with righteous wrath, the anti-Semitic press reported the incident as a plot financed by "Jews and friends of Jews," who had hired Social Democratic thugs to break up a perfectly peaceful gathering.[4] Another ready-made sensation that kept the anti-Semites in the limelight was the "ritual murder" in Xanten (Westphalia), which broke into the German press during the summer of 1891. No matter how bizarre it was, the medieval "blood accusation" that the religious prescriptions of Judaism demanded the periodic use of Christian blood continued to thrive in the nineteenth century. In 1882, the ritual murder of Tízsa-Eszlár in Hungary had rescued anti-Semites from anonymity, at least for a short time. Now, on the eve of the twentieth century, they filled their newspapers week after week with hair-raising tales and lurid innuendoes.

Recognizing the paramount need for publicity, the anti-Semites did not merely sit back to wait for such timely accidents as the Hanau riot and the Xanten murder. They attempted several projects designed to gain and hold public attention. For example, both the German Socials and German Reformers continued vigorous agitation even after the elections of February 1890, an unheard of precedent which aroused apprehension among rival political parties. The parliamentary anti-Semites also took credit for the growth of "social anti-Semitism" evidenced by the increasing number of resorts and hotels which refused Jewish guests.[5] They pointed proudly to the division of university student organizations into German and Jewish, claiming it as a direct result of their agitation.[6] Although some of these ploys were effective, they could not by themselves assure the anti-Semites of continued progress. Actually the anti-Semitic parties stood at a crucial point in their development. In 1890 they had made Germany aware of their existence. To exploit this advantage, to transform it into a permanent gain, they needed assistance, at least for the time being. They received help from the German Conservative party, which was at this time rapidly approaching a crisis of its own.

A few weeks after the election of 1890, the former chief of the German admiralty, Leo von Caprivi, succeeded Bismarck as chancellor of the Reich and minister-president of Prussia. Fully aware that by so doing he had condemned himself to unpopularity, Caprivi entered office at a time when many important decisions had to be made.[7] The new chancellor had not only to cope with his predecessor's fame but with his neglect of long-needed reforms as well. Beginning in November 1890, he presented to the Prussian parliament a reform package designed to enable the government to meet the "socialist danger" without resorting to a new, nationwide anti-socialist law. Although all of his bills contained significant concessions to Junker landowners, Caprivi could not avoid impinging on ancient preserves of privilege and power. Quickly he aroused the mistrust and then the hatred of powerful men.[8]

For a short time, the chancellor succeeded in reversing Bismarck's aggressive anti-Polish policy. His friendliness toward the Poles later earned their key support for some government bills, but at the same time caused an outcry in nationalist circles and among the Junkers of Prussia's eastern provinces. Caprivi further alienated conservative forces by withdrawing a measure that was designed to win their allegiance, the public school bill (*Volksschulgesetz,* January 1892), which, in order to combat "freethinking radicalism," allowed for the direct influence of the churches in education.[9] This last proviso provoked German liberals of every degree, men of science, university figures, artists, and writers to protest in a rare show of unity and effectiveness. Although the Centrists and the Conservatives possessed enough votes in the Prussian parliament to pass the bill over liberal objections, Caprivi, following the instructions of Wilhelm II, withdrew the draft without explanation. Wilhelm feared that the bill would create too much dissension because support from the middle parties (National Liberals, Free-Conservatives) was not forthcoming. Yet the kaiser did not shield his chancellor from the wrath of the Conservatives, and, in the resulting furor, Caprivi resigned the minister-presidency of Prussia, greatly weakening his ability to deal with critical problems.[10]

The parliamentary anti-Semites were among the first to call on Caprivi to take the "next logical step," to resign the chancellorship of the Reich also. The *Antisemitische-Korrespondenz* vehemently condemned the withdrawal of the school bill as the end result of a "liberal-Jewish conspiracy." In the *Neue Deutsche Zeitung* (Leipzig), Liebermann published a long denunciation of the chancellor, charging that he had bowed to the Jewish press and to "hidden powers." Even the supposedly radical Böckel had favored the bill because "only the Jews opposed it."[11] But more significant than the anti-Semitic reaction was the obvious disenchantment displayed by the German Conservatives. A leader in their response was Adolf Stoecker who, in 1889, had been forced by Wilhelm II to choose between his position as court chaplain and continued political activity. Stoecker had chosen to maintain his leadership of the Christian Socials which also allowed him to play a significant part in the German Conservative party.[12] In a speech to the Berlin Conservative election association at the end of March 1892, he condemned the quasi-liberal course of the government and the supporters of that policy within the Conservative party.

Stoecker's reaction to the withdrawal of the public school bill was the first open expression of a power struggle inside the Conservative party between the dominant progovernmental faction and an insurgent group led by Stoecker and Baron Wilhelm von Hammerstein, editor of the *Kreuzzeitung*. Their so-called *Kreuzzeitung* faction had slowly gathered strength among reform-minded "social conservatives" close to the Christian Social party and among ultraconservatives dissatisfied with their party's moderate leadership. Stoecker and Hammerstein had far-reaching plans for the Conservative party. They wanted to free it from dependence on a government seemingly unaware of the dangerous course it was steering toward "democracy."

They intended the party's conversion from a mere representative of the Prussian nobility into a *Volkspartei*, a broadly based party of the whole nation ready to defend German, Christian, and monarchical values against alien liberalism and socialism. In rallying voters to the "new Conservative party" anti-Semitism and possibly the anti-Semitic parties had a role to play. Anti-Semitism was already helping to keep the two poles of the *Kreuzzeitung* faction together.[13]

The aspirations of the *Kreuzzeitung* faction hinged upon the anger of Conservatives in the wake of the deepening agricultural depression of the 1880's and 1890's. The grain-producing East Elbians felt the effects of the economic crisis acutely. The moderate grain tariffs adopted in 1879 and supplemented in 1885 and 1887 failed to counteract foreign competition and falling grain prices. Predicted crop shortages in 1890 boosted prices briefly but also made an issue of agricultural protectionism in the elections of that year. The Social Democrats demanded abolition of all tariffs on food commodities and an end to "bread usury." In spite of fluctuating prices for grain, the cost of bread in Berlin, for example, had risen steadily.[14] Eugen Richter, spokesman for the left-liberal freetraders, raised the issue of protectionism on the first day of the new Reichstag session in May 1890. Throughout the next year, the antitariff clamor included widespread protest demonstrations organized by the Social Democrats. Thus, the German Conservative party, whose major area of strength lay in the grain-producing regions east of the Elbe River, found itself beset by an alliance of "Jew-liberals" and Socialists.[15]

Instead of rescuing the beleaguered Conservatives, Caprivi chose to give special support to German industry. The commercial treaties which had regulated Germany's European trade relations were about to expire. Informed opinion expected retaliation for the tariffs imposed on industrial and agricultural goods since 1879. To fend off this danger Caprivi eventually negotiated favorable trade treaties with Austria-Hungary, Italy, Rumania, Belgium, Switzerland, and Russia. The agreements granted each signatory most-favored-nation status, a reduction of some duties, and stabilization of others for a period of twelve years. The advantages for the business community were clear. Exporters could make long-range calculations based on at least one constant factor, while ruinous tariff wars, such as the one recently fought between Russia and Germany, could be avoided. However, farmers looked at the arrangements differently. The price exacted by the treaty partners was a lowering of Germany's overall tariffs on grain from a total of five to three and one-half marks per one thousand kilograms.[16]

Although the government maintained agricultural tariffs in the face of considerable popular discontent, the Conservative party regarded the commercial treaties as treachery and went into belligerent opposition. Caprivi had negotiated the first set of treaties at a time when grain prices had gone up because of predicted poor harvests. However, the actual harvests proved better than anticipated. In 1892 and 1893 good crops prevailed, sending prices sharply downward. The Conservatives interpreted the price drop as entirely the result of the new treaties. They claimed that Caprivi had sold out to public pressure, had sacrificed the interests of German agriculture, which were synonymous with the "good of the nation," to those of industry and trade. Under the influence of the antiprotectionist agitation and expected high prices for grain, the Austrian treaty had passed with a large majority; even eighteen of fifty-four Conservatives voted for acceptance, apparently unable to oppose a measure supported by the kaiser. The Italian treaty also passed with a substantial majority.[17] It became apparent, however, that any future treaty would pass the Reichstag only with the help of the left liberals and Socialists.

The *Kreuzzeitung* faction seized upon these developments to warn against the certain doom which awaited Germany when it placed trust in revolutionaries, liberals, and Jews.[18] That liberals and Socialists had already united to help pass the treaties and agitate for the withdrawal of the public school bill reinforced Conservative suspicions of conspiracy. Sensing their opportunity in the early part of 1892, Stoecker and Hammerstein launched an all-out attack against the moderates within the Conservative party because of their continuing support for Caprivi's policies.

Meanwhile, a surprising harmony between the five anti-Semites and the *Kreuzzeitung* Conservatives emerged during the Reichstag debates on the commercial treaties. Böckel ceased his Junker baiting. Instead he attacked the left and pointed out "the spiritual relatedness" of the Social Democrats and left liberals, both of whom favored Caprivi's treaties.[19] Böckel's opportunism brought a rebuke from the Socialist Paul Singer but sat well with the approving Conservatives. Liebermann von Sonnenberg "broke a lance for the agrarian cause" when he described the later Russian treaty as "an inner Jena."[20] Liebermann also defended the *Kreuzzeitung* against a sarcastic attack by Caprivi. Furthermore, the small anti-Semitic group in the Reichstag opposed all of the commercial treaties unanimously. The anti-Semites went out of their way to please the Conservatives, but they were at the same time serving their own interests. All of them represented agricultural districts in Hessenland populated by peasant smallholders. The Social Democratic and left-liberal propaganda which aimed at enlightening the smallholder about his interest in abolishing agricultural tariffs failed to take effect in Hessenland until much later. Even though the abolition of tariffs on grain would lower the cost of fodder and thus increase profits for the Hessian hog raisers, Böckel and his successors constantly advocated higher tariffs. In fact, Böckel's agricultural policy never differed from that of the Conservatives and the later Agrarian League, and his supporters always backed him fully on this issue.[21]

On the trade treaties too the anti-Semites and the German Conservatives took exactly the same line of opposition. The agreements, according to Böckel, benefited only industry and trade, "the stock exchange and the Jews." He had argued earlier that it was not high tariffs that made high bread prices, but rather Jewish grain speculators who allowed tons of wheat and rye to rot in order to make their profits.[22] Many Conservatives found it convenient to subscribe to this explanation of high food prices. The ultraconservative Hermann Kropatscheck declared angrily that only Magyars and "Jew-liberals" would benefit from the Austrian treaty.[23] The *Kreuzzeitung* devoted article after article to an anti-Semitic interpretation of the treaties.

The *Kreuzzeitung* faction and the anti-Semites shared another common interest at this time, for the anti-Semites, too, regarded Caprivi as an enemy. For them there could be no true successor to Bismarck. Furthermore, Caprivi left no doubt about how he regarded the anti-Semites. So unequivocal was his stand against anti-Semitism that the anti-Semites never attempted to recruit him as a patron of their cause, as they had done with Bismarck, Wilhelm I, and with

virtually every public figure of stature. Caprivi at first completely
ignored the five anti-Semitic deputies, then treated them with
scathing ridicule, and, finally, taking cognizance of their growing
popularity, solemnly spoke out against them and against their basic
goal:

> When the first legislative step is taken [to abolish the Eman-
> cipation Law of 1869] to this end—already a matter for anti-
> Semitic agitation outside this house—I shall use the means at
> my disposal to oppose it actively.[24]

The anti-Semites interpreted this utterance as a threat of exceptional
legislation similar to that invoked against the Social Democrats.
Whatever his ultimate designs against them, the chancellor gave no
hope of official backing or recognition. They wanted to see him
ousted.

Both the Conservative party and the anti-Semites had a good deal
to gain from active cooperation in the Reichstag and in national
politics. Although five votes in the Reichstag were normally of little
importance, anti-Semitic organizations might prove valuable to the
Conservatives, at least if Stoecker and Hammerstein were successful
in their bid for power. Both these men realized that if the Conservative party remained in opposition, it would need new bases of mass
support. Without the customary government favoritism at election
time, without a near monopoly on positions of prestige and authority,
the Conservatives would be hard put to maintain their strength, let
alone increase it sufficiently to effect a new policy. Only among two
groups could the Conservative party hope to find the popular support which would transform it into a broadly based power in national politics: the argicultural population and the *Mittelstand*.
The anti-Semites might serve as valuable recruiting agents for the
Conservatives with these two groups. Representatives of peasant
voters, the anti-Semitic deputies belonged to the urban *Mittelstand;*
their clubs were to be found in cities and large towns throughout the
empire. With funds and guidance, the *Reformvereine* might perhaps
be extended and enlarged to meet the agitation needs of the "new
Conservative party." Even without extensive reorganization, however, the anti-Semites could be useful. In the Reichstag they had
already acted as hatchet men, performing some tasks which Con-

servatives still felt beneath their dignity. Liebermann, Böckel, Zimmermann, Pickenbach, and Werner did the dirty work of opposition, attacking the chancellor in personal terms, impugning his love of the fatherland, and expressing open disdain for all of the "new course."

For the anti-Semites, a coalition with the Conservatives held out the possibility of immediate effectiveness. Anti-Semitic influence in the Reichstag clearly did not match the strength shown by the German Reformers and German Socials in the nation at large. Prior to 1890, when Otto Böckel sat alone in the Reichstag, he was able to make only four addresses to the house in three years of constant attendance. His first anti-Semitic exposé, warning against relying on Jews to provision the army, drew a merciless heckling from the left and a scolding from the president of the Reichstag for introducing the "so-called Jewish question" into a serious debate.[25] After this humiliation, Böckel almost always came last in the series of speakers after many deputies had already left and others grown tired of listening.

Following the elections of 1890, the anti-Semitic deputies learned that five Reichstag seats were no great improvement. Although they called themselves the *Fraktion der Antisemiten,* they lacked the requisite fifteen members to form a legitimate *Fraktion.* Without this status, they all suffered the disabilities experienced by Böckel since 1887. They were independents, and independents could neither propose legislation nor participate in the various Reichstag commissions which studied, revised, and prepared government bills before a plenary debate. The five anti-Semites thus remained isolated and ineffective. They could not even use the Reichstag for propaganda purposes. "Speaking out the window," in other words, to impress the electorate back home or to gain attention in the national press, was a difficult matter. According to Reichstag usage, the president determined the order of speakers on any issue. He customarily chose on the basis of *Fraktion* strength from those deputies who had previously requested the floor. If the issues merited it, two or three series of *Fraktion* representatives spoke before any independent got a chance. Under this system, the anti-Semites—"members of no *Fraktion*"—rarely got to speak until just before debate ended. Consequently, they lost many good opportunities to make their views heard.[26] The only quick way out of this impotence was to ally with a legitimate *Fraktion,* at least until the next election, which was scheduled for 1895. In the 1890's the common ground for an alliance between anti-Semites and Conservatives had emerged as a result of Caprivi's policies, an agricultural depression, and the demonstrated effectiveness of anti-Semitism as a political weapon.

From Böckel's point of view, there were political perils as well as profits attached to cooperation with the Conservative party. He ran the risk of obscuring the independent anti-Semitic identity which he had so carefully and emphatically created. Moreover, an alliance with "the Prussians" would not sit well with Hessian backers of his party. Yet the possibility of presenting an anti-Semitic bill in the Reichstag with the help of the Conservatives was extremely tempting. The next election was a long way off. Without a notable anti-Semitic success in the interim, the parties might lose the attention of German voters. If, on the other hand, Böckel could maintain his independence and still gain the cooperation of the seventy-three-man Conservative *Fraktion,* much might be accomplished in a short time.

On the side of the Conservative party, too, there was sentiment favoring and opposing partnership with the anti-Semites. Since 1887, Stoecker had gathered support within the party, especially in Westphalia and the Kingdom of Saxony, for a revision of the official party program, which would "give greater consideration to anti-Semitism."[27] Although the Saxon Conservatives appeared to be genuinely anti-Semitic, they did not count for much in the decision making of the party as a whole. However, the extreme right wing of the Conservative party, not particularly receptive to Stoecker's *Volkspartei* ideas, was nevertheless open to anti-Semitism as a way of discrediting Caprivi's policies and getting at the party chairman, Otto von Helldorf-Breda. A moderate, Helldorf opposed the use of anti-Semitism by the Conservatives and frequently spoke out against it in his personal press organ.[28] Anti-Semitism was but one of many conflicts between the moderate and the *Kreuzzeitung* factions, but it proved decisive in rallying support for Stoecker and Hammerstein. On the other hand, many powerful Conservatives suspected that cooperation with the anti-Junker Böckel might be dangerous for the party. As a prerequisite for an alliance, they wanted some measure of control over the unpredictable anti-Semites.

Throughout the imperial era, the German Conservatives always remained skeptical about the anti-Semites as possible allies. In the early 1890's, instead of demonstrations of reliability, the Conservatives had their worst suspicions confirmed. During the autumn of 1891, the most uncontrollable figure in anti-Semitic politics, Hermann Ahlwardt, appeared on the scene. Largely because of his sensational career and its aftermath, the Conservative party defined its position regarding anti-Semitism and anti-Semites.

Hermann Ahlwardt, the "second Luther," as he, too, came to be called, was born in December 1846 in a small town near Anklam (Pomerania). He attended a preparatory school in Oranienburg, was accredited as a public school teacher in 1866, and by 1881 held the post of *Rektor* (principal).[29] Ahlwardt, in contrast to Frederick the Great, with whom he frequently compared himself, spent the first half of his reign in peace and the second half in unremitting war—war on Jews, freemasons, Jesuits, the judiciary of the Reich, and, most of all, on his fellow anti-Semites. In 1884, deeply in debt, he began to embezzle from his school's picnic fund. In 1887 he spent money collected to buy shoes for poor students. He borrowed from a number of loan sharks (predominantly Christians, he later admitted) and fell even deeper into debt.[30] In 1889 his misdoings came to light, and he drew a suspension which left him on half pay until his dismissal in 1893.[31] Without enough to support his family, he cast about for a means of making a living, soon seizing upon anti-Semitic activity as a promising occupation.

His anti-Semitic career began on the fringes of the Berlin movement. But Ahlwardt quickly saw that little more could be expected from the feeble remains of organization there. He set out on his own as a public speaker and publicist. The *Rektor* charged admission to his meetings and had hawkers sell his pamphlets before and after his speech. In 1890 he produced a long description of Jewish evil which gained credibility largely because of its author's shameless confessions of personal dealings with usurers. The signs of a persecution complex, a penchant for self-exhibition and humiliation, a need to confess, reveal, and expose were present in his first work and remained characteristic until his death in 1914.[32] The second part of his first exposé, *The Oath of a Jew (Der Eid eines Juden)*, had political repercussions. The book dealt with a paternity suit concerning Bismarck's banker, Gerson Bleichröder. Ahlwardt presented the evidence in such a way as to make it appear that Bleichröder had perjured himself and been saved by the intervention of Chancellor Caprivi. When the book was proved absolutely false, Ahlwardt went to jail for four months.[33] Nevertheless, the Conservatives managed to debate the matter in the Prussian state parliament, thereby subjecting Caprivi to damaging publicity.

While in jail, Ahlwardt prepared his next sensation, a revelation which earned him yet another epithet, "the modern Arminius" *(moderner Hermann)*. This time he was cautious about putting anything down on paper. Instead, he made a whirlwind speaking tour after his release from jail, building up publicity and teasing his public. In meetings sponsored by anti-Semitic *Reformvereine,* he charged the Jewish owner of the Löwe munitions firm with delivering faulty weapons to the Prussian Army as part of a Franco-Jewish conspiracy. Ahlwardt's disclosures exceeded anything the anti-Semites had yet dreamt up. In Saxony he spoke before audiences of German Reformers and Conservatives. In Berlin, Stoecker, who had confirmed Ahlwardt's daughter and who vouched "for the honorableness of the man and his family," was instrumental in drawing the attention of the *Kreuzzeitung* faction to his usefulness.[34] In the last week of April 1892, Ahlwardt dashed off a pamphlet, *Die Juden-flinten* (Jew rifles), that revealed all. In the three weeks before its confiscation by government order, the book went through twenty reprintings. Less than a month after publication the minister of war, Hans Georg von Kaltenborn, published an official denial of its charges in the *Reichsanzeiger*. On 2 June, Ahlwardt was arrested and charged with two counts of libel against the Löwe firm.[35]

While Ahlwardt was winning popularity with the anti-Semites and making inroads into the Conservative rank and file, he began to pose a serious problem for the leaders of both groups. Undeniably the *Rektor* kept the anti-Semitic cause in the center of public attention. But both Böckel and Liebermann saw earlier than the Conservative party leadership that his revelations, when proved fraudulent, would harm their cause more than help it.[36] Although Böckel had warned five years before of the danger inherent in relying on Jewish firms to supply the army, he did his best to keep his followers clear of the *Rektor*. Liebermann hesitated longer, remaining neutral and perhaps hoping that Ahlwardt could be made into an effective and safe propagandist for the German Social party. Liebermann had difficulty keeping some of his more independent colleagues in line. The emotional Paul Förster, for example, threatened to resign his prestigious commission as officer of the reserve rather than lead his troops into battle armed with Löwe rifles. Dr. Adolf König, leader of the German Socials in Westphalia, continued to offer the *Rektor* speaking engagements even after his arrest. Despite Liebermann's denials, Ahlwardt was frequently referred to as a member of his party.[37]

Certain German Conservatives became even more deeply implicated than the parliamentary anti-Semites as Ahlwardt's rise to prominence began playing a part in the complex struggle going on inside the Conservative party. On 6 April 1892, Helldorf lost his fight against the *Kreuzzeitung* faction and resigned from the Conservative *Fraktion* in the Reichstag and state parliament of Prussia.[38] His progovernmental position and resistance to anti-Semitism no longer commanded the backing of a majority of the party. After Helldorf's resignation, Stoecker began urging the Conservatives to make their anti-Semitic sentiment public by issuing an immediate statement on the Jewish question. Ahlwardt's initial successes in April and May helped Stoecker's project along. The *Rektor* delivered the substance of what was to become his pamphlet, *Die Judenflinten*, to Otto Julius von Wackerbarth (1828–1903), Conservative deputy to the Prussian parliament and a long-time member of the party. Wackerbarth had been present when the sworn statements of some workers dismissed from the Löwe firm had been taken down and put in protocol form by Ahlwardt. In all likelihood, Wackerbarth introduced the *Judenflinten* protocol to his colleagues in the Prussian state parliament.[39] On the basis of Ahlwardt's "proof" of a Jewish conspiracy to undermine the army, the Prussian parliament's Conservative caucus voted overwhelmingly (95 to 1) in favor of incorporating anti-Semitism into the party program.[40] Men of stature within the party, like *Landrat* Wilhelm von Rauchhaupt and Wilhelm von Heydebrand und der Lasa, spoke in favor of the anti-Semitic program revision.[41] However, the instinctively cautious Conservatives resisted Stoecker's demand for an immediate declaration of anti-Semitic principle.

The Conservative party had still not publicly associated itself with Ahlwardt when the minister of war made his official denial of the charges contained in the *Judenflinten* (29 May 1892). The official *dementi* and Ahlwardt's arrest four days later produced serious misgivings among those Conservatives interested in using anti-Semitic agitation to discredit Caprivi's policies or to acquire *Mittelstand* and peasant votes. For others in the party, it was out of the question to criticize the minister of war's competence in these matters or to damage the reputation of the Prussian Army. With well over half of the caucus staying away, the Conservatives now took a new vote on the question of a party program revision. They decided by the narrowest margin (21 to 20) to postpone a revision and a full party congress because of the difficulty of formulating a position on the Jewish question at that moment.[42] After the prosecution in the Löwe suit made known its ironclad case against the *Rektor,* the notion of official cooperation or alliance between anti-Semites of any variety and the Conservative party lost all its attraction. This narrow brush with anti-Semitic fraud convinced the upper echelons of the party that too close an association with the anti-Semites was inadvisable. In the following months, Conservatives learned that such an alliance was not necessary in order to profit from anti-Semitism.

Ahlwardt's arrest, however, did not dissuade many in the lower levels of the Conservative party from agitating for an immediate revision of the party program. The Saxon Conservative party congress (13 June 1892) led the way. A resolution, which passed with a great majority, called the need for a new party platform greater now than ever before. The fight against Jewish power was too important to leave in the hands of the "anti-Semitic rabble" and rowdies like Hermann Ahlwardt.[43] During the summer of 1892, Stoecker bypassed the party leadership in Berlin to rally popular support for the revision movement in western Germany. He persuaded the Conservative club in Hamm (Westphalia) to publish an ultimatum demanding a national party congress and a new program.[44]

Meanwhile, Ahlwardt was loose again. His bail of fifty thousand marks had been raised by contribution within a week after his arrest. On 8 July, he spoke in Dresden of his martyrdom and his stay in the *"Wartburg,"* in other words, jail. The giant audience roared approval after every pause and was generous with its sympathy. The

Rektor received the first of many laurel wreaths; streets were named after him in rural villages. The *Rektor aller Deutschen* soon found himself involved in four concurrent libel suits. But justice in the case of the *Judenflinten* was too slow in catching up with the man who once confided that "when I cannot prove something, I assert it anyway."[45] Ahlwardt had still not come to trial before a backwoods Brandenburg Reichstag district fell vacant in September 1892.

Arnswalde-Friedberg was typical of an area in which anti-Semites acquired some strength. The district had no towns of over ten thousand inhabitants; between 1871 and 1912 it lost three percent of its population. Over half the arable land was in the possession of a few great landholders. In all but one previous election, Conservatives had won easy victories for both the Prussian parliament and Reichstag. The political ignorance and apathy of the rural population had become proverbial long before Ahlwardt's candidacy. In the Reichstag election of 1874, fifteen votes had been cast for the kaiser. In the eight Reichstag elections prior to 1892, participation averaged under fifty-six per cent.[46] *Landrat* Wilhelm von Meyer, representative of the district in the Prussian parliament for many years, once disclosed that his Protestant peasants' outlook was still that of the Thirty Years' War.[47]

Changes in the old attitudes of the inhabitants of Arnswalde-Friedberg were becoming evident, however. The agricultural depression prepared the peasant population for a protest. Eventually that protest, under anti-Semitic guidance, took an anti-Junker as well as an anti-Semitic turn. The German Social party, sensing an area ripe for exploitation, had organized the district the year before Ahlwardt's arrival. Without consulting Liebermann, the local organization offered the candidacy of the vacant district to Ahlwardt, the man of the hour. He promptly accepted from jail where he was serving another term for an earlier slander. Before confirmation of the rumors concerning Ahlwardt's nomination in Arnswalde-Friedberg, the Conservatives put up their own candidate, a wealthy Junker. The left liberals supported a former deputy of the Prussian parliament. The election date fell due five days before Ahlwardt was to appear in court on the *Judenflinten* suit. If victorious in the election, his parliamentary immunity would prevent him from being jailed.

In the ensuing excitement neither Liebermann nor Böckel could restrain their party followers. Whatever the possible consequences, anti-Semites flocked to Arnswalde-Friedberg. The local German Socials, agitators from Berlin anti-Semitic clubs, and Reichstag deputy Pickenbach conducted Ahlwardt's campaign for him. They played upon the sympathies of the peasantry for Ahlwardt's martyrdom to the Jews. They compared him to Christ, Luther, and Hus, carefully explaining that his freedom to go on fighting the common Jewish enemy depended on the outcome of the election. Seldom had the peasants of Arnswalde-Friedberg been made to feel so important. They responded by giving him twice as many votes as his nearest rival, but not the absolute majority requisite for election on the first ballot. The left liberal came in a poor second, slightly ahead of the Conservative. He clearly did not have a chance to win without full support from the Conservative voters. The Center party, *Reichspartei,* and National Liberal newspapers, therefore, admonished Conservative leaders to lend their help in defeating the rowdy demagogue. Instead, the whole Conservative apparatus for influencing elections was tacitly put at the disposal of *Rektor* Ahlwardt. The Berlin headquarters of the Conservative party proclaimed its neutrality, stating that the final decision rested with local party authorities. The local *Landrat,* a member of the party, acted as election commissioner; the county secretary and the director of a local seminary both campaigned actively for Ahlwardt, making use of their prestige as state officials and acting—contrary to law—in their official capacities.[48]

Although his election prospects in the second balloting were excellent, Ahlwardt's court case, which began on 29 November, looked less promising. The prosecution had gathered sixty-four witnesses. Four days after he won the runoff with a crushing eight thousand vote plurality, the court sentenced him to five months in jail, and castigated the defendant in the strongest language for "consciously endangering the interests of the state."[49] As a member of the Reichstag until 1903, he avoided serving his sentence.

Once again, Ahlwardt played a role in the formulation of an anti-Semitic position for the Conservative party. On 8 December 1892, three days after Ahlwardt's victory in the Conservative heartland and amidst the uproar it caused, the leaders of the party convened the first national congress since 1876. The convention met in Berlin's largest beer hall, the Tivoli, and from the beginning it was a wild affair. The new chairman, Otto von Manteuffel, gave free rein to the "democratic" elements present. In addition to the legitimate delegates, "party associates" also gained entrance to the hall without a check of credentials. The noisy group of German Socials under the leadership of Hans Leuss, an anti-Semitic journalist who was later jailed for perjury, helped influence debate on the projected anti-Semitic clause. Of the twelve hundred participants, the majority came from Berlin, an area in which anti-Semites and Conservatives had had close, if not always cordial, relations.[50]

Under the favorable circumstances of the moment, created largely by opposition to Caprivi's commercial treaties but exacerbated by the Ahlwardt affair, the *Kreuzzeitung* faction was able to gather a significant majority of the party. Stoecker was at the height of his powers. Through his newspaper, *Das Volk,* he led the battle to strengthen the projected anti-Semitic clause for the new program. The draft of that program, prepared by the more moderate party leaders and circulated before the congress met, read: "We combat the manifold upsurging and decomposing Jewish influence in our national life. . . . We condemn the excesses of anti-Semitism."[51] Stoecker and the delegates from western Germany conducted the floor fight to strike the last modifying sentence from the program. At a key moment in the debate, Ahlwardt's victim in the election interrupted the proceedings to declare "ten Ahlwardts, ten anti-Semites rather than one left liberal!"[52] The vote by show of hands was all against seven in favor of dropping any qualification of the anti-Semitic plank.

For the followers of Böckel and Liebermann, who suddenly found it again necessary to refer to themselves as the "independent" or "pure" anti-Semites, the Tivoli program fell far short of expectations. The single sentence did not define in a concrete way what the Jews endangered. While denouncing the harmful influence of Jewry, the Conservatives had not included any specific anti-Semitic measures or recommendations in the program. They did not promise support for the anti-Semites or recognize them as partners in the common struggle. Moreover, the behavior of the party leadership at the Tivoli congress had betrayed a lack of sincerity reminiscent of the earlier Berlin movement. For example, Chairman Manteuffel, less moderate than Helldorf but not a member of the *Kreuzzeitung* group, had first

worked for a simple renewal of the old program of 1876. After this
failed, he advocated the qualified anti-Semitic plank.[53]

Although Tivoli was taken by some as evidence of a more "democratic spirit" at work within the Conservative party, the broadly
based *Volkspartei,* built upon Christian socialism and anti-Semitism
desired by Stoecker and Hammerstein, did not come into existence.
Control remained in the same few hands. Policy making was still
anchored in a small committee of prominent Conservatives. These
leaders never lost sight of the rationale for the use of anti-Semitism:
it was no more than a political device which might win votes in
hitherto inaccessible portions of the German electorate. A few months
after the Tivoli congress, Chairman Manteuffel explained the leadership's motives for allowing an anti-Semitic plank into the party
program:

> The Jewish question was not to be avoided unless we wanted to
> leave the full wind of the movement to the demagogic anti-
> Semites; with it they would have sailed right past us.[54]

After the experience of Marburg and Arnswalde, the fear of losing
more ground to anti-Semitic rivals induced the acquiescence of the
traditional powers within the Conservative party. Not really convinced of the Jewish danger or at all interested in anti-Semitic theory,
the leadership nevertheless showed a cynical appreciation for the
usefulness of anti-Semitism. After Ahlwardt, it was too important to
neglect any longer.

First to realize the real political implications of the Tivoli program
was Otto Böckel. He accused the Conservatives of using Ahlwardt as
they had once used Stoecker in the Berlin movement, that is, for
"demagogic," not "sincerely" anti-Semitic purposes. He astutely
predicted that Stoecker would soon be pushed into the background.
Böckel also contemptuously rejected the idea that the Conservatives
would now be able to compete with the anti-Semites for peasant and
Mittelstand votes:

> A party of the nobility and great landholders is still a long way
> from being a *Volkspartei,* even though its program is patched up
> with a piece of the Jewish question.[55]

Thus, instead of a working coalition with the anti-Semites in the

Reichstag, a distinct possibility in 1892, the Conservative party had chosen to take advantage of the growth of anti-Semitic sentiment and to exploit the Ahlwardt sensation, without taking upon itself any of the potentially dangerous consequences of its irresponsibility. The party had skillfully incorporated a useful anti-Semitism while rejecting the unsavory anti-Semites.

Had the Conservative party chosen to take up the interests of peasants and *Mittelständler* and to develop an anti-Semitic program in earnest, the history of the independent anti-Semitic parties might have ended abruptly in 1892. However, the Conservatives made little actual use of Tivoli and usually ignored the implications of their anti-Semitic clause. Their lack of sincerity quickly came into public view during the election campaign occasioned by the premature dissolution of the Reichstag on 6 May 1893. In the preceding autumn, Caprivi had presented a long awaited military reform bill to the Reichstag. Although he took a much more moderate stance than Bismarck ever had on the issue of the military budget, opposition to his proposal was great. In May 1893, a compromise motion advanced by the Center deputy Karl von Huene failed to pass the house. Most of the Center and the left liberals, all the Social Democrats, and the four Böckel anti-Semites voted against the motion. Caprivi dissolved the Reichstag immediately after the vote.[56]

The dissolution had been expected for some time. The Conservatives, however, were not really prepared to fight a radically different kind of campaign. They possessed none of the necessary apparatus— local organizations, professional agitators, popular newspapers— with which to exploit the anti-Semitic potential of the Tivoli program. Conservative candidates conducted emphatically anti-Semitic campaigns only in areas where the German Social or German Reform parties had prepared the ground (Saxony, Brandenburg, Silesia, and Pomerania). In electoral districts where Conservatives competed with anti-Semites or actively cooperated with them, anti-Semitism also made its way into the campaign. In seven cases, Conservative candidates actually fought under the German Social banner, received considerable help from the anti-Semites' organization, but nonetheless "defected" to the Conservative *Fraktion* after victory in the election.[57]

Liebermann eased the way for cooperation with the Conservatives.

Although he generally approved of the government's military bill, he
touched only indirectly on the central issue of the election in his
party's election manifesto. Instead, he concentrated on the agricultural depression and the pernicious effects of Caprivi's trade treaties.
The Conservatives could, in good conscience, join the German
Socials' call

> first of all for a tax on the stock exchange, on luxury, and for
> defense. The stock exchange, i.e., the Jewish speculators,
> jobbers, and grain usurers, who lift hundreds of millions out of
> our people's pockets, who plunder the nation and still go un-
> punished—the stock exchange should bear the extra cost neces-
> sary for securing peace.[58]

Even though the two parties cooperated in seventeen electoral districts, the Conservatives chose not to make an official, nationwide
electoral alliance.

On the other hand, Otto Böckel saw immediately that the Conservatives had no intention of forwarding the anti-Semitic cause.
Moreover, the dissolution of the Reichstag relieved him of any
further need to conciliate the Junkers. If the "pure" anti-Semites
won enough seats to form a *Fraktion,* he reasoned, there would be
much less cause to court the Conservatives. Anticipating the dissolution, he had already resumed his Junker baiting. Allied now in the
German Reform party, Böckel and Oswald Zimmermann had much
to gain from a frontal attack on the Conservatives. Five of eight
mandates to be contested in the Kingdom of Saxony by the Reformers "belonged" to the Conservatives. The two remaining Conservative seats in Prussian Hesse were also due to come under assault.
Böckel and Zimmermann, therefore, purposely composed an election
manifesto to which no Conservative could subscribe:

> The German Reform party is a decisive opponent of the military
> bill because it constitutes an extra burden which the *Mittelstand*
> especially cannot bear. If the fatherland is really in danger, we
> shall answer the call to a man; but we must oppose the lingering
> extra burden, which the bill lays upon our people, with a
> decisive "No!"[59]

The manifesto underlined the Conservative betrayal of *Mittelstand* interests. Böckel expected and desired no aid from the Conservative party.

At the last minute, even Stoecker recognized that the Conservative party showed no inclination to make Tivoli a reality. Two weeks before the Reichstag elections, he published a Christian Social declaration, announcing the independence of his party, "without entering into hostile opposition to the Conservative party."[60] Stoecker had unwittingly begun his long downward slide into political obscurity. The immediate effect of his decision was to ruin his own and his party's chances of winning a Reichstag seat in 1893. For their part, the Conservatives seemed positively glad to be rid of the court chaplain. They offered him only hopeless electoral districts for a number of by-elections after 1893.[61] Stoecker had shown himself incapable of controlling the anti-Semites or exploiting anti-Semitism. He had been eclipsed by Böckel and Ahlwardt. Their rowdyism and radicalism, as far as the Conservative leaders were concerned, typified the independent anti-Semites. Moreover, the price of conversion into an anti-Semitic *Volkspartei* appeared too high. Democratization of the party would increase the influence of western German and non-Junker elements; the essential character of the party would be lost.[62]

What allowed the Conservatives to ignore the anti-Semitic implications of the Tivoli program and the whole tendency toward transformation into a *Volkspartei* was not a rediscovery of the "principles of conservatism," but the birth of a powerful new pressure group. Caprivi's treaties and the lowest grain prices of the decade combined to produce a grass-roots reaction among German farmers. Toward the end of 1892, the announcement of negotiations for a treaty with Russia, Germany's foremost grain-producing rival, gave final impetus to the formation of the Agrarian League (*Bund der Landwirte*) on 18 February 1893. In its stormy beginnings, the league expressed the anger felt by all classes of German farmers. Soon, however, the organization developed into a powerful lobbying agent for the great landholders of East Elbia. Numerically, small- and medium-sized cultivators formed a majority of the membership, but the league's impressively developed organizational network reflected the predominance of large-scale agriculture. Of the league's forty-three chairmen and vice chairmen for state and provincial branches, nineteen owned manors (*Rittergüte*), seven owned smaller manors. There were also two counts, three barons, a general, and five government officials on this level of leadership. At the peak of the organization stood a board of directors, twenty-eight of whom were aristocrats.[63]

Although forwarding their own economic interests was not yet the only concern of Conservatives, it was of major significance. To all but a few of them, agriculture came before anti-Semitism. The Agrarian League gave early promise of being more reliable and effective than the independent anti-Semites or Stoecker in the matter of getting votes for the Conservatives. Furthermore, the Conservative party and the league were bound together in numerous personal unions. Eventually the league became indispensable to the Conservative party. It financed massive election agitation, recruited mass support, and, finally, dictated the political and ideological strategy in the defense against democratic change and on behalf of the Junkers' socioeconomic privileges.[64]

From its inception, the league displayed an informal anti-Semitism. Agrarian opposition in the 1870's, prior to the passage of the grain tariff of 1879, had taken a distinctly antiliberal and anti-Semitic tone. During the 1890's the Agrarian League continued to make copious use of the literature from this earlier period of protest.[65] The league's single biggest gain in membership came in 1893 with the incorporation of the German Peasant Alliance (*Deutscher Bauernbund*). Berthold von Ploetz, leader of the alliance, set the tone for the Agrarians' agitation by declaring "war against the destructive powers of left liberalism, Jewry, and social democracy."[66] From 1894 on, the delegates to the annual general assemblies listened with glee as speakers condemned the "freetraders, liberals, and Jews." Liebermann, who drew no income from farming, nonetheless became a fixture at the annual meetings. He cultivated a relationship with the league, as he had formerly done with the anti-Semitic university students, hoping to enlist them in the struggle against Jewry. But the league was not about to become a tool of the small anti-Semitic parties. In an early statement of policy, Baron Julius von Mirbach, a high-ranking member of the league and the Conservative party, outlined the "proper" relationship which ought to exist between the Agrarians, anti-Semitism, and the anti-Semites:

We in no way deny the kernel of good in anti-Semitism; nor do we combat anti-Semitism—so far as it appears justified to us. However, we feel that it will be very difficult to keep the anti-Semitic current within its legitimate bounds. The attachment of many propertyless people to this movement conceals a possible danger that the current will turn against property as such and that anti-Semitism will sink to a species of social democracy! I certainly hope that the anti-Semites will sail clear of the snags. They will do that best by attacking the electoral districts which are in the hands of the auxiliary troops of the Jews [i.e. left liberals and Social Democrats].[67]

Much of Liebermann's ensuing career was devoted to assuring the league of his party's utter reliability. Mirbach, however, had given good warning of the kind of use the Agrarians would make of anti-Semitism and of the independent anti-Semites. Although the league had its share of "sincere" anti-Semites, especially on the staff of its most effective newspaper, the *Deutsche Tagezeitung* (Berlin), the Agrarians' brand of anti-Semitism was to prove no less "demagogic" than that of the Conservative party. Anti-Semitism remained firmly subordinated to the interests of agricultural policy.[68]

While the Agrarian League influenced the further development of parliamentary anti-Semitism, it was still too weak to make itself felt in the national elections of 1893. The organization supported candidates from the Conservative party, the right wing of the National Liberals, and the *Reichspartei,* and also helped five German Social anti-Semites. The Conservatives added only four seats to their Reichstag delegation. But the Prussian parliament elections a few months later demonstrated the potential of the Agrarian League as the Conservatives increased their representation by nineteen seats.[69] This proof of the league's strength determined the Conservatives' relationship to the anti-Semitic parties during the rest of the Wilhelminian era. For the Conservatives, the Agrarian League remained a clearly preferable alternative to coalition with any of the anti-Semitic parties.

The behavior of the Conservatives in the early 1890's drew criticism from many quarters in Germany. Liberals never tired of accusing them of prime responsibility for the spread of anti-Semitism in the empire. With more justice, the conservative *Reichspartei* scolded them for unscrupulously fishing in troubled waters.[70] Many contemporaries regarded the adoption of the Tivoli program by the Conservative party as a momentous step in the development of political anti-Semitism. Hellmut von Gerlach after renouncing his Christian Social past as a "disease of childhood" observed that anti-Semitism

> made the greatest possible gain in prestige when it was included in the Conservative program. . . . Now it became the legitimate possession of one of the greatest parties, of the party closest to the throne and holding the most important positions in the state. Anti-Semitism had moved up close to the border of social acceptability.[71]

The momentary boost in prestige afforded by the Conservatives surely helped the anti-Semitic parties to the conquest of sixteen seats in the national elections of 1893. The official statistics showed 263,861 votes for the explicitly anti-Semitic parties (German Reformers, German Socials, and Christian Socials) or 3.4 percent of the total. Including the votes of the seven who ran under Liebermann's German Social program, but later joined the Conservative group in the Reichstag, the total amounted to 342,425 or 4.4 percent. These figures, of course, do not reveal the anti-Semitic tone of many opportunistic campaigners and fellow travelers, taking advantage of the latest trend in German politics.[72] Fittingly, however, the Conservative party suffered most from its own dabbling in anti-Semitism. The Conservatives had once held no fewer than ten of the sixteen districts won by anti-Semites.[73]

In the elections of 1893, the German Socials and Reformers contested sixteen districts in Hessenland and won eight; eleven in Saxony and won six. The independent Ahlwardt triumphed in two districts, Neustettin (Pomerania) as well as Arnswalde. The double victory resulted in a by-election, in which Paul Förster "inherited" Neustettin. The anti-Semites retained all the gains of previous elections, while their vote increased six-fold from 1890. In addition to their surprising gain of six new seats in the Kingdom of Saxony, they made impressive gains in Schleswig-Holstein, the Prussian province of Saxony, Alsace-Lorraine, and the free city of Hamburg. With this indisputable show of strength, the anti-Semitic parties strode forward. Their own optimistic predictions suddenly appeared less implausible.

CHAPTER 4

A Fragile Unity, 1893–1894

So impressive a showing for the anti-Semitic parties in the elections of 1893 left contemporary politicians groping for explanations. Stoecker, a loser in two districts, cried foul demagoguery on the part of the winners, Böckel and Ahlwardt. Liberals blamed the irresponsible Conservatives or the nationalistic hysteria which the government inspired on behalf of its military reforms.[1] Most opponents preferred to find their reasons in temporary political conditions instead of conceding anything to the political capabilities of certain anti-Semites. The postmortem theorizing was clearly partisan, avoiding or brushing aside the truly essential questions. What caused the phenomenal increase in the anti-Semitic vote? Were 350,000 Germans actually willing to revoke Jewish emancipation? Who voted anti-Semitic and why? How many others would do so in the future?

For the anti-Semites speaking officially, these were simple questions simply answered. A vote for the German Socials or German Reformers meant that the voter wished primarily to revoke Jewish emancipation. At least publicly, Böckel, Zimmermann, and Liebermann never admitted the existence of a possible conflict between group interest and anti-Semitism. Only rarely in public did any of these leaders betray doubts about the motives of the "typical" anti-Semitic voter. He had come to recognize the paramount danger of Jewish power and would remain an unswerving anti-Semite for the rest of his days. According to this interpretation, the man who cast his vote for an anti-Semitic party also saw its representatives as champions of certain economic reforms that would insure final victory over the Jews. But the voter acted from idealistic motives; that his personal economic position might be improved by the anticapitalistic measures of the German Socials or Reformers was incidental and secondary to him. Even if Böckel and Zimmermann

91

recognized that the party was of the *Mittelstand* and could prosper only if it appealed strongly to the special interests of *Mittelständler* and peasants, they denied that the German Reform party was "a narrow interest group" or that its anti-Semitism was "demagogic."[2] They explained away their obvious representation of particular class and group interests by arguing that thus far the only truly reliable elements in the fight against the Jews had been the unsullied peasants and *Mittelständler*. The German Socials and German Reformers merely aimed at strengthening these two groups, which together constituted the "German economy," for the final battle with "Judah's money power."[3]

Unfortunately, information abundant enough to construct a voter profile, a description of the "ideal type" who placed his confidence in one of the anti-Semitic parties, is not available for this period of German history. Any interpretation of voter motivation, therefore, must be of tentative validity. However, why a man voted anti-Semitic in 1893 was a good deal more complex than the facile anti-Semitic explanations would have it. Certainly, a dislike of Jews must have been present in those who voted for a Böckel or a Liebermann. But how intense was that dislike? Was anti-Semitism the most compelling motive? In 1893, I believe, there were several additional reasons for voting anti-Semitic, at least as important as anti-Semitism itself.

The anti-Semitic parties had identified themselves as opponents of Chancellor Caprivi from the very beginning of his tenure. They had spoken out against the trade treaties, against his catering to the Poles, Danes, and Alsace-Lorrainers, and finally against his proposed army increases. In short, they had clearly rejected every element of the "new course" and had done so in the Reichstag, in their press, and in public gatherings all over Germany. No other party had taken so clear a stand. Just before the elections of 1893, the Conservatives had slipped back into a "governmental" position by fully supporting the military bill. On the other political extreme, the Social Democrats had weakened their reputation as the unyielding foe of the government by helping pass Caprivi's commercial treaties. Many who detested the "new course" for national reasons as well as socioeconomic ones found in the anti-Semites a method of registering their protest at recent developments. In this respect, the election came at the best conceivable time for the anti-Semitic parties. Not only did the political and economic circumstances of the moment favor a protest vote, but the anti-Semites had not yet convincingly demonstrated their complete ineffectiveness as representatives of group interests. It was not yet sufficiently apparent to the German voter that the German Socials and Reformers could simply not get things done. By the next election in 1898, the public had had ample proof of the anti-Semites' inability to realize any part of their program.

In 1893 it was still possible for the anti-Semites to capitalize on their youthful image. The sixteen anti-Semitic deputies averaged thirty-eight years of age; ten were under forty and twelve completely new to politics.[4] Brash, inexperienced, but daring and energetic, the German Socials and Reformers presented the illusion of an effective alternative to their rivals—in Böckel's words, "the old burnt-out parties." Liebermann's old slogan "new times, new parties" suddenly seemed relevant. Further, the anti-Semites had alertly prepared for the premature elections of 1893 and were able to field a full slate of candidates before the "old parties" could decide their own.

These factors constitute at best a partial explanation of anti-Semitic success in 1893. In addition, some hypotheses about the composition of the anti-Semitic vote and its territorial distribution may help round out the picture. Approximately 56,900 votes came from Hessenland. This sizeable total represented the harvest of Böckel's thorough agitation, made more effective by the ongoing agricultural depression. In Brandenburg and Pomerania *Rektor* Ahlwardt's unflagging popularity with both peasants and *Mittelständler* in spite of arrest and conviction accounted for 10,581 votes in the anti-Semitic total.[5] The most surprising development in the 1893 Reichstag elections, to the opponents of anti-Semitism, was the conquest of six new seats in the Kingdom of Saxony and an increase of ninety thousand votes there since 1890.[6] This incursion upset several old theories about the origins of anti-Semitism, its vote-getting potential, and dangerousness. Until 1893 many men with varying degrees of goodwill had viewed the rise of anti-Semitism as the more or less justified reaction of the politically immature to the real or imaginary misdeeds of Jews. This appeared a reasonable way to explain events and

pointed clearly to the best methods of defense against anti-Semitism:
enlightenment of the German public and encouragement of the
Jewish population to behave itself properly. This widely held view
rested on the assumption that if the truth were only known and if
the "cause"—Jewish misbehavior—were removed, anti-Semitism
would disappear and the parties would wither. Now, however, the
proponents of this theory had to explain the deep inroads made by
the anti-Semites into the Kingdom of Saxony, an area of Germany
where Jews constituted .27 percent of the total population.

In 1890, Saxony's Jews numbered 9,368 in a population of
3,840,000. As late as 1867, Jewish habitation had been restricted to
Leipzig and Dresden, and in 1885 almost eighty-five percent of the
Jews still lived in a few large cities.[7] A relatively large percentage of
the Saxon Jews were nonnaturalized *Ostjuden,* Jewish immigrants
from eastern Europe. Almost three-quarters of the Leipzig Jewish
community were *Ostjuden,* who earned their livelihood in petty trades
as retailers and wholesalers. Undoubtedly, the "hordes of *Ostjuden*"
who traversed Germany on the way to North and South America presented a likely target for anti-Semitic propaganda. The phantom of
a Germany swamped by eastern European Jews, although statisti-
cally groundless, haunted many Germans continuously from the
mid-nineteenth century through all the years of the Weimar Republic. Only a tiny fraction were permitted to settle permanently on
German soil.[8] But occasional expulsions and rigidly restricted naturalization procedures did not still anti-Semitic fears. Jews from the
East represented all that was inferior, sinister, and detestable in the
Jewish "race," as far as they were concerned.

Even so, the concentration of *Ostjuden* in Saxony did not provide
the "cause" that led Saxon voters to the German Socials and German
Reformers. In Leipzig, where the majority of *Ostjuden* lived, the anti-
Semitic vote in 1893 was far behind the rest of the kingdom. Anti-
Semitic victories came in places like Bautzen, Meissen, and Pirna,
towns with almost no Jewish population. In Dresden, where the
Jewish population was small and mostly of German citizenship, the
anti-Semites made a clean sweep of the three electoral districts.
Moreover, in Saxony, it was not a case of a few Jews exercising great
economic or political power. Aside from dominating the Leipzig fur
trade, the small Jewish population did not concentrate in any

particular area of commerce. The *Leipziger Zeitung* approvingly emphasized the impotence of Saxony's Jews:

> Not a single Israelite, to our knowledge, is in the Saxon civil service and not a single financial institution is in Jewish hands. There is not a trace of the predominance of Jewish capital anywhere in Leipzig. . . . The social role of Jewry is also a zero.[9]

Thus, neither the number, character, nor economic power of Saxony's Jewish inhabitants offered a convincing explanation of why the parliamentary anti-Semites had scored such a decisive victory there.

Few outside the anti-Semitic camp believed that ninety-three thousand Saxons had voted for the German Reformers or Socials with the primary purpose of revoking Jewish emancipation. Only the most fanatical could believe that in 1893 the voters suddenly awakened to the international Jewish danger, in spite of little or no direct contact with Jews. Not even the anti-Semites dared to claim that there was a Jewish problem in Saxony itself. Ironically, the very magnitude of the Saxon victory robbed the "official" interpretation of an anti-Semitic vote of any real credibility. Although they never wholly admitted it publicly, the anti-Semitic leaders must have been at least uncertain that the positive appeal of anti-Semitism was alone responsible for their success.[10]

An objective analysis of the vote for the anti-Semitic parties in Saxony in 1893 can dispense with the idea of a primary commitment to anti-Semitism per se because anti-Semitic candidates did steadily worse in subsequent elections. In 1898, they lost half of their six seats to Social Democrats; in 1903, two more. However, if ninety-three thousand Saxon voters showed only a questionable enthusiasm for the specifically anti-Jewish measures advocated by the parties, they did show a high tolerance for anti-Semitism, which, although not conforming to the anti-Semites' ideal, could nonetheless be useful to them. This receptivity to anti-Semitism had clear causes. For many years the chief agent of political anti-Semitism in the kingdom was the Saxon government itself. Discrimination in civil service appointments was the most conspicuous evidence of governmental prejudice. But the selection of privately owned newspapers to publish official information also indicated the prevailing anti-Semitic attitude of government. Deputies of the Saxon state parliament often com-

plained about "official" newspapers such as the *Dresdener Journal,
Leipziger Zeitung,* and *Bautzener Nachrichten,* which were openly anti-
Semitic and at times indistinguishable from the anti-Semitic party
press.[11] Of the major German states, only Saxony prohibited kosher
slaughtering (1892–1910) in order to discourage the immigration of
orthodox *Ostjuden.*[12]

Thus, the ordinary Saxon voter, unlike his counterpart in Hessenland or Prussia, received no indication from his government that
anti-Semitism was suspect or in any way undesirable. In addition
to the government's unambiguous discrimination, the anti-Semitism
of the prestigious Saxon Conservative party also worked to the political advantage of the German Reformers and Socials. Although the
Reformers and Conservatives often disagreed on matters of socioeconomic reform and the personal integrity of their respective leaders, the two agreed about the necessity of anti-Semitism.[13] Gradually
anti-Semitism had earned a degree of respectability in Saxony
unequalled anywhere else in Germany. From the Saxon voter's point
of view, the anti-Semitism of the German Socials and Reformers
constituted no valid reason for withholding support.

But in 1893 the anti-Semitic parties in Saxony also had something
positive to offer a prospective voter, for both the Reformers and Socials appealed strongly to Saxon *Mittelständler.* Large numbers of
them chose the anti-Semites to carry their protest against serious
economic troubles. Indeed, the economic condition of the Saxon
Mittelstand in the early 1890's merited protest. One of the most industrialized and densely populated areas of Europe, Saxony had
enjoyed a steady increase in well-being during the 1880's and 1890's.
However, the distribution of this increased wealth was far from even.
In 1886, twelve percent of the population was considered poverty
stricken (*Unbemittelte*). Those classified as *Mittelstand* formed close to
one-third of the impoverished category (about 106,000 people).
In Saxony at least, Marxist predictions concerning the *Mittelstand*
were coming true. Small-scale businessmen and self-employed artisans were becoming economically dependent wage earners. The
caste conscious *Mittelstand* was falling into the ranks of the faceless
proletariat.[14]

Driven to desperate measures, the *Mittelstand* survivors of capitalism chose the anti-Semites as a suitable means of protest. They
shared in the general illusion of the anti-Semitic parties' promise of

effectiveness and were misled by their uncompromising opposition to the Caprivi government. Furthermore, the anti-Semites appeared young and vital, willing to go further than the middle-class parties or the Conservatives, which had dominated the kingdom in previous elections and which had been unresponsive to the needs of the *Mittelstand*.[15] As in Hessenland, power in the established parties resided in a few influential persons who did not seek out constituents or expend much energy in preparing the electoral district. Once again, as in Hessenland, the anti-Semites exploited this indifference by means of incessant agitation and personal contact on the local level of Saxon politics. Although generally ignored, the organizational growth of the anti-Semites before 1893 had been steady. The Leipzig *Reformverein*, headquarters of the German Socials, nearly doubled in size between October 1891 and February 1892. The Reformers made equally impressive progress. On a single day, Oswald Zimmermann signed up two hundred and twenty new members for the *Reformverein* in Bautzen after delivering a stinging attack on the "two chief problems of the day, Jewry and social democracy." Both parties got an early start for the elections of 1893 by forming centralized agencies to map campaign strategy. Several small newspapers were purchased during the summer of 1892. The two parties also worked out a division of the kingdom into respective areas for agitation and refrained from petty backbiting until after the elections.[16]

At long last in 1893, the middle parties paid heavily in votes for their past indifference. The comparative table below gives a good idea, but no absolute certainty, of where the anti-Semites got their votes:[17]

Party	1890	1893
Conservative	129,341	126,727
Reichspartei	31,066	21,545
Center	202	518
National Liberal	112,514	49,554
Left Liberal	52,786	30,194
Social Democratic	241,187	270,654
German Social/German Reform	4,788	93,364
Others	—	139
	571,884	592,695

The German Socials, German Reformers, and Social Democrats shared the twenty-one thousand "new voters"—those who had not voted in the 1890 election or who had come of voting age since 1890—and the ninety-five thousand who defected from the middle parties. Since the Conservative vote remained virtually unchanged and the Socialists gained thirty thousand, it seems fair to assume that the majority of the ninety-three thousand anti-Semitic votes came from the distressed lower middle class, those with the most cause to switch allegiance from the ineffectual *Reichspartei,* National and left liberals. If in these statistics there was a large "hidden shift" of proletarian votes for the anti-Semites (and therefore, an equally large shift from the *Mittelstand* to the Socialists), it escaped the notice of both anti-Semites and Social Democrats. Both subscribed to the interpretation of the election results given above. Furthermore, the Reformers and Socials directed their campaign, not at workers, but at the *Mittelstand* and "the best elements" of society.[18]

Although the anti-Semites gained approximately fifteen percent of the vote in the main election, they eventually commanded twenty-five percent of the Reichstag seats allotted to Saxony. They owed their disproportionate number of mandates to election alliances in the second round of balloting. The strong showing of the German Reformers in the main elections won them the support of many National Liberals, left liberals, and Conservatives who considered an anti-Semite a lesser evil than any Socialist. Mindful of this attitude, the anti-Semitic candidates consistently presented themselves as a "dam against social democracy." Throughout the imperial era, they tried to exploit this fear and hatred of the Socialists.

In Saxony, however, exploiting the "Socialist danger" became increasingly difficult for the German Socials and Reformers. The breakthrough of 1893, although startling, proved impossible to broaden or even maintain. Apparently, Saxon *Mittelständler* had put the bulk of their faith in anti-Semitic promises of rescue from economic oblivion rather than from the "Jewish danger." After 1893 as the plight of the *Mittelstand* worsened and after the anti-Semitic parties proved politically inept, Saxon voters deserted them for a more effective protest party. Gradually, the Social Democrats strengthened their hold over "the red kingdom." Especially after a reactionary modification of the state election laws which tended to disenfranchise workers and *Mittelständler,* the Social Democrats were able to lure away *Mittelstand* votes from the anti-Semites and Conservatives.[19] All this is not to say that the ninety-three thousand Saxons who voted anti-Semitic in 1893 changed their minds about Jews by 1898. They were in all likelihood more disappointed with the anti-Semitic parties than with anti-Semitism.

A comparison between the Kingdom of Saxony and Hessenland, the two main sources of Reichstag seats for the anti-Semitic parties in 1893, reveals a few similarities and some striking contrasts. In both areas, anti-Semitic parties took root where the middle parties and the Conservatives had dominated and where their political remoteness had created grievances. The German Socials and Reformers organized extensively on the local level. Both countered the methods of the "old parties" with constant agitation and personal contact. Finally, they were able to take advantage of serious economic discontent by posing as champions of threatened economic groups. But here the likenesses between Hessenland and Saxony end. Saxony was industrial, Hessenland agricultural. Both parties relied almost exclusively on peasant support in Hessenland. But in Saxony, predominantly the *Mittlestand* voted anti-Semitic. Victory in Hessenland came in the face of stiff opposition from state officials and from special defense organizations.[20] The Saxon success took place in an atmosphere of toleration toward anti-Semitism and without real opposition. In Hessenland the Social Democrats constituted a negligible factor in politics; in the Kingdom of Saxony they posed so great a danger that many non-anti-Semites supported the anti-Semites in runoff elections. Finally, the intensity and durability of the Saxon's attachment to anti-Semitism was at least a matter of doubt outside the anti-Semitic camp. By 1893, Böckel's peasants had already proved their loyalty.

Close by one another in central Germany, the two regions which provided the anti-Semites with a considerable victory in 1893 presented glaring differences. The absence of uniform backing, revealed clearly for the first time in the 1893 election, remained an unresolved problem for the parliamentary anti-Semites. Although party membership, always a small fraction of those who voted anti-Semitic, was almost exclusively from the *Mittelstand,* support at the polls came from two separate social groups whose interests were difficult to reconcile. Neither the German Socials nor the Reformers were willing to rely on the peasants or the *Mittelstand* exclusively. By itself neither social grouping offered a large enough or a receptive enough base with which to win a Reichstag majority—the constant objective of parliamentary anti-Semitism. Yet in 1893 two essentially different groups of voters had backed the anti-Semites. How could their support be maintained and expanded without exposing their basically conflicting interests?

Oblivious to the long-range implications of this conflict, the anti-Semitic politicians preferred to tackle simpler problems. In the days after the 1893 election, the means for keeping up momentum were much discussed in the anti-Semitic press. Plans for unification of the various parties and groups into a "single fighting force" appeared with increasing regularity. In the Reichstag, the anti-Semitic deputies had gradually come to appreciate the need for unity and the rich possibilities which would open to a united party. As two separate parties in the Reichstag, they found that the gain of eleven seats since 1890 made their lot no easier.

Inadvertently, the Conservatives instructed the anti-Semites in the need for unity by withholding support from anti-Semitic measures in the Reichstag. Baron Hammerstein made it clear that help would not be forthcoming on any regular basis. He saw to it that no Conservatives helped sponsor Böckel motions.[21] As far as Hammerstein was concerned, the "wrong" anti-Semites had made off with the bulk of the spoils in 1893. Liebermann, Paul Förster, Adolf König, and Hans Leuss sat for the German Socials. All four were acceptable in Conservative circles. The official handbook of the Conservative party for 1894, the first to include a special section on anti-Semitism, expressed the preference of the party:

> With the German Social wing of anti-Semitism, as represented in the Reichstag by Liebermann von Sonnenberg, the Conservative party has many points of contact in regard to both means and ends.

On the other hand, the eleven German Reform deputies led by Otto Böckel clearly did not conform to Conservative canons of respectability:

[The existence of points of contact] holds less true for the "reform wing" and its auxiliaries. In recent times they have taken
a manifoldly unconservative stand, which does not halt at
combating the harmful influences of Jewry, but has gone over to
the attack on protected institutions and . . . leading classes
(*Stände*) of the fatherland; thus they have discredited the anti-
Semitic cause.[22]

In the hierarchy of respectability, not an inconsequential matter in
the inner workings of the Reichstag, the unaligned Hermann Ahlwardt occupied the bottom level, especially after his anti-Junker
election campaign of 1893. Their uncertain interest in the Jewish
question and the unacceptability of a majority of the anti-Semitic
deputies to the powerful Conservatives pushed the anti-Semitic
leaders in the direction of unification.

However, even before the convening of the new Reichstag, the
anti-Semites learned that a bloc of sixteen votes could have impressive effect, if skillfully employed. During the period of Caprivi's
chancellorship, sixteen votes often meant the difference between
success and failure for a government bill. The proposed expansion of
the army, which occupied first place on the agenda for the new
Reichstag, offered the anti-Semites a chance to be effective. Caprivi
had gambled by dissolving the previous Reichstag since he had had
no assurance that the voters would return a majority for his military
bill. After the elections of 1893, it was still not apparent that the bill
would pass. Hard pressed, the government actively sought votes from
the opposition, including those of the anti-Semites.[23] For this purpose
Caprivi employed a more or less unofficial press agent, Major-
General August Keim. Keim was free to act "somewhat less bureau-
cratically" than the overly scrupulous chancellor and was an ideal
man to deal with the anti-Semites. Like Liebermann von Sonnenberg, he was one of those key individuals in the Wilhelminian era
connected with almost all the important organizations of the right.[24]

Even during the Reichstag elections, Keim was already fairly
certain that the anti-Semitic deputies could be won for the bill in
spite of their campaign manifestoes. As the election results came in,
he and his wife, in good military fashion, marked a map of Germany

with blue (favorable) and red (opposed) crosses; the anti-Semitic candidates were among the blues.[25] On 14 July 1893 the anti-Semites fulfilled Keim's hopes. All thirteen deputies present voted for the amended bill, thus enabling its passage with a slim majority, 198 to 187. Anti-Semitic support had cost the government only a slight concession. Caprivi accompanied the revised bill with the promise that he would meet the increased costs for the army without raising the beer and spirits tax which weighed heavily on the "little man." Instead, the financial burden would rest upon "shoulders more capable of bearing" the expense. It was the extra expense of an expanded army, not any aversion to militarism, which had constituted the main objection of Böckel and his followers.[26] They could now vote for the bill without risking the charge of treachery from their constituents.

The educational value of the negotiations concerning the military bill was more significant for the development of parliamentary anti-Semitism than the intrinsic worth of the government's concession. For the first time, the anti-Semitic parties had gained recognition as a legitimate political force. They had learned that on certain issues they could exert an influence upon the government, if they remained unified. They expected this effectiveness to grow as their numbers swelled in the Reichstag—only a matter of time, in their opinion. But even before they acquired an "inevitable" majority, the Reichstag could be influenced in a truly anti-Semitic way. If the anti-Semites could continue to act together, a parliamentary solution to the Jewish question would soon become a reality.[27]

The yearning after parliamentary effectiveness was only one influence leading toward unification of the anti-Semitic parties. Böckel, Liebermann, and Zimmermann also came under pressure exerted from below. Formal unity had been the wish of ordinary party members ever since the late 1880's. If the anti-Semitic leaders wished to demonstrate their sincerity about solving the Jewish question, if they wanted to dispel growing suspicion about their own political careerism, then clearly they ought to bury their hate-filled rivalries and show a united front to the enemy. Such reasoning was widespread and gaining ground in the lower levels of the party membership in the early 1890's. Even after the failure of the Bochum "unity" congress (1889), attempts at cooperation and conciliation had not altogether ceased. In November 1891, for example, Böckel, Zimmermann, and Liebermann had reached full accord on respective areas of agitation and spheres of interest in Germany.[28]

Shortly after this historic meeting, however, a new and complicating factor appeared on the already confused scene of anti-Semitic politics when Paul Förster made his own bid for leadership of the movement. Formally a German Social, he nonetheless organized a new group, the Anti-Semitic Agitation Association for North Germany (*Antisemitischer Agitationsverband für Norddeutschland*), representing approximately fifty *Reformvereine* in Brandenburg, Pomerania, Mecklenburg, West Prussia, and Posen.[29] Förster hoped to mediate between the two rival parties and come out on top as the logical choice for chairman of a new party. At the first congress of the North German anti-Semites, the assembled delegates sent a solemn "instruction" to the leaders of the German Socials and Reformers demanding immediate unity.[30]

Förster's new creation certainly impeded unification efforts. But the main obstacle was still the bitter personal feud between Liebermann and Böckel. In the past, Liebermann had always shown himself more tractable than his younger rival. For example, while addressing the Silesian German Social congress of October 1892, he had expressed the desire for a long term rapprochement with Böckel and the German Reformers. After all, Liebermann correctly maintained, the parties pursued exactly the same objectives. Only a difference in tactics kept them from "marching together" as well as "striking together." Böckel conquered one electoral district after another. The German Socials, on the other hand, merely wished to tackle the Jewish question more quickly by forcing the German Conservatives, Center, and National Liberals to take an anti-Semitic stand in the Reichstag.[31] But Böckel interpreted Liebermann's moderation as a reflection of the essentially weaker position of the German Social party. He shunned all feelers from the German Socials as attempts to share in his glory. In November 1892, Liebermann, undeterred, made a new try at conciliation. He invited Böckel to address the *Reformverein* in Leipzig, headquarters of the Socials. At the meeting Liebermann dramatically announced that north Hessenland, where his party possessed some strength, would be thrown open to Böckel's Central German Peasant Association.

Rumors of imminent unification made the rounds of the daily press. Yet, once more, Böckel refused to take up Liebermann's initiative.

Behind this stubbornness lay more than Böckel's often demonstrated selfish pride. The "peasant king" had begun to falter in Hessenland. In late 1892, a number of problems emerged which two years later resulted in the complete undermining of his power. Among the difficulties which plagued him was the financing of his overextended party organization. Böckel had a poor head for business. In order to prepare Württemberg for conquest, he reportedly purchased the *Ulmer Schnellpost* for sixty thousand marks, a great strain on the slender resources of his party.[32] Professional organizers had to be paid. His so-called positive measures, the cooperative stores, insurance programs, and savings banks, which were meant to be self-sustaining, ran into serious financial trouble. After "Jewish inspired" Social Democratic typographers refused to set type for the *Reichsherold,* Böckel bought a publishing house and cavalierly outfitted it with an expensive steam-run press.[33] Bankruptcy beckoned. His only source of income to meet current expenses and short term debts came from the dues-paying membership of the peasant association. According to his own figures, he could expect no more than fifteen thousand marks annually if every peasant member met his obligations.[34] But Böckel had, from the beginning, earmarked these funds for the direct furtherance of the peasants' economic well-being. Even if he misused this money to meet the expenses of his political party, he could not possibly pay his own way. Furthermore, he had always refused to "go begging" to the rich, the way Liebermann, Bernhard Förster, Ahlwardt, and Stoecker had been in the habit of doing.[35]

At the height of his financial troubles, Böckel ran into problems of a moral nature as well. While preaching a return to Germanic virtues and urging German girls to refrain from so much as dancing with Jewish boys, Böckel himself had sired an illegitimate child. The mother sued for maintenance and involved him in a lengthy and personally damaging lawsuit. Instead of appearing in court, he sent his wife, the daughter of a minister, whom he had married in 1890. The Protestant clergy of Hessenland openly condemned him for his immorality and cynicism.[36]

Although both the financial and moral difficulties proved relatively easy to explain away to gullible peasant voters as "Jewish slander," Böckel committed one unpardonable sin. He had trained some promising native Hessians for party work, but his rapidly expanding apparatus required importation of more professional agitators. He had no choice but to recruit them from Berlin, the only training ground for anti-Semitic agitators before 1890. Starting with Wilhelm Pickenbach, he enlisted a number of shady "Prussians" into his personal circle. Not anti-Prussian himself and quite at home with the more sophisticated rabble-rousers from the North, he rapidly alienated his immediate native following. Philipp Köhler and Otto Hirschel, Böckel's disciples, managed to block Pickenbach's renomination for the Reichstag in 1893. Moreover, the employment of frock-coated Prussian foreigners gave them an issue with which they could appeal to the anti-Semitic peasants, an issue which Böckel himself had used with great success in the past.[37]

Most of Böckel's problems could have been solved by a timely merger with the German Socials and North German anti-Semites. Although the German Socials had their own financial problems, Liebermann's party had a more far-flung membership and good relations with men of wealth. The fanfare accompanying unification might also deflect attention from Böckel's lawsuit. Even the use of Prussians could be better, though not wholly, justified if the German Reformers became part of a powerful nationwide organization. But rather than unite and lose the chance for sole leadership, the prize he had fought for from the beginning, Böckel chose to risk everything. His last hope was a success in the elections which he, like many other politicians, anticipated in late 1892. If the Reformers elected enough deputies to form an independent *Fraktion* in the Reichstag, he expected to dispense with Liebermann. But Böckel made two miscalculations. Chancellor Caprivi did not dissolve the Reichstag at the end of 1892 as predicted, but attempted to pass his military bill in spite of a cold reception from the parties and the public. Reichstag debates, commission deliberations, and amendments of the bill consumed more time than Böckel had reckoned on. It was probably during this unforeseen delay that his former friends made a breach in the leader's following.

Böckel's second miscalculation was also to be his last great victory. The Reformers elected eleven deputies, four short of the number needed to form an independent *Fraktion* but seven more than his rival, Liebermann. Had Böckel chosen to negotiate a merger in the summer of 1893, right after the national elections, he would have enjoyed the advantage. Liebermann, in an open letter, admitted Böckel's superiority and spoke piously of their mutual debt "to all the anti-Semites in the country to form a *Fraktion* of united anti-Semites now."[38] But, instead of exploiting his strong position, Böckel stalled a little longer. His crony, Fritz Bindewald, won a by-election for Alsfeld in the Grand Duchy of Hesse. Böckel threw out feelers to Ahlwardt, the pariah, inviting him to join his party. He felt certain that he could pry loose either Hans Leuss or Dr. König from Liebermann. Several by-elections were also in the offing, any one of which could provide him with the fifteenth man needed for the *Fraktion*.

Kept alive by all these hopes, Böckel answered Liebermann's open letter with a point-blank refusal to negotiate.[39] Liebermann gave up trying to work through Böckel and in his desperation made overtures to Stoecker's sickly Christian Social party.[40] For Böckel, however, matters did not go smoothly. Förster resigned from the German Social party in October 1893, but chose to remain independent and began circulating his own unity program. Ahlwardt, too, showed no inclination to join Böckel. Böckel's men failed to win any more by-elections, and he had now to bear the largest part of the responsibility for the continuing impotence of the divided anti-Semites. As the foremost obstacle to unity, he began to lose popularity among anti-Semites of every party.

Well into the second session of the Reichstag (November 1893–April 1894), the anti-Semites still sat in two separate parties. Unless they banded together, their deputies could not form a legal *Fraktion*. Liebermann could bring forward a complicated legal motion to restrict Jewish immigration from Russia only with the help of the Conservative *Fraktion*, which took most of the credit. Demonstrations of weakness like this added to popular pressure for unification which began to bypass the stubborn leaders and threaten their authority. Zimmermann and Liebermann and Böckel's subordinates began negotiating behind Böckel's back.[42] They were spurred on by minor setbacks in the state parliament elections during the summer of 1893. The few successes in these elections disappointed the lofty expectations of the parties. The Reformers elected three deputies in the

Grand Duchy of Hesse. The Socials penetrated the Saxon parliament, gaining two seats. But elsewhere the anti-Semites failed completely. In Baden and Württemberg zealous campaigning yielded nothing. In Prussia the prejudicial indirect, three-class suffrage kept ten contestants from victory. In Berlin all four anti-Semitic–Conservative seats on the city council were lost; worse yet, that body now contained nineteen Jewish deputies.[43]

The outcry among local *Reformvereine* was long and loud. The absence of progress originated in a lack of unity and nothing more, according to Böckel's own Kassel *Reformverein*. The German Socials of Bromberg came forth with several unification plans of their own. The German Social state organization for Pomerania called for immediate unity at its congress in July 1894. Throughout the late summer, local organizations made their pleas and threats. In the fall, influential locals in the Rhineland, Breslau, Hamm, Hildesheim, and Nordhausen added their voices to the general call for immediate unity.[44] The most ominous development, however, took place in Böckel's home *Reformverein*. In Kassel, the German Reformers elected a new central committee for the whole party organization. Instead of reelecting Böckel, they chose Ludwig Werner, Zimmermann, and Reichstag deputy Carl Lotze. These men had all expressed their readiness to unite with the German Socials.[45]

Böckel found himself friendless. He had already sold his printing house. Now he was excluded from office in the party he had created. On 24 September 1894, he resigned the presidency of the peasant association under obvious pressure from his lieutenants. His exit from Hessian politics showed the same flair for drama as his entrance eleven years before. As he left the meeting hall, he swore never to return to Hessian soil, a vow he kept with the significant exceptions of the 1898, 1903, 1907 and 1912 election campaigns. He was the victim of his own Hessian party colleagues. Köhler, member of the Reichstag and the Hessian parliament, replaced him as president of the peasant association. In league with Otto Hirschel and Fritz Bindewald, Köhler had carried out the coup. He admitted, in an open letter, that the move had long been in preparation and that Bindewald and Hirschel had sounded out the local peasant organizations in advance. According to the letter, the reasons for the banishment of the "peasant king" were twofold:

From the first it was the weak side of Dr. Böckel to neglect the most loyal, noble, and well-intentioned of his friends and to entrust his salvation, body and soul, to more sordid elements.[46]

To Köhler's way of thinking, "body" referred to Böckel's immoralities, "soul" to his consorting with Prussians. The letter also alluded to the leader's financial mismanagement as a danger to the entire anti-Semitic movement. With Böckel ousted, the particularist tendencies of Hessian anti-Semitism were reaffirmed. The Central German Peasant Association became the Hessian Peasant Alliance (*Hessischer Bauernbund*). Henceforth, "false friends" would be kept far from Hessenland.[47]

Although Böckel could always find some support in the Hessian peasants, they offered little resistance to his dethronement. He had ignored the strong anti-Prussianism of his immediate followers and mass backing. He had also violated the common code and endangered the respectability of conventional anti-Semites beyond the borders of Hessenland. As a result, he soon found himself on the periphery of the movement. In September 1894 he moved to Berlin with the *Reichsherold,* which became a weekly, then a monthly, and finally ceased appearing with any regularity in March 1895. He lived from hand to mouth, soon compromising every one of his "ideals" in the struggle to make a living. He found employment in the statistical bureau of the Agrarian League, which he had often called the "League of Prussian Windbags."[48] He worked closely with Ahlwardt in Berlin, although he had been the first to recognize the *Rektor* as a charlatan and fool. In 1896, he sold reports of Reichstag commission meetings, few of which he ever attended, to a Jewish journalist.[49] This from the man who had declared in the Reichstag: "I have no commerce with Jews." Otto Böckel, who had campaigned under the slogan "against Jews and Junkers," did business with both.

His fall removed the last obstacle to unification of the anti-Semitic parties. Oswald Zimmermann, Liebermann von Sonnenberg, and Otto Bachler, representing the North German anti-Semites, negotiated a merger of the three parties. Two weeks after Böckel was out of the way, the union took place with deceptive ease. On 7 October 1894, the leaders convened a combined congress at Eisenach to complete formalities and celebrate the union. The one hundred and fifty participating delegates voted unanimously in favor of the unification plan proposed by their leaders. Since the failure of the Bochum congress to bring about unity, the anti-Semites had learned much. They avoided the habitual controversy over the name of the new organization. An unwieldy combination of the two major party names resulted in the Anti-Semitic German Social Reform party (*Antisemitische Deutschsoziale Reformpartei*). The congress, without debate or vote, declared Zimmermann and Liebermann to be cochairmen of the new party. Both were conveniently so overcome with emotion that a former North German anti-Semite had to make the closing speech.[50]

In spite of displays of feeling, the leaders did not lose sight of the main rationale for unification. They attempted harmony neither in ideological matters nor in political viewpoints. Only as one party could the fifteen anti-Semitic deputies (Böckel excluded) form a Reichstag *Fraktion*. To this end unity had to be achieved swiftly, while the Reichstag was still in recess. Although the party chairmen left the way open for Böckel to join the new *Fraktion*, they could have little doubt that he would scorn the opportunity. Therefore, the Ahlwardt question became more important than ever before: he was the fifteenth man. The delegates spent three hours deliberating over his status before deciding (143 to 7) that he could not become a full-fledged member of the *Fraktion*, but would be allowed "guest" (*Hospitant*) privileges. He could not vote in party caucuses but could be legally counted in the *Fraktion* of the German Social Reformers.[51]

The Eisenach congress deferred two other matters which might have led to time-consuming conflicts. A special committee took on the task of working out the "details of organization." As long as the committee deliberated, all existing anti-Semitic organizations would continue to operate in their customary fashion. With this formula the anti-Semites neatly dodged a significant problem, preferring to give assurance to vested interests that their domains would remain undisturbed, at least for the time being. In fact, the party put off the creation of a uniform organizational structure for approximately three years. When an attempt to remedy the situation did come, it dealt in half measures and remained ineffectual. For the sake of an easy union, the Social Reformers let slip the best opportunity for establishing systematic control over the anti-Semitic clubs and for defining the powers of party institutions. In their haste the delegates also postponed the formulation of a new program. Anti-Semites had always placed great faith in the efficacy of programmatic statements. The making of manifestoes, declarations, and resolutions customarily occupied much of their time. The program was, in their opinion, too important a matter to rush through at the Eisenach congress. Instead, a top-level committee was designated to draft a new program as quickly as possible.[52] Clearly, the union of anti-Semitic parties constituted little more than a tactical maneuver to increase parliamentary effectiveness. At birth the German Social Reform party appeared makeshift and destined for a short life, a party without an organization or a program.

CHAPTER 5

Organization and Ideology:
The German Social Reform Party, 1894–1898

In the years after 1894, the leaders of the German Social Reform party had the opportunity to give substance to the hastily executed unification of Eisenach. They had at their disposal the raw materials with which to build a significant political force: a network of political clubs, a highly developed press, and a dedicated group of activists. Otto Böckel had shown how these three elements could be welded into a powerful organization, and how they could be used reciprocally to expand his movement. Now it was the job of Liebermann and Zimmermann to apply Böckel's principles on a nationwide basis. But under their slipshod leadership the opportunity was squandered. Instead of laying the groundwork for success, they prepared the failure of parliamentary anti-Semitism in the German Empire.

Incoherent organization remained the hallmark of the parliamentary anti-Semites, even though they had developed a unique and potentially powerful institution—the *Reformverein*. This anti-Semitic political club differed considerably from those of other parties. Until the twentieth century, the local political organizations of the liberal and conservative parties led irregular existences, springing up before elections and disappearing soon afterward.[1] But the anti-Semitic *Reformvereine* that took root in the early 1880's did not concern themselves solely with election agitation. They were permanent institutions dedicated to anti-Semitic education, political propaganda, and fund raising as well as electioneering. They usually formed around strong personalities. Liebermann controlled the Leipzig *Reformverein*; Zimmermann, that of Dresden; Ludwig Werner, the one in Kassel; Köhler, the Marburg and Giessen clubs. All the major leaders established and maintained their relations with the grass-roots, club level of the movement. After unification, the number of *Reformvereine* remained fairly stable at 140, although a few new ones occasionally appeared and a few old ones vanished. Approximately twenty clubs refused to associate officially with the new party, and a few others kept their old party names.[2]

Zimmermann and Liebermann did not tamper with the *Reform-vereine*. Instead, they concentrated their efforts on the middle levels of anti-Semitic organization, the creation or remodeling of state and provincial bodies.[3] In Prussia, organization followed provincial boundaries except in the eastern portions of the kingdom. For East Prussia, West Prussia, and Posen, the party relied upon individual *Reformvereine* in Königsberg, Thorn, and Bromberg in order to communicate with a sparse membership. Pomerania, Silesia, Brandenburg, Schleswig-Holstein (and Hamburg), Hanover, the Rhineland, and Prussian Hesse (including Waldeck) all possessed *Provinzial-verbände* (provincial associations) with presidents, vice-presidents, secretaries, and treasurers. Each *Verband* held its own congress at irregular intervals to elect officers and discuss regional matters. Largest among the Prussian provincial associations was that of Brandenburg, which sported a central committee as well as the full complement of offices.

In Prussia the law forbidding combination of associations for political purposes (*Vereinsgesetz*) prevented the subordination of local *Reformvereine* to the provincial associations. The Associations Law, part of the Prussian Constitution of 1850, was in force until 1900. The enforcement of the law was the option of the government, so a great deal depended upon the good will, or the lack of it, on the part of state officials.[4] However, any organization which regularly opposed the government, such as the Social Democratic party, the Agrarian League, or the German Social Reform party, had to protect itself from possible dissolution. All these organizations tried to avoid appearing to be a union of local chapters under central control. Therefore, according to the fiction adopted by the Social Reformers, the provincial association was just one more totally autonomous anti-Semitic club. As a result of this expedient, however, the party leaders were unable to tighten their control over the *Reformvereine* and provincial associations of Prussia.

Outside Prussia, where the *Vereinsgesetz* was less strictly enforced or nonexistent, the organization could be more effectively centralized. *Landesverbände* or state associations operated in Bavaria (after 1896), Baden-the Palatinate-Alsace-Lorraine, the Kingdom of Saxony, the Grand Duchy of Hesse, the Duchy of Brunswick, Magdeburg-Merseburg-Duchy of Anhalt, and east and northwest Thuringia. In addition, the Lübeck and Münster *Reformvereine* acted as central "state" associations for their surrounding areas. Strongest among the *Landesverbände* were Saxony, with thirty-three *Reformvereine* divided into subgroupings, and the Grand Duchy of Hesse, where chapters of the Hessian Peasant Alliance counted as local party organizations. In most of the state associations, the chain of command and channels of communication were more clearly defined than in Prussia.

The elaborate structure of the German Social Reform party developed slowly and in careful imitation of the established parties. An eclectic creation, it made no innovations in the German party system. Theoretically democratic, the party was in fact an oligarchy. Real power over national policy, the use of funds, and, in most cases, even the choice of candidates lay with the Reichstag *Fraktion* and a clique led by Liebermann. Liebermann's powerful personality, long experience in anti-Semitic politics, and possession of key posts at each level of the party structure assured him of overriding influence. With Böckel gone, he was the natural choice for chairman of the party, an office he grudgingly shared with Zimmermann. Liebermann was the guiding force in the party directory, which was composed of the two chairmen and the Reichstag *Fraktion*. He directed the central committee (chairmen, directory, presidents of state and provincial associations, and state parliament deputies), and kept firm control over the provincial association for Pomerania. Finally, at the lowest level in the party structure, he retained the presidency of the Leipzig *Reformverein*. Similarly, Zimmermann, Philipp Köhler, and Ludwig Werner held positions of power on all levels of the party hierarchy.

Democratic bylaws could not stop these men from working their will upon the party, so long as they stuck together. During the short history of the party, actual practice counted more than theory, and, for this reason, democratic safeguards were regularly ignored and easily undermined by the leadership.[5] For example, the central committee, designed to moderate the power of the directory and to keep top leaders informed about the will of the rank and file, failed to do its job. The duplication of personnel in the directory and the central committee effectively negated the power of the latter. Not only did the entire directory belong to the committee, but most directory members were at the same time presidents of state and provincial associations. The duplication extended even further down the chain of command to the *Reformverein* level; every member of the directory was at the same time a chairman or officer in a *Reformverein*.[6] The same few individuals also managed to hamstring the theoretically democratic annual congress, an institution copied from the Social Democrats. Here, too, the directory usually kept the upper hand, for it set up the agenda and provided the documentation for debate. One of the party chairmen presided over the meetings. Furthermore, by virtue of their offices in state and provincial associations and in the *Reformvereine*, members of the directory exerted great influence on the choice of delegates to the congresses. Despite these precautions, however, the party congresses sometimes proved embarrassing to the leadership. "Unauthorized issues" crept into debate. The *Fraktion* position on certain questions came under fire. Even members of the ruling clique were occasionally subjected to sharp criticism from rank-and-file delegates.[7]

One of the most common sources of conflict within German political parties, the selection of candidates, caused a great deal of trouble among the German Social Reformers, too. The party paid lip service to the concept of local autonomy but nevertheless tried to work out a system of authorized candidacies. Initiative in the choice of contestants, according to the bylaws, came from local *Reformvereine* in the electoral district or from special agents in cases where the district was without an anti-Semitic club.[8] But the directory often wished to bestow candidacies upon influential anti-Semites, friends, or possible financial backers. These "dictated" choices often went unrecognized by local anti-Semites. On the other hand, the directory was not always pleased with the autonomously chosen candidates. With so many disreputable characters constantly issuing from the ranks of the anti-Semites, the possibility of wildcat candidacies, such as Ahlwardt's in 1892, had to be outlawed for the sake of anti-Semitism's good name. Now that only one anti-Semitic party existed, it would be impossible to shunt off responsibility on the "other party." The Social Reformers therefore adopted a formula used by Liebermann since the Ahlwardt affair. The directory would grant its blessing only if a prospective candidate's public statements conformed to "German Social Reformist or intellectually related anti-Semitic tendencies." In spite of the formula, the party and its successors continued to be plagued with double candidacies in which anti-Semites ran against anti-Semites, wildcat contestants, and nominees who later switched party allegiance.[9]

Another significant organizational failing was in the field of anti-Semitic journalism. Potentially a source of great strength, the twenty-two newspapers of "German Social Reform persuasion" reached a wide audience. Three of the strongest papers were Liebermann's *Antisemitische-Korrespondenz,* Zimmermann's Dresden daily, *Deutsche Wacht,* and the *Staatsbürger-Zeitung* of Berlin. Together, they had approximately twenty-five thousand subscribers in the 1890's. However, subscription statistics do not accurately reflect the number of people who came into contact with the anti-Semitic press. Coffeehouses, taverns, and hotels often provided free copies to their customers. Secondary circulation was at least as large and perhaps larger than the number of paying subscribers.[10] Still, the anti-Semitic newspaper business was a perilous enterprise. Relatively easy to establish, they proved extremely difficult to keep going. Only the *Antisemitische-Korrespondenz,* the *Staatsbürger-Zeitung,* and the *Deutsche Reform* managed to survive until 1914. All three changed ownership, publisher, or location on a number of occasions. The mortality rate among anti-Semitic newspapers was astounding. Between 1890 and 1897, the period of political anti-Semitism's flowering, thirty-six new papers appeared; by 1898, only seven were still in operation. The average life span for the individual newspaper was two years.[11] This lack of staying power, combined with the continual appearance of new competitors, naturally vitiated the effectiveness of the anti-Semitic press.

Instead of supporting the two or three newspapers of proven durability, the anti-Semitic leadership left the press untouched. The reasons for this hands-off policy were complex. Traditionally, journalism provided anti-Semites with their first practical experience in the movement.[12] As a preparatory school and an introduction to the limited number of ideas required by aspiring anti-Semites, the many newspapers served a definite purpose. However, the main reason for leaving them unregulated had less to do with the future training of recruits than with the vested interests of the moment. Anti-Semitic politicians used newspapers as props for personal power. In 1894, eight of the sixteen Reichstag deputies owned or edited an anti-Semitic sheet. A newspaper was the indispensable weapon in the arsenal of anyone with leadership pretensions. All the major personalities acquired personal press organs to make sure that their opinions got the proper airing. Liebermann, already heard in the pages of the *Neue Deutsche Zeitung* (Leipzig), purchased the *Anti-semitische-Korrespondenz* from Theodor Fritsch in 1894. Köhler and Otto Hirschel consolidated their positions as the successors of Otto Böckel by founding a newspaper in Offenbach, the *Deutsche Volks-wacht*.[13] Oswald Zimmermann owed his rise to cochairmanship of the party to skillful handling of the *Deutsche Wacht*.

Zimmermann's case illustrates the importance of the press in anti-Semitic politics. Under his direction since 1887, the *Deutsche Wacht* became a lively affair. Its editor was an able journalist and phrase-maker. After being attacked by the Saxon Conservatives, Zimmer-mann menacingly dubbed them "Cohn-servatives." He was also quick to see the effectiveness of Böckel's agitation in Hessenland. In a stroke of good timing, he associated himself with Böckel's Hessian organization before the elections of 1890. Zimmermann was not as forceful a speaker or as original an organizer as Böckel. Yet he had one indisputable advantage over his partner, a regular income. In 1893, at the crest of the anti-Semitic wave, he made the *Deutsche Wacht* a joint stock company. Although the *Deutsche Wacht* corporation never paid a dividend and in fact began running a deficit im-mediately, Zimmermann, as its director, earned an annual salary of approximately six thousand marks. He had, moreover, overcapital-ized the company and kept ten percent of its shares.[14] By means of this shady dealing, he gained for himself the prestige of a personal newspaper and a comfortable income.

The *Deutsche Wacht* was one of the few anti-Semitic newspapers to enrich anyone. But while it was normally an unlucrative occupation, anti-Semitic journalism did provide a minimal economic existence for many who had no time to pursue another vocation. A very high proportion of the anti-Semitic Reichstag deputies listed their profession as "journalist" in the official handbook.[15] Until the Reichstag instituted per diem allowances in 1906, the leaders of the anti-Semitic parties showed little inclination to exert control over or to clean up their press. Always on the verge of extinction, the numerous shabby papers did nothing to enhance the respectability of the movement. Despite deep-seated yearnings for respectability, the conventional anti-Semites never allowed themselves to understand why their newspapers had to purvey scandal, sensationalism, and crime in order to appeal to their readers. They seemed not to recognize that their own press was riddled with all the defects for which they condemned the "Jewish press"—superficial, biased, and often inaccurate reporting, "coarseness of tone," and a proneness to libel suits.[16]

The regulation of the press, central control over candidacies, and organizational restructuring, important though they were, depended to a great extent upon another problem, that of finances. Acquiring funds for the party remained a basic and pressing problem, recognized but not remedied by the anti-Semites. Once again, the leaders were primarily responsible for failing to put the party on a sound financial basis. In feudal fashion, they refused to distinguish between public and private sources of income, a vitally important distinction because most of them lived off some aspect of their anti-Semitic activity. Accusations of mismanagement and malfeasance frequently caused internal rifts and damaging publicity. Calling leaders to account for the use of "party funds," a vaguely defined term, produced schisms, resignations, and purges. Part of the problem was legal. The Prussian Associations Law hampered the centralization of finances because a hostile public prosecutor could cite the regular payment of dues to a central treasury as evidence of an illegal coalition for political purposes. Anti-Semites, therefore, resorted to various expedients to get around the law. Because individual *Reformvereine* could not contribute to a national political organization, the president of the local club gave the collected funds in his own name and as a private individual. But this device begged for abuse. The president and treasurer of a *Reformverein* could cheat both their own members and the national party treasury by delivering less than they had collected. The party's national headquarters made no systematic check of income sources on the *Verein* level. Many of the clubs conducted their financial business in a very lax manner, trusting too steadfastly in their officials' "Germanic sense of honor."[17]

The problem was not one of mechanics alone, however. The German Social Reformers needed more money. The cost of political activity mounted steadily in imperial Germany. Salaries for professional agitators, the printing and distribution of propaganda material, and the manifold expenses of Reichstag, state parliament, and municipal elections drained the treasury. As election campaigns, the main expense of the party, grew more sophisticated, they grew more costly.[18] In 1893, the various anti-Semitic parties contested 128 electoral districts. For most they undertook no serious agitation, and therefore spent almost nothing. But in Neustettin and Arnswalde-Friedberg the North German anti-Semites spent 11,700 marks, 4,000 marks in the runoffs alone.[19] In the other seriously contested districts, the expenditures probably stayed well below this level. However, because anti-Semitic candidates rarely won on the first ballot, the party actually had to pay for two campaigns in almost every district it conquered.

To improve the financial situation, the directory defined party membership in explicitly monetary terms: all who paid dues to a *Reformverein* or directly to the central treasurer (where no local club existed) were formal members of the German Social Reform party. The party, like most others in the *Kaiserreich,* never divulged its total membership. However, on the basis of figures for some of the *Verbände* and *Reformvereine,* it is possible to arrive at an estimated strength of thirty to thirty-five thousand members, or about ten percent of the anti-Semitic vote during the mid-1890's.[20] Theoretically, one-half of the dues paid to local *Reformvereine* was earmarked for use by the national party. At the height of its powers, the Social Reformers probably had an annual income of no more than fifty thousand marks.[21] Like their political competitors, the anti-Semites tried to raise additional funds. Their insistent pleas for money alternated between pathos, anger, and admonitions to be like the Jews, who allegedly gathered vast sums to prosecute their war on Germans. The parliamentary anti-Semites devised special funds for frequent election campaigns and monuments to German heroes. However, the official receipts of such "one-time" gifts, acknowledged in special columns of their newspapers, rarely amounted to more than a few thousand marks in any year.[22]

The anti-Semites were in a unique position. No party was as bereft of wealthy supporters as the Social Reformers and their successors. The German Conservatives represented the interests of great landowners. By the end of the 1890's, the expenses of agitation in the interests of agrarian conservatism were borne by the Agrarian League, whose membership stood at over three hundred thousand. Local Conservative magnates customarily financed elections in their districts. The *Reichspartei,* representing both big business and big landowning, had ample resources with which to finance its small organization. The National Liberals spoke for the wealthiest sectors of German society. Their Reichstag and state parliament deputies regularly contributed a third of the party's annual budget. Even the left liberals, whose mass following came from the same groups as that of the anti-Semites, could tap powerful freetrade interests by championing laissez-faire economic policies in the parliaments of Germany.[23] The anti-Semites, on the other hand, represented only peasants and *Mittelständler,* whose individual capacity for monetary sacrifice was not great. Yet the collective wealth of these two sectors of German society was adequate for the tasks set by the parliamentary anti-Semites. Had the party aroused the enthusiasm of these groups, had it spread the anti-Semitic message to greater numbers and awakened the spirit of sacrifice as the National Socialists were later able to do, the nagging problem of finances could have been overcome.

The leaders of the party, however, were content to cut corners while waiting for anti-Semitism to catch on as a mass movement. Most of the parliamentary anti-Semites assumed that this wait would be short, involving only a few years of hard times. In the meantime, German Social Reformers continued some very questionable practices. Charging admission for public speeches, one of Ahlwardt's innovations, gained general acceptance in the party. Liebermann charged thirty marks to address smaller gatherings and fifty marks for larger ones. For a typical month in 1895, he could have raked in one thousand marks.[24] What he did with this income became a constant source of concern within the party and ridicule from its enemies. The fear of adverse publicity probably kept the Social Reformers from going quite as far as Böckel and Ahlwardt's briefly revived *Antisemitische Volkspartei,* which charged an entrance fee to its own party congress in 1895.[25]

This laxity in financial matters and willingness to wait for the situation to remedy itself damaged the credibility of the German Social Reformers as a political party. Prior to 1906, Reichstag deputies received no salaries or per diem allowances to help pay their expenses in Berlin or for frequent travel to and from the capital. The lack of income seriously affected the conduct of the anti-Semitic *Fraktion.* While the Social Democrats were able, by means of their tight organization and mass following, to support their *Fraktion* members in Berlin with modest allowances, the anti-Semites got no help at all. Part of the explanation for the anti-Semitic deputies' hyperactivity lay in their great need to make a living. Charging fees to speak to supporters contributed to their perilous livelihoods, although certainly not to the prestige of the party. Furthermore, the poorer anti-Semitic deputies were frequently absent to make public appearances or conduct their newspaper businesses. They usually appeared in Berlin only for crucial votes. The other parties, with the exception of the Social Democrats, normally put up candidates who were self-supporting and who did not have to tend to business during Reichstag sessions. This alternative was not open to the anti-Semites. Instead, they hunted for state parliament seats, which usually entailed some form of payment. Those few anti-Semites fortunate enough to hold both Reichstag and state parliament mandates rarely attended sessions in Berlin. Köhler in the Grand Duchy of Hesse and Zimmermann in the Kingdom of Saxony sometimes missed entire sessions of the Reichstag in order, it was suspected, to collect their state parliament allowances.[26]

Until 1898, the anti-Semites fought desperately to make do with their own sources of income. But in that year the directory took steps to tap resources outside the party. Liebermann announced the creation of the Receipt Club *(Quittungsmark Verein),* open to any German Christian inside or outside the regular party structure. One-fifth of the Receipt Club's income would be spent on the organization's own administration, publicity, and projected expansion. Two-fifths was destined for general agitation and enlightenment of the German public on the Jewish question; the remaining two-fifths was to be saved for regular Reichstag elections and by-elections. With typical optimism, the directory voiced the hope that all who had voted anti-Semitic in 1893 would feel qualified to join the new club.[27]

Ultimately, the German Social Reform party's financial feebleness opened it to extraparliamentary and even non-anti-Semitic influences. The perils of cooperation with parties and groups that were not primarily dedicated to combating Jews had been well demonstrated by the Berlin movement and by the Conservatives as recently as 1892. In such arrangements the anti-Semites always tended to become the anvil instead of the hammer. Many rightly feared such cooperation as a threat to their independence. To accept financial aid from outside sources threatened to besmirch further the idealism of the party. On the other hand, to do without it might mean bankruptcy and impotence. Slowly, the party began falling under the sway of the Agrarian League, one of a few organizations in Wilhelminian Germany both willing and able to help the anti-Semites. After its founding in 1893, the league grew steadily in size and strength, showing singular capability in the raising of funds and conducting of massive propaganda. Its large network of strictly controlled local chapters staffed by paid professionals made it the most powerful lobbying agent in the empire.[28]

The exact relationship between the German Social Reform party, its successors, and the Agrarian League was of great concern to friends and enemies of the party. Liberal opponents of both the anti-Semites and the league insisted on regarding the anti-Semites as nothing but pawns of the Agrarians.[29] Yet the relationship was not that simple during the 1890's. The anti-Semitic politicians proved anything but tractable servants of the Agrarians. For its part, the league was very selective about which anti-Semites earned its support. This often acrimonious relationship played a vital part in the development of parliamentary anti-Semitism and its eventual fragmentation in 1900. For the time being, however, some anti-Semites found in the league a means of moral and financial support. While the league was in its infancy, the anti-Semites and Agrarians developed a theoretical division of labor. The German Social Reformers were to deal with the cities and towns, where the Agrarian influence remained weak; the league would take care of agitation in rural areas, with the exception of Hessenland.[30]

Even before all these organizational arrangements went into

effect, anti-Semitic leaders were at work on the second matter left
unresolved by the Eisenach unity congress, the writing of a party
program. The top-level drafting committee, composed of Liebermann, Zimmermann, and Paul Förster, took approximately four
months to produce the three-thousand-word document, which came
to be called the Erfurt program. Its ten "guiding principles" and
nineteen "demands" contained all the flaws of previous German
Social and German Reform statements: great length, logical incon-
sistency, and the mixing of lofty principle with niggling detail. Upon
publication in early 1895, the draft elicited considerable criticism
from the regular German press. One or two of the "practical demands," especially those regarding court reform, earned condescending praise as "worth looking into" or "worth further study."
For the most part, however, the press of every political tendency
found the statement confused, a hodgepodge of unoriginal and
conflicting ideas.[31] The Erfurt program met adverse criticism largely
because its authors were unable or unwilling to address themselves to
an audience that did not share their assumptions concerning the
Jewish question. As rhetoric, it was a complete failure. It spoke only
to the convinced.

The document was most consistent, and least successful, in its
attempt to portray the German Social Reformers as a true *Volkspartei*,
a party of the whole nation. The method of its adoption played a
part in this image building. The draft appeared in several anti-
Semitic newspapers well in advance of the scheduled ratification
congress. Throughout the early part of 1895, *Reformvereine* all over
Germany debated and amended the program and sent their recommendations to the committee. In this manner the party aped the
democratic procedures employed by the Social Democrats in the
adoption of their program of 1891. However, the "democracy"
proved a sham, the outward trappings of a party that wished to appear grounded in "the people." On 21 October 1895 at Erfurt,
Liebermann, always annoyed by theoretical discussion, gaveled
through acceptance of the program with virtually no changes and
no debate.[32]

In content, too, the anti-Semites thought that their new program
conformed to the contemporary idea of a *Volkspartei*. Although the
anti-Semites in the Reichstag always supported high tariffs and

agricultural protectionism in general, they claimed to act on the "basis of German nationality," and not in order to help the big landlords at the expense of the masses.[33] The anti-Semites did not feel that such a position impaired the democratic image, which they further cultivated by demanding retention of universal, equal, and direct suffrage and legal safeguards for a secret ballot (pt. 1). The advocacy of democratic voting rights in national elections reflected the Social Reformers' confidence in the German electorate and in their own future: the party would move steadily forward at the polls and eventually achieve its programmatic goals. So certain were they of anti-Semitism's mass appeal that they demanded the transformation of the right to vote into an obligation to do so. Liebermann insisted that the anti-Semitic victory of 1893 would have been even greater had everyone been forced to vote.[34]

Advocacy of democratic suffrage made its way into the Erfurt program, not from any commitment to democracy, but because it appeared useful to the anti-Semites. They were not so certain about the usefulness of equal, direct, and secret voting in the state parliaments, however. In 1890 Otto Böckel had called for the extension of the Reichstag suffrage to the state parliament elections, aiming especially at abolition of the prejudicial three-class franchise of Prussia. At Erfurt a few anti-Semites raised this demand again. Several Saxon party members objected, explaining that although this democratic principle was "justified" in national elections, in state elections it would overwhelmingly benefit the Social Democrats of heavily industrialized Saxony. This undemocratic but no less useful position received full support from Liebermann, and the Erfurt program made no mention of electoral reform for the states.[35]

For the same combination of pseudodemocratic and utilitarian motives, the program supported freedom of speech and assembly, freedom of religion and political association (pts. 2–3). The German Social Reform party and its predecessors felt victimized by bureaucratic arbitrariness in the exercise of their basic rights.[36] Point five of the program thus called for: "Elimination of the ruling bureaucratism; occupation of the higher administrative positions by professional and knowledgeable officials." But posing as champions of the basic freedoms and the rule of law did not prevent the anti-Semites from denying those freedoms to political opponents and

Jews. Censorship of the "Jewish press," for example, was a moral necessity, a safeguard for the purity of the German spirit (guiding principle 2). Freedom of religion also had its limits: Jewish religious practices were to be allowed only in so far as they did not arouse public anger or break the law (pts. 3 and 4). Ever since the publication of Wilhelm Marr's *Victory of Jewry*, anti-Semites had striven unsuccessfully to free themselves from the stigma of religious intolerance. Their predilection for racial theories stemmed largely from the desire to avoid being branded as reactionary religious bigots. Racism, they felt, put the matter on a higher, a nonreligious plane. In fact, they ought to be regarded as "progressive" and even "scientific."[37] Racists, however, believed that the whole religion of the Jews was inextricably bound up with the Jewish spirit, with "Jewish blood." Working from this premise, they necessarily failed in the attempt to differentiate between Jews as a racial and as a religious group. Anti-Semites found it impossible to escape the "moral obligation" of attacking the Talmud, kosher butchering, the Kol Nidre prayer, and other usages of the Jewish religion. In so doing, they appeared intolerant and bigoted instead of "progressive" to those not yet convinced of the Jewish danger—still the vast majority of imperial Germany.

As another element of its democratic facade, the Erfurt program tried to erase the popular image of a party dedicated exclusively to peasant and *Mittelstand* interests. Pious statements about the need for unity and cooperation between Germany's warring economic and social groups (guiding principle 4) were intended to show the German public that the Social Reformers earnestly wanted to unify the nation. The program addressed "the whole German nation without difference of class or religious denomination." Point 15, as well as the guiding principles, dealt with the plight of all honest, "productive" labor. The call for a progressive income tax would supposedly appeal to the proletariat as well as the impoverished *Mittelstand* and peasantry (pt. 8). Point 12, on agriculture, was obscurely worded enough to appeal to both peasants and great landholders. A commitment to "extensive tariffs" on manufactured goods assured industrialists and laborers that the party was also aware of their vital interests (pt. 9).

However, the mere enumeration of everyone's aspirations did not suffice to dispel the *Mittelstand* and peasant character of the party. Ten of the program's nineteen points dealt with the supposed interests of these two social groups. The *Mittelstand*, the more likely of the two to be influenced by a written program, received minute attention. The party showed its concern for the pettiest interests of every segment of the *Mittelstand*, specifically including small-scale merchants, artisans, bureaucrats, teachers, shop clerks, and noncommissioned army officers. In order to rescue the struggling class of self-employed artisans, point 13 of the program demanded obligatory guilds, elimination of "unrestrained" occupational freedom, the founding of cooperatives (presumably for marketing), abolition of competitive penitentiary labor, and an exclusive preference for master artisans in state-owned factories and in the fulfillment of state contracts. For the small merchant the Social Reformers were willing to go equally far (pt. 14).

Unsurprisingly, the program failed to win allies from other segments of German society. Supporting a graduated income tax recruited no friends in Conservative circles, which persistently fought against direct taxation all through the Wilhelminian era. Declaring war on "mobile capital" and the stock exchange, while pleasing elements of the *Mittelstand*, alienated big industry and high finance. On the other hand, advocating high tariffs, which, in fact, favored manufacturers and agriculturalists, drew the scorn of workers and the urban *Mittelstand*. The individual measures to be taken on behalf of the working man came almost word for word from the Christian Social party program of 1879 and were to prove every bit as ineffective in winning the allegiance of proletarian voters.[38] The German Social Reform party also did injury to liberal and humanitarian sentiments. While appealing to animal lovers by prohibiting "cruel" kosher slaughtering, the anti-Semites showed less pity for human beings; they welcomed penal colonies (pt. 18) and condemned convicts to idleness. The Catholic Center party might take pleasure in the anti-Semites' federalism (guiding principle 10), advocacy of freedom of religion, and the maintenance of Christian influence in public schools (pt. 4), but the Center strenuously objected to depriving Jews of civil rights and the free practice of their religion.[39] In summary, if a German citizen did not subscribe to the basic tenet of the anti-Semites, there were many reasons for him to regard the German Social Reform party as no true servant of himself or the nation.

The Erfurt program matched this failure as rhetoric with a much more significant failure. The program did not even satisfy the *Mittelstand*, or to a lesser extent, the peasantry, the two groups most open to anti-Semitism. The German Social Reform party and its successors never captured a majority of either group. The fault was not entirely with the Erfurt program, although it might have helped its cause by a less detailed statement. The contradictions and conflicts of interest within and between the peasantry and *Mittelstand* were the results of economic developments over which the anti-Semites had no control. However, the Erfurt program emphasized rather than obscured these virtually unresolvable conflicts. The party, for all its explicitness, erred by posing as all things to all men. In order to defend shopkeepers and artisans, it promised to prohibit consumer cooperatives, which were condemned by these two segments of the *Mittelstand* as "socialistic gravediggers of monarchy, a Jewish invention." But consumer cooperatives had been one of Böckel's "positive measures" for the Hessenland peasantry; his successors announced that they had no intention of giving them up.[40] On the other hand, agricultural tariffs, still favored by the anti-Semitic peasants, were considered "bread usury" by the urban *Mittelstand*.

Considering the *Mittelstand* alone, the Erfurt program merely served to emphasize the fragmentation of *Mittelständler*. In fact, the *Mittelstand* had almost no uniform interests, and for that reason no party ever won its allegiance or successfully represented it in the Reichstag of imperial Germany. True, all were in some sense the victims of capitalism. But each of the substrata of the *Mittelstand* possessed a recognized position in German society, a status to which it clung tenaciously. Moreover, many of them had long-standing antipathies toward one another which made them more aware of their differences than their common bonds. Here the Erfurt program provided no help at all. The few common interests binding civil servants, sergeants in the army, and primary school teachers became obscured in the detailed measures advocated for each of them. What the individual groups within the *Mittelstand* desired from a political party was that a clear choice be made between them. This the Social Reformers refused to do.[41]

Only in its anti-Semitism was the Erfurt program unambiguous. While the rest of the program simply underlined the divisiveness of the party's mass backing, anti-Semitism was meant to act as the integrating factor. The common struggle against Jewry would draw *Mittelstand,* peasant, nobleman, *Bürger,* and proletarian together. In dedication to the "higher cause" material conflicts of interest would lose importance. During the imperial era this integration on the basis of anti-Semitism never took place.

The Erfurt program's anti-Semitic planks were basically the same as those enunciated in the Anti-Semites' Petition of 1880. Point nineteen contained the kernel of the party's demands: "Abolition of the civil equality of Jews living in Germany." Like all its predecessors, the German Social Reform party demanded the revocation of Jewish emancipation, after which Jews were to be put under a strictly administered aliens law. The reasoning behind this platform had remained constant for the last twenty years. Equality for a racial minority had proved unhealthy and unworkable. The Emancipation Law of 1869 still stood as the cardinal stupidity of liberalism. According to the law, the anti-Semites falsely maintained, Jews were to have renounced their Judaism in order to become "good Germans." Clearly, at least to anti-Semites, the Jews had characteristically failed to honor their part of the contract.

Taken as a whole, the programmatic statement of the Social Reformers revealed an extraordinarily naive faith in the power of legislative action. The program put overriding emphasis on domestic affairs because they could be affected by legislation. The party's interest in foreign affairs, a realm clearly beyond the influence of parliament, remained minimal until the turn of the century. Yet at Erfurt, and for that matter, well before the formation of the united party, the conventional anti-Semites expressed some important views about the rest of the world. Most had been pan-German before the founding of the Pan-German League (1890). The Erfurt program called for the protection and cultivation of Germandom in foreign lands (guiding principle 9) and fully shared the "greater German" outlook of the Pan-German League. Liebermann, Zimmermann, Ludwig Werner, Paul Förster, and many others became active members of the league and occasionally acted as its spokesmen in the Reichstag.[42] During the greater part of its activity in she *Kaiserreich,* however, the Pan-German League did not reciprocate by openly forwarding the cause of parliamentary anti-Semitism. Even after Heinrich Class became its leader in 1908, and the majority of the main leadership *(Hauptleitung)* was anti-Semitic, the organization remained strictly neutral on the Jewish question. Until 1910 it accepted Jews as well as anti-Semitic members. As late as 1915 there was a Jewish member on the governing board. The league was a respectable association of professionals with some impressive names on its membership rolls. An anti-Semitic episode in the Berlin branch during the early 1890's had caused considerable criticism among the members.[43]

The reluctance of the Pan-Germans to espouse anti-Semitism deeply grieved the anti-Semites. But the league was not an isolated example. The Erfurt program embodied the goals of another organization which also refused to support anti-Semitism. Although the anti-Semites had, for years, warned of the dangers of Polonization in Germany's eastern regions, although they had denounced the moderation of the Caprivi government toward the Poles, a special organization devoid of anti-Semitism took root in 1894. The *Deutscher Ostmarkverein* remained steadfastly neutral on the Jewish question. Anti-Semitism may have appealed to many in the organization, but its leaders clearly recognized the usefulness of the Jews in Posen, West Prussia, and Silesia who normally stood in the camp of Germandom. Periodically, the *Ostmarkverein* leaders admonished members to have nothing to do with anti-Semitism.[44] In some eastern areas of the empire, almost complete unanimity among Germans was necessary in order to elect a German instead of a Pole to the Reichstag. The anti-Semites who frequently contested these electoral districts were a greater menace to the cause of Germandom than the Jews, who customarily voted "German."[45]

In 1898, Liebermann lamented the formation of "overlapping" organizations, such as the *Ostmarkverein* and the Pan-German League.[46] He could have added several more to the list of right-wing associations whose interests were clearly represented in the Erfurt program. Before 1900, the anti-Semites espoused the main objectives of the Agrarian League, the Colonial Society (1887), the Naval League (1898), and the Shop Clerks' Union (1893). Yet, instead of joining with the anti-Semites, these representatives of special group interests continued a separate existence. The Shop Clerks and

Agrarians forbade membership to Jews and actively engaged in "anti-Semitic education," but neither joined the struggle of the German Social Reformers as forthrightly and energetically as Liebermann hoped they would. Other right-wing groups were even less helpful, abstaining from overt anti-Semitism, cultivating it more or less in private, or dabbling in the "demagogic" variety.

In the Wilhelminian era, few Germans outside the anti-Semitic parties regarded the Jewish problem as the most significant one facing Germany. Although many shared the anti-Semites' dissatisfaction with economic liberalism, with the lack of unity among Germans, with "moral decay," and even with "upstart" Jews, this discontent was not enough to drive them into the anti-Semitic movement. Unless one felt certain, as the anti-Semites did, that the Jews were at the bottom of all troublesome developments, the Erfurt program spoke only for specific group interests and revealed a "one-issue" party. Only the anti-Semites believed that unity "among the sons of one race," economic harmony, moral rebirth, and the expansion of German power could be had by denying civil rights to Jews. The parliamentary anti-Semites, moreover, failed to convince their most likely allies on the German right of the necessity for "sincere" anti-Semitism. In the *Kaiserreich*, the German Social Reform party did not succeed in becoming a "holding company" for the right or in enlisting those organizations which could have supplied the party with money, prestige, and influence. Thus, the unification at Eisenach, partial reorganization, and formulation of the Erfurt program provided the party with none of the prerequisites for success.

CHAPTER 6

The Anti-Semites and Their Opponents

Study of the opposition to anti-Semitism, like the study of parliamentary anti-Semitism, has suffered much because of the near-successful extermination of European Jews by the Nazis. Just as the activities of the anti-Semites have been described as an uninterrupted progress on the road to Auschwitz, stretching from the Second through the Third Reich, so the resistance to them has been portrayed as a long series of inept tactics and catastrophic mistakes. Because the failures of political anti-Semitism in the German Empire have been considered merely a prelude for later successes, no adequate discussion of the resistance, its philosophy, method, and effectiveness has been thought necessary. Yet there is special value in an investigation of the opposition forces within the milieu that created them, for during the Weimar Republic and in the early stages of the Third Reich, the methods and philosophy of resistance remained what they had been in imperial Germany. One of the reasons the resistance failed so drastically in the Weimar era was that in the earlier epoch it appeared to succeed so well.

Except for the efforts of rival political parties, to be discussed separately in the next chapter, defensive action against anti-Semites before the election breakthrough of 1890 had been sporadic, often more dramatic than effectual. In the early 1890's, however, several German state governments and two "anti-anti-Semitic" organizations became systematic and active opponents of the anti-Semitic parties for a variety of motives.

Determining the attitude of "the state" toward Jews, anti-Semites, and anti-Semitism poses several difficulties. The Bismarckian constitution stressed the federal nature of the empire, which was composed of twenty-five sovereign states. Although the Reich supervised administration of the law and could exercise a direct administrative competence, it normally depended on state administrations to execute most legislation. This unwieldy relationship between state and Reich appealed to Bismarck for complex political and economic reasons.[1] However, the chief result of his system, for the purposes of this study, was the striking variation in the treatment accorded to Jews and anti-Semites in the individual German states. There simply was no single "state attitude." The first and last uniform national policy on the Jewish question was the Emancipation Law of 1869, and even this statute was executed in quite different ways by the states.

In the Jewish question, as in many other areas of German life, Bismarck's strange federalism enhanced the importance of Prussia. Because of its size, efficiency, and prestige, Prussia exerted an overwhelming influence on the rest of Germany. The anti-Semitic parties, too, felt this influence because of the nature of their goal. To revoke Jewish emancipation meant changing the constitution of the Reich. But according to Article 78 of that document, only fourteen votes in the *Bundesrat* were needed to defeat constitutional amendments. Prussia's seventeen *Bundesrat* delegates, appointed representatives immune to universal suffrage, held veto power over constitutional change. Therefore, a Prussian government favorable to the anti-Semitic cause was absolutely essential to success. Not merely the Prussian masses, but their rulers, too, had to be won over.

The first organized effort of the anti-Semites, the petition of 1880, allowed the Prussian government to take a position on anti-Semitism. While the petition circulated through Germany, the left-liberal deputy to the Prussian lower house, Albert Hänel, addressed the government with a formal interpellation, touching off two days of unusually intense debate in November 1880. Hänel prefaced his question with a condemnation of the "regrettable excesses" accompanying the petition agitation. Enumerating the anti-Semites' demands, he asked: "What position does the royal state government take on those demands that aim at setting aside the full constitutional rights of Jewish citizens?" Although the petition had not yet reached his office, the vice-president of the state ministry, Count Otto zu Stolberg-Wernigerode, answered for the government:

> . . . the state ministry does not intend to advocate a change

in the legal conditions or the existing legislation which declares equality of status among the religious denominations in civil matters.

(Bravo! from all sides of the house.)[2]

Left liberals expressed dissatisfaction with the government answer. The left-liberal *Fortschrittspartei,* target of Court Chaplain Stoecker's attacks since 1879, wanted an all-embracing condemnation of the anti-Semitic agitation. Although Stoecker's Christian Social party had not organized the petition, the chaplain had signed it. Hänel had hoped for a repudiation of Stoecker as well as of anti-Semitism. Instead, the official statement, according to left-liberal interpretation, tacitly encouraged the anti-Semites by merely announcing that no immediate action would be taken against the rights of Jews.[3] But the left liberals were mistaken in believing that the government acted in sympathy with the demands of the anti-Semites against the Jews. The coldly detached reply to the interpellation probably had more to do with the official attitude toward left liberals than with either anti-Semites or Jews.

Bismarck's feelings about the petition, his role in the answer to Hänel, and his general attitude on the Jewish question, like most of the important questions of his career, are a matter of debate. His was certainly the most important opinion in Prussia and remains the most difficult to pin down. He was absent on leave—probably on purpose—when the interpellation fell due. He never chose to answer the petition in person, either as Prussian minister-president or chancellor of the Reich. Unlike his successors in office, he never spoke out officially against the anti-Semites. Only his private and behind-the-scenes utterances give some idea of his own position.

As the *Kulturkampf* waned in importance in the late 1870's, Bismarck deftly switched political enemies. He confided to his press secretary, Moritz Busch, himself an active anti-Semite: "The Center party has moved off target . . . the left-liberal . . . Jews with their money are now the Center."[4] Bismarck also acknowledged the usefulness of Stoecker against the new enemy, the *Fortschrittspartei:*

> At first, I did not want this agitation for Stoecker *qua* anti-Semite. Now, however, I am glad about it. He is active, fearless, manly, and has a trap [*Maul*] that is not to be shut.[5]

He was willing to use Stoecker and anti-Semitism against his foes of the moment. That these same foes had sponsored the Hänel interpellation influenced the kind of answer given by Count Stolberg. Bismarck simply refused to give the *Fortschrittler* any concessions. Although the chancellor appreciated Stoecker's usefulness, he began to dislike him as early as June 1880. While responding to hecklers at a particularly stormy meeting, Stoecker insulted Bismarck's personal banker, Gerson Bleichröder. Bleichröder, a man always conscious of his dignity, complained directly to Kaiser Wilhelm I in a private letter, perhaps at the suggestion of Bismarck. The chancellor later prevailed upon the reluctant Wilhelm to reprimand his chaplain for attacking individuals of great wealth and creating unrest.[6]

Contemporaries of Bismarck and modern critics both have blamed him for not putting an end to the anti-Semitic movement in its infancy. They argue that a word from him at the opportune time would have squelched the anti-Semites. More seriously, Eugen Richter, leader of the left liberals, accused him on several occasions of financing the entire Berlin movement from the "reptile fund," money derived from the confiscated property of the former king of Hanover and kept beyond parliamentary control. Hellmut von Gerlach, at first a Christian Social and zealous anti-Semite, later an outspoken opponent of anti-Semitism, picked up Richter's accusation.[7] Neither Richter nor Gerlach ever substantiated their contentions with anything but circumstantial evidence. Going even further but also without direct evidence, Massing has suggested that Bismarck, operating behind the scenes, initiated the anti-Semitic attacks of the *Germania* and *Kreuzzeitung* (1875–1876) in order to create a new coalition in the Reichstag, and that he intended welding the Conservatives and the Center party together by means of anti-Semitism.[8] Yet even though the two parties often cooperated with each other and the government after 1879, freeing Bismarck from dependence on the liberals, this single fact cannot prove Massing's case. At the time of the *Kreuzzeitung-Germania* articles, the chancellor was deep in the *Kulturkampf*. Furthermore, both papers attacked him directly as a tool of the Jews, a pawn of his "ruling banker."

Actually, the chancellor was by no means a free agent in the manipulation of the anti-Semitic agitation. The anti-Semitic attacks on him in the 1870's had been damaging. His great prestige notwithstanding, he could not afford to come under such criticism too frequently. In 1885, according to Bleichröder, Bismarck thought it more expedient to acquiesce in a stock exchange tax than risk revival of the anti-Semites' accusations. A few hints in the *Kreuzzeitung* about his favoring Jewish financiers recalled all too vividly Joachim Gehlsen's defamatory newspaper, the *Reichsglocke* (1876).[9] Moreover, Bismarck soon grew wary of Stoecker and on at least two occasions worked behind the scenes to have the Christian Socials placed under the antisocialist laws.[10] His displeasure with Stoecker grew more acute in 1887 when it appeared that Prince Wilhelm, later Kaiser Wilhelm II, was falling under the sway of a clique around the court chaplain and Count Alfred von Waldersee, whom Bismarck regarded as a possible rival for the chancellorship. Stoecker, keenly aware of the chancellor's enmity, always attributed it to his own "fighting of the Jews." Although Bismarck later denied any personal animosity, his opposition to Stoecker certainly had little to do with principle.[11] The court chaplain had once been a tolerably useful political tool that had become less useful and even somewhat dangerous.

What is virtually certain about Bismarck's hostility toward Stoecker is that it was not motivated by concern for the Jews of Germany. The chancellor operated with his own peculiar version of the Jewish stereotype. His comments on Jews ranged from the obscene to the pro-Jewish. Rich Jews were good, state-supporting citizens of Germany and sure taxpayers. But they were offset by the upward-striving, radical, have-not Jews. His personal physician, banker, and lawyer were Jews. Yet he spoke contemptuously of the "Jew press" and the "Jew cities" (Frankfurt am Main, Breslau).[12] Doubtless, he shared many of the sentiments of his class about alleged Jewish "money grubbing," lack of physical courage, and so on. But he was not a racist. Like many of his contemporaries, he borrowed from the racist vocabulary without drawing any of its built-in conclusions.

Aside from Stoecker, to whom he never gave an interview or sent a letter, the chancellor did not even mention the independent anti-Semitic leaders by name. His position toward them, unsurprisingly the same that the Prussian administration adopted, rested on two observations made early in the Berlin movement. As a result of the Bleichröder affair in 1880, Bismarck lodged a complaint with the kaiser and the *Kultusminister* Robert von Puttkammer. The memo dealt with Stoecker's activity but can also be applied to the independent anti-Semites closely associated with him in the Berlin movement. He condemned Stoecker's handling of the Jewish question, recommending "serious censure." However, the court chaplain's sowing of hatred was not the worst of it. Bismarck worried about the movement getting out of control. The anti-Semites' anticapitalism, in reality little more than criticism of the remnants of laissez-faire economic policies, smacked of socialism as far as the chancellor was concerned. He feared that anti-Semitic politicians were unwittingly doing the work of the revolutionary Socialists, that they were nurturing the seeds of unrest already present in the masses. Furthermore, the goals of the anti-Semitic parties, so far as they touched upon Jews, were highly impractical, unnecessary, and ill advised: "We certainly cannot expel the Jews, and we also cannot launch a St. Bartholomew's Night against them." Keeping Jews from positions of authority, he pointed out, would just make matters worse. They would then concentrate in commerce and the professions to a greater extent than was now the case. What the anti-Semites complained about actually was no more than "the Jews' superiority at making money," according to Bismarck. This, like "Jewish diligence and parsimony," was an inborn trait which could not be corrected by legislative proposals.[13]

While a few conventional and several revolutionary anti-Semites had doubts about Bismarck's loyalty to their cause, they simply worshipped the old kaiser, Wilhelm I.[14] Indeed, at least the parliamentary anti-Semites fared slightly better with him than with any other high personage. On the eve of his birthday in 1882, Wilhelm received Stoecker and other prominent personalities in the Berlin movement, a definite mark of distinction. By 1883, however, he reluctantly had to chastise the court chaplain after his anti-Semitic preaching nearly created an international incident in London. Liberal Londoners forced the lord mayor to revoke permission for Stoecker to use Mansion House for his speech. When a new meeting hall was chosen, many exiled German Socialists appeared for his performance which ended with Stoecker's quick exit by a back door. Later, a series of damaging libel suits involving Stoecker further diminished the kaiser's regard. Such disreputable behavior was not the kind of prop for authority which Wilhelm sought and which had once gained his tacit support for the Berlin movement. As in the case

of Bismarck, Wilhelm's disenchantment with Stoecker had nothing
to do with respect for German Jews. In a letter to another court
chaplain, the kaiser expressed his position on the strivings of the
anti-Semites as well as his feelings about Jews. Although desirable,
it was no longer possible to abolish Jewish emancipation or to revoke
the "many too many" rights "furnished the Jews."[15]

Wilhelm's successor, Friedrich III, reigned only three months
before dying in June 1888. The shortness of his rule was a blessing
for the anti-Semites. However questionable the supposed liberalism
of Friedrich, the sincerity of his opposition to anti-Semitism was
beyond serious doubt. While attending a concert at the dedication
of a new Berlin synagogue, a widely noted mark of public respect, he
described anti-Semitism as "the shame of the century." Stoecker
recognized him as an opponent and tried without success to win him
over.[16] Later the conventional anti-Semites, who considered themselves supporters of monarchism *par excellence,* tried in vain to deny
Friedrich's well-documented opposition to their efforts.[17]

Kaiser Wilhelm II appeared to be the anti-Semites' hope in the
years before his accession. After one of Stoecker's libel suits ended
with an unfavorable judgment, it was Wilhelm who successfully
intervened with the old kaiser on behalf of the court chaplain. Wilhelm seemed to be very much under the influence of Waldersee,
Stoecker, and several other participants in the Berlin movement.
His sympathy for this clique earned him a critical article in the
Norddeutsche Allgemeine Zeitung, a paper close to the government.
The liberal press pursued the opening, believed to have emanated
from Bismarck, and caused Wilhelm some embarrassment.[18] Anti-
Semites flocked to his defense. Theodor Fritsch dashed off a pamphlet entitled "Why is Crown Prince Wilhelm Defamed?" Later,
Liebermann greeted his accession triumphantly: "For the freeing of
our nation from impoverishment, strangulation, and poisoning by
alien parasites."[19] But Wilhelm soon betrayed all these hopes. Although his verbal nastiness about Jews is abundantly documented,
the new kaiser refrained from open association with anti-Semitic
groups. He certainly gave no comfort to the parliamentary anti-
Semites during his reign.[20]

Bismarck, Wilhelm I, and Wilhelm II all held remarkably similar
opinions about anti-Semites and Jews. In their view, no specific

Jewish danger existed. Rich Jews were not a problem; in many ways they were an asset to the empire. Those Jews who stirred up the masses or "behaved insolently" were no more or less a problem than those anti-Semites and Social Democrats who did the same. For a long time, many Jews and most anti-Semites tried hard to believe that all three men were allies of their own cause. In reality, all three disliked most of both groups. The "neutrality" of the highest personages in the state naturally influenced the administration of their government. More importantly, official neutrality made possible both anti-Semitic and anti-anti-Semitic governmental policies.

In Prussia, the government administration was often accused of lending open support to anti-Semites. During Caprivi's tenure in office, for example, several *Landräte* (county directors) exerted their influence on behalf of anti-Semitic candidates. This obvious abuse of governmental authority by the *Landrat,* however, originated in Conservative party sympathies rather than in any illegal instructions from the state government. On the other hand, the central administration was slow to censure such actions. In isolated instances the conclusion that government officials supported anti-Semites, especially when they opposed left liberals or Socialists, was inescapable. Yet, the arbitrary powers of the *Landrat* often turned against the anti-Semites as well. For example, Hermann Ahlwardt, after becoming anti-Junker, was flatly denied entrance to the district of one outraged Pomeranian *Landrat.*[21]

The alert administration of Prussian Hesse, unlike that of Pomerania, kept careful tabs on its anti-Semitic problem, opposing both the anti-Semitism and the "radicalism" of Otto Böckel. Early resistance from the administration took the form of a confidential circular letter from *Landrat* Risch of Kassel. Risch advised formation of election committees from all sections of Hessian society to combat anti-Semitism and to prevent the penetration of known anti-Semites into communal and district offices of government, an effort that proved successful.[22] In 1892 the official *Reichsanzeiger* of Kassel instructed school inspectors to proceed against subordinate teachers who encouraged anti-Semitic incidents in the schools.[23] After 1887, Böckel found his meetings supervised by police officials who frequently dissolved them. On balance, however, the resistance to Böckel put up by the state administration was not very successful. At most, it influenced him to take his agitation over the border to the Grand Duchy of Hesse. He was also able to turn such state harassment to his own advantage, using it to exacerbate the anti-Prussian feelings of his peasant followers. The Social Democrat, Philipp Scheidemann, contended that this kind of opposition from conservative state authority in Prussian Hesse had made a martyr of Böckel.[24]

After Bismarck's dismissal in March 1890, opposition efforts of the Reich government usually emanated from the chancellor's office. For example, prior to the Tivoli congress (1892), the *Norddeutsche Allgemeine Zeitung* spoke out against the adoption of an anti-Semitic plank by the German Conservative party. In a typically "neutral" way, the paper described the early outburst of anti-Semitism (1873–1881) as the outraged expression of the German people against Jewish immorality and dishonesty. Now, the paper went on, mobism had penetrated the anti-Semitic movement:

> Anti-Semites today are as revolutionary as the Social Democrats and should be rejected by the Conservative party as completely contrary to the principles of conservatism.[25]

Although Caprivi conceived of the anti-Semitic danger in exactly the same fashion as had Bismarck, his stinging denunciations of anti-Semitism were made publicly. He attacked anti-Semites the more bitterly because they were among his most vocal opponents. However, he went far beyond what self-defense demanded of him in this matter. Reacting to the growth of the movement in 1893, Caprivi delivered a long speech to the Reichstag, which charged the anti-Semites with abetting the Socialists, the equivalent of high treason from his conservative point of view:

> The method by which you anti-Semites seek to spread your views through the country is decidedly demagogic. And, gentlemen, that is dangerous. . . .
>
> For where does anti-Semitism lead, what does it want? Indeed it is—to use the often employed phrase once more—the early fruit [*Vorfrucht*] of social democracy. All who generate dissatisfaction today work to the good of the Social Democrats. (Quite right!)

Caprivi continued to lump the Socialists and anti-Semites together as enemies of the state:

The anti-Semites have begun with agitation against Jews; they have not stopped there. They go further. They persecute Jews back to the third and fourth generation. They begin to mix religious with racial anti-Semitism; and what is left but an anti-Semitism directed toward capitalism? This is the most dangerous. The circles they address are not inclined to or capable of making distinctions.[26]

Neither the anti-Semitic parties nor the misled masses, he stated, would stop at hostility toward "Jewish capital"; they would go on to anticapitalism in general and, perhaps, to revolution.

Caprivi's constant and widely publicized opposition made no impression on the anti-Semites or the Conservatives, the anti-Semitic students or peasantry. His attacks were interpreted as "philo-Semitism" by his enemies, merely one additional reason to work for the chancellor's downfall. His successor in 1894, Prince Chlodwig zu Hohenlohe-Schillingsfürst, proved much more difficult to attack, even for these groups. He was "neither conservative nor liberal, neither ultramontane nor *Fortschrittler,* neither churchman nor atheist."[27] Hohenlohe never made enemies as easily as Caprivi. He was acceptable to almost everyone, perhaps because of his innocuousness. On the Jewish question, too, his record was clear, though unfortunate from the anti-Semites' point of view. As minister-president of Bavaria, he had actively worked for the emancipation of Bavarian Jews and thus stood opposed to the basic goal of the anti-Semitic parties. His successors as chancellor and minister-president, Bernhard von Bülow (1900–1909) and Theobald von Bethmann Hollweg (1909–1917) conformed more nearly to the pattern of Bismarck. Both were reported to have made anti-Jewish remarks. Both occasionally made willing use of anti-Semites in the Reichstag. But—an exception to the Bismarck precedent—on a number of occasions both men dealt out severe scoldings to the anti-Semites.[28]

Although slow in starting, the resistance efforts of the Grand Duchy of Hesse were far more systematic than those of Prussia or the Reich. From haphazard prohibitions of meetings, musical parades, and banners and fines for those who protested injunctions, the government of Prime Minister Jacob Finger (1884–1898) moved to a more concerted opposition against Böckel. Prior to the 1890 Reichstag elections, provincial and district officials adopted set procedures to regulate their anti-Böckel actions. Local mayors were instructed to prevent Böckel's rallies by withholding the rights of hospitality. The official *Giessener Anzeiger* refused to print notification of the time or place of an anti-Semitic meeting. If a gathering took place despite these precautions, a special police commissar was assigned as overseer and instructed to disperse the meeting in case of "any excess."[29] Finger backed up this program with two formal decrees to his subordinates. The Civil Servant Decree of October 1892 forbade the participation of state officials in anti-Semitic party activity of any sort. The order was aimed specifically at primary and secondary school teachers. It remained in effect until World War I and resulted in several disciplinary proceedings. One such case, the transfer of a Mainz school teacher who campaigned for Böckel's party, led to an angry debate in the Hessian parliament. Philipp Köhler, a member of the parliament from 1890 until his death in 1910, maintained that the government had no right to curb the political rights of its employees. Finger took advantage of the opportunity presented by Köhler to denounce anti-Semitism. Since Hessenland had been the scene of some vandalism against Jewish property and disturbances of a more serious nature, according to Finger, the government viewed anti-Semitism as a special threat to public peace.[30] Succeeding Hessian governments continued to put the anti-Semitic movement in this special category, long after the threat of violence had subsided.

The view of anti-Semitism as a danger to public peace provided Finger with the basis for his second decree, issued in December 1890. The ordinance originated in an attempt to keep Böckel from overrunning Starkenburg, the largest province of Hesse and site of Darmstadt, its capital. Instructing the local public prosecutors to give special and relentless attention to the anti-Semitic agitation, the decree also facilitated the bringing of public suits against libelous attacks upon Jews. This decree, too, remained in force for the duration of the empire. Böckel indirectly admitted its effectiveness in 1892, when he complained that he and his newspaper were fighting fifty-two lawsuits. In this way, the Hessian government added greatly to his financial problems. The *Reichsherold* admonished the anti-Semites: "Avoid lawsuits like fire."[31]

Finger had the full and immediate support of the head of state, Grand Duke Ernst Ludwig (1892–1918), who early in his reign announced his opposition to the anti-Semites' "reprehensible persecution" of Jews.[32] Finger also got moral support from the upper levels of both the Catholic and Protestant churches, whose spokesmen denounced Böckel and anti-Semitism. An order from the upper consistory of the Evangelical Church (1890) forbade the participation of Protestant clergymen in the Böckel movement, which "catered to the darker instincts of German Christians." Blaming Jews for all the ills of the rural population, according to the statement, "encouraged the peasants to disregard their own errors and their own considerable guilt."[33] But church resistance came too late to do much good in the Grand Duchy. By 1893, a Protestant minister lamented that "in Hesse, Dr. Böckel has won such regard in town and country that clergymen dare not oppose him even when he pursues his false anti-Semitism."[34] Clearly, a great many Protestant clerics made no effort to restrain their flocks. Several ministers sympathized openly with Stoecker's Christian Socials, and a few even participated in Böckel's movement. Not so the Catholic Church in Hessenland whose hierarchy deplored the "dishonorable and unchristian parties" that attacked Jews.[35] In the face of such opposition, anti-Semites were never able to conquer an electoral district in the heavily Catholic province of Rheinhessen or in the Catholic districts of Starkenburg. Here the control exerted by parish priests was paramount and totally impervious to undermining by the anti-Semites.

The Grand Duchy of Baden's resistance proved more effective than that of neighboring Hesse. When Böckel and Liebermann began agitation in Baden, they found stiff resistance. Grand Duke Friedrich I (1852–1907) made his opposition known immediately. From 1881 on, he appointed prime ministers hostile to anti-Semitism. Moreover, Baden was the one state in the Reich where a professing Jew, Moritz Ellstätter, held a ministerial post. An order similar in content to the Hessian Civil Servant Decree came in time to prevent the defection of secondary school teachers to the anti-Semitic cause.[36] In Baden the state instituted the measures that Böckel had used to win over the Hessian peasants. State savings banks, cooperatives, and agricultural chambers were already operating before the German Socials and Reformers were ready to "open up Baden." The German Social Reform party and its successors never came close to winning a Reichstag seat in the Grand Duchy. The Social Reformers did gain two state parliament seats, exploiting political conditions discussed in the next chapter. They could not hold onto those seats, however, and eventually all such efforts were abandoned. Baden offers the only example of resistance efforts by a German government which succeeded in quashing the anti-Semitic threat.

But even where the states put up no formal resistance, the anti-Semitic parties did not do well. Although able to win a few state parliament seats, they could not extend their influence beyond the legislative branch of government. They never penetrated above the lowest levels of the executive and judiciary of any state. After the collapse of the Berlin movement, anti-Semitic politicians, with few exceptions, could not make contact with highly placed officials sympathetic to their strivings. They consistently met an informal resistance, perhaps nothing more than snobbishness, but nonetheless effective. Those in power or close to the seat of power, the rich, and the "established" of the *Kaiserreich* bestowed scant attention on them. When discussed by the powerful, anti-Semites were objects of scorn, "little men," climbers and strivers who were using "democracy" and demagogy to claw their way up the social ladder. According to this view, anti-Semites were like Social Democrats; both employed slogans in which they had not the slightest faith.[37]

Disdain for the anti-Semites did not provide the soundest basis for proceeding against anti-Semitism. Clearly, much more pressure could have been brought to bear against the anti-Semitic parties, especially in Prussia. But the will for such action and the proper concern for the dangers inherent in anti-Semitism were missing in the wielders of state power. In Hessenland and Prussia, opposition to the anti-Semites had more to do with the fears of authoritarian governments about a movement that appeared "too democratic" than it did with the rights of Jews to live with dignity. In fact, none of the state government matched their disdain for anti-Semites with any special understanding or sympathy for their victims. Most pursued their own brand of anti-Semitism in the filling of civil service appointments. In this area, theoretical equality of opportunity could make little headway against a much older and more potent tradition of exclusion. The Jews of imperial Germany, in spite of constitutional equality, formed a group of distinctly second-class citizens.

The anti-Semitism of the civil and military service of Prussia rested on one fairly ancient and one more recent prejudice. The hoarier of the two was a belief in the ethical inferiority of Jews. The trend toward Jewish assimilation had done little or nothing to weaken this belief. The more modern prejudice had to do with the political unreliability of Jews. From the mid-nineteenth century, "Jew" and "liberal" were synonymous terms to many Germans. In associating with liberal parties, and later, with the Social Democrats, Jews identified themselves as enemies of government policy, opponents of conservatively oriented state administrations, and, in Prussia, as thorns in the flesh of Junker privilege. During the 1870's the unsuccessful attempts of liberal reformers in the Prussian parliament to break Junker domination of the civil service triggered much ill will. However, more than revenge was involved in the transformation of the civil service into a bastion of conservatism during the 1880's. The purge of liberal elements from the administration was part of a full-scale defense of the traditional power structure against the forces of modernization. One of its by-products was a great diminution of the number of Jews in the Prussian bureaucracy. Gradually, they were excluded, dismissed, or pensioned off. In the 1890's the policy of exclusion or nonadvancement for those not yet driven out made it clear that political docility counted for more than ability.[38]

Naturally, anti-Semites often tried to make use of the official mistreatment of Jews. They suggested and wanted to believe that, deep down, those in authority sided with them against the common enemy. Liebermann continually pointed out that the government of Prussia was already achieving some demands of the anti-Semites in its administrative practice.[39] Such rhetoric, however, lacked power. The government gave sufficient indication of its dislike for anti-Semites to dispel the idea of a secret alliance with them. Furthermore, the Prussian authorities did not act on racist principle. Jewish converts almost always received preference over the unbaptized, even in the lower levels of the civil service. Most importantly, the Prussian government would not openly acknowledge its anti-Semitism. Singling out Jews for special treatment was a violation of the Prussian Constitution of 1850 (Article 12).[40] But it was *de jure* discrimination on racist principle that the anti-Semites yearned for. That the authorities feared to admit they were acting illegally was no victory for justice or the Jews. Yet clandestine bigotry, by itself, presented no significant opportunities to the anti-Semites. Clearly, the government acted neither at the behest of the anti-Semitic parties nor in response to anti-Semitic public opinion, but rather on its own initiative. It misguidedly insisted upon a religiously and politically homogenous civil service.

The anti-Semites only rarely tried to take credit for the decrease of Jews in the civil service, the true extent of which was generally unknown. Spokesmen for the anti-Semitic parties constantly expressed dismay at the lack of thoroughness in excluding Jews and periodically renewed demands for a complete cleansing of the bureaucracy. One extremist group contended that Jewish power could not be fully broken until government officials who had married Jews were also purged.[41] However, such extremism was unusual, more typical of the Weimar era than the conventional anti-Semitism of the imperial period. Before the turn of the century, with the exception of Hessenland, conventional anti-Semites rarely accused their government of working secretly on behalf of Jewish power. Although they did not often pause to consider the logical consequences of their allegations, they instinctively shied away from depicting German policy as a conspiracy between the highest state officials and the Jews. Such a charge, made so frequently and effectively during the Weimar Republic, would have been too revolutionary for the anti-Semites of the *Kaiserreich*. When disappointed with their rulers' lack of attention to the Jewish danger, they preferred the polite fiction that the kaiser, king, or grand duke was being advised poorly by ignorant, rather than malicious men.

Later, after many anti-Semites began to suspect a conspiracy, they found it difficult to persuade their countrymen of a deal between Jews and government. Evidence of the governments' independence of Jewish power was too manifest. Ironically, official discrimination against Jews gave the official defense measures against anti-Semites a credibility with the general public that the better intentioned Weimar Republic never equalled. Moreover, in the political dimension of government anti-Semitism there lay another irony. For those Germans who objected to the rapid social rise of Jews, but who were otherwise unconcerned about a racially conceived Jewish peril, government anti-Semitism may have sufficed to allay their anxieties and may have even rendered the anti-Semitic political parties redundant.

Certainly, any such positive effects of government anti-Semitism were accidental. In the *Kaiserreich*, national and state governments never fully appreciated the corrosive effects of anti-Semitism. Not merely the anti-Semites' breeding of hatred and suspicion, but their poisoning of political life with slander and innuendo were contrary to the ultimate interests of government, no matter what its officials felt about Jews. Furthermore, no legitimate excuse can be found for the injustice perpetrated upon German Jews by their government. To grant them constitutional equality and yet withhold their rights mocked the constitution and unmasked an arbitrary conception of the rule of law.

Yet it is not helpful to judge the resistance and nonresistance of the state out of context. In the Wilhelminian era, anti-Semitism did not appear to be a major problem. Its most vocal proponents did not openly threaten authority. The growth of socialism seemed far more grave to all governments and most of the governed. Rightly or wrongly, they saw in the Socialists and workers a threat of bloody revolution. Beside this nightmare, the anti-Semites appeared relatively innocuous. Only so far as their activity resulted in violence or the threat of violence did governmental authority evince an interest in them. Whatever the harmful and self-defeating effects of the governments' discrimination toward their Jewish citizens, they drew a line beyond which few German anti-Semites dared to go. Finally, in overestimating the danger from the left and underestimating the danger from the right, German governments were neither the first nor the last to make this error.

Not all Germans were as shortsighted or as devoid of a sense of justice as their governments. From the time of the Anti-Semites' Petition in 1880, many eminent German Christians openly deplored anti-Semitism as a blight on national life. In answer to the utterances of Treitschke and Stoecker and as a counter to the petition itself, thirty distinguished Germans published a statement in the major dailies of the Reich (14 November 1880).[42] Among those who decried the resurrection of the "deeply shameful . . . racial hatred and fanaticism of the Middle Ages" were men of science and scholarship like Theodor Mommsen, Rudolf Virchow, Johann Gustav Droysen, Rudolf von Gneist, and Albrecht Weber, as well as political leaders like Max von Forckenbeck and Heinrich Rickert. The signatories felt that the protection of civil equality was "not merely the province of the tribunals, but of the conscience of every single citizen." Ten years later, many who had signed the "Declaration of the Notables" also subscribed to the founding of a new organization, the specific purpose of which was an active fight against anti-Semitism. On 14 December 1890, at a meeting in Berlin, Rickert, Gneist, Theodor Barth, Albrecht Weber, Wilhelm Förster, Erich Schmidt, Isidore Löwe, and Charles L. Hallgarten composed an invitation to form the *Verein zur Abwehr des Antisemitismus* (Association for Defense against Anti-Semitism). The invitation and manifesto published in January 1891 bore the signatures of five hundred and thirty-five Germans and eloquently called upon Christians of both churches to help erase the shame of anti-Semitism by joining the organization.[43]

Although open to all faiths and all parties, membership in the *Abwehr-Verein* remained predominantly non-Jewish. Unlike its Austrian counterpart founded in June 1891, very few members of the German organization came from the nobility. By November 1893, thirteen thousand Germans, most from the liberal middle class, joined the organization. The geographical distribution of members reflected the strength of Otto Böckel's agitation; almost two-thirds came from south and west Germany. Later, the emergence of Hermann Ahlwardt promoted a sharp increase in membership from north Germany as well. The organization opened independent bureaus in Berlin and Frankfurt am Main and branch offices in Cologne, Marburg, and Kassel. The *Abwehr-Verein* functioned until the war and then reduced its activity. It sprang back to more active life after 1918 and continued until its dissolution in November 1933.[44]

Eventually, the *Abwehr-Verein* fought anti-Semitism in two ways. It sought to enlighten the German public by means of apologetic publications, and it intervened in election districts that had been won or were being threatened by anti-Semites. Initially, however, the organization experimented with a more direct kind of combat. Members went into Böckel's strongholds and attempted to reason with his peasant adherents. The response was usually hostile and more often uncomprehending. Neither archivist Georg Winter nor Professor Stengel, one of Böckel's former teachers at the University of Marburg, accomplished much with this method. Böckel found it too easy to make them seem ridiculous intruders: "Archivists, lawyers, scholars, anthropologists—what do they know of our life and how the Jews rob us?"[45]

Because the *Verein* failed to make meaningful contact with Böckel's peasants, it fell back on an indirect approach. In preparation for the 1893 elections, the Frankfurt bureau tried to reach the peasants through intermediaries who possessed some authority with them. The bureau distributed one and a half million pamphlets to town dwellers, university students, municipal officials, local priests, and ministers in areas where Böckel was active. In addition to communicating with the peasantry, however inadequately, the *Verein* hoped to keep the educated from joining Böckel, thus depriving him of valuable allies. The brochures enumerated the failures of his consumer cooperatives and recommended insurance companies. They also countered anti-Semitic propaganda with statistics, showing that usury was not a Jewish monopoly and that the Jews' alleged carving up of peasant farms was largely mythical.[46]

In election contests against Böckel and Ahlwardt, the *Abwehr-Verein* lent its full support to candidates who opposed the anti-Semites, mainly to left liberals, the most outspoken foes of anti-Semitism. The organization distributed literature and made small financial contributions to chosen candidates. In 1898 the Berlin office presented seventeen thousand marks to anti-anti-Semitic candidates. In 1907 and 1912, special fund-raising drives, to judge from published receipts, did not do very well. In 1912 only forty thousand marks from the special election fund were available for distribution to twenty candidates, a relatively small sum in light of soaring campaign costs. The truth was that, although often accused of being no more than a front for "moneyed Jewry," the *Abwehr-Verein* never possessed substantial financial means.[47]

Although direct intervention by the *Verein* wherever anti-Semites ran for the Reichstag infuriated the anti-Semitic parties, the general effectiveness of these endeavors is almost impossible to evaluate. In 1892 and the election year of 1893, it is certain the infant organization suffered severe setbacks. Böckel triumphed in Hessenland. Ahlwardt won two districts in spite of the group's determined efforts to stop him. The *Verein* analysis of these defeats reveals something of its outlook. According to Georg Winter, in several electoral districts the cutthroat competition between National Liberals and left liberals gave victory to the anti-Semites. Instead of putting up one common candidate, the divided liberals split the liberal vote, allowing an anti-Semite to reach the second balloting. In the runoffs, anti-Semites could draw votes from those who preferred them to Conservatives or Socialists. Such had been the case in Eschwege and Waldeck in 1893. The obvious way to put an end to this situation was for liberals to unite. The *Abwehr-Verein* made constant pleas for liberal unity and saw no better starting point than in the fight against anti-Semitism. In reality, however, the *Verein* faced a more serious obstacle to effectiveness than liberal disunity. From left to right on the German political spectrum, all parties deemed the anti-Semites a lesser evil than the Social Democrats. When anti-Semites confronted Socialists in runoff elections, not only National Liberal, but left-liberal voters—the most loyal allies of the *Verein*—often helped the "lesser evil" to a Reichstag seat. In 1893, left-liberal voters supported anti-Semites in Stralsund, Alsfeld, Giessen, and Erbach.[48] Repeatedly, the *Verein* found itself in the embarrassing position of aiding candidates who, having lost out in the main election, threw their own support to anti-Semites in the runoffs.

Courageously, the *Abwehr-Verein* under the leadership of Theodor Barth, editor of the liberal periodical, *Die Nation*, went against the majority opinion. The practical goals of the anti-Semites, according to Barth, were far more harmful than the "theoretical statements" of the Social Democrats. Though liberals rejected any call to revolution, they shared much in common with the Socialists in regard to basic human rights. They also held similar opinions on political issues, like reform of the Prussian suffrage, abolition of church influence in public education, and a lowering of protective tariffs. In 1904, Barth formulated a new principle regulating *Abwehr-Verein* support for candidates in national and state elections. In order to qualify for help, a prospective candidate had to give assurance that, in case of a failure to make the second balloting, he and his party would support any non-anti-Semitic candidate, even a Social Democrat. The formula met stiff resistance from within the *Verein*. Several members of the executive committee never fully accepted it. Most preferred abstaining if it came to a contest between anti-Semite and Socialist.[49] In 1907, Georg Winter, who had risen to vice-president of the organization, contested Eisenach for the National Liberals. Failing to qualify for the runoff, he asked his supporters to vote for the anti-Semite rather than the Social Democrat in the second balloting. A man keenly aware of the dangers of anti-Semitism, Winter could not bring himself to see it as a greater danger than the Socialists. Deeply wounded, Barth requested and received Winter's immediate resignation. Like the resistance efforts of the German states, those of the *Abwehr-Verein* were weakened—although to a lesser extent—by fear of the left.

In the *Kaiserreich*, the *Abwehr-Verein* contributed more effectively in the struggle against anti-Semitism by its publication of polemical works than by its election intervention. Pamphlets about the ritual murder accusation, comparative analyses of Jewish criminal statistics, exposés written by renegade anti-Semites, scientific treatises on the humaneness of kosher butchering, histories of Jewish participation in Germany's wars—these formed the staple publications in the *Verein* catalogue. Its main production was the *Antisemiten-Spiegel. Die Antisemiten im Lichte des Christentums, des Rechtes und der Moral (Anti-Semite Mirror. The Anti-Semites in Light of Christianity, the Law, and Morality)*.[50] The *Antisemiten-Spiegel* took its format from Theodor Fritsch's *Antisemiten-Katechismus* (later *Handbuch der Judenfrage*), which was already in its eighteenth edition in 1892. An encyclopedia of anti-Semitism, its alphabetically arranged articles dealt with virtually every facet of the anti-Semitic agitation. Its method was simple and straightforward. The *Antisemiten-Spiegel* debunked the outright lies and half-truths of the anti-Semites with documented accounts from authoritative sources. The book enjoyed a measure of popular success, reached a great number of Germans, and proved a valuable and reliable source of information for those actively engaged in fighting the anti-Semites. From 1892 onward, the *Verein* sent the *Antisemiten-Spiegel* and its series of pamphlets to schools, youth groups, and to seven hundred priests and ministers.[51]

The most expensive endeavor of the *Verein* was its weekly newspaper, *Mitteilungen aus dem Verein zur Abwehr des Antisemitismus* (News from the *Abwehr-Verein* or *MVA*). From 21 October 1891 until 1 January 1911, the paper appeared from Berlin every Sunday; in 1911 it became a fortnightly.[52] The small full-time staff of the *MVA* made a conscious effort to imitate the *Antisemitische-Korrespondenz*, which came close to serving the anti-Semitic parties as an official organ. The layouts of the two newspapers were identical. Both ordinarily began with a long feature article dealing with the Jewish question in a theoretical way. A discussion of upcoming election tactics, anal-

yses of recent elections, or an essay of topical interest relating to the
Jewish question might also serve as lead articles. In the *Antisemitische-
Korrespondenz* a permanent column was "Israel [matched in the *MVA*
by Anti-Semites] in Conflict with the Law"; "Mosaic" in the *Antisemitische-Korrespondenz* dealt with the latest Jewish misdeeds to go
unpunished. The *MVA* answered by investigating the allegations
where possible, printing the true story, or as was often the case,
pointing out that the accused was not Jewish. The *MVA* gave close
attention to the contributions of Jews to German culture, science,
commerce, and political life. The *Antisemitische-Korrespondenz* indicated its special slant on this topic in "The Conquest of Germany
by the Jews: Infiltrations into Medicine, Law, and Teaching." Both
papers carried news about anti-Semitism in foreign lands, book
reviews, and quotations from famous men about the Jews. The *MVA*
enjoyed one advantage over its anti-Semitic competitor. It could expose the internal backbiting, squabbles, and scandal within the anti-
Semitic parties, something from which the *Abwehr-Verein* was notably
free.

The positive value of the *MVA* as a weapon of resistance is open to
question. It is likely that the paper spoke only to those already
convinced of the dangers and disgrace of anti-Semitism. At most it
may have given support to those whose convictions had begun to
waver in the face of constantly repeated anti-Semitic accusations. In
circulation, the *MVA* made sporadic progress corresponding to the
palpability of the anti-Semitic threat. By 1897 it had eight thousand
subscribers, more than the *Antisemitische-Korrespondenz* but far fewer
than the anti-Semitic press as a whole.[53]

The avowed goal of the *Abwehr-Verein* was the defeat of anti-Semitism. In arriving at a judgment of its success, the special vulnerability
of the *Verein* must be considered. Although members of the Conservative, National Liberal, and left-liberal parties sat on the original
executive committee of the organization, the overwhelming majority
belonged to one of the left-liberal groups. Even before the death in
1895 of the first president, the National Liberal Rudolf von Gneist,
left liberals exerted the predominant influence in the executive.
From 1896 to 1933, the presidents of the organization, Heinrich
Rickert (1896–1902), Theodor Barth (1903–1909), and Georg Gothein
(1909–1933), were all leaders in the left-liberal parties. The *Verein*

tried to keep the combating of anti-Semitism on a nonpartisan basis. Yet both its sympathies and its politics were left-liberal. In the Reichstag and Prussian state parliament Barth, Rickert, and Gothein took upon themselves the task of rebutting anti-Semites or interpellating the government about its discriminatory practices. This close association between left-liberal parties and the *Verein* made it easy for enemies to discount the organization as an auxiliary of specific political groups. The identification was unfortunate because the left-liberal parties already had the reputation of being "Jew parties." The anti-Semites thus employed a ready-made argument, declaring that the *Verein* was but another machination of the Jews who had managed to bribe men "posing as Germans."[54]

The liberal outlook of the organization also limited its effectiveness in other ways. It was an unfruitful liberal prejudice, after all, to look upon anti-Semites as relics of the Middle Ages, the last elements of a futile resistance to enlightenment and the triumph of reason. To the liberals of the *Abwehr-Verein*, anti-Semitism was nothing more than "the work of a community of bigoted and egotistical reactionaries."[55] The liberal opponents of anti-Semitism, in general, relied altogether too much on the efficacy of human reason. They predicated their actions on the firm belief that if the facts were known, men would act accordingly. Since the facts about the Jews and about the anti-Semites were clear and led to obvious conclusions for any reasonable man, the *Verein* had but to enlighten the public in order to bring about the defeat of anti-Semitism. These articles of faith led the organization to frequent use of stock liberal answers for very complicated questions. Thus, the *MVA* found a reassuringly simple explanation for Ahlwardt's success in Arnswalde-Friedberg in 1893, after his several arrests and convictions. The people of Arnswalde were poorly informed, dependent on a Conservative and an anti-Semitic newspaper. But, surely in this case, Theodor Mommsen was closer to the truth when he said: "Reason is useless on a man who votes for Ahlwardt."[56] Unable to face this unhappy possibility, the *Abwehr-Verein* flooded Arnswalde with its enlightenment publications and distributed the *MVA* free of charge. Ahlwardt was nevertheless reelected in 1898.

However, the *Verein* considered its methods correct and, indeed, the only ones honorable men could employ. Even though the anti-

Semites catered to the irrational instincts of their followers, they always couched their arguments in a logical way. They used statistics and also thought that one of their functions was enlightenment of the German public. Parliamentary anti-Semites were as unaware of or as unwilling to admit the strong irrational appeal of anti-Semitism as the members of the *Abwehr-Verein* were. Unlike the later Nazis, they consistently defended anti-Semitism as a *logical* necessity. Parliamentary anti-Semites tried to refute the claims of the *MVA* with "facts and figures." Appeals to "the blood," to listen only to racial instincts and thus hate Jews, to ignore the "one or two" morally respectable Jews one might know—all familiar Nazi techniques—were far less prevalent although not totally absent in imperial Germany. Conventional anti-Semites made few such attempts to exploit unreason. Thus, as long as the anti-Semites were willing to "debate" the Jewish question, it made sense for the *Abwehr-Verein* to contest the issue in the only way it knew how.

At least during the *Kaiserreich,* the *Abwehr-Verein* served a useful purpose and made a valuable contribution to the defeat of parliamentary anti-Semitism. The organization set itself limited goals. It quickly gave up the hopeless task of trying to convert the outright anti-Semite. Rather, it aimed at containing the contagion and keeping the poison from spreading. To do more, the *Verein* would have had to reach "the masses," and this it never accomplished. Its many reasonable arguments never gained the ear of the people who believed anti-Semitic lies. Yet Mommsen may have been overly pessimistic about the ineffectiveness of reasonable argumentation. Some of the organization's reasoning may well have had strong appeal for Wilhelminian Germans and may have helped undermine the anti-Semitic parties, if not anti-Semitism itself. The literature distributed by the *Verein* consistently portrayed the anti-Semitic agitation for revocation of Jewish emancipation as an overthrow of the constitution, a demand with undertones of revolutionary illegality. The *MVA* gave ruthless publicity to the criminality, double-dealing, and general lack of respectability among anti-Semites. Stoecker's notorious letter to Hammerstein, which outlined a plan for driving a wedge between Kaiser Wilhelm II and Bismarck, the three-year sentence meted out to Hans Leuss for perjury, Hammerstein's embezzlement and writing of bad checks to the tune of two hundred thousand marks—all these the *MVA*, among others, exploited fully and effectively, along with hundreds of less sensational misdemeanors. Anti-Semites regarded scandals like these as a very serious threat to their cause. They expended vast quantities of ink and abuse to counter *Verein* publicity. Böckel and Liebermann accused the organization of everything from hiring rowdies to beat up anti-Semites to shielding Jewish ritual murderers. The amount of attention the *Verein* received is a good indication of how seriously the anti-Semites took the organization's activities. The parliamentary anti-Semites were kept on the defensive. They never felt secure enough to let the *Verein* accusations go unchallenged.[57]

Ultimately, the most important contribution of the *Abwehr-Verein* in the fight against anti-Semitism was the character of its membership. Men like Rickert and Barth were widely respected. By calling the *Verein* into existence, they served no personal interests. They brought down upon themselves epithets like "Jewish auxiliaries" and "lackeys of the Jews." Nonetheless, with great courage, they lent their prestige and influence to fight what they saw as "a menace to freedom and the future of Germany."[58] In imperial Germany they helped stigmatize anti-Semitism.

The progress of parliamentary anti-Semitism in the early 1890's, which had awakened state governments and the *Abwehr-Verein* to resistance, also spurred a large percentage of German Jews to action. A specifically Jewish resistance had been slow in forming for a number of significant reasons. A monolithic "Jewry" existed nowhere but in the imagination of anti-Semites. The extreme fragmentation of Germany's Jews made it nearly meaningless to speak of "a Jewish community." The legal status of the Jewish religion and religious organizations in the German states was quite confused. Without acknowledged leaders who could speak for "the community," concerted action against anti-Semitism remained difficult. However, the silence of the Jews, a matter of extreme regret to the *Abwehr-Verein*, rested on more than just the difficult mechanics of common action.

This silence seemed to contemporaries to be a confirmation of anti-Semitic allegations. In fact, it was a product of the historical experience of emancipation. The tortuous granting and withdrawing of legal equality for German Jews during the nineteenth century helped keep them in perpetual insecurity. When emancipation came in 1869, it was not the fruit of revolution or the result of Jewish power but a gift from the liberally minded North German Reichstag. Like their anti-Semitic enemies, many Jews believed that Jewish emancipation was conditional, a contractual agreement. Civil equality, according to this view, was not essentially an inalienable right. Jewish emancipation had come because non-Jews had finally recognized their worthiness. Implicit in emancipation, to German Jews, was the faithful fulfillment of their side of the contract—continuing to be exemplary citizens and demonstrating the capacity to become good Germans.

In their anxiety to show themselves good Germans, Jews hesitated to defend their own cause, fearing to appear to non-Jews as a special interest group that needed protecting. To make a fuss would only give more ammunition to the anti-Semites. To ask openly for special intervention by the states would be tantamount to asking for a privileged status, akin to that enjoyed by "court Jews" of earlier centuries. Before the 1890's, Jews made relatively slight response to anti-Semitic attacks and preferred to rely on the good offices of "unimpeachably objective" Christian defenders.[59] Individual Jews, speaking for themselves, constantly countered the more infamous pamphlets of the anti-Semites. On the other hand, outstanding public figures such as Eduard Lasker and Ludwig Bamberger remained silent. At the height of the Berlin Movement in 1880, Bamberger published an essay, *Deutschtum und Judentum* (*Germandom and Jewry*), which timidly warned against the impeding of complete Jewish assimilation by the anti-Semites. The worst thing he could say about the anti-Semites was that they kept "some Jews" from becoming "fully German and enjoying those special blessings."[60]

Notwithstanding the indications of animosity in official quarters, discussed above, most German Jews preferred to rely upon government for their defense. Over the years, Jews in western and central Europe had become accustomed to depend on state authority to fend off the mob.[61] For Jews in Germany to rely upon the state to defend them was not totally unwarranted. It had given them liberty and had assured them in answering Hänel's interpellation that that liberty would be maintained. In the most important matter, that of physical safety, the state had proved its utter reliability by using troops to quell riots in Neustettin (1881), Xanten (1891), and Konitz (1900), and by handing out stiff punishments to rioters.[62] With this assurance of personal safety, Jews could live in relative peace. They hoped that the less congenial aspects of the Wilhelminian state, primarily its discrimination against Jews in civil service appointments, might be overcome some day.[63] If Jews continued to be model citizens, they reasoned, the state would have to grant this last measure of confidence, too. They wanted, with Bamberger, to be accepted as good Germans and to "share those special blessings."

In the 1890's, only a few German Jews saw the need for something more, an organization to combat anti-Semitism openly and to obtain the rights guaranteed in the constitution. On New Year's Day 1893, Raphael Löwenfeld, journalist and founder of the Schiller Theater Society, published a pamphlet which proved seminal in its basic ideas. Entitled *Schutzjuden oder Staatsbürger?* (*Protected Jews or Citizens?*), the pamphlet hotly advocated no other protection for Jews than that afforded to all law-abiding citizens. Löwenfeld maintained that the relationship between Jews of Germany and Jews of other nations was no different than the one between German Protestants and those of other lands. To bring this point home, he coined a phrase which gave expression to the unformed thoughts and emotions of most of the Jews of Germany: "We are not German Jews but German citizens of Jewish faith."[64] Jews shared only a common, or fairly common, set of religious beliefs and practices. Once and for all, Löwenfeld rejected "collective responsibility for unworthy acts of individual Jews."

As Löwenfeld's ideas elicited favorable and unexpectedly intense response throughout the winter and spring of 1893, an active resistance group, including a number of noted lawyers, bankers, and businessmen, began to take shape. After preliminary meetings attended by approximately two hundred notables, an advertisement appeared in the big German dailies, calling for the formation of the *Centralverein deutscher Staatsbürger jüdischen Glaubens* (Central Association of German Citizens of Jewish Faith). Löwenfeld's theses in slightly amended form served well as the new organization's credo and as a means of recruitment for what became the largest Jewish voluntary association in Germany. By 1903 the *Centralverein* spoke for twelve thousand individuals and one hundred affiliated groups, a total membership of one hundred thousand. Its 177 chapters and many local agents kept tabs on regional anti-Semitic activities. Much of the intelligence thus gathered made its way into the organization's newspaper, *Im Deutschen Reich* (*IDR*), which appeared monthly until 1922 whereupon it became the weekly *CV-Zeitung.*[65]

In the postemancipation era, the *Centralverein* represented a renewed search for Jewish identity. The persistence of anti-Semitism and its attendant humiliations rendered useless the older solutions to the ongoing identity crisis.[66] The *Centralverein* committed itself to a public defense of Judaism, to a dignified assimilation, and to full participation in German life. Although silent reliance on progressive Christians came to an end, evidence of a lack of self-confidence among German Jews was still apparent. The *Centralverein* attitude toward Zionism, for example, revealed the continuing ambiguity of the Jewish position. From the publication of Theodor Herzl's *Der Judenstaat* (1896), the organization showed consistent hostility toward what it branded as "racial Semitism." The Zionists' conception of a separate Jewish *Volk* played right into the hands of anti-Semites. Even though the movement never gained many adherents in Germany, the *Centralverein* was embarrassed by its "excessive nationalism" and annoyed by its assertion that Jews could not truly belong to the German nation. This was the wrongheaded reaction of hotheads to the emergence of political anti-Semitism.[67]

The feebleness of Zionist organizations in Germany illuminates not only the peculiar attitudes of German Jews, but another failing of the anti-Semitic parties as well. The growth of Zionism in Austria, Russia, and Rumania came in response to active, often violent anti-Semitic agitation. But in Germany, the vast majority of Jews, although deeply hurt by anti-Semitism, maintained and perhaps even intensified their allegiance to German nationality. The anti-Semites failed to create even a "negative solidarity" among German Jews. Consequently, throughout the Wilhelminian era, the *Centralverein* offered German Jews a more agreeable way of meeting the anti-Semitic threat than did the Zionists.

The practical resistance to anti-Semitism developed by the *Centralverein* followed the liberal pattern. Unlike the warring anti-Semitic factions, the *Centralverein* and the *Abwehr-Verein* maintained close and cordial relations. Minor disagreements about tactics never marred their cooperative efforts. The *IDR* borrowed articles freely from the *MVA*. The two organizations instituted a common election fund in 1912. Both usually persented the activities of the other in the best possible light.[68] In fact, the activities of the *Abwehr-Verein* and the *Centralverein* were largely the same in content and conception. The Jewish defense association also faced many of the same problems as its sister organization. The *Centralverein,* too, found it difficult to endorse Social Democrats, even when they opposed anti-Semites. Not until 1903 did it insist that its members vote against an anti-Semite, no matter who his opponent happened to be.[69] For exemplary, patriotic citizens such "treasonous" behavior came very hard.

The organization published "enlightenment materials," practiced political intervention in national and state elections, and provided documentation for Reichstag and state parliament debates. The *Centralverein* added only one unique feature to the fight against anti-Semitism. From the beginning, it put great emphasis on its legal protection bureau (*Rechtsschutz-Kommission*). The bureau composed of highly qualified lawyers and legally trained members read virtually all of the anti-Semitic press looking for prosecutable material. The research and investigation of likely cases preceded the decision of the main committee on whether or not to intervene. Eugen Fuchs, first chairman of the bureau and one of the chief spokesmen for the *Centralverein,* set rigorous standards to govern intervention on behalf of individuals. The organization rendered aid only if the "rights and interests of Judaism itself" were concerned in the case. The defense of Judaism, not just individual Jews, remained the chief task of the bureau.[70]

German law posed many obstacles to this kind of work. Legal technicalities as well as the fragmentation of the Jewish population made convictions for libel against "Jews as a whole," rather than individuals or particular Jewish communities, difficult to obtain. Such suits usually ended with sentencing for "gross misconduct" (*grober Unfug*), which carried only minor penalties.[71] The legal resistance of the *Centralverein* depended heavily on the degree of good will to be found in the judicial authorities. During the last two years of Caprivi's chancellorship, the tempo of legal prosecution and the much needed cooperation of the public prosecutor improved noticeably.[72] Yet the interpretation of the law as well as its execution varied from place to place and was ultimately in the province of men who regarded anti-Semitism in ways far different from the *Centralverein*. Nonetheless, the legal protection bureau enjoyed some notable successes. It obtained several convictions against anti-Semites who alleged the defilement of meat by Jewish butchers, the torture of animals by kosher slaughterers, and the "religious necessity" for Jews to commit perjury and ritual murder. Sometimes the bureau achieved its goal by merely informing the proper state authority of an illegality. As a result of such information, the Prussian minister of the interior frequently confiscated anti-Semitic newspapers, pamphlets, and postcards. Without going to court, the *Centralverein* brought the attention of officials to the occasional slanders of state institutions in the anti-Semitic press.[73] Sooner or later, the legal protection bureau counted nearly every major anti-Semitic leader among the victims of its vigilance.

The *Centralverein* had no illusions about legal prosecution as the ultimate weapon against anti-Semitism. According to one of its last governing officials, Alfred Wiener: "Nobody in the ranks of the *Centralverein* ever thought that such legal actions would eliminate the roots of anti-Semitism."[74] In one respect, legal activities had only dubious success. Very soon after the legal bureau got to work, personal attacks upon individual Jews ceased appearing in anti-Semitic newspapers. Similarly, defamations of the Jewish religion became rarer.[75] But the anti-Semites merely resorted to innuendo, Aesopian language, or "quotation" from foreign anti-Semitic newspapers. In the long run, the lack of factuality in the attacks of anti-Semites probably did little damage to their cause. Their followers were usually ready to accept assertions in place of solid proof.

In another way, however, the *Centralverein* legal measures took a heavy toll among anti-Semites. Willi Buch lamented the "many hard sentences" pronounced against his colleagues and the time spent in jail because of unpaid fines.[76] The existence of the legal protection bureau kept the anti-Semites from acting with impunity, placed a drain on their slender finances, and damaged their public image. They responded to the "denouncers' league" with special vehemence. But the *Centralverein* had the law on its side and this counted for a great deal in imperial Germany. In Germany especially, according to Alfred Wiener, conviction and sentencing had great influence on the general public.[77] Signs of decay in reverence for the law were already apparent in the Wilhelminian period, but nowhere and at no time did this degeneration reach the levels common in the Weimar Republic. Among Wilhelminian anti-Semites, a serious brush with the law almost always sufficed to hamper or even end the influence of the guilty individual within the party or affiliated organizations. Moreover, the parliamentary anti-Semites were usually far more respectful of the law than the mass of their voters. The peasants of Arnswalde-Friedberg might be willing to ignore Hermann Ahlwardt's numerous convictions, but his fellow anti-Semites in the Reichstag wanted as little to do as possible with the "rowdy."

The extent of the anti-Semites' troubles with the law did not derive exclusively from the efforts of the *Centralverein*. State authorities initiated lawsuits on their own, as did many individuals. The public prosecutor became increasingly active in the pursuit of anti-Semites. According to partial figures compiled from the *MVA* and *IDR* between 1893 and 1915, 537 individuals with known anti-Semitic affiliations stood trial.[78] The courts sentenced them to a total of 135 years in prison and fines of 56,200 marks, exclusive of court costs, which convicted libelers had to pay. Most offenders were anti-Semitic journalists; many were identified as party agitators and local *Reformverein* leaders. Not a single "big-name" anti-Semite escaped conviction, although Liebermann and Zimmermann got off rather lightly for their infrequent offenses. The crimes ranged from murder, assault, and robbery (14 cases) to extortion and embezzlement. Libel, defamation, and slander were the most frequent offenses (240). Convictions for incitement to class hatred or violence, fraud, bad checkwriting, usury, and perjury (66) occurred with an embarrassing regularity for those caught committing the very crimes they deplored as "specifically Jewish."

Although pronouncedly nonpartisan in its principles, the *Centralverein* had the same inclination toward left liberalism as the *Abwehr-Verein*. It, too, had members who belonged to and voted for most of the parties. But the predominant tone of its public statements was left-liberal, and the majority of its members voted for middle-class liberal parties in the *Kaiserreich* as well as in the Weimar Republic.[79] The organization occasionally supported left liberals for the Reichstag and state parliaments. The influential Fuchs and Maximilian

Horwitz, director of the *Centralverein* since 1894, were both members of the left-liberal *Fortschrittliche Volkspartei* and had at one time favored the formal attachment of their organization to a left-liberal party.[80] Any attachment to a specific political party, however, would have been cause for dissatisfaction on the part of some faction within the *Centralverein*. Moreover, in the 1890's, the left liberals had begun to waver under anti-Semitic pressure. Almost imperceptibly, they ceased putting up Jewish candidates, except in certain large cities and in Posen.

The knowledge that the left liberals were not anti-Semites and that they acted from legitimate political motives—putting up the man with the best chance of winning—did not mollify the *Centralverein*. The other major parties either put forward no Jews at all or Jewish converts who, though occasionally found defending Jewish rights, could not be regarded as representative of German Jewry. The few unbaptized Jews in the Reichstag were Socialists, chosen by their party without regard to creed. But most of these Socialists were Jews only from the anti-Semitic or racist standpoint. As far as the *Centralverein* was concerned, Social Democrats who had severed their connections with Judaism were no longer Jews. To make the situation more annoying, anti-Semites like Stoecker were fond of boasting that the Prussian parliament, where the Social Democrats had no deputies until 1908, was *judenrein*, free of Jews. He counted this as one of the triumphs of his movement. Goaded by this boast and as a protest against liberal timidity, the *Centralverein* leadership supported its own Jewish candidates in the Prussian parliament elections of 1898.[81]

As a consequence of this action, an immediate controversy developed inside and outside the organization. The debate focused on the accusation that the *Centralverein* leaders wanted to create a special Jewish political party. The controversy soon died down, although it reemerged periodically.[82] The arguments for and against a special party to represent Jewish interests raised basic questions and led to a redefinition of purpose for the *Centralverein*. One of the ideas behind the backing of Jewish candidates in 1898 was the achievement of parity for German citizens of Jewish faith. Under the slogan of "*Parität*," the Center party had long struggled for Catholic *Landräte* and a proportional number of administrative posts for Catholics in heavily Catholic areas of Prussia. However, in the formulation of Hugo Preuss, later the chief author of the Weimar Constitution, the idea of parity possessed a loftier character:

> Parity is not clericalism's false idea of proportional participation of religions, but the absolute insignificance of religious denomination for the holding of public office. This parity is legally right; the exact opposite, at least regarding Jews, is the fixed administrative practice.[83]

The struggle for equality became the great positive work of the *Centralverein*. Recognition from the state and a realization of constitutional guarantees gradually grew more important than confronting the anti-Semitic parties which were steadily losing power in Germany. Still the defender of Judaism, the *Centralverein* began the fight against government anti-Semitism. In its battle for implementation of the constitution, the organization acted not only in defense of Jewish rights, but in the interests of every German citizen. Therefore, the *Centralverein* conceived of the struggle for parity as another proof of good citizenship, not as the selfish strivings of a "Jewish Center party."[84]

But no sooner than formulated, Preuss's principle met with official opposition. Between 1899 and 1902, the governments of several German states made decisions regarding administrative appointments, especially in the justice department, which smacked of anti-Semitism. By refraining from the appointment of Jewish judges, the Hessian government appeared to be giving in to the anti-Semitic sentiments of its citizens. A protest by Jewish citizens brought only the assurance that the government intended to uphold civil equality, a phrase that had begun to sound hollow even to the most patient.[85] Justice Minister Karl Heinrich von Schönstedt of Prussia, "unknown when he came, unloved when he left," revealed in the state parliament that Jewish lawyers had to wait longer than non-Jews to be appointed to the office of notary. He also confessed to appointing fewer Jews to this office than might be warranted by their competence. Appointment of Jews in proportion to the number of Jewish lawyers would, according to the justice minister, "irritate a considerable segment of the Christian population" which "naturally sought out Christian officials." The left liberals, Martin Peltasohn and Theodor Barth, responded angrily to the justice minister's subjective interpretation of the common good. Both men doubted that the anti-Semitic public opinion alluded to was anything more than a pretext for the government's flagrant violation of the Prussian and Reich constitutions, that is, for its own anti-Semitism.[86]

The storm raised by Schönstedt's remarks at first vented itself in plans for an organized protest demonstration. But Horwitz, Fuchs, and other Jewish notables channeled the unprecedented anger among German Jews into the formation of a long-planned cover organization, a Jewish congress, that aspired to encompass all major German Jewish groups. Jews had come to feel the need for a broadly based organization to speak out more energetically for Jewish interests than the left liberals were willing to do. The *Verband der deutschen Juden* (Association of German Jews), which began operations in April 1904 and disbanded in 1922, was meant to answer this need. The *Verband* never lived up to expectations, although it did contribute to the fight against government anti-Semitism. Two of its committees, heavily occupied by members of the *Centralverein*, undertook careful studies of the various branches of the civil service.[87] In 1906 the *Verband* concentrated on the fairly common practice of passing over Jews for jury duty. In 1907 the first minor success for one of its protests came from the least likely quarter, the Kingdom of Saxony. The Saxon minister of justice admitted that exclusion was widespread and contrary to the law. He agreed with the letter that many Saxon Jews were certainly qualified to serve by their level of education. He promised to inform the courts and committees, which chose jurors, of the justified wishes of the parties concerned.[88]

Upon further study, the *Verband* substantiated with statistics what many had only suspected. Clear cases of discrimination in the civil service were verified, although it was impossible to determine whether Jews were kept back because of religion, "race," party affiliation, or class. The constitution, of course, admitted none of these pretexts. Extensive research revealed a depressing picture of the lack of fair play. Only in the railroad department of the Reich was there a considerable number of Jews; they, however, did not advance beyond a certain rank.[89] The field of primary education retained a strong religious emphasis in most of the states. Only in Baden, where non-denominational schools were the rule since 1878, did Jews readily find employment. In the category of secondary school teachers (*Ober-lehrer*), the states and municipalities of Germany appointed ninety-seven Jews out of a total of 8,377 in the years 1875–1895. More than half this number taught in Jewish parochial schools. For all of Prussia, Jewish secondary school teachers never exceeded twelve in number at any one time.[90] In the ranks of higher education around 1900, there were two hundred Jewish faculty members in German universities. They represented ten percent of the instructors (*Privat-dozenten*); seven percent of the assistant professors; and two percent of the professors (20–25). No Jews ever held a full professorship in German language, literature, or classical philology. Teaching was one of the few fields where religious conversion—"the victory of hypocrisy over intolerance"—proved no great advantage.[91]

In the judicial branch of government the story was much the same. Although often highly qualified, unbaptized Jews rarely rose to the higher levels of the judiciary.[92] Bavaria showed less discrimination in this area of state service; in 1900 thirty-one of its one thousand judges were unconverted Jews. From 1880 to 1914 Prussia appointed approximately two hundred Jewish judges, who constituted three to four percent of the total number.[93] However, because Jewish lawyers could find only limited employment by the state, there were twice as many in private practice as in the civil service. The exact opposite ratio operated among Protestants.[94] Once again, government discrimination had political repercussions. Nonemployment by the state helped concentrate Jews in private law practice and gave fuel to the anti-Semitic politicians' constant complaints about "the Jewified law profession."

Caste consciousness, religious intolerance, and the protection of social status appeared indisputable in the Prussian Army. No Jews, converted or unconverted, were to be found on the general staff of the Prussian Army from the late 1870's until the early years of World War I.[95] Another aspect of military discrimination against Jews, the absence of Jewish officers of the reserve, cast doubt upon their patriotism and social acceptability, two matters about which they cared a great deal. Since 1880, twenty to thirty thousand one-year volunteers of Jewish faith (those with certificates from secondary schools) served in the regular army. Following their active service, none achieved officer of the reserve status, a highly prestigious title in Wilhelminian society. However, three hundred of the twelve to fifteen hundred converted Jews who served did become reserve officers.[96] Armed with facts and figures and individual case histories, the left liberals made a major effort to rectify this situation. They plagued successive defense ministers with interpellations about discrimination in the army. They met with feigned ignorance of any wrongdoing or outright deception concerning the steps being taken to remedy the obvious discrimination. In 1908, the Prussian minister of war, Karl von Einem, tried to silence his critics by alluding to an order from the kaiser forbidding the rejection of qualified men because of their religious affiliation. Einem's successor, Josias von Heeringen, adopted an apparently conciliatory attitude on this question in his yearly appearances before the Prussian parliament and the Reichstag.[97] But nothing really changed. The army's imperviousness to agencies of popular control proved impossible to overcome.

Outside the military sphere, however, the forces fighting for Jewish civil rights had some successes. Under constant pressure from the resistance organizations and from the left-liberal parties in the German parliaments, the various state governments began to modify their discriminatory policies. In 1906 and 1907, the Prussian minister of justice, Maximilian von Beseler, appointed four Jewish associate justices to the courts of appeal, among them Fuchs of the *Centralverein*. The Grand Duchy of Hesse appointed its first Jewish judge (*Amtsrichter*) in 1910.[98] Such minor victories did not tempt the resistance organizations to diminish their efforts. They accepted the slight improvements as token of a different policy, a policy which would take time to implement fully. But as long as a matter of principle was at stake and some Germans were denied full constitutional rights, the *Centralverein* and the *Abwehr-Verein* continued to prod those in power.

Opposition to the anti-Semitic political parties in the imperial era unfolded in a number of ways and for a variety of reasons. Uncoordinated defense efforts and differing attitudes toward the enemy make it, perhaps, illegitimate to speak of a single "resistance." State governments could combat anti-Semites while discriminating against Jews, that is, undermine the anti-Semitic parties while fostering anti-Semitism. With few exceptions, the governments cared only about the methods and not the arguments employed by the anti-Semites. Only the defense organizations combated anti-Semitism as well as the anti-Semitic political parties. But the high-minded fight put up by the *Abwehr-Verein* depended too much upon an inadequate understanding of anti-Semitism and an inability to reach the people who were most prone to anti-Semitic blandishments. The *Centralverein* and *Verband der deutschen Juden* carried on a double battle against anti-Semitism and for real equality, but they did so from a position weakened by their own lack of self-confidence. They never demanded strongly enough what was theirs by right. Like the men of the *Abwehr-Verein,* their trust in the triumph of reason vitiated the effectiveness of their counterattack. Yet, in spite of their short-comings and the lack of a united front, all these oppositional forces contributed to the defeat of the parliamentary anti-Semites in the *Kaiserreich.*

CHAPTER 7

The Parliamentary Solution is Tested

The agencies of opposition did valuable work in the struggle against parliamentary anti-Semitism, especially by helping to discredit the political capacities of the anti-Semites. Of course, the anti-Semitic politicians were their own worst enemies in this matter. Virtually the entire bid for support made by Böckel's and Liebermann's brand of anti-Semitism depended upon the promise of effectiveness in the Reichstag. Keeping that promise, however, proved much more difficult than any parliamentary anti-Semite had dared imagine. In 1894 the German Social Reform party entered the Reichstag with fifteen deputies. A year later, the party added another in a by-election for Waldeck, a tiny principality adjacent to Hessenland. This allowed it to jettison Ahlwardt for the sake of respectability while remaining a legal *Fraktion* with access to all the means afforded by the Reichstag for the implementation of its program. Fifteen votes did not, of course, amount to much in a total of 397. Yet the Poles, the Socialists before 1890, and the various left-liberal splinter groups between 1893 and 1910 possessed approximately the same strength as the anti-Semitic *Fraktion*. All were far more successful than the anti-Semites in gaining concessions from the Reich government, in keeping their causes before the public, or in exerting an influence upon the proceedings of the Reichstag. The Social Reformers could no longer, in 1894, hide behind the excuse of too few numbers. They had to produce some palpable success, show some sign of a future solution to the Jewish question through parliamentary action.

The anti-Semites proceeded straightforwardly in the Reichstag. During the sessions of 1893–1898, the party made use of its *Fraktion* prerogative to initiate four legislative motions which it regarded as anti-Semitic. In March 1894, Liebermann reintroduced a complicated measure to restrict Jewish immigration from eastern Europe.

He and the German Conservatives had attempted a similar move in 1893. Tactically, the motion seemed sound. It might very well attract support from other deputies as a way of opposing the last of Caprivi's trade treaties. Liebermann argued that the pending treaty with Russia would inundate Germany with *Ostjuden* because, according to the first article of the agreement, citizens of either country who settled or stopped in the other would enjoy the same rights as citizens of countries with most-favored-nation status. Such an opportunity would draw Russian Jews to Germany like a magnet, he asserted. It was the duty of every patriotic German to avert this possibility.[1] But Chancellor Hohenlohe's foreign secretary, Adolf Marschall von Bieberstein, easily convinced the Reichstag that the overrunning of Germany by Russian subjects was not a real danger. He pointed out that the treaty left the German government entirely free to prevent Russians from entering Germany or to expel them after entry. The German Social Reformers' bill eventually went down to defeat 167 to 51.[2] As a tactic, however, the motion may have gained a little temporary prestige for the anti-Semites. The party had drawn support from the Conservatives and *Reichspartei* and elicited the Pan-German League's only plainly anti-Semitic bill, a related measure presented by the president of the league, Ernst Hasse. But Liebermann soon made a nuisance out of the motion, persistently reintroducing it long after it had become clear that very few *Ostjuden* were being allowed to settle permanently in Germany.[3]

Only one other German Social Reform motion actually reached the stage of plenum debate during the Reichstag of 1893–1898. The *Fraktion* presented what amounted to Liebermann's pet project, the reintroduction of denominational religious oaths for sworn witnesses in jury trials. Although the bill had little overt anti-Semitism attached to it, Liebermann interpreted it in his own way. Typical of the conventional anti-Semitic outlook, the measure attempted to remedy the ominous decay of German morality by legislative means. Since so many false oaths had come to light lately, the oath-taking ceremony had to be reinvested with every sort of religious significance and solemnity. As everyone knew, said Liebermann, primary responsibility for oath breaking rested with the Jews who were able to hide behind the uniform, nondenominational oath instituted in 1877: "I swear by the almighty and all-knowing God. . . ." The revival of the traditional Protestant and Catholic oaths, which mentioned Christ or the Gospel, would serve to identify Jewish witnesses, thus affording a defense against creeping Jewish cynicism. Although Liebermann did not admit it, he probably hoped that some Germans would refuse to take a Christian oath before a Jewish judge "for reasons of conscience." But Liebermann dared not spell out all the anti-Semitic implications of his motion, for he knew that crucial supporters would put no anti-Semitic interpretation on the bill whatsoever. In fact, both the Conservative and Center party spokesmen for the bill specifically denied anti-Semitism as a motivation for the support of their respective parties. With their votes, the only measure ever proposed by an anti-Semite and adopted by the imperial Reichstag became law in April 1897.[4]

With each new session, the anti-Semites tried to get at least one bill debated before the house. Aside from the immigration motion, the most frequently attempted measure demanded the prohibition of kosher slaughtering. The anti-Semites always portrayed this practice as a racially conditioned desire in Jews to inflict pain upon animals. The party sensed a "sweet issue," one which no other party could argue against, without appearing to be animal haters, vivisectionists, or worse. But once again, the anti-Semites oversimplified matters and fell victim to their own impassioned thinking. In 1899, during the Reichstag debate of their motion, the anti-Semites learned that most veterinarians thought kosher slaughtering humane and that many butchers in the Prussian Army used the method because of its efficiency. Moreover, Ernst Lieber of the Center party interpreted the motion as interference in religious freedom. He branded the anti-Semites as religious bigots and announced that the Center would oppose the bill.[5] Thus, what had appeared a perfectly safe issue to exploit turned into a damaging fiasco for the anti-Semites.

The German Social Reform party undertook one other purely anti-Semitic enterprise on a fairly regular basis. Petitions from local *Reformvereine* bombarded the state parliaments and the Reichstag with the demand that the Talmud and the Schulcan Aruch be translated and studied at state expense. In these sacred writings of rabbinic Judaism, anti-Semites were sure there lurked prescriptions for ritual murder, cheating of gentiles, and conquest of the world. In trying to get this issue before the Reichstag, however, the party demonstrated a fundamental lack of understanding about the workings of parliament and an equally important flaw in party organization. The status of *Fraktion* entitled the German Social Reformers to send members to all of the Reichstag commissions. Deputy Julius Müller of Waldeck, one of the least capable members of the party, sat on the petition committee. The post possessed little prestige but could have been quite important, especially for the anti-Semites. A systematic effort by the party's one hundred and twenty *Reformvereine* could have launched a petition that would have been difficult to ignore. With a capable man on the petition commission, the anti-Semites would have been able to portray the need for state translation as a deep-felt concern on the part of masses of Germans. But Müller sat mute and the uncontrolled *Reformvereine* acted independently of one another. Their many individual petitions failed to make an impact on Germany's parliaments.

Efforts to prosecute the Jewish question directly ended in consistent failure for the German Social Reformers. However, a frontal attack was not the only method open to them in the Reichstag. The leaders of the party, backed by delegates to the Halle congress (11–12 October 1896), advocated an "indirect" approach to the Jewish question. By emphasizing the socioeconomic demands of the Erfurt program, the party, it was hoped, could make up for initial setbacks and regain public attention.[6] But this shift in strategy was no longer to be accomplished easily. The Reichstag record of the Social Reformers in support of their own program planks had already proved quite uneven. For example, a spirits tax designed to benefit small-scale farmers and businessmen split the anti-Semitic vote: three yes, six no, and six absent. A majority of anti-Semites also voted against laws dealing with unfair competition, consumer cooperatives, fair business practices, and a revision of the sugar tax—all interpreted at the time as favoring the *Mittelstand*.[7]

Perhaps the most startling contrast between the words and deeds of anti-Semites came over the reform of the civil code. The full-scale revision of the *Bürgerliches-Gesetzbuch* or civil law was one of the great achievements of the imperial Reichstag. It required months of intensive labor by a special Reichstag commission that studied government proposals, debated various alternatives, and made reform suggestions of its own. In the Erfurt program, the German

Social Reformers had come out strongly for "creation of a civil code rooted in German legal principles" to replace a legal system they regarded as inadequate. In 1896, they sent their only lawyer, Georg Vielhaben of Hamburg, to represent the anti-Semitic point of view on the special commission. The newcomer, known for his ultraconservatism, was quickly intimidated by the number of legal experts on the commission. During debates on the position of "the little man" and the forwarding of "German legal principles," Vielhaben sat silently, letting the National Liberals and Centrists take the lead and reap the glory. He made only two recommendations during all the months that the commission sat. He called for reintroduction of the right to total distraint of a debtor's worldly goods, including furniture and kitchen utensils, a measure condemned by the Erfurt program because it dealt too harshly with indebted *Mittelständler*. His other suggestion, according to the National Liberals on the commission, served the exclusive interests of the great shipowners of Hamburg, making the impounding of their ships virtually impossible. When the projected civil code came to a final vote on 1 July 1896, eight German Social Reformers absented themselves, six abstained, and deputy Heinrich Lieber voted in favor, whereupon the rest of the *Fraktion* expelled him.[8]

By the end of the legislative period 1893–1898, the German Social Reform party had given its enemies plenty of ammunition for critical barrages. The party's unity of purpose extended no further than the anti-Semitic planks of the Erfurt program. That program offered neither a plan of action nor specific and concrete goals which could guide the *Fraktion*. The voting record of the German Social Reformers in matters which did not touch on anti-Semitism revealed their inner divisions and conflicting interests. In the eighty rollcall votes of the 1893–1898 Reichstag, the party voted unanimously only forty-six times. Furthermore, phenomenal absenteeism weakened an occasional show of unity. For the eighty roll-call votes, the German Social Reformers, not counting Ahlwardt or Böckel, were absent 398 times. Of these absences, less than one-third were legitimate according to Reichstag rules.[9]

Clearly, the anti-Semites had been unable to exploit their presence in the Reichstag. Even after forming their own *Fraktion* and therefore gaining a place in the series of speakers, they found that their oratorical skills were seldom appreciated. The clichés and patriotic slogans that met with thunderous applause at anti-Semitic rallies brought laughter and ridicule in the Reichstag. For all its shortcomings and lack of real power, the Reichstag operated according to high standards of germaneness and efficiency. Work in the commissions demanded competence and in some cases a good deal of expertise, neither of which the anti-Semites ever succeeded in acquiring. Their critics scornfully pointed out these glaring weaknesses, identifying the anti-Semites as a do-nothing party that betrayed its own program and failed to achieve anything either for the "whole nation" or even for the narrower interests of the *Mittelstand.* Anti-Semitic deputies made a minimal contribution to the hard work of the Reichstag commissions. The party demonstrated not only ineptness and disunity, but could not even fulfill its obligation to attend Reichstag debates with any regularity. Critics never ran short of reprehensible anti-Semitic deeds to expose and condemn. Moreover, criticism came from all quarters, not just from the *Abwehr-Verein, Centralverein,* or left-liberal parties. No matter what the critics thought of Jews, they were united in their denunciation of the "dilletantish demagogy" of the anti-Semites.[10]

Even if the German Social Reformers did recognize their impotence in the Reichstag, few saw reason for despair. The next election in 1898 would undoubtedly relieve the situation. If, however, the party made no progress at the polls, it had two alternative methods of exercising an effect on German life: it could seek an alliance with a stronger party or parties in the Reichstag; or, in order to save face and make the headlines, the party could turn on the institution of the Reichstag itself, declare it unrepresentative of the German people, and systematically try to discredit it. In an isolated instance, when Bismarck was refused an ovation motion on his eightieth birthday in 1895, the parliamentary anti-Semites became incensed with the Reichstag. This was not, however, the beginning of a new and calculated policy of undermining parliament. The sense of outrage proceeded from genuine feeling in those who considered themselves the most loyal upholders of Bismarckian tradition.[11] True, they helped to coarsen the proceedings. They were for the most part coarse men. Anti-Semites often heard the president's bell of censure but not a great deal more frequently than many others who went beyond the parliamentarily acceptable. Ineffective though they were, the anti-Semites adapted themselves to the accepted forms and customs of the Reichstag. They mastered its intricate protocol and imitated the debating techniques of its acknowledged experts. The Reichstag, after all, was a creation of the revered Bismarck. Systematic obstruction and the belittling of the institutions of the *Kaiserreich,* on the other hand, belonged to the tactics of revolutionary Socialists and a few misguided revolutionary anti-Semites, like Fritsch or Dühring. Long after respect for the institutions of the empire had weakened among them, the conventional anti-Semites still hesitated to make a mockery of the Reichstag or to use it as a vehicle of propaganda for their cause.[12] Furthermore, had the conventional anti-Semites adopted such a plan of action, they would have had to wipe from memory the thorough humiliation of Hermann Ahlwardt.

In March 1893, Ahlwardt made insinuating accusations concerning the administration of the fund for disabled veterans *(Invalidenfond)*. He claimed to have proof—weighing two hundred pounds—that embezzlements from the fund lined the pockets of Jews. Corruption in high places, he asserted, had helped the Jews to steal the money that by right belonged to those crippled while fighting for German unity. But Ahlwardt's attempt to launch a parliamentary version of the *Judenflinten* episode foundered on the resistance of the left liberals, Richter and Rickert, and Manteuffel of the Conservative party. All three demanded to see the proof. On 25 April the *Seniorenkonvent,* made up of a high-ranking member from each *Fraktion,* examined the evidence and found nothing incriminating. The *Rektor* then demanded an investigation by a special commission, which delivered the same verdict a week later.[13] The affair ended with a severe tongue-lashing by the Conservative president of the Reichstag. To fellow anti-Semites the Ahlwardt affair provided another object lesson in the need for respectability. A revolutionary use of the Reichstag was not a real alternative for men of their stamp.

The first alternative, an alliance with a more powerful party, appeared much more dignified and reputable. The best chances for help in the realization of anti-Semitic goals still lay with the Conservative party. But even Liebermann could no longer be in doubt about the dangers of exploitation at the hands of the Conservatives. Cooperation with them, whether in the Reichstag or at election time, called for extreme caution. In early 1896 they gave new evidence of their lack of "sincerity" concerning anti-Semitism. The Conservative party's ruling committee of eleven confronted ex-Court Chaplain Stoecker with a demand that he publicly censure the newspaper of the Christian Socials, *Das Volk*. The paper, which advocated many of the same economic changes as the German Social Reformers, had begun to make suggestions about improvements in the lot of agricultural workers, an issue which directly touched the interests of Conservative Junkers. Rather than condemn *Das Volk*, Stoecker severed his relations with the Conservatives on 2 February 1896.[14]

The committee of eleven's decision proved epoch making for the Christian Social party, which remained virtually helpless until after the death of Stoecker in 1909, and for the Conservative party, too. The dropping of Stoecker underlined the victory of agrarianism within the Conservative party. The Agrarian League's swift progress impressed Conservative leaders far more favorably than the court chaplain's uncontrollable following or an association with the unreliable German Social Reformers. The league provided the Conservatives with a vote-getting apparatus and funds for massive agitation on behalf of agricultural interests, and it managed this without seriously disturbing the traditional, oligarchical power structure of the party. By 1896 the league was doing its job well enough for the Conservative party decisively to reject "social conservatism," that is, conversion into a social reform party. Stoecker and the parliamentary anti-Semites were simply not vital to a party of this nature.[15] The Conservatives and especially the Agrarians continued to use anti-Semitism and even the anti-Semites periodically. But after 1896, the possibility of a formal relationship between the German Social Reformers and the Conservatives—one that would stress anti-Semitism instead of agrarianism—virtually disappeared.

Yet, despite significant differences between the Conservative and anti-Semitic parties in social composition and their divergent stands on important issues such as fleet building, colonial expansion, universal suffrage, and the graduated income tax, the Conservative party was the only one that deigned to make frequent use of the German Social Reformers. Total agreement in agricultural matters bound the two together. Moreover, by 1898 the anti-Semites' financial straits were beginning to play a role in their relations to the Conservatives and Agrarians. Many German Social Reformers had become directly or indirectly dependent upon the league for a livelihood, a hard fact which tended, by the turn of the century, to limit their freedom of action and to impair their independent image.[16]

To the consternation of the Conservatives, the anti-Semites at times slid over to the left side of the house, voting with the Social Democratic party on a few issues.[17] In the Naval Fleet Bill of 1898, for example, the anti-Semites and Social Democrats voted unanimously in favor of meeting the costs of naval construction by means of a graduated income tax. Isolated instances of cooperation between anti-Semites and Socialists in a by-election for Giessen (1911) and in elections to the Baden and Prussian state parliaments (1899, 1901, 1903) were made possible because the two parties preferred each other's candidates to those of the Conservative, National, or left-liberal parties.[18] But these were altogether rare occurrences. The peasant populism of Böckel and the anticapitalism of the anti-Semites in general often led the liberal defense organizations to accuse the German Social Reformers of being little better than the Socialists. But Böckel and his successors in Hessenland were, to the contrary, aggressively opposed to the Socialists. The Hessians always presented themselves as a national antidote to the un-German, peasant-hostile Social Democrats.[19] Similarly, a large measure of the anti-Semitic program in the Kingdom of Saxony consisted of a fervent antisocialism. For the mass of anti-Semites, the Socialists were misguided dupes of the wily Jews.[20]

On the other hand, the Social Democratic attitude toward the anti-Semitic parties, resting on the standard interpretation of the Jewish question by Karl Marx, wavered between condescending toleration and open hostility. In Marx's formulation, anti-Semitism was a manifestation of bourgeois society. Upon the imminent destruction of bourgeois society, both anti-Semitism and the materialistic "Jewish parasite" would disappear forever.[21] Basing themselves on Marx, who wrote before the incorporation of anti-Semitism into political party platforms, Social Democratic leaders adapted his thoughts to explain the relatively new phenomenon. Typical of this outlook was the speech of Paul Singer (1844–1911), for many years one of the floor leaders of the party in the Reichstag. Born of Jewish parents, Singer frequently came under nasty personal attack from anti-Semitic deputies. His speech of 12 January 1892 addressed Stoecker, but it applied to all the anti-Semitic parties:

> . . . No, gentlemen, anti-Semitism has far different causes. A foreign colleague of ours . . . has hit the nail on the head with his description of the origins: "Anti-Semitism is the socialism of stupid clods [*der dummen Kerle*]" (laughter), and that is wholly correct. . . . I believe that I judge anti-Semitism correctly when I say that it combats phenomena with which Jewry as such has nothing to do. . . . The fact is that a large number of people believe that to create bearable conditions for the have-nots and the poor, steps must be taken toward effective legislation protecting the worker and toward realization of those social adjustments recommended by us. These people, by means of their own thinking and because of further development of economic conditions, will come to social democracy. Instead of coming where they belong . . . the Jew-hunt initiated by Stoecker and his colleagues has enticed them to abide with anti-Semitism temporarily.[22]

Singer defined the "temporary anti-Semites" as exclusively petty bourgeois. The workers were far too class conscious to be kept from their ultimate goals or to be misled by anti-Semitism.

Singer's presentation paralleled in remarkable fashion the thoughts of Bismarck and Caprivi. He, too, felt that the anti-Semites played into the hands of the Socialists, that they were stirring up unrest already present in German society, and that their agitation could only benefit his party. But Singer was careful to delineate the temporary anti-Semites within the anti-Semitic party. His colleague, Philipp Scheidemann, whose early political career brought him into close contact with the anti-Semites in Hessenland and made him somewhat of a party expert on the Jewish question, showed no such reserve:

> In spite of everything they [the *Mittelstand* and peasantry] have

become at least politically interested, thanks to the anti-Semitic
demagogy; thus, it won't be long before they must come to a
clear decision: either they become reactionary, *in a word,* Conservative, or they must recognize anti-Semitism for its complete
wretchedness and cast their eyes to the future. That means to
learn how to *think* politically and to become Social Democrats.[23]

Misled by their ideology, the orthodox Social Democrats could not
conceive of a "permanent" anti-Semitic threat or one that required
more than verbal denunciation from them.

What aroused the active concern of the Social Democrats was
certainly not the anti-Semites' "near socialism," not their attacks
upon the civil rights of Jews, and not even their demagogic promises
to the *Mittelstand* and peasantry. Only direct attempts by anti-Semites
to win the workers away from socialism stirred the party to action.
Because Court Chaplain Stoecker had made such an attempt during
the Berlin movement, he remained the center of Socialist attention
long after his influence had waned. After Stoecker's direct threat had
been repelled in the early 1880's, anti-Semitism became a wholly
secondary problem for the Social Democrats. The growth of socialism, internal conflicts between radicals and revisionists, administration of the giant organization that had come into being after 1890—
all these matters were far more urgent than the activities of a handful
of anti-Semites. This setting of priorities left little time for dealing
with the problem of anti-Semitism. In 1890, for example, the party
congress quickly tabled a resolution from the Marburg delegation
asking that measures be taken against Böckel's increasingly effective
agitation in Hessenland.[24]

The only other time representatives of the whole party concerned
themselves with anti-Semitism was at Cologne in 1893. There
August Bebel delivered what was to become the standard interpretation of the problem, quoting from Marx's *Zur Judenfrage* and exhibit-
ing the same confidence as Singer and Scheidemann. Bebel accepted
much of the stereotyped picture of German Jews. He spoke of their
"indwelling intelligence and hustle," considered them a race, and
indulged in some mildly anti-Jewish witticisms. Despite all the weaknesses of his approach, he was one of the few critics of the anti-Semites
to take them at their word. He examined their program, "a veritable

herring salad of demands," and believed that the anti-Semites in reality aimed at a revocation of Jewish emancipation. He called the anti-Semitic leaders demagogues and hucksters, but also evaluated their stated and implied objectives with care. He drew the proper conclusions concerning anti-Semitic racism, that a racist should not be satisfied with anything less than annihilation, expulsion, or very thorough socioeconomic isolation. Like the vast majority of his contemporaries, including the anti-Semites, Bebel could not imagine the implementation of the first or second possibilities. The third possibility, social and economic isolation of Jews, according to him, could be realized only by means of an exceptional law or an anti-Semites' revolution. The first would fail to solve the Jewish question as it had failed to solve the "Socialist question." The second, an anti-Semites' seizure of power, was "not even to be thought of." Although he refused to see parliamentary anti-Semitism as totally harmless, he, too, clearly regarded it as a secondary problem, one which would solve itself and ultimately redound to the benefit of social democracy.[25]

The Social Democrats eventually printed Bebel's speech in amended and corrected form, improved the tone, and distributed it as a pamphlet. For the mass of party members, it remained the official word on anti-Semitism throughout the *Kaiserreich*. However, some less orthodox Marxists in the party disagreed about the seriousness of the problem. The revisionist, Eduard Bernstein, cautioned against complacency, even though he, too, thought that the anti-Semitic parties acted as temporary stopping places for people on the way to socialism. Georg von Vollmar, an avowed reformist, was one of the first to call for a more concerted attack on anti-Semitism. He was also one of the first to fight government discrimination against Jews in the civil service. In Hesse, despite his myopic theoretical stand, Philipp Scheidemann led an active fight against the anti-Semites there.[26]

Yet the record of the Socialists is not without its blemishes and deviations from the party's official opposition to anti-Semitism. Isolated individuals and newspapers occasionally indulged in diatribes against *Ostjuden* and Jewish capitalists. Like the anti-Semites, some Socialists distinguished between capital and "Jewish capital." The overwhelming support Jews gave to bourgeois liberal opponents of the Social Democrats also nettled some. Like most Germans, the

Socialists, too, had grown up with the traditional and ingrained stereotype of the Jew. Private prejudices and "under the rug" anti-Semitism undoubtedly existed and periodically rose to the surface.[27]

With these qualifications in mind, it must still be recognized that the Social Democratic party rendered great services in the fight against parliamentary anti-Semitism. Even though most Socialists did not see anti-Semitism as a great danger, the party by its very existence acted as a strong deterrent to the spread of parliamentary anti-Semitism. Of all the German parties, only the Socialists managed to keep their followers virtually untainted. From the days of the Berlin movement through the Weimar Republic, the party rank and file consistently rejected anti-Semitic appeals.[28] Fending off the anti-Semites was no small achievement. Neither Marxist nor other socialist movements were automatically immune to anti-Semitism, as the uneven record of the French and Austrian socialist parties adequately demonstrates.[29]

The appearance of parliamentary anti-Semitism conformed to Marxist expectations. But to liberals it was a disturbing, unexpected phenomenon. Racism, the persecution of a minority, the irrational appeal of anti-Semitism, the revival of "medieval superstitions"—all these clouded the liberal's vision of human progress. In the defense of their world view, the left-liberal parties became the most dedicated opponents of the anti-Semitic parties in the Reichstag and state parliaments. The belief in the efficacy of human reason, a conviction which made sense out of the world for liberal men, demanded opposition to the anti-Semites who threatened the most sacred principles of liberalism. However, unlike the Socialist Bebel, left-liberal spokesmen could not take the anti-Semites at their word. They almost always conceived of anti-Semitism as a roundabout way of attacking liberalism itself. Left liberals could never convince themselves that anti-Semitism was more than a pernicious plot by the Conservatives. Basically, what they saw was a reactionary attempt to destroy the liberal outlook which worked itself out, almost incidentally, upon the Jews.

Although they cared about standing up for the rights of Jews, self-defense, too, drew left liberals into the fight. Like the Social Democrats, the left-liberal parties became the object of concerted anti-Semitic competition during the 1880's. After Stoecker's threat to the Social Democrats evaporated, the anti-Semites never again tried to penetrate the ranks of Socialist labor. But the threat to the left liberals continued unabated for the duration of the empire. Consequently, only the left liberals showed a continuous concern with parliamentary anti-Semitism from its beginnings in Berlin.[30] Alive to the specific dangers of anti-Semitism for the future of their party, left liberals were nevertheless surprised by the swift progress of the anti-Semites in the 1890's. In February 1893, five months before the general elections, which brought the anti-Semites sixteen seats, the left liberals faced a direct challenge in the Liegnitz (Silesia) administrative district, an area in which they usually held nine of the ten Reichstag seats. Local anti-Semites put up Hermann Ahlwardt's defense lawyer, Gustav Hertwig, who received campaign support from German Socials and Reformers in a by-election for Haynau-Liegnitz. The *Abwehr-Verein,* recognizing the significance of the anti-Semites' attempt to penetrate the left-liberal stronghold, actively supported Georg Jungfer, Hertwig's rival. The election took on symbolic overtones, a test of strength between the forces of light and darkness, as far as the *Abwehr-Verein* was concerned. The forces of darkness did far better than anyone expected. In 1890 an anti-Semite had polled 151 votes. Hertwig, in 1893, qualified for the second balloting with 8,553 votes. He lost only because the third strongest candidate, a Socialist, threw his support to Jungfer.[31]

Hertwig's near victory presaged greater dangers. Although the *Abwehr-Verein* remained alert and gave evidence of sensing the threat to left liberalism, the left-liberal party paid too little attention to this storm signal. Forgetting the attempted anti-Semitic incursion, the party divided over the issue of Caprivi's military bill. In May 1893, a minority of left liberals who favored the government bill formed the *Freisinnige Vereinigung* under the leadership of Heinrich Rickert. Eugen Richter renamed the remaining majority the *Freisinnige Volkspartei.* Entering the elections of June 1893, the fragmented left liberals suffered a drastic loss in representation, falling from seventy-six to forty-eight seats.[32] The Conservatives and Agrarians took away many once liberal peasant votes. The anti-Semitic parties cut deeply into the urban *Mittelstand.*[33] The defenders of liberalism and the foremost opponents of anti-Semitism therefore met what proved to be the most serious anti-Semitic challenge in a weakened condition.

From the 1890's, Barth, Richter, and Rickert led the battle against anti-Semitism and in defense of liberal principles. Although respected and even feared for their abilities, these men were not popular with the German public and, in fact, inherited the unpopularity of their party. Since the Prussian constitutional crisis of the 1860's, left liberals had stood in fairly constant opposition to the governments of the Prussian king and German emperor. Their championing of laissez-faire economic policies, once a point of agreement between them and government, had turned into another oppositional issue after the adoption of tariffs in 1879. During the 1880's and 1890's, left-liberal stands against army expansion and fleet building chafed against the growing nationalism of Germans. To their contemporaries, they appeared eternal and inflexible naysayers, the proponents of unpopular causes.

One such cause was the achievement of real civil equality for Jews. Rickert's *Freisinnige Vereinigung,* allied closely to the *Abwehr-Verein* through many personal unions, fought stubbornly to attain equal status for Jews in all branches of the civil service. Richter's group was also active in the fight. In 1907, his *Freisinnige Volkspartei* formally demanded that employment and promotion in the civil service be based on talent alone.[34] In 1912, the reunited left liberals of the *Fortschrittliche Volkspartei* published a strongly worded protest against the denial of constitutional rights to Jews.[35] Moreover, between 1901 and 1914, the Reichstag and state parliament deputies of the left-liberal parties brought up the issue of discrimination against Jews in the military, judicial, and academic branches of civil service on nineteen separate occasions. Their interpellations of various state and Reich ministers, usually at the time of the annual budget debates, not only embarrassed the government, but at least twice led to a serious discussion of constitutional reform.[36] The left liberals always attempted to make the government see the larger consequences of its discrimination. For them the issue was more than just whether one liked or trusted Jews. A hallowed liberal conception of the rule of law was at stake.

In direct combat with the anti-Semites in the Reichstag and Prussian parliament, Richter, Rickert, and Barth answered every anti-Semitic speech and countered every accusation. In well-documented speeches and with great wit, these and other left-liberal spokesmen demolished the vague assertions of the parliamentary anti-Semites. In the Reichstag as well as the parliaments of Prussia, Hesse, and Baden, left liberals were a force to be contended with. Deputies from other than the anti-Semitic parties who had used anti-Semitic slogans to get elected were customarily cautious once inside the Reichstag. Even the anti-Semites moderated their tone and often avoided the Jewish question altogether. Although the German Social Reform party made considerable use of the right of *Fraktion* members to speak on every issue, in the Reichstag of 1893–1898 only 30 of their 425 speeches could be construed as openly anti-Semitic. Deputies of the Conservative party contributed approximately 15 more. Considering that the Reichstag met in 506 sessions in this period, very little of the house's time was wasted on anti-Semitism.[37] The left liberals, an articulate and informed minority, were largely responsible for making the Reichstag unreceptive to anti-Semitic tirades. Although they did not change many minds about Jews, Rickert, Richter, and Barth made their colleagues in the Reichstag certain that no anti-Semitic attack would remain unchallenged.

The crucial shortcoming of left-liberal opposition was the same as that of the defense organizations. Many adherents of the various left-liberal parties could think of no greater threat to Germany than the Social Democrats. Although no left liberals ever got themselves elected by using anti-Semitic slogans, the majority of them were willing to participate in an antisocialist coalition which included anti-Semites. In 1907 and 1908, they joined with the National Liberals, *Reichspartei,* Conservatives, and anti-Semites to support the government's colonial policy against the opposition of the Center and the Social Democrats.[38] The experiment was short-lived and not repeated during the *Kaiserreich,* but the numerous betrayals of liberal principle in the 1907 Reichstag elections stained an otherwise praiseworthy record. By the time of the 1912 Reichstag elections, however, left liberals had resumed their opposition to anti-Semitism. Leaders instructed their followers to vote for no party tinged by anti-Semitism and, in fact, for no party right of the National Liberals.[39]

The National Liberals never opposed anti-Semitism with the same rigor or steadfastness as the left liberals. They also let slide the defense of liberal principles. Once considered "the party of the Jews," the National Liberals grew less liberal and more national during the

Wilhelminian era. They found room for Pan-Germans like Dr. Hasse and extreme agrarians like Diedrich Hahn (until 1894). Many National Liberals held simultaneous membership in a wide range of rightist organizations. Liebermann had been quick to recognize the difference between liberals, especially after the secession of the National Liberal party's left or "Lasker wing" in 1880. With the departure of Bamberger and Lasker, Liebermann suddenly discovered "healthy elements" in the party. Still distrustful of the National Liberal leaders in Berlin, he began to distinguish between them and the rank and file, whose "sound instincts" he came to respect.[40]

In certain areas of Germany, National Liberals had a long record of collaboration with anti-Semites. In the Kingdom of Saxony the party frequently united with Conservatives to support anti-Semites against Social Democratic opponents. These alliances could not be ascribed entirely to political expediency or a loathing of socialism. They often corresponded to the feelings of many right-wing National Liberals. Formal pronouncements from this "healthy element" differed little from those of the anti-Semites.[41] Indirectly, the party fostered the growth of the anti-Semites in the Grand Duchy of Hesse, one of the places in Germany where the National Liberals enjoyed a clear majority in the state parliament. In the early 1890's, they used a ten-seat majority to keep deputies of rival parties from seats on commissions or from participating in government to the degree their strength would have warranted. As a result of this practice, left liberals, Socialists, Centrists, and anti-Semites united against the National Liberals in 1896. The anti-Semites doubled their representation to six deputies. Not only did the National Liberals lose their majority, but thanks to their power politics, they also enabled the anti-Semites to become the second strongest party in Hesse, a position of power they maintained long after losing out in national elections.[42]

In Reichstag elections, too, the Hessian National Liberals consistently came to terms with anti-Semitic feeling in Hessenland. The "Worms Corner," a group of influential National Liberals that included Count Waldemar Oriola, Artur Osann, and Baron Cornelius Heyl zu Herrnsheim, was well represented in the Agrarian League and maintained close relations with Otto Böckel. In 1911, these right-wingers caused a party crisis by ignoring pleas from National Liberal newspapers to refrain from supporting an anti-Semite in a by-election for Giessen.[43] Pockets of conservative agrarians and extreme nationalists within the National Liberal party help explain its very uneven record in the matter of anti-Semitism. Indeed, Liebermann had good reason to hope for some sort of cooperation from the right-wing liberals. The party had shown itself opportunistic enough in the past to warrant his faith in the "healthy elements."

The Center party was more consistently opposed to parliamentary anti-Semitism than the National Liberals. But its record, too, is not without anti-Semitic episodes. The ingredients for a specifically Catholic anti-Semitism were present in Germany. Centrists never forgot or forgave the deeds of Jewish politicians and the "Jewish press" during the *Kulturkampf.* Anti-Catholic legislation, supported by liberal newspapers and carried out in the Prussian parliament and Reichstag on the strength of liberal votes, threatened to alienate Catholics and Jews for all time. Catholics, like other Germans, were willing to believe that Jews had profited from and perhaps planned the crash of 1873. The anti-Semitic articles in the *Germania* were as scurrilous as those of the *Kreuzzeitung* or Glagau.[44] During the 1870's August Rohling, a Catholic canon, became famous on the basis of his pamphlet, *Der Talmudjude,* an absurd plagiarism which nonetheless earned him a professorial chair in Semitic languages at the University of Prague. Before Rohling revealed his thorough ignorance of the Talmud in the courtroom (1885), he saw his pamphlet widely distributed, especially in the Catholic areas of Germany.[45]

A continuing Catholic animosity for Jews fostered by the Church hierarchy and the Center party would certainly have aided the parliamentary anti-Semites. The Center occupied a key place in the configuration of German politics. A true *Volkspartei,* it gathered voters from all classes and economic groups. Undoubtedly, among them were many with anti-Semitic views. Yet what bound German Catholics together was not anti-Semitism but the *Kulturkampf.* This experience united them in steady support of the Center party. Between 1874 and 1912, nearly one hundred Centrists were returned to the Reichstag in every general election. The Reichstag could form a majority without the Center, but only if the other mutually hostile parties joined together. Only twice after 1879 did the government of the Reich attempt to dispense with the long-term cooperation of the Center (1887–1890 and 1907–1908). Therefore, the Catholic party's position on the Jewish question was of immense importance to the parliamentary anti-Semites.

The Center became one of the most unyielding opponents of the anti-Semitic political parties, thanks largely to the efforts of Ludwig Windthorst (1812–1891). Former minister to the king of Hanover, leader of the Center party, and foe of Bismarck, he spoke out against the inflammatory nature of anti-Semitic agitation. In the debate which followed the Hänel interpellation of 1880, Windthorst deplored the blanket indictment of all Jews for the misdeeds of some. During a session characterized by insulting accusations and ad hominem argument, his speech stood out as calm and reasoned. He recognized the problems created by a Jewish minority in a "Christian state" and did not engage in condescending philo-Semitism. In Germany, he argued, political and religious tolerance could be the only sane basis of the state. His speech was all the more remarkable because most of his party colleagues wanted to avenge themselves on the "Jew liberals" who had engaged in the *Kulturkampf*. But Windthorst saw the dangers of discriminatory legislation. German Catholics, too, were a minority, one still suffering under the effects of exceptional laws. He was admonishing his own party as well as all Germans to cease baiting each other because of religious differences. He urged all the pious to band together in order to root out the godless and to resist any interference from any quarter in the constitutional equality of the faiths.[46]

It took Windthorst's forceful leadership to wean the Center away from political anti-Semitism. To be sure, there had been key differences between Centrist anti-Semitism and that urged by the independent anti-Semites. Even the Centrist Peter Reichensperger, who had given free rein to his anti-Semitism in the Hänel debate, balked at infringing upon or revoking the constitutional rights of Jews. Moreover, Catholic politicians looked upon Jews primarily as adherents of a contrary religion. They never accepted the racists' contention that Jewish converts to Christianity were unassimilable. In 1881 the Center distanced itself from the Berlin movement and expelled the author of the anti-Semitic *Germania* articles, Joseph Cremer, specifically because of his anti-Semitism.[47] During the

1880's, Windthorst's unflinching defense of religious liberty won converts within his party.

Two factors in addition to strong leadership went into making the Center turn against anti-Semitism as a political weapon. Although German Catholics constituted a much larger minority (30 percent) than Jews (1–1.25 percent), it was quite difficult to deny Jews what the Center demanded for Catholics. This held true not only in the matter of religious liberty, but in the parity question, too. The differing definitions given the term did not diminish the importance of the community of interests between Catholics and Jews, especially in Prussia. Both resented the near monopoly enjoyed by Protestant Junkers in the army, the diplomatic corps, and in the upper echelons of administration. Both demanded a fair share of those offices. Even if Catholics and Jews possessed little love for one another, they were, at least for a while, in a similar situation. They were natural allies in the search for just treatment from a sometimes hostile state power.[48]

The second reason that induced the Center to oppose the anti-Semites was provided by the anti-Semitic politicians themselves. Periodically, they threatened to unleash the full force of their wrath upon the Center. Very early the Catholic party had fallen under Liebermann's censure for being insufficiently "national." "The feet stand in Germany," he scolded, "but the head is in Rome." Paul Förster identified the Center as part of the "black-red-gold international," that is, the clerical-socialist-Jewish conspiracy, bent on undermining the "German idea."[49] Oswald Zimmermann, a dissident Catholic (who did not accept the doctrine of papal infallibility) usually led the German Social Reformers' attacks on political Catholicism. The only Catholic among the anti-Semitic leaders, Zimmermann chastised the Center for not acting like the clerical parties of France and Austria. The Dreyfus affair in France and the cautious treatment of it in the German Catholic press particularly galled him.[50] The anti-Semites were never able to understand why the Center party refused to go anti-Semitic. They failed to appreciate Windthorst's reasoning or to see how deeply the experience of *Kulturkampf* discrimination had affected German Catholics.

Certain facts about the Center's solid support from the Catholic electorate were inescapable even for anti-Semites like Zimmermann,

who could normally remain unaware of unpleasant truths. Wherever
Catholics constituted the majority of an electoral district, anti-
Semites did not get elected and usually ran poorly. This held true even
in Hessenland, where the Catholic peasant population suffered from
the same problems as their Protestant neighbors. Unable to make a
dent in the Center's ranks, anti-Semites alternated between carping
complaints and "idealistic" condemnations of the Catholic party.[51]
Only rarely did they view the unshakeable loyalty of Catholic voters
with a proper appreciation for the seriousness of the situation:

> German anti-Semites can go no further by kowtowing to the
> Center. Unless they make an energetic front against the party,
> the flag of the true Germans [*Deutschnationalen*] will never wave
> in Catholic electoral districts; and we shall remain without
> significance.[52]

This anonymous analyst at least faced the problem forthrightly. He
recognized that if the anti-Semitic parties were cut off from the
votes of both Socialist working men and German Catholics, the
party would never gain the mass following with which to elect a
Reichstag majority and achieve its legislative program.

However, the anti-Semites formulated no consistent policy regarding the Center's loyal electorate. They attempted neither the
seduction of the Catholic masses nor a courting of the hierarchy.
Admittedly, after the waning of the *Kulturkampf*, the parliamentary
anti-Semites would have found it difficult to convert Catholic
leaders to their cause. These highly respected men saw too clearly
that the greatest danger to the free practice of their religion lay not
with the Jews, but with Protestant Prussia and "godless liberalism."
Quite aside from the moral questions involved, they would have been
foolish to overlook the real danger by indulging in anti-Semitism.[53]
The anti-Semitic parties could find no way out of this problem.
For the duration of the empire, they continued to threaten and then
"kowtow." Liebermann, for example, disavowed the article quoted
above for fear of offending the Church.[54] None of the anti-Semitic
parties aimed their propaganda at Catholics. They preferred to wait
for the unavoidable logic of anti-Semitism to penetrate the Catholic
grass roots.

Windthorst's successor as leader of the Center, Ernst Lieber (1838–

1902), was a zealous opponent of the anti-Semites in the Reichstag. He consistently rejected any attempt to inhibit the free practice of Judaism, to prohibit kosher butchering (1899, 1901), and to have the state translate the Talmud or Schulcan Aruch (1901). He spoke out scathingly against Ahlwardt in 1893, against the attempt to prohibit Jewish immigration in 1895, and in favor of appointment of Jewish military doctors in 1898.[55] Under his leadership, no Center deputies ever helped sponsor anti-Semitic motions. From 1880 on, in fact, the record of the Center party in the Reichstag was one of unbroken opposition to anti-Semites and anti-Semitism.

The Reichstag opposition of the Catholic party was valuable in the fight against the anti-Semites. But equally important was its defense of Bavaria. The inability of the anti-Semites to gain a foothold in Bavaria, the second largest state in the Reich, was largely a result of the resolute Center party and Church hierarchy. Bavaria, which later became the hotbed of Nazism, remained relatively free of the anti-Semitic blight before the war. However, the motives and methods for the Catholic opposition there and elsewhere in Germany present some problems for the historian. Was that resistance anything more than a cynical appreciation of political necessity? Did the Center overcome the appeal of the anti-Semitic parties by injecting a fair amount of anti-Semitism under its own auspices, especially in Bavaria?[56]

In Bavaria the Center party actually sponsored an anti-Semitic bill. In 1901, Dr. Georg Heim, Center deputy in the state parliament, called for a *numerus clausus* in the appointment of Jewish judges, thereby launching one of the rare debates on the Jewish question in the Bavarian lower house. In defending his bill against the objections of the Bavarian minister of justice and an unfavorable report from the parliamentary commission appointed to study the bill, Heim emphasized his distance from the parliamentary anti-Semites and pointed to his record as a defender of Jewish religious rights. Nonetheless, his speech traversed the well-worn path of anti-Semitic cliché, blaming the Jews for not having lived up to German standards of morality and honesty. Following an attack on the motion by the left-liberal deputy, Günther, which misguidedly made an issue of Center party solidarity, the house accepted the bill (77 to 51), with a majority of the Center voting for it.[57] Yet to emphasize Heim's motion, one of the few open manifestations of Centrist anti-Semitism, is somewhat unfair.

The leader of the anti-Semitic party in Bavaria, Ludwig Wengg, was never able to expand his small branch of Böckel's organization in the face of Center opposition. Wengg therefore left Böckel to associate with the Agrarian League. Under his direction, the Bavarian branch of the league assumed an especially anti-Semitic tone to compensate for the lack of it in the Center's peasant organizations.[58] But even with league help, Wengg could not extend his base of support to the countryside. His party remained restricted to its original small following in Munich, Würzburg, Nuremberg, and Homburg (Prussian Hesse). He adopted desperate devices just to keep going. For example, he used Ahlwardt, long after he had fallen into disrepute with other anti-Semites, as a speaker in Munich and Nuremberg, where the price of admission could fill empty party coffers. Nonetheless, the Center was dramatically successful in beating back the anti-Semitic attack. Wengg's followers never won election to the Reichstag or state parliament. Their best showing was in 1903 when twelve candidates drew a miserable 3,187 votes.[59] By 1912 they had ceased campaigning altogether.

As significant as the Center's success at the polls was its refusal to resort to anti-Semitic electoral campaigns. An occasional anti-Jewish article in the *Bayerischer Kurier* or *Augsburger Post* usually brought an immediate scolding from the *Kölnische Volkszeitung*, the watchdog of the Catholic press in Germany. The *Abwehr-Verein*, especially exacting about the Catholic party's opposition to anti-Semitism, was quick to pounce on any deviation in the matter of anti-Semitic speeches or slogan mongering. While the *MVA* carried an occasional story about anti-Semitic speeches by Catholic priests and politicians, these appear to have been infrequent—certainly not part of a concerted election strategy by the Bavarian Center party. Even in the more regional arena of the state parliament, the Center numbered many outspoken opponents of anti-Semitism, chief among them Abbot Franz Schädler.[60] Furthermore, many German Jews held the Center in high regard. In Bavaria, a sizeable orthodox Jewish vote for the Center was customary. As late as 1912, a Jewish newspaper wrote: "It would be unjust not to concede that our coreligionists in Bavaria have fared quite well under the rule of the

Center party." On the other hand, complaints were frequent in the *Allgemeine Zeitung des Judentums,* an organ historically concerned with Jewish rights.[61]

This rather murky picture of the Center's relationship to the anti-Semites and anti-Semitism becomes somewhat clearer when motives are examined. The Bavarian Center was defending its territory, not striking a blow against anti-Semitism. That Wengg's followers were mostly Protestant also made it incumbent upon the Center to resist them. In short, it was politically opportune for the Center to oppose the anti-Semites. The Centrists' lapses into anti-Semitism depended on their reading of the political situation and the advantages or disadvantages of the moment. A clear instance of this opportunism occurred at the Bavarian state congress of the party in 1905. In answer to Wengg's agitation and the more threatening espousal of anti-Semitism by the Bavarian Peasant Alliance, several Center deputies proposed a resolution condemning "Jewish exploitation of the rural population." The same Georg Heim who had four years earlier suggested the *numerus clausus* in the judiciary now came down on the other side of the issue. He presented a counterresolution which was eventually victorious, calling upon the state to punish all misdeeds, "no matter the position, class, or faith of the wrong-doer."[62] Another "hot and cold anti-Semite" was Matthias Erzberger, who was not above the use of anti-Semitic slogans in mass meetings or polemical pamphlets. He did not speak out against anti-Semitism until 1913. When an anti-Semitic Reichstag deputy accused him of being an anti-Semite at heart, Erzberger flatly denied the charge and then launched a defense of the constitutional rights of Jews in the matter of reserve officer appointments.[63]

Such reversals point out the self-serving nature of Catholic anti-anti-Semitism. Neither the party nor the Church attempted to inculcate a loathing for anti-Semitism in their followers or to put their own opposition on a truly principled basis that could with-stand a radical shift in political conditions. On behalf of the Center party and the Church, it must be said, however, that the lack of principled opposition made them no less effective against the parliamentary anti-Semites in the *Kaiserreich.* Keeping the masses of Catholic voters from supporting the anti-Semitic parties was instrumental in the failure of parliamentary anti-Semitism.

As the above survey shows, the relations between the major German political parties and the parliamentary anti-Semites possessed a degree of consistency. No party was above dealing with them outside the Reichstag, especially at election time. For most parties, the anti-Semites were a lesser evil than some other rival party. A majority of every party to the right of the Socialists frequently found anti-Semites preferable to the Social Democrats. However, collaboration usually went no further than election day. In the Reichstag itself, the German Social Reform party and its successors could expect no *Fraktion* to render regular help. Even the Conservatives offered no reliable support for the party's anti-Semitic or reform measures. The two mass parties that kept their adherents from cooperation with anti-Semites, the Center and the Social Democrats, also had much in common at least in this matter. Respected leaders, in one case the Catholic clergy and Center leadership, in the other case, trade union officials, party functionaries, and socialist theoreticians, kept their respective flocks safe from anti-Semitic wolves. This similarity between Catholics and Socialists highlights a great weakness in German political life and in the political maturity of Germans. Those groups in the empire most vulnerable to anti-Semitic myths and most prone to take action against Jews were the Protestant peasants and a segment of the urban *Mittelstand,* exactly those who exercised their political rights directly, who possessed no organization, no intervening spiritual or secular hierarchy, to tell them how to vote. Left to themselves, they proved deficient in political intelligence, to say nothing of moral judgment. Finally, and even more disturbing for the future, among all the German political parties only the left liberals and Social Democrats saw the necessity of combating anti-Semitism as well as the parliamentary anti-Semites.

Most of the anti-Semites were slow to realize that their relations to the other political parties had become fixed. Even when the more perceptive Social Reformers recognized that several of the parties had to be included in the forces of opposition, few were ready to concede defeat or give up their cause. The optimistic remained hopeful that all parties would come to see the necessity of solving the Jewish question. Yet the experience of the German Social Reform party during the period 1893–1898 began to affect at least some of the anti-Semitic politicians. Signs of doubt appeared first in the Reichstag *Fraktion,* where there developed an impasse that was difficult to ignore. Incapable of achieving any part of the Erfurt program under its own power, unable to make alliances with other parties, unskillful in winning sympathy for its cause, the *Fraktion* began to disintegrate. Hans Leuss's perjury conviction and the voiding of Dr. König's election because of campaign irregularities had already removed two German Social Reformers from the Reichstag, but the party hung on to the two seats in by-elections. In July 1895, however, Felix Haenichen resigned his Dresden mandate for personal reasons; in the by-election his seat went to the Socialists. The *Fraktion* expelled Heinrich Lieber because of his vote on the civil code. In July 1897, one of the founding members of the party, Paul Förster, felt honor-bound to resign. An inveterate quitter, he had already left Liebermann's German Socials in 1893, and would eventually leave still another party.

Förster set forth his reasons for resigning in an open letter to cochairman Zimmermann. He expressed deep disappointment in the party's poor performance, for which he blamed the lack of proper procedure, unsatisfactory relations with the press, neglect of regular caucus meetings, *Fraktion* inaction, and absenteeism.[64] He made a number of other serious and petty criticisms, but his colleagues chose to vent their anger at his washing of their dirty linen in public instead of examining the validity of his critique. His rejection of the Erfurt program, which he had helped write, as too narrowly *Mittelstand* and inappropriate for a "party of the whole nation" passed without comment. This resignation had a deeper significance for the party than merely leaving the *Fraktion* another man short of the requisite fifteen members. A conventional anti-Semite, Förster was moving toward a crisis that many others would soon experience. Still, in 1897, he could not bring himself to ask the ultimate question: could a parliamentary party working in the framework of the Reichstag effect a solution to the Jewish question? Did conventional anti-Semitism have a future in Germany?

Förster's malaise about the parliamentary solution to the Jewish question was not the only kind of reaction from anti-Semitic deputies. The independent Böckel and Ahlwardt considered leaving an inhospitable Germany. Although Böckel's departure never got beyond the planning stages, Hermann Ahlwardt actually tried to transplant his anti-Semitism to America while absent without permission from the Reichstag.[65] Those intrepid anti-Semites who stayed at home had serious problems with which to deal. Reduced to twelve men, the Social Reformers resorted to the first of many compromises in order to maintain the status of *Fraktion*. Liebermann persuaded several independent deputies and some members of the Bavarian Peasant Alliance to join with his party in the Reichstag. The *Fraktion*, already sharply divided on matters not pertaining to the Jewish question, now incorporated avowed non-anti-Semites for the first time. Several of these independents went out of their way at election time and in the Reichstag to deny any anti-Semitic conviction.[66] Thus, the German Social Reform party had remained an independent *Fraktion* of anti-Semites for only three years.

Its weakened condition did not prevent the party from unleashing a great flurry of activity preparatory to the 1898 elections. During 1897 the Social Reformers held 720 separate meetings in 630 locations. Speakers carried their agitation to every state in the Reich except for the Mecklenburgs. By the end of the election year of 1898, the party had strained every fiber of its strength; the treasury reported only 185 marks.[67] In spite of four years of parliamentary ineffectiveness and no well-grounded hope for future achievement, the German Social Reformers entered the 1898 elections with high expectations. Liebermann predicted a half million more votes and twice as many mandates as in 1893.[68] The actual results were disappointing. The party suffered a definite setback, winning only ten seats. Liebermann, Ludwig Werner, Georg Vielhaben, Emil Gräfe, and Carl Lotze were successful on the first ballot. In the runoffs, Fritz Bindewald, Philipp Köhler, Julius Müller, and Gustav Gäbel were reelected. Friedrich Raab, a porcelain painter from Hamburg, provided the one bright spot with the first victory in Schleswig-Holstein (Flensburg), the result of a hard-fought campaign. But some alarming omens of future developments also emerged from the elections of 1898.

Three of the six anti-Semitic seats in the Kingdom of Saxony, including both Dresden districts, went to the Socialists. Oswald Zimmermann, cochairman of the party, lost his mandate. The German Social Reform party held its own only in Brandenburg, where voter participation fell below seventy percent. In Hessenland, the anti-Semites lost 9,000 votes and, more significantly, two seats. In Baden, Bavaria, and Württemberg, the vote sank from already low levels. The official statistics reported a total of 284,250 votes under the rubric "anti-Semite." But this included approximately sixty thousand votes for the Christian Social party and Böckel and Ahlwardt, both reelected in narrow runoff races. The German Social Reformers proper got 222,447 votes compared to the 263,861 of 1893. Although the total anti-Semitic vote increased slightly over the 1893 level, the German Social Reformers faltered, losing votes and six Reichstag seats.[69]

The signs of reversal went beyond the ranks of the Social Reformers. The Christian Socials seemed to be in their death throes. Expulsion from the Conservative party in 1896 did not mean that Stoecker had opted for a program of radical social reform. Instead, he purged the young radicals, Friedrich Naumann, Hellmut von Gerlach, and Heinrich Oberwinder and instructed the new editor of *Das Volk* to steer a course "more conservative than the Conservatives, more rightist than the right."[70] Still the party did not prosper. Its twentieth anniversary celebration in January 1898 was a morose affair. Stoecker, naturally the main speaker, dwelt on the past and the heroic days of the Berlin movement. As for the future, he could only voice pious hopes.[71] Stripped of its dynamic young men and cast out by the Conservatives, the Christian Social party mustered only thirteen candidates and 48,814 votes in the 1898 elections. Nearly half this total came from two utterly hopeless contests in Berlin.[72] Stoecker returned to the Reichstag after a five-year absence but as the sole representative of his party.

Within the shaken German Social Reform party the gloomy task of analyzing the causes of the setback became the occasion for airing old and new grievances. The semiofficial *Antisemitisches Jahrbuch* put the blame on the party leadership, without naming anyone in particular. The *Jahrbuch* had become a center of dissension within the party. In its pages, newcomers like Otto Böckler and Wilhelm Giese made some oblique criticisms of the veteran anti-Semite leaders. From Giese's point of view, "a radical overestimation of our powers and the underestimation of those of the old parties" lay at the bottom of the poor showing. Liebermann retorted that the main error had been trying to go it alone. In 1893 the various constituent parties of the German Social Reform party had concluded thirty-eight election alliances. In 1898, according to Liebermann, the party had chosen to test its independent strength too soon.[73] In this arid debate, which continued throughout most of the year 1899, were concealed the seeds of a future schism.

Tactical errors and overconfidence recommended themselves as more tolerable reasons for the setback than other possibilities. None of the party analysts ever suggested that the Reichstag record of the *Fraktion* had anything to do with the loss of votes. Yet the defection of twenty thousand voters in the Kingdom of Saxony ought to have made the anti-Semites aware of danger. One-quarter of those who had found the anti-Semitic parties a suitable means of protest in 1893 no longer found them so in 1898. Certainly, the four years of nonachievement in the Reichstag had had something to do with their change of heart. Even if the particulars of the record were unknown to German voters, the resistance groups and political competitors of the anti-Semites had gone to great lengths to present a general idea of their ineptitude. Pamphlets, newspaper articles, and speeches portrayed them as bumbling fools and harmful individuals. Such contentions were backed up amply with episodes from the past four years.

CHAPTER 8

Breaking the Pattern:
Schism and Radicalization, 1898–1903

Had we only kept the matter constantly before us, we would be the mightiest and most influential party in the country. Unfortunately we have too often placed the "personality question" above the Jewish question.

Johannes Wilberg (1901)

Far from a debacle, the elections of 1898 nevertheless worked devastatingly upon morale. Whatever the explanation, the setback itself stood as established fact. Even the most zealous German Social Reformers could not deceive themselves about the "uninterrupted progress of the party toward victory." The election results of 1898 and the ensuing year of inaction exploded this important myth for all time. Rocked by the shock waves of that explosion, the party faithful could no longer regard their anti-Semitic activities in the same old way. They began to doubt swift victory over the Jewish enemy. Although it took little to reinvigorate them with new hope, an irreversible process had begun, the end result of which was a radicalization of conventional, parliamentary anti-Semitism. Signs of revolutionary disaffection and a loss of faith in the Reich and its institutions began to appear with increasing frequency. A few parliamentary anti-Semites had finally perceived the possibility of failure.

The election returns of 1898 coupled with the previous four years of undramatic action drove strong allies away from the German Social Reformers. The *Mittelstand* youth groups of the *Deutsche Jugendbünde* and the anti-Semitic university students in the *Verein Deutscher Studenten,* which had provided the anti-Semitic parties with youthful agitators and dedicated organizers in the late 1880's and early 1890's, grew cold and even hostile.[1] The legislative program of

the Reichstag anti-Semites seemed piddling and intellectually bar-
ren, especially when compared to the world-historical musings of
Wagner, Lagarde, or the latest celebrity, Houston Stewart Chamberlain. Chamberlain urged his readers to view the Jewish problem
from a "loftier standpoint than political considerations."[2] Beside
Chamberlain's cosmic perspective, Liebermann's practical anti-
Semitism had become dull. Too readily he and his followers had
become bogged down in the trivia of party politics. Youthful activists
were growing impatient, not only with the conventional anti-Semites,
but with the political parties in general. These were simply incapable
of dealing with the truly vital national questions. By the turn of the
century, *völkisch* youth had withdrawn from parliamentary politics.
Their "purified" anti-Semitism expressed itself in ideological specu-
lation and *völkisch* ritual. Helpless before this defection of young
"idealists," Liebermann referred to them acidly as "salon anti-
Semites."[3]

A more immediate and no less damaging effect of the 1898 setback
was the strengthening of small rival anti-Semitic groups outside the
party. Friedrich Lange, at heart a revolutionary like Theodor
Fritsch, had nonetheless remained on the fringes of anti-Semitic
parliamentary politics. He kept his tiny *Deutschbund,* founded in
1894, out of the German Social Reform organization. But Lange
himself observed from on high and occasionally tendered advice to
the parliamentary anti-Semites through his newspaper, the *Deutsche
Zeitung* (Berlin). He advocated a nonviolent revolution of German
life, a kind of Fabian anti-Semitism that called for long, patient
preparation and exposure of influential men to a knowledge of the
Jewish danger.[4] After 1898, his group, which considered itself the
intellectual elite of anti-Semitism, and others like it siphoned off one-
time Social Reform activists. As the conventional anti-Semitic parties
continued to demonstrate the unfruitfulness of their parliamentary
methods, a host of "nonpolitical" splinter groups like Lange's sprang
up in Germany.[5]

However, during the period of stagnation and frustration following
the elections, the legislative solution to the Jewish question still retained strong appeal for German anti-Semites. Even radicals
spawned by the earlier failure of the Berlin movement and members
of "nonpolitical" groups who looked upon parliamentary parties as

an evil of modernity could be persuaded to give conventional politics one more chance. It was out of these elements that an ex-naval officer named Hans von Mosch fashioned a new political party, albeit a well disguised one. His *Deutscher Volksbund* (German Folk Alliance) adopted an elaborate masonic structure. In its mature form the organization was led by three grandmasters, Mosch, Paul Förster, and, as of December 1901, Otto Böckel.[6] The grandmasters coopted seven masters who, with thirteen jurors *(Freischöffen)*, formed the council of twenty-three. The council, absolute in its powers, appointed elders and agitators and acknowledged "friends," well-wishers who remained anonymous. Unlike the German Social Reform party, the *Volksbund* did not even pretend to be democratic. It was to be something different, a "tightly knit, closed organization." Mosch also refused to call the new group a political party, although its political intentions were clear. He sensed the need for an alternative to the discredited "old parties," a rubric which now included the German Social Reform party as well as the others.[7]

Long before the *Deutscher Volksbund* openly declared itself a political party in April 1900, Mosch and Förster were contesting Reichstag by-elections under the organization's banner. Profiting from the failure of Liebermann and Zimmermann's party, the *Volksbund* grew rapidly, claiming five thousand members in thirty-five local lodges.[8] Led by the grandmasters, it posed a genuine threat to the German Social Reform party, representing not only competition but, more importantly, a danger to the respectability of conventional anti-Semitism. Mosch, in particular, was an embarrassment. When challenged in public debate, he frequently lost his self-control and became violent or incoherent. Mosch's doggerel poems, his favorite mode of political discourse, not only villified Jews, but also accused the kaiser of selling out Germany and reviled the Reichstag as a parasite on the body politic.[9] Such startlingly radical utterances would ordinarily have sufficed to make him an outcast, a violator of the conventional anti-Semites' code. But after 1898, the mass of conventional anti-Semites became more receptive to this sort of extremism. Mosch and his party typified the kind of radicalization that was slowly eating away at the parliamentary anti-Semites' fundamental respect for the *Kaiserreich*.

Beset from the outside, the German Social Reform party was also quietly crumbling from within. Its ad hoc organization and brittle unity could not withstand the combined pressure of electoral defeat, criticism from outside, and dissension within. Dissatisfaction with the party leadership became intense and widespread. Once loyal party men began hinting at a conspiracy which involved their own leaders.[10] In a large segment of the party, sentiment was building against the policies of Liebermann. His popularity continued to sink in the year and a half following the 1898 elections, as his every move came under increasingly bitter criticism from dissidents within the German Social Reform party and from Hans von Mosch. Critics seized upon his plan to fill out the party *Fraktion* with Stoecker and a number of Agrarians as a typical example of his arbitrary ways and his willingness to compromise the party's anti-Semitic purity. Mosch dredged up Böckel's old charge that Liebermann was "leading the party constantly to the right . . . to make it an appendage of the Conservative party and Agrarian League."[11]

Liebermann's close connections on the right made him susceptible to such accusations. If it were true that he aimed at submerging the anti-Semites in an expanded Conservative party, then he could well expect the rank-and-file Social Reformers to be provoked. In 1897 the Conservatives and Agrarians had united to replace six anti-Semitic deputies to the Saxon state parliament with their own more reliable men. In the national elections of the next year, the two again worked actively to exclude anti-Semites in Saxony from a union of the "parties of order." In the same year, the Agrarian League also expelled from its membership three anti-Semitic politicians, creating much ill will. A close friend of Liebermann's, Baron Conrad von Wangenheim of the Agrarian League, raised a storm among the anti-Semites when he publicly questioned the rationale for the party's continued existence.[12] The past betrayals by the Conservatives and the league were still fresh in the memory of the rank and file of the German Social Reform party; they were by no means as willing as Liebermann to forgive and forget.

A good deal of circumstantial evidence fed the suspicions regarding Liebermann's plans for the party. Over the years he had, by means of anti-Semitic politics, carved out a powerful position that no longer depended upon the existence of an independent party. An impoverished, landless Junker, he could never have risen to such eminence in the Conservative party. By the turn of the century, he had come to occupy a key mediating position for the organizations of the right in the *Kaiserreich*. A member of the Agrarian League and frequent speaker at its general assemblies, board member of the Pan-German League, and an influential politician who could get favors done, his fortunes were no longer tied exclusively to the success of the Social Reformers.[13] Certainly, he stood to lose little if, as his friend Wangenheim seemed to suggest, the party gave up its identity and merged with the Conservatives and Agrarians. In July 1899, Liebermann added to the growing doubts about his reliability with a front-page article in the *Antisemitische-Korrespondenz*. For the first time in party history, he allowed some guarded pessimism to creep into the pages of his newspaper. He spoke of the need for new methods, new issues, and a new will to get free of the doldrums into which the party had drifted. He closed his somber analysis with a phrase that outraged his party colleagues: "The great national anti-Semitic movement has momentarily arrived at a dead point which must be overcome."[14] If Liebermann knew anything at all about his colleagues' sensibilities, he realized that the public confession of a "dead point" would raise hell.

His actual plans for the party were probably not as sinister as his critics suggested. Without changing any of his fanatical views about the Jews, he had matured as a politician. Thus, he drew the only proper conclusion from the 1898 election: the German Social Reform party could no longer go it alone and hope to accomplish any part of its program. In light of this truth, he plotted a seizure of power within the party. Its unruly elements, the successors of Otto Böckel currently under the leadership of Oswald Zimmermann, had either to be subordinated to his sole authority or to be forced out. Purged and brought to order, according to Liebermann's standards, the party would become acceptable to the powerful Agrarian League and Conservative party. If the purged or reorganized anti-Semites maintained enough strength, the Conservatives and Agrarians might be cajoled into a formal relationship with them.[15] Instead of remaining subject to the occasional and conditional interest of those powerful groups, the reformed party might earn reliable partners and guaranteed support.

Liebermann readied himself for the crisis which his comment about the "dead point" kindled. He had his loyal lieutenant, Friedrich Raab, present a detailed reform plan designed ostensibly to revitalize the party. "Raab's reform plan" was a thinly disguised power grab. It spoke of the reorganization of state and provincial associations and greater centralized control, which would enable a rationalization of local party activity and give greater direction to the activities of *Reformvereine*. What the reform amounted to in actuality, however, was a renaming of certain state and provincial associations and an attempt to load the leadership levels in Schleswig-Holstein, Prussian Hesse, and Brunswick with Liebermann's own men.[16] Liebermann's crucial measures for the upper levels of the party leadership were not spelled out in Raab's program. These concerned the directory, which held formal control over national policies. Until the 1898 election, the *Fraktion* and the directory were virtually identical in personnel. But in 1898 Zimmermann lost his bid for election to the Reichstag and consequently was no longer a member of the *Fraktion*. Liebermann intended replacing the directory, to which Zimmermann still belonged, with the *Fraktion*. He justified this transparent attempt at a coup by pointing out the need for greater harmony between the activities of the party and the *Fraktion*. That his main rival for leadership of the party would thereby be removed from power escaped no one.[17] However reasonable his intentions, Liebermann's methods for making the Social Reformers worthy of the Conservatives and Agrarians were bound to reduce the struggle to a question of personalities and personal loyalties.

In the ensuing struggle, Liebermann overestimated the security of his position within the party. His schemes backfired and foundered on popular resistance. At the Hamburg congress in September 1899, all the issues—Wangenheim's statement, the "dead point," and Raab's reform plan—came out into the open. Anxiety and controversy about the immediate future brought 130 delegates and 350 interested participants to Hamburg, the best attended congress since the Eisenach unification of 1894.[18] Without mentioning his behind-the-scenes maneuvering against Zimmermann, Liebermann presented his ideas about the future of the party. He spoke with confidence, expecting to prevail upon the delegates as usual:

We must come out of our isolation. . . . *The baiting of related groups, which has been introduced consciously by our opponents, must cease.* We must strive to bring about better relationships. While we protect our full autonomy and independence, we must also be active in cultivating friendly neighbor relationships with parties and organizations which pursue similar goals—such as the Christian Social party, Conservative party, and Agrarian League.

After breaking out of their isolation, the Social Reformers, according to Liebermann, would make formal election alliances with the named groups and set about the conquest of liberal and Socialist constituencies. "On this path alone can we succeed to the parliamentary influence which we need."[19]

The delegates at Hamburg rejected Liebermann's plan. They voted down Raab's reform measures one after another; on the total plan the vote was 48 to 76.[20] A serious rift in the top echelons became visible to the party as a whole. Ranged against Liebermann, Raab, and a few others were Zimmermann, Fritz Bindewald, Ludwig Werner, and Philipp Köhler—the direct successors of Otto Böckel—and a group of radical Berliners, Wilhelm Giese, Wilhelm Bruhn, and Otto Böckler. These men opposed Liebermann for three reasons. First, if he succeeded in reforming the party according to his plans, they would occupy subordinate positions at best. Second, they all represented the Kingdom of Saxony, Hessenland, or East Elbia, where right-wing organizations had proved anything but helpful in recent state parliament and Reichstag elections.[21] Third, nothing in Liebermann's plans suggested that the "related groups" were to renounce their traditional "demagogic" anti-Semitism or that they would be asked to show their readiness for "sincere" anti-Jewish efforts.

On the second day of the Hamburg congress it was the turn of Liebermann's enemies to suffer defeat. Wilhelm Giese, already thought of as a troublemaking intellectual because of his journalistic attacks on the "reactionary, obscurantist bureaucracy," presented a set of seven remarkably radical theses for general consideration. Clearly shocked, the delegates laboriously emasculated all of them. It was the seventh, a Dühringesque diatribe against Christianity,

that allowed Liebermann to rise once more in defense of respectability, practical labor, and "reasonable anti-Semitism." To the
conventional majority, these arguments were still compelling. The
seventh thesis was entirely dropped, but not before insults, accusations, and threats passed between the warring factions.[22] When the
Hamburg congress dispersed, the Social Reformers were still one
party. Liebermann, however, had gained only a little time.

After Hamburg, the struggle continued unabated in the newspapers of the various opponents. Never was it more important for an
anti-Semite to have a newspaper at his disposal. Liebermann's
Antisemitische-Korrespondenz and Raab's *Deutsches Blatt* (Hamburg)
joined battle against Zimmermann's *Deutsche Wacht* (Dresden) and
Bruhn's *Staatsbürger-Zeitung* (Berlin). Meanwhile, outside the party,
Hans von Mosch hammered away at the once unassailable position
of Liebermann from his newspaper, *Deutsche Reform,* and then in the
official organ of the *Volksbund,* the *Deutsche Hochwacht* (Neustettin).
The existence of so many newspapers, each representing a different
point of view, made it almost impossible to halt the process of disintegration.

Liebermann, however, would not retreat. On 21 January 1900, at
a meeting of the central committee, he seized the initiative once
more, insisting on new elections for the party directory. The central
committee, never very observant of the party's bylaws, had not
bothered to elect a new directory since 1895. Liebermann, posing as
the champion of correct procedure, tried in this manner to remove
his rivals from the directory and replace them with his allies. But
once again he failed. His foes Bindewald and Ludwig Werner gained
reelection by narrow margins, while Raab went down to defeat for
three separate offices. In a surprise move, Liebermann resigned cochairmanship of the party. Still a party member and *Fraktion* leader,
he restated his position in ominous terms. It was up to the next congress to choose the correct strategy and resolve the crisis. A matter of
tactics, not ideology, he correctly asserted, was driving a wedge into
the party and threatening to destroy it.[23]

But more was involved. Liebermann's statement failed to do justice
to the personal dimension of the struggle. He ignored the increasing
number of enemies he had been making. As the only anti-Semite on
speaking terms with the high and mighty of the Reichstag, he had

grown haughty in recent years. He became impatient with his own colleagues, who often undid the good impression he had carefully made upon a section of the Reichstag. In a much publicized instance of short temper, he ordered Fritz Bindewald to shut up or be thrown out of the chamber. As *Fraktion* leader he prevented Emil Gräfe from speaking on all but the most inconsequential matters. Personal animosities hastened the party toward schism. In addition to tactless attacks on friends and enemies, Liebermann continued trying to make the Social Reformers acceptable to the "friendly neighbor" parties. Speaking in the name of the *Fraktion,* he commanded the retraction of an anti-Agrarian League article which was to appear in the *Antisemitisches Jahrbuch* for 1900. The directory refused to meet his demand.[24] It was obvious to the leaders that the party had reached a state of internal paralysis.

Prior to the fatal congress at Magdeburg in September 1900, Liebermann delivered an ultimatum. If Raab's reform plan were not adopted, he would leave the German Social Reform party completely.[25] At the opening of the congress, instead of submitting humbly, Gräfe, Bindewald, and Giese used the regular report of *Fraktion* activity to air their personal grievances against Liebermann. Violent arguments erupted. A vote of confidence in Liebermann was called for and failed (75 to 85), whereupon he majestically announced: "The schism is completed—Hail! Hail! Hail!" Zimmermann countered with "better small but pure!" (*lieber klein, aber rein*). Forty-six delegates stomped out of the hall with Liebermann. Zimmermann's group retained the name "German Social Reform party" and over one hundred delegates, mainly from the Kingdom of Saxony and Hessenland.[26]

The outcome of the congress could not have surprised Liebermann. He had already reserved another hall in Magdeburg with the specific intention of reconstituting the German Social party, a task that took less than two hours. Underlining the lack of ideological motivation for the schism, both parties adhered to the old Erfurt program. The resurrected German Socials elected Liebermann chairman and chose a five-man directory. Raab settled for the office of treasurer and the naming of his newspaper and the *Antisemitische-Korrespondenz* as the official organs of the new party.[27] Apparently, little had changed in the six years since unification. In 1894, the German Socials had been by far the weaker partner in the union. In 1900 it was still so. They counted four Reichstag deputies to the six of the German Social Reformers. Liebermann's strength centered in Schleswig-Holstein, Hanover, and Hamburg. The "purer" Social Reformers came out of the split with what Zimmermann too boldly described as undiminished strength. He shared chairmanship of the party with Carl Lotze, who also served as *"Fraktion"* leader.

In view of Zimmermann's obvious preponderance, the German press began speculating on Liebermann's future. He would, it was widely thought, bring his German Socials into the fold of the Conservative party and Agrarian League and occupy the position Stoecker had once enjoyed as the Conservatives' "expert on Jew baiting."[28] Based only on the supposed desires of Liebermann, the theorizing failed to consider the views of the Conservatives and Agrarians on this matter. Neither proved anxious to recruit the remnant of "respectable anti-Semites" as a group. Neither offered the German Socials the kind of guaranteed support Liebermann had desired. Commenting on the "purge" of the party, the *Konservative Korrespondenz* congratulated Liebermann on ridding himself of the disreputable anti-Semites like Zimmermann. But above all the split showed, according to the paper, the fruitlessness of a purely anti-Semitic party.[29] The Conservatives simply had no great need for an anti-Semitic party with the size and stature of the German Socials.

The anti-Semites had always had more to offer the Agrarian League than to the Conservative party. The league made more constant use of anti-Semitism. Furthermore, the anti-Semitic parties could help recruit the votes of the *Mittelstand* and the peasantry in Westphalia, Hessenland, Saxony, and the Thuringias, areas in which the Agrarians were not strong. In recognition of its value, Heinrich Suchsland, a director of the league, had at one time advocated the incorporation of the whole German Social Reform party into his organization.[30] But that was before the schism. After the schism, the Agrarian League proved as hardheaded as the Conservative party. Liebermann's German Socials were neither more valuable nor more reliable than Zimmermann's rump party. The case of Friedrich Raab, a loyal Liebermann man, gave the league good cause to doubt the dependability of the German Socials. In 1898, as a common candidate of the anti-Semites and the Agrarians, Raab won election from Flensburg, a largely peasant constituency in Schleswig-Holstein. In the same year, he ran for a seat in the city-state parliament of Hamburg. To the horror of the Agrarians, he announced a tax and land reform program that promised direct taxation, state ownership of property, confiscation of large estates, and land redistribution.[31] After such a performance, it made little sense for the league to throw in with one of the anti-Semitic parties exclusively. Moreover, because both anti-Semitic parties represented peasants and *Mittelständler*, the league could not be prevailed upon to alter its policy of selective support in order to help only the German Socials. If an individual anti-Semite could do the Agrarians some good, he received their endorsement and perhaps financial aid at election time. Such had been the case with the German Social Reformers, Werner, Lotze, and Gräfe in 1898. All Liebermann's entreaties notwithstanding, the Agrarian League continued to keep a free hand in doling out support to anti-Semites of either party.[32]

Soon enough it became clear that the schism had not strengthened the hand of either party with regard to the German right. Furthermore, the timing of the split also proved damaging to the anti-Semitic cause. With a solid front, an anti-Semitic party might have been able to make real progress with the German electorate as the new century opened. For, shortly before the schism, two ready-to-be-exploited and dramatic issues suddenly gained the fervid interest of masses of Germans: the Boer War and the Konitz ritual murder. Even without unity, the German Socials, Social Reformers, and *Deutscher Volksbund* were able to insure their separate survivals by means of the emotions they whipped up over these two events. However, the gradual radicalization born of the frustrations of 1898 and 1899 did not disappear with the return of "good times." Faith in the effectiveness of a parliamentary solution to the Jewish question had suffered permanent damage. Thus, agitation at Konitz in eastern Prussia and on behalf of the Boers exhibited revolutionary overtones with open, sometimes violent criticism of the Reich. Only a few individuals from all three parties conducted their agitation in an implied or overtly revolutionary way. But in the fragmented state of anti-Semitic politics, revolutionary and rowdy individuals could find a home where they might remain as long as they wished. The small parties kept them on because they needed every man and because they had become more receptive to radical solutions, more willing to listen to alternative ways of solving the Jewish question. Although the majority plodded along in the fashion that had become traditional, the effects of unsuccessful, conventional methods began to make themselves felt. Radicalism, which began with a few tolerated individuals, wormed its way into all levels of the anti-Semitic parties.

Since the last sensational case in Xanten during 1891, the anti-Semitic press had never really lost interest in the most hair-raising sign of Jewish evil, the alleged practice of ritual murder. Judging from the number of ritual murder stories and the amount of space devoted to them, the blood accusation appealed powerfully and consistently to the readers of the anti-Semitic press. In the ten years between 1891 and 1900, the *Abwehr-Verein* counted 120 separate ritual murder stories covered extensively in anti-Semitic newspapers.[33] The cumulative effect of such often repeated charges ought not to be underestimated. The stories were invested with hints of sexual violation as well as cruel death. Among the gullible and backward, these accusations spread fear of the Jews and cultivated hostility toward them. Even among the more sophisticated, who scoffed at such fantasy, these horror stories may have left a residue of suspicion.

The Konitz murder of March 1900, a particularly grisly case, provided anti-Semites with the most favorable opportunity in years. Their exploitation of the situation proved at once more adroit and more radical than ever before. At the time of the Xanten case, individual agitators had been satisfied merely to stir up hate and suspicion. In Konitz, the anti-Semitic parties attempted to reap permanent political benefits from "the new flood tide of anti-Semitic feeling in Germany."[34] Several anti-Semites came to prominence as a result of their Konitz agitation, among them Wilhelm Bruhn and a soon defrocked Protestant minister, Karl Krösell. The excitement also brought Otto Böckel back to active political life as a grandmaster of the *Deutscher Volksbund*.

The murder was especially well suited to the purposes of the anti-Semites. The facts of the case were uncertain; the murder itself remained unsolved. On 11 March the dismembered body of a student, Ernst Winter, was found near the house of a Jewish kosher butcher.

That the deed was done near the Jewish Passover holiday and by a ritual slaughterer was in keeping with anti-Semitic expectations. Jews needed the blood of a Christian boy like Winter in order to fulfill the obligations placed upon them by the Schulcan Aruch. In May 1900, Liebermann arrived in the Konitz area and announced himself a candidate in the upcoming by-election for the Prussian state parliament. In personal appearances before anti-Semitic audiences composed of Germans and Poles, Liebermann demanded election so that he could confront the Prussian minister of justice "with the clear indications of a blood murder."[35] But the veteran campaigner also needed the votes of the well-to-do Germans and Jews of Konitz in order to win. Liebermann did not appear before Jewish audiences, but he did aim some reassuring campaign literature at them which only hinted at the "ritual nature of the murder." To the more respectable German elements in Konitz, he merely suggested that somewhat incompetent state officials were moving too slowly in a case that bordered on emergency.[36] But, like all his attempts to get into the Prussian parliament, this one, too, ended in failure.

Liebermann's behavior in the Konitz affair had followed traditional anti-Semitic lines. He had tried to garner some political advantage for himself and his party, without causing too much of a ruckus. But other anti-Semites were no longer willing to follow in his path. Bruhn and Pastor Krösell were also present during the month of May 1900, stirring up crowds and paying special attention to the Polish population in and around Konitz. Both men capitalized on the complex resentments existing between Poles on the one hand and Germans and Jews on the other. Although programmatically committed to an anti-Polish policy, the anti-Semites could not refrain from attempting to use the Polish masses. In Konitz the presence of anti-Semitic agitators led to disturbances in June. Serious riots, involving mainly Poles, broke out, and the synagogue went up in flames. The Prussian government declared martial law, sent in troops, and made mass arrests.[37]

In former days, such an outbreak of violence would have been cause for disavowal and disengagement by the anti-Semites. At Konitz, however, their efforts and activities increased. More disturbances in which local anti-Semites acted as ringleaders occurred in October, this time on a minor scale. As the excitement died down, insinuations of collusion between Jews and Prussian state officials began to get wide circulation in a number of anti-Semitic newspapers. Hans von Mosch proclaimed that perhaps five or six dozen ritual murders went unsolved and unpublicized every year.[38] Bruhn rashly condemned "the shielding of Jews by Prussian bayonets." The government defended itself in court, convicting several anti-Semites for defamation of the whole Prussian civil service as well as disturbance of the peace, incitement to violence, and a host of lesser charges. Bruhn and the editor of his *Staatsbürger-Zeitung* drew particularly heavy sentences, a total of eighteen months in jail between them. Altogether, the sentences arising from the Konitz disturbances amounted to over fifty years in jail.[39]

The lessons of the Konitz agitation gradually gained recognition in anti-Semitic circles. Liebermann's conservative and, by anti-Semitic standards, still respectable efforts failed completely. His German Socials benefited only indirectly from the "new flood tide of anti-Semitic feeling." But Mosch's *Volksbund* and the Social Reformers, thanks to a complete lack of scruples, reaped immediate advantages. The *Volksbund* registered the new impulse by formally becoming a political party. In August 1901, the Social Reformer, Fritz Bindewald, seized public attention with his "Program for Protection against Ritual Murder," which appealed to the righteous anger of German parents. The anti-Semites, in Bindewald's program, appeared as the upholders of German moral values, striving nobly to master their justifiable wrath. He hinted at a desire for counterviolence, but settled for a long-range solution that demanded expulsion and expropriation of suspected "bands of murderers."[40] In its impassioned language, suggestion of violence, and radical social demands (to be applied to Jews only), the statement contrasted strongly with the Erfurt program of 1895. Neither the German Social Reformers nor the *Volksbund* went so far as to suggest that anti-Semites take the law into their own hands. The proper legislative changes had to be made before vengeance could be taken. The conventional anti-Semites were still thinking within the legal framework, but quite clearly their fantasies had taken an ominously violent turn.

The exploitation of the Konitz affair exhibited the anti-Semites' expanded conception of what was permissible. Bruhn, however, soon stepped beyond the permissible, as far as most anti-Semites were concerned. Unlike Bindewald, he had not bothered with programmatic statements. Instead, he found a goldmine in the deranged religious fanatic, Count Pückler. Bruhn acted as a booking agent for the personal appearances of the "scythe count" (*Dreschgraf*), who was later pronounced insane. Pückler advocated mass murder as a way of staving off the "ascension of Cohn I to the throne of Europe."[41] Although condemned from all sides for his manipulation of a lunatic, Bruhn was not legally responsible for the count's actions. When, after his nineteenth court appearance, Pückler became too embarrassing for his agent, he was left to his own devices.[42] Unquestionably, Pückler's activities were simply not acceptable to the mass of anti-Semites. Yet Bruhn's contravention of the unwritten code of conventional anti-Semites was no longer enough to disqualify him from leadership in the German Social Reform party. As long as he was able to maneuver around legal responsibility, he was regarded as a regrettable but acceptable phenomenon by his colleagues.

Commitment to legality and faith in the institutions of the Reich, both strong while the anti-Semitic parties seemed to be rising to power, had weakened as a result of the setback of 1898 and the inability to accomplish anything of importance in the Reichstag. The Konitz affair and the scythe count led anti-Semites into more radical actions because, they discovered, the kinds of "issues" which brought the greatest response from their supporters were exactly those which could not be exploited in parliament. In the Reichstag Liebermann circumspectly referred to Konitz as "a murder committed out of superstition" and passed on to several other matters. Ludwig Werner's interpellation of the minister of justice in the Prussian parliament came two years after the event. He showed extreme caution, denied that he had ever accused the Jews of the murder, and sought to gain sympathy for the harsh sentence meted out to his colleague Bruhn. Werner got no satisfaction whatsoever from Justice Minister Schönstedt, and no sign of sympathy from the deputies.[43] Because Germany's parliaments were not places where one could debate "ritual murder" seriously, the idea that parliament was perhaps unsuited to deal with the Jewish danger—and therefore gravely deficient—gained ground among conventional anti-Semites.

A sudden interest in foreign affairs provided another indication that the anti-Semitic parties were turning away from customary ways of expressing their discontent. Inability to achieve results in domestic affairs helped turn men like Ludwig Werner and Zimmermann into self-acknowledged experts on foreign policy. Until the outbreak of the Boer War, anti-Semites had concerned themselves exclusively with the colonial aspect of foreign policy, the one area in which they had always felt competent to instruct the government and everyone else.[44] The parliamentary anti-Semites were extreme German nationalists; pan-Germanism was written into the program of all their parties. A good part of the coming furor, occasioned by official treatment of the Boers, stemmed from the inability of anti-Semites to conceive of a situation in which reasons of state could preclude support for "Germanic race brothers." Leaders and followers were slow in recognizing any conflict between the interests of imperial Germany and "Germans" everywhere in the world. Thus, anti-Semites complemented their simplistic domestic policy with an equally facile foreign policy. Moreover, they discovered in foreign affairs an area where they could maintain ideological purity by simply and irresponsibly demanding the utmost, the "visionary," the impossible.

The complexities of the international situation leading up to the Boer War eluded the anti-Semites. They were aware of an increased tempo in German colonial expansion after the resignation of Chancellor Caprivi in 1894. Like many Germans, they regarded England as the prime obstacle in Germany's rise to the status of world power. Like most, they had thrilled to the kaiser's confrontation with the English at the time of the Jameson Raid in 1895. The telegram which Wilhelm sent to President Paul Krüger, congratulating him on the defense of the Transvaal against the raiders, symbolized a growing animosity toward England felt widely in the German public.[45] As the dominant power in Europe, England had awakened anti-English feeling not only in the anti-Semites, but in Germany as a whole. Therefore, a degree of Anglophobia and a definite sympathy for the Boers was to be expected among nationalistic Germans of all parties. However, the anti-English sentiments of the anti-Semites knew no bounds, no moderation. This depth of feeling differentiated them from the other producers and consumers of German Anglophobia. Although often confused with the Pan-German League, especially by English public opinion, the anti-Semites were even more consistent than the Pan-Germans in the purveying of England hate.[46] Moreover, the league, unlike the anti-Semites, couched its Anglophobia in the language of power politics, *raison d'etat,* and the protection of Germandom. The Pan-Germans were not, at the time of the Boer War, overtly anti-Semitic. The anti-Semites, on the other hand, did not doubt for a moment that the Jewish world conspiracy lay at the bottom of "England's robber war" against South Africa. For them, to be pro-Boer and to hate the English were just two more ways of fighting the main enemy, the Jews.[47]

The anti-Semites were never more bizarre than when they gave expression to their detestation of the English. Hatred of England was virtually automatic with them. Fritsch, Liebermann, the Förster brothers, Böckel, Mosch, Lange, and Zimmermann, conventional and revolutionary alike, shared a loathing of the English that predated the Boer War by several years, by decades in some cases. England was the home of laissez faire and liberalism, a thoroughly Jewified place. According to Paul Förster, the English were "Jews six days a week and Christians on one."[48] What further proof of England's Jewishness was needed after one stopped to consider that the nation had been ruled alternately by two Jews, Benjamin Disraeli and William Glattstein, alias Gladstone?[49] During the war, statements in the anti-Semitic press and at anti-Semitic protest meetings exceeded anything expressed elsewhere in Germany. Cecil Rhodes was, according to Bindewald, "a genuine Jew" (*waschechter Jude*). Rich Jews stood behind the Prince of Wales and the colonial secretary, Joseph Chamberlain. Mosch saw the English paving the way for Jewry: "The Transvaal question is for the most part also the Jewish question." Böckel rejoiced in the death of Queen Victoria's grandson in battle—"a just punishment from God."[50] Anti-Semitic passions had never risen to such a pitch.

In the days following the opening of the war, the German Social Reform party, in conjunction with the Pan-German League, organized a massive protest meeting in Hamburg to give a clear expression of public support for intervention on behalf of the "race-related" Boers. Another meeting, organized by Oswald Zimmermann in Breslau, urged that the German government act against England. In Leipzig Liebermann organized a mass rally which made the same plea for prompt intervention.[51] However, other more sound considerations guided the actual makers of German foreign policy. Anti-Semites could not know that complex negotiations between England and Germany were taking place or that a possible alliance between the "Anglo-Saxon and Teutonic races" might be the outcome of this delicate diplomacy.[52] Yet it is doubtful that a much wider knowledge of the facts would have greatly altered the anti-Semites' "foreign policy." Their rabid involvement in the Boer cause made a calm evaluation of Germany's foreign policy alternatives unlikely. The anti-Semites, who had compromised most of their principles in domestic matters for the sake of temporary political advantages, remained desperately inflexible on the war. The German government's strict neutrality naturally prompted a particularly passionate reaction from them.

Foreign policy was so clearly a prerogative of the crown and a function of the chancellor and foreign office in the *Kaiserreich* that to criticize it required a change in attitude among the conventional anti-Semites. From the beginning of his reign Wilhelm II had taken a prominent part in foreign affairs. The convenient pretext of poor advice or incompetent ministers, which had served so long and so well in domestic matters, could not really exonerate the emperor in the eyes of the anti-Semites. To criticize German neutrality in the Boer War was to criticize the monarch as well. His callousness toward the plucky Boers, his official visit to England, in short, his whole conduct during the war proved a shocking disappointment to German anti-Semites. Unable and unwilling to stifle their emotions, they began to attack the foreign policy of the Reich and the kaiser personally. Such criticism of the monarch would have been unthinkable before the process of radicalization had been set in motion by the failures and frustrations discussed above. Now, however, the conventional anti-Semites were less inclined to make excuses for the kaiser or the institutions of the Reich. Something was gravely wrong in a German state that allowed the English to extirpate the Boers.

At first, the attacks upon the kaiser remained oblique. Philipp Köhler, for example, used extravagant praise for Queen Wilhelmine of the Netherlands as a foil against Wilhelm:

> She alone has never closed her royal heart to the bitter deadly peril of the heroic, courageous Boers. She has remained noble

and brave while many others have groveled in the dust before England.[53]

The government confiscated issues of several anti-Semitic newspapers because they expressed their scorn for Wilhelm too openly after he refused to receive "the most honorable and noble of all patriots," Paul Krüger.[54] Liebermann carried criticism of the kaiser to the Reichstag itself. During the debates over expansion of the German fleet in June 1900, he dared to express his chagrin with Wilhelm II— at least metaphorically. Liebermann spoke in favor of expanding the German Navy in order to help the Boers. But he wanted it clearly understood that voting for a larger fleet should in no way be construed as approval for Wilhelm's foreign policy. To make his criticism of the kaiser unmistakable, he dwelt at length upon the glories of Bismarck's conduct of foreign affairs. While assuring the house of his staunch monarchism, he nonetheless closed with a veiled threat: "I hope that a fresh breeze will blow away the English fog which has settled between throne and *Volk*."[55]

Once again, however, the anti-Semites' handling of a potentially explosive issue, the neutrality of the government in the face of overwhelming pro-Boer sentiment among Germans of all parties, was more effective outside the Reichstag than inside it. Even though the German Socials and Social Reformers were counted as one *Fraktion* after the schism of September 1900, constant quarreling and vindictiveness hampered their efforts on behalf of the Boers. Each party refused to support the other's motions, so that these rarely got beyond the planning stage.[56] Unable to rise above petty squabbles, the anti-Semites were not as notable in defense of the Boers in the Reichstag as were the National Liberals or the representatives of the Pan-German League. In the end, the anti-Semites' championing of the Boers was limited to individual feats of oratory, with Liebermann taking the lead. His chauvinistic chest-thumping occasionally impressed his Reichstag colleagues, many of whom shared his pro-Boer sympathies. But frequently he succeeded in embarrassing even his fellow anti-Semites by indulging in "excessive criticism of imperial foreign policy."[57] With one such performance in the Reichstag on 10 January 1902, he created an international incident.

The background of Liebermann's speech is important. By January

1902, to all but diehard anti-Semites, the cause of the Boers appeared indeed hopeless. In five months' time South Africa would come under British sovereignty according to the Treaty of Vereeniging (May 1902). Anti-English feeling, which had fluctuated greatly in Germany between 1896 and 1902, was at a momentary low. However, during the last stages of guerrilla warfare waged by the Boers, word came back to Europe of English atrocities and of inhuman conditions prevailing in English-built concentration camps. Rumors and the accounts of refugees initiated a new wave of Anglophobia, which was fed continually by the anti-Semitic and Pan-German presses. As the latest wave of hatred gathered force, it engulfed even the more responsible German newspapers.[58] In October 1901 Joseph Chamberlain, reacting to the charges of an increasingly hostile European press, reminded England's critics that other wars, including the Franco-Prussian War, had been equally barbarous. These aspersions on the honor of the German Army in the War of 1870–1871 went straight to the heart of Liebermann von Sonnenberg. The ex-lieutenant and holder of the Iron Cross had enshrined the experience of that war in his memory. Moreover, Chamberlain had never convinced anti-Semites that he had not himself instigated the Jameson Raid of 1895. To many, he seemed responsible for the whole South African War. Such "vile accusations" as those made by Chamberlain had to be answered and answered dramatically. Liebermann appointed himself to do the job.

Chancellor Bülow, although advised not to do so by the German ambassador in London, also felt it his duty to answer the slur upon German military honor. On 8 January 1902, he made his concession to an aroused German public in a Reichstag speech.[59] Liebermann, far down on the list of speakers, had to wait two days before he got his turn. During this time, the English press reacted quite unfavorably to the chancellor's "peremptory tone" and all "too-ready credulity" in the matter of atrocities.[60] As Bülow entered the Reichstag on 10 January, Liebermann had just begun to speak on the Boer question. He complained of the chancellor's slowness in answering the Chamberlain insult. Ignoring the frequent laughter, he presented his own wild interpretation of responsibility for the continuation of the Boer War, casting blame on the Russian Tsar for "false humanitarianism" and on the French for their customary treachery. Professing his satisfaction with the chancellor's "refutation of the Chamberlain libels," Liebermann gradually worked himself into a rage, began to contradict, and then repeat himself:

> . . . [Chamberlain] will be burdened with the guilt for this most atrocious of all wars—and not without some inner justification. Colonial Minister Chamberlain as owner of many dynamite and armament stocks, as owner of Transvaal gold and diamond shares, as friend of Cecil Rhodes and Jameson, can justly be looked upon as the embodiment of the evil instincts which unleashed this robber war and stamped their character dreadfully upon it. If I should pronounce the judgment of the German people upon Chamberlain and his slander of our army, I must use these words: *Minister Chamberlain is the most infamous rogue who ever profaned God's earth.* (President's bell)[61]

Much alarmed, Bülow rose and administered a controlled but severe scolding to Liebermann, which met with loud bravos from the whole house.

However, the damage was done. The English press, already annoyed, refused to be mollified by Bülow's reprimand of Liebermann. The *London Times* conducted itself more moderately than most, but even the *Times* was incensed:

> Herr Liebermann von Sonnenberg is a fair specimen of the meaner sort of anti-Semite. . . . Mr. Chamberlain made no attack on anyone; he only answered as they deserved people like Herr Liebermann von Sonnenberg, of whom there are far too many in Germany and elsewhere at present.[62]

Less restrained English papers simply equated "the extravagancies of the stentorian anti-Semite" and his "contemptible boorish insinuations" with German public opinion in general.[63] Liebermann had thus contributed to the poisoning of German-English relations. In the Reichstag on 14 January, he tried rather lamely to justify his speech, claiming that his rudeness truly expressed the feelings of the German people, whose deputy he was. Nevertheless, in a rare show of unanimity, the press of every political party, the Pan-German League, and several anti-Semitic papers condemned him. The *Kreuz-*

zeitung and *Germania* had unusually sharp words for "the meddling of the anti-Semites."[64]

As with the Konitz murder, the anti-Semites bungled their attempts to exploit the Boer War in the Reichstag. Again, all their most successful actions were extraparliamentary. Perhaps their greatest moment of glory in the Wilhelminian era came when Liebermann and Stoecker received the defeated Boer generals Dewet, Botha, and Darley in Berlin during October 1902. Liebermann delivered a panegyric on the heroic generals and rode in the lead carriage with General Dewet, basking in the publicity he loved. Like the mass protest meetings, this was a kind of "street action" in opposition to official government policy, which had ignored the generals' presence. A group of anti-Semites present at the reception gave their opposition a pointedly antimonarchical tone by gathering later on *Unter den Linden* and refusing to doff their hats to Wilhelm II, a traditional mark of respect.[65]

Anti-Semites naturally began to compare the relative effectiveness of action in the Reichstag and "in the streets." Suddenly, leaders of the parties began to worry about the revolutionary sentiments they had helped foster within their conventional colleagues. Dreading the growth of radicalism, Liebermann, Bindewald, Bruhn, and Ludwig Werner began reaffirming the nonrevolutionary nature of the parties and their commitment to finding legislative solutions to the Jewish question.[66] However, the unsettling effect of German neutrality and the delving into foreign affairs could not be undone so easily. What the leaders needed most to stem their followers' alienation was a parliamentary success. And this continued to elude them.

At the same time that the Konitz affair and the Boer War further weakened conventional respect for the *Kaiserreich,* they were also reactivating the anti-Semites and helping to keep their organizations from disintegrating in self-pity and frustration. But more than this the two causes could not provide. The public hysteria could not go on indefinitely, and the Wilhelminian anti-Semites were by no means as adept at creating issues as the Nazis later proved to be. Gradually, interest in Konitz faded. No permanent gains, no impetus to new growth resulted from the exploitation of the murder or the war. In the years between 1901 and 1907 no new *Reformvereine* were established. The strength that anti-Semites might have drawn from

Konitz and the Boer War was squandered in schismatic battles.

Furthermore, neither the German Socials nor the Social Reformers improved their general credibility as political parties during the agitation or immediately afterward. Following the schism, Liebermann arranged a short-lived "Free Economic Group" (*Freie wirtschaftliche Gruppe*), which included several non–anti-Semites as well as the German Social Reformers in one *Fraktion*. The group functioned poorly and with manifest disunity. Only twice between 1900 and 1903 did it vote unanimously. Absenteeism reached scandalous proportions. Philipp Köhler rarely appeared in the Reichstag; in the legislative period 1898–1903, he missed 153 of 188 votes; his last speech had been in 1893. The attendance records of Lotze, Gäbel, and Gräfe were scarcely better than that of the chronically absent Ahlwardt.[67]

This sorry situation finally prompted Liebermann to action. In contrast to the leaders of the German Social Reformers, he made far-reaching changes in the organization of his party. He streamlined its bureaucracy, consolidated state and provincial associations, and insisted upon personal control. The German Social party was small, but it was obedient. Its strength lay in the west and north of Germany: the Westmark Association comprising *Reformvereine* in the Rhineland and Westphalia; the Southmark with locals in Baden, the Palatinate, and Alsace; and the Association for Prussian Hesse and Waldeck. The Northmark Association, the parent organization which provided the others with a model, remained the strongest, with about 1,050 members and 8,000 marks in annual dues. In 1902 the party added a new organization, the Lower Saxony Association, which included *Reformvereine* in Hanover and Brunswick.[68]

The German Socials attracted most of the promising "young" talent within the ranks of the anti-Semites. In fact, Count Ludwig zu Reventlow (b. 1865), Wilhelm Lattmann (b. 1864), and Wilhelm Schack (b. 1869) did not constitute a new generation of anti-Semites. They were simply closer in age to Böckel (b. 1859) than to Liebermann (b. 1848). All of Liebermann's new men began anti-Semitic careers in their mid-twenties or early thirties. The most carefully cultivated was Reventlow, the German Socials' dauphin and Liebermann's hand-picked successor. A declassé nobleman, Reventlow was a practicing lawyer and in 1901 became the vice-chairman of the

Agrarian League for Schleswig-Holstein.[69] Lattmann had served in
the bureaucracy of Prussian Hesse from 1887 until his active entrance into anti-Semitic politics in 1901.[70] He was of above average
intelligence and possessed some organizational ability. His public
speaking, however, lacked the polish of his master. Reventlow and
Lattmann resembled their leader in so far as they respected the conventions of the day, sought the company and favor of powerful men,
and kept their personal lives relatively free from scandal. None of
these characteristics could be attributed to the most important of the
"new men," Wilhelm Schack.

Schack was a gifted agitator and organizer, a man of tireless
energy. After graduating from a Hamburg secondary school, he
attended various commercial schools and taught in them between
1884 and 1887.[71] He showed an early affinity for anti-Semitism by
becoming an activist in Hamburg's *Deutscher Jugendbund*. In 1894,
he became interested in a new, emphatically nationalistic organization of shop clerks. From its beginnings in Hamburg, the National
German Shop Clerks' Union (*Deutschnationaler Handlungsgehilfen-
Verband*) developed hand in hand with the anti-Semitic movement.
Like many of the *Mittleständler* attracted to anti-Semitism, the shop
clerks had lost faith in the ability of the liberal parties to rescue them
from economic woes. Strongly caste conscious and fearful of pro-
letarianization, they were drawn to the anti-Semitic parties. The
anti-Semites Raab and Zimmermann recruited members for the
union by adroitly comparing it to rival socialist organizations. While
Jewish-inspired Social Democrats preached internationalism and
foresaw only economic extinction for the *Mittlestand,* the union and
the anti-Semitic parties stood ready to champion the rights of honest
German clerks.[72]

The debt owed to anti-Semitism for the expansion of the Shop
Clerks' union beyond Hamburg into the rest of Germany was
acknowledged in important ways. Paragraph 7 of the union's bylaws, a statute which needed a three-fourths majority as well as
unanimous consent from the board of directors to amend, excluded
Jews from membership in the association. "Lack of courage, greed
for profits, sultry sensuality, lack of honor and cleanliness" were,
according to the official handbook, "unacceptable Jewish traits."[73]
Moreover, a good deal of the union's noneconomic activity consisted

of *völkisch* education for its members and a wider German public. Yet the union, perhaps for the sake of recruitment in areas where liberal, socialist, and conservative organizations already existed, declared itself politically neutral. The shop clerks, in fact, kept their anti-Semitism strictly subordinate to their material interests.[74]

Schack rose to the presidency of the Shop Clerks' union in 1896. An ally of Liebermann and Raab, he became secretary of the German Social Reform party's state organization for Hamburg and Schleswig-Holstein and a member of the party directory. But his main task was making the shop clerks a powerful ally of the party. During his presidency, membership tripled, reaching 115,000 dues-paying clerks organized into 1,172 locals.[75] By 1900 the income from dues alone stood at close to six hundred thousand marks annually. The suspicion that Schack siphoned off some of these funds for anti-Semitic party purposes, at least at election time, seems well founded. Yet, as in the case of the Agrarian League, the evidence for the frequently made allegation is not conclusive. However, Schack was accused of the misuse of funds by more than just the hostile defense groups. "It is certain," wrote Wilhelm Giese after the schism, "that Herr Schack can dictate his will" in any branch of the German Social party. Giese's claims may have been little more than sour grapes. But some of Schack's own colleagues in the union complained of unwarranted use of organization funds for Reichstag candidacies. A one thousand mark contribution to Friedrich Raab's 1904 election campaign, for example, raised a protest inside the union.[76] Nevertheless, to say that the union financed the German Social party and directed its policies seems unjustifiable. Schack was no goldmine, and the German Socials still had to continue the hectic public pursuit of funds.

Although the exact financial relationship between the union and Liebermann's party remains elusive, Schack's membership in the German Social party and his control of the Shop Clerks' union was valuable in several ways. The union's own publishing house printed the two German Social papers, the *Deutsches Blatt* and the *Antisemitische-Korrespondenz*, free of charge. The party directory found it profitable to shift its headquarters from Berlin to the Hamburg offices of the union. Further, according to Giese, shop clerks who remained in the *Reformvereine* of the German Social Reform party were notoriously sympathetic to the German Socials. Their presence was one of many factors working to weaken Zimmermann's party.[77] Schack kept the group actively anti-Semitic, working to get out the vote. Liebermann could well congratulate himself on recruiting so valuable a personality.

In the Reichstag, Liebermann ingratiated himself with the Conservatives and Agrarians, delivering his four German Social votes on almost every occasion. The four anti-Semites voted with the Conservatives to abolish the distillery tax and against a new international sugar agreement.[78] When the Caprivi commerical treaties were about to fall due for renewal in 1902, the German Socials, Conservatives, and Agrarians joined together to push for the highest possible tariff protection. Liebermann and his party thus became publicly associated with what many regarded as the Agrarian League's most extreme venture. Although some Conservatives felt constrained to support a tariff compromise, the German Socials remained conspicuously loyal to the Agrarians, voting against any moderation.[79] On none of these issues did the German Socials truly serve the best interests of their peasant and *Mittelstand* constituents. Small-scale farmers drew little benefit from high tariffs which, in the case of livestock raisers, merely served to raise the cost of feed. Abolition of the distillery tax relieved Junkers but at the same time added to the burden of indirect taxation already weighing heavily on *Mittelständler*. Now, more than ever, the German Socials seemed to be turning their backs on the people they pretended to represent.

In spite of his complete surrender, Liebermann proved no more successful than before in gaining the active moral and financial support of the Conservatives and Agrarians. Although he placed his speaking talents and his four votes at their disposal, he received personal rewards rather than political ones. Grateful for his loyalty on the tariff question, the Agrarian League instituted an honorary fund in his name, which drew some impressive cash contributions. The official league history lauded his "gripping oratory."[80] Nevertheless, the Agrarians continued to refuse exclusive attachment to his party. The league, thoroughly anti-Semitic though it was, kept its anti-Semitism firmly harnessed to the political and economic objectives of large-scale agriculture. To "sincere" anti-Semites the league remained lamentably "demagogic."

Unlike Liebermann, the German Social Reformers saw no need to tighten up the organizational structure of their party after the schism of 1900. They retained most of the *Reformvereine* in the heartland of parliamentary anti-Semitism, Hessenland and the Kingdom of Saxony. Moreover, Wilhelm Bruhn, disreputable but dynamic, succeeded in reviving anti-Semitism in Berlin with the aid of Count Pückler and his scandal sheet, the *Staatsbürger-Zeitung*. He engineered a merger between the East German Association of the German Social Reform party and the resurrected German Anti-Semite Alliance of Berlin.[81] As chairman of this new body, he became a force within the national party and a direct threat to Oswald Zimmermann's leadership.

From the point of view of the Agrarian League, the schism had solved nothing. Liebermann's party was dependable enough in the Reichstag. But the uncontrollable and hostile Social Reformers spoke for more peasant voters. The Hessian organization built by Böckel was still a power. In view of the stalemate, it was natural for the Agrarians to bypass both parties and to attempt to gain direct control of the Hessian peasantry. Demonstrating its thick skin, the league ignored years of abuse heaped upon it by Böckel and his successors, as it actively sought to incorporate the Hessian Peasant Alliance. The leader of the alliance, Philipp Köhler, had made many pronouncements giving the league's agricultural platform full support while rejecting political cooperation. In 1903 this attitude had cost Köhler his Reichstag seat in Giessen where the league supported his National Liberal opponent. Köhler was anxious enough to regain his mandate to risk offending the anti-Prussianism of his peasant followers. In 1904 he reversed the policy of many years, agreeing to the incorporation of the alliance.[82] Unconvincingly, he glossed over the surprising about-face by describing his new partners as "the ancient German nobility, not . . . the Jewified peasant-catching Junkers." For the wily leaders of the Hessian peasants there were clear advantages in the deal. Köhler, Otto Hirschel, and Michael Wolf VI became paid employees of the Agrarian League. The league, on the other hand, came out second best. Although the agreement called for a disbanding of the peasant alliance and its re-formation into Agrarian League chapters, Köhler was still refusing to fulfill this part of the bargain as late as 1909.[83]

Neither the schism nor the manipulations of the Agrarian League disheartened the anti-Semites. The German Socials, Social Reformers, and *Volksbund* approached the 1903 elections with complacency. The hubbub and ferment of Konitz and the Boer War agitation had receded, but all the politicians expected to profit from the anti-Semitic renaissance which had surged through Germany. Their renewed optimism, however, met with even greater disappointments than in 1898. Whether or not there had been an upsurge in anti-Semitic feeling, the parties failed miserably when it came to converting that feeling into more Reichstag seats. Eleven anti-Semites entered the Reichstag of 1903, but, to the amusement of their enemies, they represented no less than four parties: Liebermann, Reventlow, and Lattmann for the German Socials; Bruhn, Böckler, Ludwig Werner, and Gräfe for the German Social Reformers; Pastor Krösell and Ernst Fröhlich for the *Deutscher Volksbund;* Stoecker and Georg Burckhardt for the Christian Socials. Since the last election the total anti-Semitic vote dropped by close to fifty thousand.[84] A drastic change in personnel removed eight of the twelve anti-Semites who had served between 1898 and 1903. Veterans like Ahlwardt, Böckel, Raab, Müller, Bindewald, Lotze, Gäbel, and Köhler failed to return.

Another veteran, Adolf Stoecker, was more successful in his bid for reelection to the Reichstag, where he was joined by the general secretary of the Christian Social party, Georg Burckhardt. Yet the Christian Socials had undoubtedly suffered a further erosion of support. Their ten candidates won only 23,155 votes, a drop of more than 25,000 since 1898. Moreover, the two victories in Westphalian districts depended upon election help from the Center party. This help had to be repaid with Protestant votes for Catholic candidates elsewhere in Westphalia, even when Catholics were in a minority. At least one orthodox Protestant newspaper found it disgraceful that these Protestant votes were denied to "the truly national parties" just so the Christian Socials could elect two candidates. Such a cost "raised serious doubts" about the continued existence of the party.[85]

The more radical parliamentary anti-Semites of the *Deutscher Volksbund* did no better than the Christian Socials. None of the three grandmasters got into the Reichstag. Although Otto Böckel had begun to run again in Marburg, he retired from the race early. Ironically, he had come full circle. The personal contact and full-time presence in the district, which had brought victory in 1887, 1890, and 1893, now characterized the conduct of his main opponent, Hellmut von Gerlach. Böckel showed up in Hessenland only for elections. Paul Förster campaigned untiringly, holding 140 separate meetings in Hanover. He drew only 5,300 votes, not enough to gain a berth in the runoffs. Hans von Mosch was equally unsuccessful with 4,300 votes in Erfurt.[86] Of the party's two successful candidates one was a defrocked clergyman; the other quit the *Volksbund* almost immediately.

The decline of the German Social Reform party was the most marked of all. Neither of its cochairmen, the colorless Lotze or the unscrupulous Zimmermann, came close to winning. Zimmermann contested Marburg, the constituency of his "old comrade" Böckel. He drew a pitiful 2,400 votes in what was once the focal point of anti-Semitic politics.[87] Even more fateful for the party was the election of Wilhelm Bruhn, to whom Hermann Ahlwardt had bequeathed Arnswalde-Friedberg. The *Rektor* had finally exhausted the gullibility of both his Brandenburg and Neustettin backers, but they found his logical successor in Bruhn. With a seat in the Reichstag, his challenge to the leadership of Zimmermann grew more insistent, further dividing an already fragmented party.

Only Liebermann could find some consolation in the outcome of the 1903 elections. The way in which Reventlow and Lattmann won seats in the Reichstag justified his conception of correct strategy. None of the German Social candidates had opposed a member of the Conservative party or Agrarian League. The two winners had faced Social Democrats in the second balloting where each was supported by the right, the National Liberals, and some left liberals. Although Wilhelm Schack, the other rising star in the party, and Friedrich Raab did not get elected, they made very strong showings and eventually won by-elections in 1904 and 1905. Furthermore, in the 1903 elections, the German Socials had emphasized their antisocialist character more than their anti-Semitism. However constant Liebermann's ultimate aim, the abolition of Jewish emancipation, he nonetheless realized that cooperation with the right would yield the best results. Because the right in imperial Germany was much more concerned with the Social Democratic threat than with the "Jewish danger," the German Socials accommodated themselves to this preference. Lattmann's case, in particular, showed the efficacy of this tactic. In the Kassel district his Socialist adversary outpolled him two to one in the first ballot, without, however, winning the necessary absolute majority. In the campaign for the second ballot Lattmann ignored his anti-Semitism and gathered sufficient support from the other parties.[88]

Events following the elections seemed to bear Liebermann out. His connections to the Agrarian League and Schack's control of the Shop Clerks' union operated as a lure for anti-Semites only loosely committed to the German Social Reformers and *Deutscher Volksbund.* As a result of the election, the German Social Reform party suffered its first major defection in October 1903. The Berlin Electoral Association of the party formally changed its affiliation to the German Social party. In January 1906, the largest state organization of the Social Reformers, that of Hessenland, came over to the German Socials. Hirschel and Köhler maintained their power over the Hessian organization, but Liebermann could exult in finally getting hold of Böckel's creation.[89] This significant change in the balance of power between the two anti-Semitic parties left Liebermann on top once again. Among the anti-Semitic factions it was his German Social party, with its distinctly rightist orientation, that showed faint signs of energy.

CHAPTER 9

Decline and Dissolution, 1903–1914

Despite occasional talk of an anti-Semitic revival, the real strength of the anti-Semitic political parties declined steadily from about 1896. The deterioration of Reichstag strength from sixteen seats in 1893 to twelve in 1898 and eleven in 1903 was not the most telling symptom of this decline, for in 1907 the number of anti-Semites in the Reichstag actually surpassed the 1893 level. More indicative of the degeneration of parliamentary anti-Semitism were shrinking membership in the fragmented parties, the growing dissatisfaction with German institutions evidenced by conventional anti-Semites, and their recognition that the purely anti-Semitic part of the program had become an obstacle to election. After 1903, even the most optimistic individuals could read the danger signals. The extensive grass-roots organization which had sustained the parties through failure in the Reichstag and the schism of 1900 was falling apart. Liebermann's reorganization of the German Socials came too late and covered too small a portion of German anti-Semites to reinvigorate the movement. His new men failed to live up to expectations, while the ageing leaders remained as cantankerous as ever. The anti-Semitic parties had exhausted and outlived their youthful image.

Following the elections of 1903, the parliamentary anti-Semites parted company in the Reichstag. The German Social Reform party readopted the name German Reform party but made no arrangements for gaining *Fraktion* status.[1] Liebermann, on the other hand, received endorsement from the Agrarian League to form a multiparty bloc in the Reichstag under his leadership. Angered by defections in the tariff controversy of 1902, the league, whose own candidates usually joined the Conservative or National Liberal blocs in the Reichstag, called for creation of the separate Economic Union (*Wirtschaftliche Vereinigung*) in the national and state parliaments. With two by-election victories, the five German Socials became the largest subgroup and consequently set the tone for the Economic Union in the Reichstag. In addition to the German Socials, there were four members of the Agrarian League, two Christian Socials, Pastor Krösell of the *Volksbund,* and a few deputies of the Bavarian Peasant Alliance. The German Reformers remained aloof. A "colorless dwarf party" sitting on the right side of the house, the Economic Union grandiosely claimed to represent all productive labor in Germany.[2] In reality, it acted as the parliamentary agent of the Agrarian League and incidentally provided Liebermann with the advantages of *Fraktion* membership. However, neither the Economic Union nor the German Reformers showed any inclination to pursue the Jewish question in the new Reichstag. Neither party presented an anti-Semitic motion during the years 1903–1907. Both had more pressing problems of survival to face.

Again, Liebermann was more effective than Zimmermann in salvaging what was to be salvaged. His reorganization, although it relied heavily on defecting German Reformers, produced some temporary benefits for the German Socials. With the backing of Conservatives and Agrarians, Wilhelm Lattmann won a seat in the Prussian parliament.[3] Friedrich Raab joined the German Socials in the Reichstag after a by-election victory in 1904. The finances of the party also improved. By 1907, Treasurer Raab reported an income and expenditure of 50,000 marks and a membership of ten thousand.[4] In November 1905, Wilhelm Schack finally entered the Reichstag via a dramatic by-election victory in Eisenach-Dermbach (Thuringia). Schack aimed his extraordinarily intensive and innovative campaign at small occupational groups with similar interests. Invited to separate and closed meetings, they listened to promises carefully tailored to their particular needs. Schack never published a platform for the whole electorate. Like all the anti-Semites, he promised all things to all men. But this time he did so in private and to one faction at a time. In the safety of closed meetings he could also denounce the Social Democrats, especially strong in Thuringia, while escaping a physical confrontation. To defeat his Socialist rival in the runoff election, he toned down his anti-Semitism and went after Centrist, National Liberal, and left-liberal voters. In the closing days of the campaign, his urgent warnings of an imminent red uprising brought out the police of Weimar and Eisenach. The victory was impressive, but Schack's methods were far too expensive for the German Socials to employ on a wide scale.[5]

These signs of well-being among the German Socials were deceptive, however. In May 1906, Reventlow died after undergoing surgery for a kidney ailment. The dauphin was lost. The party retained his seat, but his successor was the lackluster Richard Herzog (b. 1868), mayor of a small town in Schaumburg. At the time of Reventlow's death, an ominous development in German politics confronted the anti-Semitic parties. New and competitive *Mittelstand* organizations, the strongest of which was the *Mittelstandsvereinigung* founded in 1904, appeared unwilling to let the anti-Semites remain the political representative of their interests.[6] To counter the appeal of this group and others like it, the anti-Semitic parties hastily revised their programs.

Since the schism of 1900, the Socials and Reformers had complacently used the old Erfurt program of 1895, although it had grown less and less viable. Clearly, it was not the desire for innovation in solving the Jewish problem that prompted the German Socials to adopt a new program in 1905 and the German Reformers to follow suit a year later. Neither party had any new anti-Jewish proposals to make. Their demands remained the same as those first expressed twenty-five years ago in the Anti-Semites' Petition. No new proposals on the Jewish question had gained wide acceptance in the interim. But there were considerable changes in the revised programs. Demands made on behalf of the *Mittelstand* received even greater emphasis than at Erfurt. To meet the challenge of the *Mittelstandsvereinigung* and satisfy the doubts of their *Mittelstand* supporters, both parties made detailed suggestions for tax reform, including the demand for a graduated income tax.[7] The old planks concerning the stock exchange, insurance system, the lot of petty civil servants, store clerks, and white-collar workers were supplemented and given refurbished wording. As in the past, both the Socials and the Reformers backed the Agrarian League's most extreme demands for agriculture. In short, the parliamentary anti-Semites had learned nothing in approximately ten years. The new programs, like the old, accentuated the conflicting interests of supporters instead of glossing over them. Furthermore, as a maneuver

meant to reassure *Mittelständler* that the anti-Semites were still active
on their behalf, the hasty revisions could not stand up against a long
record of betrayal in the Reichstag.[8]

A second threat posed by the *Mittelstandsvereinigung* appeared
especially grave to the anti-Semites. The Agrarian League and the
Conservative party began showing a solicitous interest in the new
organization. They were accused by liberal publicists of having
gained the upper hand financially as early as 1905.[9] The anti-Semites
could not sit idly by while the league and the Conservatives went
about gaining control of what might possibly become their replacement, at least in the cities. Therefore, anti-Semitic spokesmen began
attending recruitment meetings, became more prominent at the
general assemblies of the group, and eventually gained positions on
its central committee. However, the *Mittelstandsvereinigung* never
showed a united front on the question of anti-Semitism. While
Liebermann, Bruhn, and Fritsch were active in the group, the
"Düsseldorf wing" (including Mainz, Wiesbaden, and Frankfurt
am Main) allowed Jewish members and officers.[10] Defense against
economic extinction and the Socialists, rather than the Jewish
danger, appeared to be the organization's only unifying factor.
Luckily for the parliamentary anti-Semites, the *Mittelstandsvereinigung*
proved even less reliable than the German Socials or Reformers.
Conservatives and Agrarians cried betrayal when the organization
advocated equal, direct, and secret suffrage in Prussia and when it
came out strongly for a graduated income tax. During the finance
reform of 1909, the break was complete when the group sided openly
with the *Hansabund,* an association closely tied to the moderate wing
of the National Liberal party.[11] Although the threat that the *Mittelstandsvereinigung* might steal the affections of the Agrarians and
Conservatives eventually disappeared, the evolution of the organization toward the National Liberals was scarcely less alarming to
the anti-Semites. If more than a mere episode, this return to more
liberal attitudes on the part of the *Mittelstand* would sorely hurt the
anti-Semitic parties in their traditional recruiting grounds.

These problems and fears notwithstanding, the anti-Semites
elected seventeen deputies in the 1907 election. Their strong showing, however, was not a result of successfully fending off *Mittelstand*
rivals, program revisions, reorganization of the German Socials, or

the altered balance of power between the two major anti-Semitic parties. More than any other single factor, the unusual and transitory political constellation which developed shortly before the elections played into the hands of the German Socials and Reformers. Late in 1905 the able and ambitious Centrist, Matthias Erzberger, began to criticize government colonial policy, the immorality of colonial officials, and their abuse of the natives in German Southwest Africa. Because Germany had been at war with the Herero tribesmen since 1904, Erzberger's sudden concern in 1906 was taken by contemporaries as a mere pretext. He was suspected of raising the price of the crucial cooperation of the Center party in the Reichstag. In May 1906, the Centrists and Social Democrats refused to support the government request for supplementary funds to make an independent ministry out of the colonial office. In September, a new director of colonial administration plunged into battle with the Center in the Reichstag. The party answered by demanding a reduction of war credits for the Herero War.[12]

Meanwhile, Chancellor Bülow, having noticed that the left liberals were adhering to his colonial policy, decided to end government dependence on the Center, replacing it with a coalition of left liberals, National Liberals, Conservatives, German Reformers, and the Economic Union. To this end, he dissolved the Reichstag on 13 December 1906. Although the "Bülow bloc" did not come into existence until after the elections, it was operative in many electoral districts during the campaign. In the six weeks between dissolution and the new elections, the progovernment "parties of order" fought a fiercely nationalistic contest, both anti-Catholic and antisocialist. These two "internationalist" elements, the government maintained, were trying to deny Germany's right to world power and possession of colonies.[13] On such a platform the anti-Semites could thrive. Their unsullied chauvinism and antisocialism stood them well. Moreover, the fight against anti-Semitism was eclipsed by the maneuvering of Erzberger and Bülow and by the unusual alignment of political forces.

The Center party withstood the assault much better than the Social Democratic party which lost nearly half the eighty-one seats it had won in 1903. Both the conservative parties and the National Liberals made moderate gains. In the 1907 elections Liebermann's good relations with the right helped his party. All eight German Social victors were simultaneously candidates for the Agrarian League. In Prussian Hesse, where the Socials and Reformers competed, the agitation apparatus of the Agrarians came to Liebermann's rescue. Elsewhere, the league supported the six victorious German Reformers as second-round candidates for the "parties of order." For the first time since the early 1890's, anti-Semites also received help from official sources in isolated cases. In Eisenach, for example, the district commissar of Weimar, the mayors of several villages, and other state officials campaigned openly for Schack's reelection.[14]

Once again, dread of the Socialists played into the hands of the anti-Semites in 1907. For years, they had presented themselves as an antidote to red revolution and "a dam against social democracy." They were also members in good standing of a powerful new organization formed in 1904 and dedicated to a "nonpartisan, nondenominational struggle against social democracy." The Reich League against Social Democracy (*Reichsverband gegen die Sozialdemokratie*) drew most of its two hundred thousand members (1909) from the *Reichspartei*, National Liberals, and Conservatives. Its board of directors boasted generals, bankers, industrialists, bureaucrats, and landowners with, so it was rumored, easy access to the highest levels of government. Of course, the parliamentary anti-Semites could never hope to exercise a leadership role among such high and mighty personages. And, in fact, the Reich league, like so many other extraparliamentary right-wing organizations in the *Kaiserreich*, found no advantage in anti-Semitism. Nevertheless, in the elections of 1907, several anti-Semitic candidates qualified for direct help from Reich league organizers. As opponents of the Socialists, anti-Semitic candidates received favorable treatment in the press service of the organization which reached some 1,275 local and provincial newspapers.[15]

Membership in the Reich League against Social Democracy helped make the anti-Semites acceptable to the right as compromise candidates against Socialists. Yet there was still work to be done in this area. The German Socials, for example, set about wiping away all vestiges of "radical democracy" that had somehow survived until this time. Universal suffrage and electoral reform in the states of the

Reich were deemed dangerous by the German Socials because the gullible masses, as the *Antisemitische Korrespondenz* complained, "blindly go along with the stupidities of their Jewish or Jewified leaders. . . . "[16] Obviously pleasing to the Conservatives and Agrarians, this about-face marked an important step in the decay of parliamentary anti-Semitism: the largest anti-Semitic splinter group had lost faith in the German electorate. Meanwhile, the German Reform party, too, did its best to cash in on the antisocialist coalition. The Reformers had already dropped *sozial* from their name so as not to be confused with the Socialists, especially in rural areas. Talk of expropriating Jewish property in cases of ritual murder vanished from their publications. The German Socials went further, promising to protect "the private property of native Jews as well as that of Germans so that every citizen can enjoy his property in peace."[17]

To make themselves more acceptable to the left side of the anti-socialist coalition, the anti-Semites, for the first time, systematically veiled their anti-Semitism. Very few fought truly anti-Semitic campaigns. Some went to extraordinary lengths to appear respectable, in other words, not anti-Semitic. For example, Wilhelm Lattmann made a bid not only for liberal support, but for the Jewish vote as well. In a Kassel newspaper he described himself as "no anti-Semite in the current sense of the word." He urged Jews as "members of the *Mittelstand*" and "our common fatherland" to vote for him.[18] Friedrich Raab, facing a union of all liberal forces in Eschwege (Prussian Hesse), fought his customary campaign until the second balloting against a Social Democrat, whereupon he pocketed his anti-Semitism and won two-thirds of the votes that had originally gone to the liberal candidate. In Weimar-Apolda, Meissen-Grossenhain, Eschwege, Rinteln, and Eisenach the muffling of anti-Semitism and fear of the Social Democrats combined to win National Liberal and left-liberal voters even when party headquarters forbade cooperation or urged abstention. In at least four districts the left-liberal vote was instrumental to anti-Semitic victory against Socialists.[19]

Together, all anti-Semitic parties polled 267,205 votes, an increase of 9,000 over the 1903 total. Although their percentage of the total vote decreased slightly, the number of anti-Semitic mandates rose by six, from eleven to seventeen. The German Socials elected eight, largely because of Liebermann's judicious policy of accommodation. Of the seven German Socials who eventually won in runoff elections, five competed against Socialists.[20] The German Reformers were less accommodating and therefore less successful. On 29 December 1906, just before the election, the Reformers and the *Deutscher Volksbund* dramatically announced a merger of the two parties. For the German Reformers this was anything but a politic decision. The *Volksbund* had long been the gathering place for the disaffected among parliamentary anti-Semites. Zimmermann himself had described Mosch's group as "ripe for the public prosecutor." For many like Paul Förster, it was the last stop before complete withdrawal from political life. The incorporation of the group brought little strength to the Reformers and only underscored their own reputation for unreliability. In 1907 all the *Volksbund* candidates lost in the first balloting; it was expelled from the German Reform party and perished soon thereafter.[21] In spite of association with the *Volksbund,* the Reformers elected Zimmermann, Bruhn, and Gräfe in the first balloting. All ran as virtually unopposed compromise candidates against the Social Democrats. Of the Reformers' three runoff victories, two came against the parties labeled "antinational," the Social Democrats and the Center. Thus, no more than those of the German Socials, could the Reformers' victories be attributed to uncompromising anti-Semitism. The Christian Social party also made somewhat of a comeback at the polls in 1907, electing Stoecker and two others. Although the ex–court chaplain remained true to his nonracist brand of anti-Semitism, this doctrine was fading in significance for the Christian Socials. A faction in the party had already begun working for a reorientation of the Christian Social program designed to make cooperation with the Center party more extensive and more fruitful. Such a reorientation raised serious questions about the acceptability of Stoecker's anti-Semitism.[22]

In the history of parliamentary anti-Semitism, the 1907 elections were a significant milestone. Success at the polls was not a fluke or "merely an inconsequential episode."[23] The 1907 election was Liebermann's vindication, as 1893 had been Böckel's. Liebermann's neighborly relations with like groups, his dream of a coalition extending from the healthy kernel of the National Liberal party to the Conservative party, supported by the Agrarian League and Shop

Clerks' union, resulted in partial victory. For the first time, his party gained more seats than the Böckel-Zimmermann wing, which followed an essentially similar policy of accommodation during the election. The nationalism, antisocialism, and anti-Catholicism of the 1907 campaign corresponded very nearly to the ideal circumstances Liebermann had outlined as early as 1882. Böckel had insisted upon an independent anti-Semitic party and in 1893 elected sixteen deputies. Liebermann had stressed compromise and cooperation, and in 1907 seventeen deputies were elected. However, it could be and frequently was said of this election that it proved only one thing about anti-Semitism: that its political drawing power and even its political usefulness to others had been exhausted.[24] The seventeen anti-Semites had not won election because of their anti-Semitism, but in spite of it. The parties were able to increase their representation in the Reichstag only because they were willing to fight the battles of others. Their own special cause—the abolition of Jewish emancipation—had temporarily to be concealed and, in some cases, even denied. Furthermore, Liebermann's method was not significantly better than Böckel's in getting men elected, and as far as the anti-Semitic cause was concerned, it was probably far worse.

In 1907, had the Christian Social, German Social, and German Reform deputies united, their seventeen Reichstag seats would have entitled them to an independent *Fraktion*. The sad six-year history of the German Social Reform party, however, had shown the futility of an independent anti-Semitic *Fraktion*. Little or no cooperation from the other parties, a lack of specialized knowledge which would have enabled anti-Semites to influence Reichstag commissions, open hostility expressed by the great majority of deputies toward the basic aims of the anti-Semites—these factors were still operative in 1907 and made the formation of a single anti-Semitic party pointless. No one even suggested such a course of action. The Christian Socials and German Socials secured *Fraktion* status by virtue of the Economic Union. In February 1907, the German Reformers obtained full rights in the Reichstag by being counted with the conservative *Reichspartei*.[25] Voluntarily, all the anti-Semitic parties had ceased functioning autonomously. With little hope of success, they greatly reduced the direct struggle against Jews. A few old motions were tried again, but no new anti-Jewish legislation was presented in the Reichstag of

1907–1912. Instead, as members of the Bülow bloc, the anti-Semites emphasized the "positive" aspects of their program.

Although they could justify cooperation with the Conservatives, Agrarian League, *Reichspartei*, and National Liberals, the anti-Semitic deputies were acutely embarrassed when called upon to collaborate with the left liberals, also members of the bloc. In Liebermann's ideal coalition, there was no room for the archenemy. The left liberals, in spite of numerous defections in the election of 1907, were still the most articulate and consistent enemies of anti-Semitism in Germany. But neither the Socials nor the Reformers possessed weight enough to force their bloc partners to do without the left liberals. Should the forty-nine left-liberal deputies go over to the other side, the bloc majority would be endangered. Nonetheless, anti-Semites soon began to grumble against the left liberals. Zimmermann opened the attack in the Saxon state parliament by bringing up the usual charges against the "party of the Jews" and by accusing certain left-liberal newspapers of trying to "spring the bloc." Stoecker's son-in-law, Reinhard Mumm, flooded the press of the right with criticism in the same vein.[26] In early 1908, cries of "*Los vom Block*" echoed from the provincial organizations of the German Socials. The Westmark Association requested its leaders to limit cooperation with the bloc to "purely national matters"; in economic and social reform, on the other hand, the German Socials and Economic Union had to keep a free hand.[27]

Yet pursuit of an independent policy in the Reichstag was beyond the feeble powers of the anti-Semites. The Economic Union under Liebermann's leadership consisted of eighteen members, only eleven of whom were avowed anti-Semites. The six-point program of the Economic Union said nothing about the Jewish question but did pledge its members to intercede on behalf of the *Mittelstand* and sound agriculture. The Socials, however, proved less capable than ever of arbitrating between the contending groups among their own supporters. Too weak to do anything on their own, the German Socials followed the path of least resistance. On almost every vote in the legislative period 1907–1912, the party did the bidding of the Conservatives and Agrarians.

In vain the anti-Semitic deputies sought to present at least an illusion of political effectiveness in the Reichstag. This was still no easy matter. The German Reformers were not allowed by their *Fraktion* hosts to present any of their own motions. Those of the Economic Union got nowhere. Forced to ignore the Jewish question, the anti-Semites tried to compensate by speaking on all issues and at greater length than any other party. They merely succeeded in provoking their Reichstag colleagues with overblown and ungermane speeches.[28] While the dangers of obscurity again loomed large, the parliamentary anti-Semites had to keep clear of men like Pastor Krösell and Hans von Mosch, whose activities bordered on illegality, violence, and implicit revolution. Even during the 1903 election campaign, Krösell had led bands of roughnecks, whom he dubbed "storm columns" and who greeted their leader with "*Heil!*" Mosch, too, yearned for a more violent approach to the Jewish question, a desire barely concealed in Aesopian language: "As bees throw out the drones, so must Germany destroy its parasites." Criticism of imperial institutions became more direct. Köhler, for example, openly referred to the Reichstag as "a bunch of eunuchs." Such sentiments, though spreading, were still not the norm among parliamentary anti-Semites. Krösell was shunted aside and left the country. Mosch was driven into isolation after the collapse of his *Deutscher Volksbund.*[29]

Yet, even among the conventional, radical criticism of the Reich and calls for drastic change became more typical. The need for a radical cure of Germany's ills was far greater than most anti-Semites had believed back in the 1880's. The implications of their impotence were becoming clear to them. Through no fault of their own, the parliamentary anti-Semites simply did not have the power they deserved. Clearly, the Reichstag, not the anti-Semitic record, was responsible. If the Reichstag were truly representative of the desires of the German people, then, certainly by now, anti-Semites would have been well on the way toward a solution to the Jewish question. On the basis of such invulnerable logic, the balance between conventional and revolutionary anti-Semite was being shifted. Anti-parliamentary revolutionaries like Fritsch were making important converts to their conception of the Jewish question and its solution.

The change in Otto Böckel was both dramatic and influential. In the 1880's he had championed the parliamentary solution of the

Jewish question. In 1898, exiled from Hessenland, he reminisced warmly about his ten years in the Reichstag, still full of respect for the personalities and feats of the German parliament, in which anti-Semites had "achieved great deeds."[30] However, the Boer War, his incompetent colleagues, and growing bitterness all helped change his outlook. First he reversed his stand on democratic suffrage laws for the Reichstag and state parliaments. The democratic franchise had already produced a Reichstag unwilling to help the peasant, a Reichstag which sooner or later would be dominated by alienated, antinational city workers. When some deputies obstructed passage of a higher grain tariff schedule in 1902, Böckel urged a coup d'état and an unspecified change in the electoral laws. In March 1902, he delivered lectures under *Volksbund* auspices, stressing the decline of parliamentarianism in Germany. By 1903, after his withdrawal from the Marburg election race, he had a more radical solution than suffrage reform: "It would be better if the parliamentary gang were abolished and the money saved. World history is made with the sword and the plow, not the tongue."[31] Theodor Fritsch's comments on the "bankruptcy of the Reichstag" and a coup that "would be regarded by millions as salvation" seconded Böckel's thoughts and penetrated more frequently into the parliamentary anti-Semites' newspapers.[32]

Liebermann was not yet ready to scrap the Reichstag. But even in this pillar of conventionality, pressures were building up: the task of pleasing both his electorate and the "friendly neighbor" parties was proving too exacting. Continued participation in the bloc and the muffling of anti-Semitism were damning the anti-Semites in the eyes of their own followers. Simultaneously, competition from the new *Mittelstand* organizations threatened to render the German Socials useless to both Conservatives and Agrarians. The anti-Semites very much needed a cause, one which would make them the center of public attention. In October 1908, they received a windfall in the form of a royal indiscretion. Wilhelm II allowed an English acquaintance to publish an account of a confidential talk between the two in the London *Daily Telegraph*. The kaiser, seeking to allay English fears about the German fleet, assured his friend that it was a defensive weapon and that, furthermore, he, unlike the majority of his subjects, was a firm friend of England. He had shown his friendship during the Boer War, for example, by sending Queen Victoria, his grandmother, a campaign plan that eventually brought victory. Wilhelm had also refused to join France and Russia in intervening in South Africa, as they had suggested. The *Daily Telegraph* affair, as it came to be called, advertised the dangers of Wilhelm's personal regime. The kaiser aggravated anti-German feeling in England by arrogantly claiming the credit for victory in the Boer War and by confessing that his people were anti-English. He also gratuitously betrayed the confidence of France and Russia.[33] Moreover, he provided the parliamentary anti-Semites with their last moment of public prominence.

Resentment of Wilhelm had deep roots among anti-Semites. Even before the kaiser's refusal to aid the Boers, he had come under fire for the ennoblement of Jews. As recently as 1906, he celebrated his silver wedding anniversary by raising four Jews to the nobility. Oswald Zimmermann referred contemptuously to the "bank and stock exchange nobility" and to the growth of Jewish influence in the kaiser's immediate circle. Liebermann coined the term "Ballinism" to disparage the kaiser's social hobnobbing with men like Albert Ballin, director of the Hamburg-Amerika Line. Wilhelm Bruhn reacted to the appointment of Bernhard Dernburg as director of colonial administration by hinting darkly at a plot to Jewify Germany (Dernburg's paternal grandfather was Jewish).[34] Anti-Semites of all parties were coming close to accusing the kaiser of being a tool of the Jewish conspiracy. So far had the devolution of the German Empire progressed in their eyes.

The *Daily Telegraph* episode angered the German people and all the political parties. Once again, as in the case of the Boer War, anti-Semites felt themselves to be part of the majority. This infrequent feeling produced its usual consequences. The exhilaration led the anti-Semitic Reichstag deputies too far. Left liberals and Social Democrats wanted to proceed against the personal regime of Wilhelm. Yet neither party showed a determination to destroy the monarchy. Both tried to channel public outrage into a demand for constitutional change, the institution of responsible parliamentary government.[35] Liebermann and Zimmermann had no such positive goal. They wanted primarily to make a splash and to vent their long simmering wrath upon the kaiser, without regard for the consequences. This they did during the formal interpellation of Chancellor Bülow in the Reichstag on 10 November 1908. Liebermann spoke not only as floor leader of the Economic Union but as a member of the Pan-German League. Once again he appointed himself tribune of the people, the man most closely in touch with the German masses. He congratulated all previous speakers. However, the inordinate delicacy, the "minor key" of their remarks, did not correspond to Liebermann's mood or the mood of the land. After a few comments about his innate monarchism, he launched the nastiest, the most personal, and most tasteless attack of the day. Not only had the kaiser squandered public and international trust in Germany, but he was also responsible for Germany's serious financial crisis. Instead of acting as an example of thrift and common sense for the people, he kept an unnecessarily luxurious court. He was too impressionable, too prone to take on the color of his surroundings. Liebermann warned that the German people had been alienated by the kaiser, and perhaps irretrievably so: "The English fog settled between throne and *Volk,* which I mentioned years ago in a speech, has thickened still more."[36] He ended on a particularly offensive note, alluding to the kaiser's friendship with Prince Maximilian von Fürstenberg and his questionable entertainments. At this point, Bülow hurried out of the Reichstag. The next day, Zimmermann continued the attack on the same themes. He spoke of "anglicization" (*Verenglanderung*), and the royal court's preference for foreigners and millionaires. He demanded removal of "the court eunuchs," a reference to a homosexuality scandal involving close friends of the kaiser, and their replacement by "German men."[37]

The extremism of the anti-Semites immediately sobered the Conservative party. The committee of eleven, ruling body of the party, had earlier published a declaration signed by most of the high-ranking Conservatives, imploring the kaiser to show more restraint in the future. Although conceding Wilhelm's good will, the declaration mentioned the dangerous misinterpretations which some of his statements seemed to invite. On the day after Liebermann's speech, however, the party backed off. Oskar von Normann, leader of the Conservative *Fraktion,* announced that he and his friends were fully satisfied by Chancellor Bülow's answer to the interpellation of 10 November.[38] Liebermann should have read the signs of Conservative retreat, but he did not. The Economic

Union presented a motion calling for a formal address to the kaiser listing all the grievances of the nation. Although the idea of an address had not originated with the anti-Semites, Liebermann sought to stay in the forefront of the matter in order to reestablish the anti-Semites' reputation for fearless championing of the German people. Instead of accomplishing this, he saddled himself with a good share of the responsibility for the proceedings against Wilhelm, something the monarch was slow to forgive even his dearest Conservative friends.[39] Liebermann had associated the anti-Semites with those elements most critical of Wilhelm II, the Socialists and left liberals. Although all the parties were angry with the kaiser, none but the anti-Semites showed a willingness to sponsor an address.[40] Liebermann finally came to his senses, recognizing that the pursuit of a policy opposed by the Conservatives would jeopardize the continued existence of the German Social party. The *Daily Telegraph* affair thus marked the last independent action taken by the German Socials in the Reichstag. From the end of 1908, the party became in reality what liberal critics had always accused it of being, a pawn of the Conservatives and Agrarians.

During the extended Reichstag debate on finance reform, the anti-Semites in general and Liebermann in particular demonstrated their thralldom and the hopelessness of their dilemma. The *Mittelstand* supporters of the German Socials and Reformers definitely needed relief from the heavy load of indirect taxation. Germans paid more for food items than other Europeans as a result of the high agricularural tariffs. Excise taxes on beer and tobacco made these staples relatively expensive too. From the beginning of their activities, all the anti-Semitic parties had stressed the need for financial reform. The introduction of a graduated income tax and the curbing of indirect taxation had long been planks in all anti-Semitic party programs. The *Mittelstandsvereinigung* and Shop Clerks' union demanded reform along these lines. Even as Liebermann castigated the kaiser, he had called upon the Reichstag to reestablish the nation's fiscal soundness. Zimmermann had come out unequivocally for a national income tax and direct property tax in the Saxon parliament.[41] The constituents of the anti-Semitic parties had no reason to doubt that their deputies stood for some form of direct taxation and opposed any increase in indirect taxes.

From 1879 until 1900 the Reich had lived well within its means, the revenue from customs duties and other sources of common income. However, after the turn of the century, deficits rather than surpluses had come to be the rule. To meet the growing needs of army expansion and fleet building, the Reich had customarily resorted to indirect taxation or loans. By March 1906, the national debt had reached approximately three and one-half billion marks. A financial reform bill in 1906, which resorted once again to raising indirect taxes and increasing postal rates, had yielded only half of what was expected.[42] Although the Conservatives represented the main opposition to direct taxation, Chancellor Bülow hoped to tackle the job of financial reform with the combined forces of the bloc. In 1909 the Reichstag began working on a government package that included suggested increases in several indirect taxes and a modest death dues, or what amounted to an inheritance tax on fortunes over ten thousand marks.

In the Reichstag finance commission, the German Socials and Reformers tried to work on behalf of their *Mittelstand* supporters in a way which would least offend the Conservative party. But on the floor of the Reichstag, when matters came to a vote, the anti-Semites bowed to the Conservatives.[43] Much to their surprise, this double-dealing got extensive publicity. The National Liberal newspaper, *Liberale-Korrespondenz,* published a special series containing the anti-Semites' record in the commission and in the Reichstag. The facts spoke for themselves, not only in numerous newspapers of National Liberal orientation but in special pamphlets for the Reichstag elections of 1912 and in anti-Semitic defense group publications.[44] Even without the liberal exposé, the anti-Semites would sooner or later have been forced into an open stand on the various measures of the bill. Liebermann and Zimmermann perhaps hoped that anti-Semitic votes would not be vital and that, therefore, the Conservatives would not be unduly upset if the anti-Semites voted according to their programs and the expectations of their supporters. However, on several of the eighty-nine votes concerned with the reforms, the twenty-four deputies of the Reform party and Economic Union were crucial. Well before the final voting began, the Agrarian League general assembly in Kassel made clear that the Agrarians intended to exact a price for their previous election aid. Those anti-Semites who received league help in 1907, that is, all of the deputies, were now commanded to vote against the projected inheritance tax.[45] Individuals like Raab, Zimmermann, Herzog, and Lattmann dared not renege on their frequent public statements. But how could the anti-Semites satisfy their political allies without permanently alienating their popular support? As usual, they tried to have it both ways. On 24 June 1909, a majority voted for the inheritance tax provision. However, Liebermann, Bindewald, Köhler, and three members of the Economic Union voted against it. These six votes meant the difference between success and failure, for the provision fell through 186 to 194.[46]

Not only did the most significant part of the finance reform fail, but the Bülow bloc, already sorely strained, split apart. Bülow himself resigned. Because a majority of anti-Semites had, true to their programs, voted for the inheritance tax, the German Socials and Reformers were willing to risk voting in favor of the less publicized indirect tax measures, thus satisfying the Conservative party and Agrarian League. Accordingly, a majority of anti-Semites voted for higher coffee and tea import duties, for a tax on matches and lighting fuel, for extension of the duty on sugar, for an increased tobacco excise without compensation to unemployed tobacco workers, for a brewery and liquor tax, and against a measure raising the salaries of civil servants in the middle and lower ranks.[47] At every turn, anti-Semitic deputies sacrificed the interests of the *Mittelstand* to those of the great landholders of the Conservative party.

Predictably, this "compromise solution" pleased only the Conservatives and the Agrarians. The anti-Semites' performance in the vote on finance reform, their role in Bülow's fall, and their sellout to the Conservatives and the league produced turmoil. For the first time, anti-Semitic voters made known their anger on a large scale. Tumultuous protest meetings and demands for resignation were widespread. Wilhelm Lattmann was the target of a recall petition from his Kassel constituents. Throughout 1909, open hostility reigned between anti-Semitic deputies and their voters. One member of the Economic Union needed police protection in order to address a meeting in his home district. Raab received assurances from a group of anti-Semitic artisans in Hamburg that they would certainly never vote for him again.[48] Total parliamentary ineffectiveness had been made public; disillusionment among anti-Semitic voters was manifest; desertion of both peasant and *Mittelstand* backers was accelerating. These indications of approaching dissolution erased any lingering doubts about the survival of parliamentary anti-Semitism.

Scandal, too, contributed to the downfall. Personal respectability, more slowly affected by the process of radicalization than any other part of the conventional code, hit a new low. Not since the heyday of Ahlwardt and Böckel had so many anti-Semitic leaders stood naked before German public opinion in all their tawdriness. The National Liberals revealed that Adolf Stoecker, who unceasingly cried out against "unproductive Jewish capital," had himself made approximately one hundred thousand marks profit from an opportune investment in a Jewish-owned corporation. In July 1908, Otto Hirschel went to jail for embezzlement. Throughout 1907 and 1908, the council of twenty-three tried to bribe Hans von Mosch into relinquishing control of the *Volksbund* treasury. He was later taken to court by his party for absconding with the dues of two thousand members.[49] Scandal also adhered to the name of Wilhelm Bruhn. Following his lucrative promotion of mad Count Pückler, Bruhn sold the *Staatsbürger-Zeitung* in 1905 and brought out a new paper, *Die Wahrheit,* which like its predecessor purveyed sex, violence, and anti-Semitism. It was so offensive and damaging to their self-respect that Bruhn's own anti-Semitic colleagues in the Reichstag urged the minister of the interior to ban it from railroad stations.[50] In 1909 the paper's star reporter was sentenced to eighteen months in jail for attempted blackmail. Bruhn stood trial on the same charge but got an acquittal. The adverse publicity, however, led to withdrawal of advertising and falling circulation for *Die Wahrheit,* which ceased publication before the war.[51]

Over the years, enough cases of anti-Semitic scurrility had come to light to damn the whole enterprise as far as respectable opinion was concerned. One scandal, however, did do considerable further damage to the already tainted reputation of the parliamentary anti-Semites. The so-called *Triole* affair quickly removed Wilhelm Schack, the dynamic leader of the Shop Clerks' union and most likely successor to Liebermann, from the political scene. Under the name *Triole,* Schack advertised in a newspaper for a young lady to enter his household. When a rather naive girl answered the ad,

Schack sent her some more information concerning her future duties. Qualifications for the job included bisexuality and a willingness to share the "joys of love, both physical and spiritual." The girl showed the letter to her father, who instituted a police investigation. Schack was caught, and his guilt was undeniable. For years he had played the keeper of public morals, had denounced the "sultanic desires" of Jewish shopkeepers, and had described Jewish shops as "preparatory schools for the bordello."[52] The subsequent sensation and public outrage, fed by full exposés and lengthy condemnations in several German newspapers, had an immediate effect. The German Social party congress, already scheduled for October 1909, was cancelled. In September 1909, Schack resigned his Reichstag seat and presidency of the Shop Clerks' union. His anti-Semitic colleagues urged him to plead insanity and proceeded to do so for him in their press. He eventually entered a mental hospital and never returned to public life.[53] The *Triole* affair meant more than the loss of a Reichstag seat and financial aid from Schack's organization. It demoralized the anti-Semites and seemed to take the fighting spirit out of them.

Anti-Semites could not bring themselves to admit that their cause drew more than its share of the undesirable, the rowdy, and the abnormal. Looking over the list of celebrities like Ahlwardt, Pückler, Bruhn, and Schack, the Magdeburg *Sachsenschau* explained the fatal fascination of anti-Semitism for the unstable by blaming the German masses, who could not tolerate less spectacular but more efficacious anti-Semitism. With fanatical narrowness of view, the newspaper refused to see any other cause for the number of disreputable anti-Semites than the immaturity of the German public.[54] The *Sachsenschau* and the practicing parliamentary anti-Semites had dropped all democratic pretenses. They assumed an attitude toward the German people which Theodor Fritsch had long held and which the Nazis later subscribed to as well: Germans were foolish, somewhat naughty, and irresponsible children, playing at the edge of the abyss of Jewish conquest; should they continue in their childishness and refuse to listen to the few adults in their midst, then they, and Germany with them, would perish.[55]

If the situation were really as bad as the *Sachsenschau* portrayed, a parliamentary anti-Semite had only a few alternatives open to him.

He could stick to the old ways no matter how slim the chance of success. Or, if he admitted that the German public was not ready for the right kind of anti-Semitism, he could join with Fritsch or Friedrich Lange, who had been saying this for many years. He could work patiently to prepare Germany for a total revolution and the subsequent solution of the Jewish question. Another possibility, one which the *Sachsenschau* chose, was to quit. In 1912, the newspaper renounced parliamentary anti-Semitism, though not anti-Semitism per se, and publicly regretted its role in the past two decades.[56] This last choice appealed to many individual anti-Semites in the *Kaiserreich*—just exactly how many it is impossible to ascertain. What had been the German Social Reform party lost at least half of its approximately thirty thousand members by 1912.[57] Those who espoused the revolutionary approach of Fritsch, Lange, and a number of other "nonpolitical" groups by no means accounted for all the defections from the German Socials and Reformers.

Even the practicing parliamentary anti-Semites seemed to grow disinterested in their cause. In 1909 they perfunctorily resurrected the motion to prohibit Jewish immigration. When it came to a vote, over half of them were absent from the Reichstag.[58] Many were sick and growing old. Leaders now found time for a great flourishing of literary activity, something they had been too busy to pursue since the dark days after the Berlin movement and before the emergence of Böckel. Liebermann worked on his nostalgic memoirs, a well-written account of the Franco-Prussian War, which, with two exceptions, did not even mention his anti-Semitic career or dwell on the Jewish question. Otto Böckel, too, began his final withdrawal from active politics, devoting himself to his first love, the study of folklore. In his own melodramatic words, he was attempting to "revitalize the weary spirit, full of disappointed hopes, like so many dried leaves."[59] His continuing attachment to the anti-Semitic cause rested upon his never-ending need to make a living. Occasionally, he found work as a traveling agitator for the Saxon branch of the German Reformers and later for the Conservative party and Agrarian League. In the 1912 Reichstag election, he returned to Marburg as an independent candidate. Scarcely remembered by a new generation, he drew only twenty-five hundred votes in spite of a heavy turnout.[60] He retired to Michendorf, near Berlin, remained there through the war, and died a paralytic in 1923. Since his trip to America, Hermann Ahlwardt had exercised his enterprising mind in many endeavors, most of which victimized his fellow anti-Semites. Selling "*Judenflinten* cigars for the anti-Semitic smoker" and phony mining stocks to non-Jewish capitalists occupied his declining years. In 1914, he was run over by one of the first motorized meat trucks in Leipzig. "His death," wrote the *Staatsbürger-Zeitung*, "was as strange as his life."[61] Paul Förster, another of the pioneers, finally left the ranks of parliamentary anti-Semitism after his unsuccessful bid in the 1907 elections. Until his death in 1925, he devoted himself to fighting the Jews by other than political means. In the early 1920's, he could still be found lecturing on the dangers of the Schulcan Aruch or advocating the protection of animals.[62]

In the space of three years, death left the conventional anti-Semites without their traditional leaders. Stoecker resigned his Reichstag seat in February 1908 and died a year later. Reinhard Mumm was unable to maintain the ex–court chaplain's traditional seat in Siegen. Oswald Zimmermann died in May 1910; his mandate went to the Social Democrats. Philipp Köhler followed Zimmermann to the grave, but his district elected the Hessian school teacher and anti-Semite, Ferdinand Werner (1876–1961). In September 1911, Liebermann died. The Fritzlar-Homberg district, which had voted anti-Semitic in every election since 1890, eventually chose a National Liberal in Liebermann's place. Between 1903 and 1914 death removed Bachler, Pickenbach, Gehlsen, Marr, Wilberg, Rohling, and Müller. The high mortality rate among party leaders and prominent individuals underlined a weakness in parliamentary anti-Semitism apparent since the turn of the century. Personal rivalry and dreams of grandeur had made Böckel, Zimmermann, and Liebermann unwilling to train successors or tolerate competitors. Liebermann had tried to correct this deficiency but chose his disciples imprudently. Reventlow's early death and Schack's instability left only Lattmann, the least promising of the three above-average German Socials. Ironically, Ferdinand Werner, schooled in Böckel's Hessenland anti-Semitism, eventually gained control of Liebermann's party. The Christian Social party had been without a youth wing since the purge of the "Young Christian Socials" in 1896. Although Friedrich Naumann and Hellmut von Gerlach had originally objected to Stoecker's conservatism far more than to his anti-Semitism, they had gradually moved into the left-liberal camp in which there was no room for Jew baiting.[63] In the German Reform party the vacuum created by the death of Zimmermann remained unfilled.

By 1911, all three parties were in peril. Since the turn of the century, the Christian Socials had moved farther away from the German Socials and Reformers. Even after Stoecker's death, his party remained impervious to the kind of radicalization eating away at the conventional anti-Semites. Although the Christian Socials had rallied support for the Boers, Stoecker never indulged in attacks on the kaiser. During the *Daily Telegraph* affair crisis, the Christian Socials remained silent. The central problem of the party was, as always, its relationship to the Conservatives. Although nominally independent since 1896, the party—or the largest part of it—never took this separation seriously. Led by Stoecker, Party Secretary Burckhardt, and the editor of *Das Volk*, Oertzen, these Christian Socials maintained that only a slightly greater emphasis on social problems divided the two parties and that, otherwise, they shared vital common values.[64] For another, smaller group in the party, those involved in the Christian Trade Union movement launched in 1894, the matter was not so simple. They knew that continued reliance on the Conservatives for funds and sympathy meant continuing stagnation.

After Stoecker's retirement from active politics in 1907, the party displayed great uncertainty as to what course to follow. From 1909 to 1912, the new chairman, Franz Behrens (1872–1943), was able to steer the Christian Socials into closer cooperation with the Center party. Behrens and his allies wished to foster the growth of the interdenominational Christian trade unions. Intended as a defense against "godless Marxism," the Christian unions were predominantly Catholic. Only 70,000 of the 345,000 members were Protestant.[65] In spite of the numerical weakness of the Protestant unions, the Center party found them useful and therefore lent the Christian Socials valuable election support in 1907. However, to move closer to the Center, that is, to concentrate the energy of the Christian Social party on the trade union movement, meant jeopardizing the relationship with the Conservatives, who feared the extension of unionism to rural proletarians.[66]

Under Behrens' guidance, the Christian Socials seemed ready to embark on a new course. Had they carried through on it decisively, they might have freed themselves from the deadening grip of the Conservatives. But a general revision of the program of 1895, part of the new tack, revealed the same old ambiguities. In 1909, the party congress tabled a discussion of the Jewish question until the next year. The new program ultimately deleted the anti-Semitic phraseology of the "guiding principles" but, rather puzzlingly, retained the specific anti-Semitic demands of the 1895 statement.[67] A similar lack of decision appeared in the rest of the program. There were the traditional archconservative sentiments regarding throne and altar, public morality, and creeping materialism. Yet the new program also gave greater weight to social and economic reform and thus widened the gap between the Christian Socials and Conservatives. Such a program could scarcely be construed as a clean break with the Conservatives. Nor did the party appear fully ready to drop the anti-Semitism it had ignored for years in order to throw in with the Center.

What amounted to a partial reorientation of the Christian Social party underwent the acid test of national elections in 1912. Party candidates campaigning on the new program maintained complete silence on the Jewish question. With clear conscience, the Center party delivered unstinting support. Of the 101,887 votes cast for the Christian Socials, an estimated eighty percent came from obedient Center voters.[68] Still, the party failed to increase its Reichstag delegation beyond three deputies. These results, although an improvement over 1903 and 1907, were not convincing enough to guarantee the new orientation or still the objections of the pro-Conservative faction. Behrens resigned and was replaced by Pastor Philipps, a man repelled by the idea of cooperation with the "antinational" Catholics. Philipps apparently yearned to return the party to its traditional position as the powerless appendage of the Conservatives, a wish accomplished near the end of the war by the total disappearance of the Christian Socials into the Conservative party.

While the Christian Socials hovered between the Center and Conservative parties, the German Socials thrashed about helplessly. In October 1910, at the last party congress over which Liebermann presided, the desperation of his party surfaced despite a public show of equanimity. For the Reichstag elections due in January 1912,

Liebermann, as usual, advocated the closest possible cooperation with the parties of the right. This time he received active opposition to the traditional tactic. Ferdinand Werner objected to cooperation with the Agrarian League, which had never gained the trust of the Hessian peasants. Lattmann complained of the loss of 140 members in his district alone because of the German Socials' record on the financial reform.[69] The Conservatives and the league had dictated this policy, but the German Socials were suffering the consequences. In 1908, the Conservatives had abruptly demanded and collected Lattmann's Prussian parliament seat as payment for supporting him in the Reichstag election of 1907.[70] During Liebermann's last years, the Conservative party became increasingly hardhearted in its dealings with the German Socials. Fresh evidence of anti-Semitic unreliability, the resignation of Carl Böhme from the Economic Union in 1909, was the final straw. Elected in Marburg as a common candidate of the German Socials and Agrarian League, Böhme quickly accepted a position on the governing board of the liberally oriented German Peasant Alliance (founded in 1909). In 1911 he advocated electoral reform in Prussia and, citing Böckel as precedent, announced his intention of defending peasant interests against the Conservatives and Agrarians.[71] Acts of treachery such as this were not solely responsible for driving away the Conservatives. They had already begun to keep a safer distance since Liebermann's attacks on the kaiser. After his death, the German Socials and Reformers moved down a step on the social scale and began maligning the German nobility. Advertisements in their newspapers called attention to the *Semi-Gotha*, "genealogical handbook of the whole nobility of Judaic origin." A reader of the *Semi-Gotha* and similar publications learned that eight popes, numerous cardinals, Theodore Roosevelt, Jack Johnson, Leopold von Ranke, and several centuries' old Junker families sprang from Jewish blood.[72]

In the *Kreuzzeitung* obituary for Liebermann, the Conservatives seemed to be about to write off the German Socials. According to the paper, Liebermann, by force of character and by virtue of his "genuine German heart," had kept his party fairly respectable. Except for Schack, he had not attracted "adventurers and fortune-hunters" or the "morally impure," in the way the Reformers had so obviously done. The obituary hinted that, with the leader gone, the German

Socials would now take on the same objectionable characteristics as the Reformers and that both would soon vanish.[73] Judging from the new edition of the Conservative handbook for 1911, the party had changed its attitude on several significant issues since 1894. Conservatives still regarded Jewish influence on German life as essentially pernicious. As in 1894, the handbook again advocated assimilation of Jews by means of Jewish self-regulation. But until such assimilation became reality and in view of the danger from Socialists and atheists, the handbook acknowledged the need for retaining a "piece of anti-Semitism" as part of the Conservative outlook. The Conservative appraisal of the anti-Semitic parties was considerably more derogatory than in 1894. Parliamentary anti-Semitism as practiced by the German Socials and Reformers had done more harm than good, according to the manual. The specifically anti-Semitic parties had outlived their usefulness. By rowdyism, excess, and exaggerated agitation, they had inhibited the process of Jewish assimilation, had even promoted an unwanted Jewish solidarity. Instead of recommending support for the German Socials, as the handbook of 1894 had done, the new edition conspicuously ended its article on anti-Semitism without any suggestion of future assistance.[74]

Wilhelm Schack's Shop Clerks' union also deserted the anti-Semites. Hans Bechly, the new president, abstained from party politics in accord with the original intentions of the bylaws. A new generation, still interested in anti-Semitism but above "vulgar anti-Semitic politicking," had come forward. Almost seventy-five percent of the membership now consisted of white-collar workers whose concerns were predominantly occupational. The shop clerks stopped providing the German Socials with free printing of the *Antisemitische-Korrespondenz* and with personnel for election campaigning. The party tried to salvage its valuable connection to the association by electing Alfred Roth to its central committee. Roth, also a member of the shop clerks' governing board, had substantial anti-Semitic credentials, but, as one of several board members of the union, he did not enjoy nearly the same degree of influence as Schack once had. Moreover, Roth disapproved of the union's withdrawal from politics and ultimately broke with the organization.[75]

Although nominally a part of the German Social party, the Hessian

Peasant Alliance had long neglected its anti-Semitism in favor of the peasantry's economic interests. After Hirschel's imprisonment and Köhler's death, the "*völkisch*" character given the organization by Otto Böckel grew less noticeable. "*Völkisch* education" had more or less ceased in 1904 after the merger with the Agrarian League.[76] The Hessian organization made use of anti-Semitism sporadically— less in the state parliament than in Reichstag elections. Among Hessenland peasants, the commitment to finding a solution to the Jewish question had lost all force. Anti-Semitism was now an expedient, the use of which was becoming more and more circumscribed.

Liebermann's choice in 1900, the closest possible association with the Conservative party and Agrarian League, had not produced lasting improvement in the position of his party. At his death, it too was at the point of extinction. Membership had remained stationary at approximately ten thousand from 1905 until 1911.[77] This stagnation was all the more ominous when compared to the rejuvenation apparent among the National Liberals and left liberals. The left liberals, united again in one party, had once more begun putting forward Jewish candidates. In the Prussian parliament seven Jews sat for the liberal parties at Stoecker's death, and in 1912 the number rose yet higher.[78] After 1907 the sporadic and expedient nature of National Liberal opposition to anti-Semitism yielded to a more principled and constant fight against it. Pushed by the Young Liberal movement, the *Hansabund,* and the German Peasant Alliance, the party became more competitive in an era of growing political participation. The expansion of liberal clubs, the inclusion of peasants and *Mittelständler* on election committees, and a general intensification of activity made the National Liberals more attractive to groups which had been prone to parliamentary anti-Semitism. Although all these developments were resisted by powerful elements within the party, the National Liberals once again began nominating Jewish candidates in districts with good prospects of victory. From 1911, important National Liberals spoke out in parliament against the military's anti-Semitic policies.[79]

The German Socials, however, were too preoccupied with their own decline to deal with these signs of liberal revival. In 1910 the Hessian State Association of the party discussed the possibility of its complete collapse in the next Reichstag election. An ever-decreasing party membership pointed in this direction. In the Reichstag, German Social strength was slipping away; the delegation dropped from eight to five members. The party suffered setbacks in the other German parliaments as well. In 1909, the German Social-Conservative-Agrarian majority in the Grand Duchy of Weimar was shattered by a victory of the left. Schack's withdrawal meant the loss of the last German Social seat in the Hamburg municipal parliament; Raab and another German Social had already lost their places in 1904.[80]

The situation of the German Reformers looked gloomier than that of the German or Christian Socials. Even before Zimmermann's death in 1910, the Reformers could no longer compete with the German Socials. The defection of the Hessenland organization left the party without one of its strongest props. By 1906, the Reformers' diminished strength lay in Saxony and Brandenburg. The Saxon Reformers were reduced to a budget of fifteen thousand marks contributed by 3,750 members. In the Dresden municipal elections of 1908, the combined German Reformer-Saxon Conservative list of candidates lost control of the city government for the first time since the 1880's. The new elections for the Saxon parliament necessitated in 1909 by a revision of the franchise laws were disastrous for the Reformers. All seven lost in the first balloting.[81] The Brandenburg wing of the party, weaker to begin with, fared no better than the Saxons. At the last national congress of the party in 1908, the delegates under Zimmermann's direction voted Wilhelm Bruhn out of the central committee. But Bruhn was not so easily got rid of. After Zimmermann's death, he forced his way back into a leadership position. His very presence drove out two experienced Reformers, Bindewald and Gäbel.[82] Bruhn's erratic behavior emphasized the lack of central control in the German Reform party. As long as he possessed Arnswalde-Friedberg and controlled the Brandenburg organization, he was irreplaceable and irremovable. The party had grown so weak in numbers and in financial power that it simply lost control over its members. To get away from Bruhn, the Saxon branch elected its own president, held separate congresses, and thus put an end to the Reformers as a national party.

Not even the anti-Semites doubted that they were heading for a full-scale disaster in the 1912 elections. For the first time since 1890, the customary predictions of success did not appear in the struggling anti-Semitic newspapers. The history of the past few years gave no grounds for optimism. Of the nineteen by-elections contested by the parties between 1908 and 1911, only one had resulted in success. Furthermore, the political alignments governing the 1912 elections were unfavorable for the anti-Semites. Election agreements between the National Liberals, left liberals, and Social Democrats, aimed primarily against the Centrists and Conservatives, severely limited the chances of the anti-Semites. Although the complex election alliances worked less smoothly than anticipated, the anti-Semitic candidates were unable to exploit the fear of the left. Even in the second balloting, they received almost no liberal votes. The Social Democrats conquered 110 seats, an overwhelming victory after the setback of 1907. The National Liberals and left liberals, while increasing their vote total, lost seventeen seats between them. The blow to the right was far more serious. The Conservatives forfeited seventeen mandates; the already small *Reichspartei* lost ten additional seats, the German Reformers and German Socials, eight.[83]

The Reformers mustered enough resources to contest only nine districts, winning three of them in close runoff battles. They retained one deputy in each of the former areas of strength, Ludwig Werner in Hessenland, Bruhn in Brandenburg, and Gräfe in the Kingdom of Saxony. The whole party drew 51,928 votes, or 0.4 percent of the total. The German Socials also managed to produce three winners, Ferdinand Werner, Johann Rupp, and Richard Herzog. Three veterans, Lattmann, Raab, and Bindewald, performed miserably, losing on the first ballot. The seventeen German Social candidates received 78,923 votes, or 0.6 percent of the total.[84] The following table measures the electoral decline of the anti-Semites in the traditional areas of strength.[85]

	1893			*1903*			*1912*		
	Con-tests	*Votes*	%	*Con-tests*	*Votes*	%	*Con-tests*	*Votes*	%
Brandenburg (and Berlin)	16	37,084	5.4	5	28,798	3.2	4	9,548	0.7
Prussian Hesse	12	32,678	15.2	9	40,083	13.0	6	42,027	9.7
Gr.D. of Hesse and Waldeck	10	26,309	13.8	4	15,434	7.6	2	15,598	5.9
Kingdom of Saxony	11	93,364	15.5	7	73,656	9.8	3	37,160	4.0

Returns from Schleswig-Holstein, West Prussia, and the Province of Saxony, areas in which the anti-Semitic parties had once shown promise, stayed well below the one percent level. Hanover, Württemberg, the Rhineland, Alsace-Lorraine, and Posen fell into the same category as Baden and Bavaria—out of bounds for the anti-Semitic parties. Thus, thirty years of hectic activity produced a total of 130,841 German voters who, perhaps, wished to legislate Jews out of German life in 1912. Instead of acting as the vanguard of a mass movement, the German Socials and Reformers had become impotent fragments without political significance or future.

In the last imperial Reichstag, five of the six anti-Semites allowed themselves to be counted with the Conservatives.[86] On 22 March 1914, "the marriage of the lame and the halt," the reunification of the Reformers and Socials took place after protracted negotiations. Wilhelm Lattmann and Ferdinand Werner wrestled for leadership of the new *Deutschvölkische Partei,* which became the last refuge of those who would not or could not renounce parliamentary politics. Unlike the unification of 1894, the creation of a new party of anti-Semites made no impact on friend or foe. During the war, the six anti-Semites joined the *Deutsche Fraktion,* exponents of annexation and a "peace of victory."[87] In 1918, anticipating the elections for the National Assembly, the anti-Semites realized that their brand of parliamentary anti-Semitism could no longer win elections. On 15 December 1918, the party gave up its independent identity and joined the successor to the Conservatives, the German National People's party, in which it played a role of slight importance.[88]

Conclusion: The Aftermath

> It is unthinkable that either in Europe or America anti-Semitism could ever bring about legal disabilities for Jews. Any such legislation would be a direct break with the political tradition of the nineteenth century, and no state could well take such a step. . . . Jews, as a race, are beyond the reach of legislation.
>
> Arthur Ruppin (1913)

The organized defenders against anti-Semitism rejoiced in the 1912 election defeat of their enemies. But, while conceding that the anti-Semitic parties were as good as dead, neither the *Abwehr-Verein* nor the *Centralverein* overestimated the victory. Leaders of both organizations focused their attention more than ever on the German Conservative party, claiming that the Conservatives and their Agrarian allies were and would remain the major vehicles of political anti-Semitism. Ludwig Holländer, eventually the last director of the *Centralverein*, carefully analyzed the victory of 1912 and warned that anti-Semitism was still a tool by which declining political parties could "put new wind in their sails." Thus, the welcome election statistics did not signal the end of the struggle. The *Centralverein* still had work to do, even though the independent anti-Semitic parties had been ruined.[1]

Immediately after the elections of 1912, the defense organizations had good cause to be concerned about a revival of anti-Semitism in national politics. The outcome of the elections, in which the Center and Conservative parties faced coalitions of liberals and Socialists, provoked an anti-Semitic reflex reaction. Martin Spahn, son of the Center party leader, Peter Spahn, wrote a bitter article for the Catholic journal, *Hochland,* complaining of Jewish proclivities toward radicalism and socialism, demonstrated so ominously in the recent campaign. The response of the Conservatives to Socialist gains and their own considerable losses was more petulant than that of the Center. The *Kreuzzeitung* spoke of the "Jew elections" and attacked the "incursion of Jewish capital" into politics. Furthermore, the Conservative press identified the two meddling defense organizations, the liberal parties, the *Hansabund,* and the Social Democrats as blatant examples of "Judah's money power." Soon after the election, Baron Conrad von Wangenheim, influential member of both the Conservative party and Agrarian League, predicted a rebirth of "purified anti-Semitism."[2]

Despite these omens, the expected revival of "demagogic" anti-Semitism did not occur. The Center's bout of bad temper passed and the party returned to the anti-anti-Semitic principles of Windthorst and Lieber. Public expressions of wrath by the Conservatives also ceased quickly. From their point of view, the parliamentary anti-Semites had outlived their usefulness years ago. Of this there could no longer be any doubt. But by the spring of 1913, the Conservative party seemed about to go further, renouncing, at least temporarily, the utilization of anti-Semitism per se for the achievement of political goals. After the sting of election losses had subsided, delegates to the 1913 party congress refrained from discussing the Jewish question at all, a notable departure from precedent. A more telling indication of the new tactic was the directive issued to the staff of the *Kreuzzeitung* by the general secretary of the party, Bruno Schröter. In the name of the newspaper's supervisory board, Schröter instructed reporters and editors to curb their anti-Semitism, the tone and principles of which were "better left to other papers." Unable to desist wholly from its Jew baiting, the *Kreuzzeitung* occasionally reprinted anti-Semitic articles from the newspapers of the Agrarian League.[3] In general, however, the paper followed the directive. The anti-Semitism of the Conservative party had never owed much to principle. Its rejection was similarly based on an objective view of the usefulness of anti-Semitism for the purposes of the party. Thus, in the elections for the Prussian state parliament of 1913, the Conservatives did not employ the customary anti-Semitic arguments or slogans because these had become inopportune. No single fact provides such convincing evidence of the failure of parliamentary anti-Semitism in the empire as the behavior of the opportunistic Conservatives in 1913.[4]

The primary responsibility for this failure rested with the parliamentary anti-Semites themselves. Although some of their problems seemed beyond human control, most were, in fact, the result of rigid attitudes and misconceived policies. The lack of financial resources, a popular explanation of failure cited by the anti-Semites, is just such an apparent cause of the defeat. It is true that neither the German Socials nor Reformers possessed a fraction of the financial resources available to their rivals. In the national elections of 1912, they contested fewer districts than other parties. While their enemies distributed well over one hundred million polemical pamphlets, brochures and calendars, the anti-Semites had to make do with two million of Theodor Fritsch's tracts, which bore slight relevance to the programs of either party.[5] But the leaders of the German Social Reform party had once been in a position to remedy the problem of finances, at least partially, by improving the yield and collection of membership dues. They had preferred to let matters slide rather than risk disturbing vested interests. Moreover, Otto Böckel had once shown that an anti-Semitic party did not necessarily need great resources in order to accomplish a great deal. He made up for the lack of money with daring and imagination. The convenient excuse of insufficient funds was not the main reason the anti-Semites fell behind their competitors.

The main cause of their enfeeblement was the inability to progress beyond the Böckel era. In the 1880's and 1890's, the anti-Semitic parties had begun as innovators, using the mass meeting, local organization, and extensive personal contact to rouse the politically apathetic and neglected. The anti-Semitic parties managed to hold onto a sizeable fraction of these "new voters" until 1898. But, having pointed the way, they were soon left behind as the older and larger parties implemented the new techniques far more effectively.[6] Instead of responding to this competition with imaginative new techniques, the anti-Semites stayed rooted to their old ways. Notwithstanding the severity of the 1912 election defeat, those remaining in the parties were unconvinced of the need for radically new departures. The German Socials merely brought out a slightly revised program in 1913, which repeated the same demands made in the Anti-Semites' Petition of 1880. Oswald Zimmermann's successor as chairman of the Saxon Reform party proposed the familiar cures for anti-Semitic ills: a program revision, creation of a strong press, and strengthening of the most anti-Semitic classes in German society by legislative means.[7] By 1912, the anti-Semites had, beyond all reasonable doubt, exhausted the potential of the old measures and methods.

Contrary to the often stated but never proven view, the steady decline of the anti-Semitic parties and their total lack of success in enacting anti-Jewish legislation were not inevitable in the German Empire.[8] A prohibition of Jewish immigration from the East or a *numerus clausus* in the professions might have been achieved if the anti-Semites had been able to enlist the help of the German right. Liebermann von Sonnenberg was the only leading anti-Semite who had shown an awareness of how important the right was to anti-Semitic plans. But his attempt after 1898 to ally the German Social Reformers with stronger right-wing groups was both half-hearted and one-sided. He demanded no commitment to the specific goals of the anti-Semites from would-be allies and thus failed to assuage the fears of most of his party comrades regarding cynical exploitation of their cause. Far from revitalizing parliamentary anti-Semitism, Liebermann's strategy resulted in schism, loss of independence, and revolt from out of the ranks of anti-Semitic voters. This inability to win the German right to the cause of "sincere" anti-Semitism was the anti-Semites' most serious failing. Converting these "natural allies" from "demagogic" into "sincere" anti-Semites, in order to counteract the forces of resistance and the competition of rival political parties, should have been the first priority for the parliamentary anti-Semites. It was, instead, a job which they never undertook in any systematic way.

By 1914, the anti-Semites had not succeeded in creating the proper climate for their cause. They alone felt anti-Semitism to be the most burning issue of the day. Tied to a single issue, the anti-Semitic parties suffered under severe handicaps. Even when they won sympathy for their main cause from diverse socioeconomic groups, this was soon alienated by their handling of practical political questions. On issues devoid of anti-Semitism, the anti-Semitic parties had no inherent position, showed no unity, and followed a willy-nilly course. They were too ineffective in the art of politics to expand their support beyond a segment of the peasantry and *Mittelstand*. With the recovery and growth of the German economy during the mid-1890's, the problem became not one of expansion, but of survival. The parties had prospered in adversity. Economic well-being did them no good at all.

The number of anti-Semitic party members and voters, the size of

Reichstag delegations, the enactment of anti-Jewish legislation, and
the winning of powerful allies—these direct indicators of political
strength should not be the only criteria for judging the success or
failure of parliamentary anti-Semitism. Indirect influence on political
life ought also to be considered. For example, how much impact did
anti-Semitic agitation have on the sharp decrease of liberal Jewish
Reichstag deputies or the purge of Jews from civil and military
service? While several historians attribute these "achievements," at
least in part, to the anti-Semites, the anti-Semites themselves were
uncharacteristically modest in their own claims.[9] They found little to
boast about in the Reichstag of 1912–1918 with its seven professing
Jews. Anti-Semites, it must be remembered, insisted upon "racial"
definitions and had therefore to count four converts and seven dissidents, which raised the total to eighteen "Jewish" deputies, twice
as many as in the heyday of Lasker and Bamberger. Even the twenty
year absence of National and left-liberal deputies of Jewish faith, a
source of pride to anti-Semites, had come to an end in 1912. Both
liberal parties had begun running Jewish candidates again, either in
spite of anti-Semitic voters or, as I believe, because anti-Semitic
sentiments had declined in importance.[10] The Prussian parliament
election of 1913 presented a yet darker picture of failure, with thirteen
Jews sitting for the liberal parties and two for the Socialists. Similarly,
the civil services of the German states and the Reich, when measured
"racially," could not but disturb true anti-Semites. From their point
of view, the purge of Jews from public service had been carried out
for the wrong motives and with regrettable lack of thoroughness. In
light of these retrogressions, the anti-Semites could not even pride
themselves with having alerted the German government or German
people to the Jewish peril. Nearly thirty years of passionate political
activity resulted in abject failure, at least according to the parliamentary anti-Semites' own terms.

In terms of later generations, however, the matter of anti-Semitic
failure is not so certain. Did the anti-Semitic parties of the empire
really fail, or did they, as many have assumed, lead the way to Nazi
"success?" Did Otto Böckel and Liebermann von Sonnenberg in
some sense make a lasting contribution to the attempted annihilation
of European Jews? Measuring the long term effects of conventional
anti-Semitism on German-Jewish relations admits of no precision.

Whether by 1914 the parliamentary anti-Semites had succeeded in increasing anti-Jewish feeling in Germany is equally a matter for conjecture. A few things are certain, however. The conventional anti-Semites pounded away at the Jews, disseminating the Jewish stereotype in press and pamphlet. It is reasonable to assume that such incessant propaganda helped poison German-Jewish relations and promoted an atmosphere of ready tolerance for anti-Semitism which the National Socialists were able to use effectively. Yet the parliamentary anti-Semites had neither invented the Jewish stereotype nor created the animosity against Jews. Moreover, by the turn of the century, they were no longer the main propagators of Jew hatred. The publications of the Agrarian League and Theodor Fritsch reached a far greater audience than the crippled vehicles of the anti-Semitic parties.[11] True, *völkisch* thought and the "science of racism" had become more popular, filtering out from small groups of intellectuals into the many youth organizations of the middle class and the newspapers of powerful pressure groups. But the meager theoretical writings of the conventional anti-Semites had had next to nothing to do with this development. Their underemphasis of ideology and boring political maneuvers had alienated both young and old enthusiasts.

From a position of supreme importance in the development of political anti-Semitism the anti-Semitic parties had declined into virtual insignificance. Their defeat did not, however, mean the disappearance of German anti-Semitism in general. On the eve of the war, anti-Jewish sentiment was widespread in German life, although not as overtly a part of national politics as it had been in the 1870's or 1890's. The groups in German society most likely to politicize their anti-Semitism were still the *Mittelstand* and elements of the German right. During the 1890's the progress of the anti-Semitic movement had compelled the attention of right-wing political parties, several professional and propagandistic associations, civil and military bureaucracies, and the organizations of heavy industry and academic youth. Even as the parties declined, these elements of the German right continued to harbor and cultivate anti-Semitism out of a variety of essentially economic motives. To the parliamentary anti-Semites this was "demagogic." But these powerful rightists objected only to the forms developed by the anti-Semitic parties, not their anti-

Semitic content. Under the right conditions and with the right leadership, the deadly political potential of this "demagogic" anti-Semitism was enormous.

Ironically, the manifold failures of the parliamentary anti-Semites of the imperial era helped a more broadly and powerfully based anti-Semitism come into existence. The disintegration of the anti-Semitic parties cleared the way for the reemergence of a man who had never lost sight of ultimate goals. Theodor Fritsch's day had finally dawned. Once and for all, the 1912 Reichstag elections substantiated what he had fanatically preached for decades: political parties and parliamentary methods could achieve nothing against Jews. For this reason he had fought the politicalization of the German Anti-Semitic Alliance in 1886, opposed Böckel, and left the German Social party. As he had feared, premature involvement in party politics squandered the first opportunity and diverted the energies of the anti-Semites along false paths. In 1912, Fritsch stood ready to pick up the pieces left by the anti-Semitic parties. Anti-Semitism reorganized, not in a "party-political sense, but in a much more practical and effective way, would reach all levels of the population without crossing over (old) party boundaries." For the task of reorganization Fritsch had already created the necessary cadre, the subscribers to his journal, *Hammer-Blätter für deutschen Sinn* (1901, Hammer Papers for the German Way). In 1912 the *Hammer* readers, already meeting in local discussion groups for several years, were united by Fritsch into the *Reichshammerbund.* This select band studied his ideas about revolution, the abolition of the Reichstag, the removal of the kaiser, and the need for strong powers in the hands of a "leader, a constitutional dictator." Following the "Jew elections" of 1912, the *Hammer* became more menacing. Fritsch began preparing the *Reichshammerbund* for action. Its task would be to kill the revolutionaries (Jews and Socialists) at the very start of the leftist revolution he expected momentarily. From its ranks would be chosen the holy *Fehme,* a band of vigilantes who were to deal out swift justice to the revolutionary criminals and thus save Germany from chaos.[12]

Fritsch was still talking to *Mittelständler* who were too weak to change things by themselves. "Daniel Frymann"—in reality, Heinrich Class of the Pan-German League—addressed a similar set of revolutionary and anti-Semitic ideas to the most powerful sectors

of German society in his brutal *If I Were Kaiser* (1912). All the book's
demands regarding Jews had been voiced earlier by the anti-Semitic
parties.[13] But Class struck a new and ruthless tone in the name of
"objectivity." His anti-Semitic "reforms" were an important part of
the total program of the *Kaiserbuch,* although still only one of many
indispensable changes to be made in Germany's foreign and domestic
policies. Angered by the whole course of German development since
Bismarck's fall, Class espoused a frankly pan-German, imperialist
policy. To this he tied drastically reactionary plans for domestic
enemies—Jews, Socialists, and liberals. The Reichstag, elected by
Jewish capital and grown unrepresentative of the educated and
propertied elite, had to be brought to heel. This *Reichsreform* could be
accomplished either by a coup d'état or a successful war, certainly
not by parliamentary politics or, in all likelihood, by the kaiser's
timid government.[14]

Before the war, the closely related thoughts of Fritsch and Class
were reflected in new radical groups. The masonically organized
Germanen-Orden and the *Verband gegen Überhebung des Judentums* (Association against the Arrogance of Jewry) attracted men whose
primary allegiance had never been with the anti-Semitic parties.
Their methods, views, and intentions were far from conventional.
Whether they represented "a new *völkisch* phase of anti-Semitism"[15]
or merely the reappearance of the always present revolutionary
element of imperial anti-Semitism in a new situation is a moot
question. By 1914 there no longer existed a conventional, parliamentary brand of anti-Semitism that could withstand the appeal of
the revolutionaries. The failure of the anti-Semitic parties left the
field open to Fritsch, Class, and their friends.

However brilliant the future for this kind of anti-Semitism, the
revolutionaries did not thrive prior to the war. The *Mittelständler*
remained isolated in tiny groups of disaffected intellectuals. The
Reichshammerbund, for example, had perhaps one thousand members
at the outbreak of the war.[16] In the spring of 1913, the steadfast
Fritsch sounded the same somber tones of retreat from an inhospitable Germany as had Bernhard Förster thirty years before:

> If we lack the power to undertake a great cleansing of the air in
> the Reich as a whole or to fill the whole environment with a new

spirit, ought we not still try to secure for ourselves a physically and spiritually pure atmosphere on a sheltered piece of land far from the great thoroughfares of the vulgar?

But Fritsch's "Cooperative Settlement Homeland," like Förster's *Neu-Germanien* before it, proved a flop, unable to lure the saving remnant of Germandom from its hostile surroundings.[17]

The reaction to Class's *Kaiserbuch* was certainly more enthusiastic than to any of Fritsch's schemes. Twenty-five thousand copies of the book were in circulation by the spring of 1914, and all the important organs of right-wing opinion discussed it at length. Various segments of the right approved heartily either the author's domestic or foreign program or both. But there was also much objection to the anti-Semitic portion of the *Reichsreform*. The German Conservatives, *Reichspartei, Verein Deutscher Studenten,* and big businessmen regarded these demands as unrealistic, immoderate, impossible, and something out of a fairytale.[18] Few right-wing critics found it theoretically abhorrent to degrade and disenfranchise Jews, who played too large a role in the press, cultural life, and, as of 1912, in parliamentary politics. Yet in the last peaceful years of the *Kaiserreich,* only the Agrarian League, which made a fetish out of its lack of respectability, used political anti-Semitism unstintingly. For others on the right, anti-Semitism was still neither respectable nor important enough to adopt wholeheartedly and openly as a political weapon. Leaders of the *Ostmarkverein,* the Reich League against Social Democracy, and Class's own Pan-German League, men who considered themselves anti-Semites, nonetheless hesitated to take their associations into overt anti-Semitic politics. To do so, they felt, would have meant the end of their effectiveness as national organizations.[19] This reluctance is not really surprising. In 1914 the German right, despite all its grumbling, still had many ways of defending vital interests—a government at its beck and call, a reliable military force to keep the "social peace," or even the possibility of a short, successful war with conquests enough to buy off all those demanding democratic change. By 1918 all these options had disappeared in war and revolution. Much of the German right thereupon lent itself, with some hesitation, to a violent anti-Semitic mass movement.[20]

Even without the war, the tensions present in German society which made the right receptive to anti-Semitism were likely to remain and intensify. Aware of this, the defense organizations were properly cautious in interpreting the 1912 election defeat of conventional anti-Semitism. However, they misinterpreted the revolutionary anti-Semitism of Fritsch not from overconfidence, but rather from a lack of comprehension. Fritsch's conspiracy was an open secret. His freely available writings evidenced willingness to do violence to Jews and the law of the land. Yet his plans seemed too bizarre to take seriously. The usually observant defense groups paid him little attention, merely reprinting an outrageous antiparliamentary or antimonarchical tirade from the *Hammer*. The *Centralverein* and *Abwehr-Verein* continued to devote the greater part of their energies to the "normal" political manifestations of anti-Semitism. They feared the effects of state discrimination toward Jews, and they feared the by now remote possibility that parliamentary anti-Semites and their allies might win over the uneducated masses. But revolutionary anti-Semites like Fritsch had necessarily to make their appeal to the educated minority, a few solitary intellectuals who seemed to pose no immediate threat.

The liberal opponents of anti-Semitism failed to see the significant difference between Fritsch and Liebermann von Sonnenberg. True, the gap between revolutionary and conventional anti-Semite had narrowed considerably over the years. Yet the differences between the two types were still apparent in 1912. The techniques developed by the defense organizations were at least partially effective against the conventional, parliamentary anti-Semite because he shared most of his values of his contemporaries. He was embarrassed by scandal. He yearned for respectability and wanted to be thought of as progressive. Most of all, he respected the institutions of the Reich, although that respect had steadily deteriorated because of his failure to make them work against Jews. But Fritsch and the Nazis rejected the validity of the institutions surrounding them. They were truly revolutionary. Censure in the Reichstag, appearances in court, the ridicule of respectable opinion left them unabashed because they utterly rejected the "decadent" state and society which used these devices for the promotion of Jewish conquest. The Nazis refused to abide by the rules that the general climate of opinion had forced upon the conventional anti-Semites of the *Kaiserreich*. Against the

Nazis, therefore, the defense organizations that continued to fight bravely in the Weimar Republic remained ineffectual and, in fact, became largely counterproductive.

The defeat of parliamentary anti-Semitism in the 1912 elections thus possessed a shadowy side. Although convinced that the battle was not yet wholly won, the defense organizations were certain that their methods for combating anti-Semitism had received ultimate vindication. During the Weimar Republic, a few leaders of the *Centralverein* recognized the need for new techniques. Yet their single deviation from tried and true measures had to be carried out secretly, to fend off bad publicity and condemnation from the group's own members.[21] The *Abwehr-Verein* remained even more settled in tradition because the difference between revolutionary and conventional anti-Semite wholly eluded both leaders and led. On the fortieth anniversary of the *Verein* in 1931, the enemies still appeared much the same as they had in the days of the empire:

> . . . there is an interesting parallel to the present. The German Conservative party and the specifically anti-Semitic parties which arose in those days are the exact analogues to what we see before us in the German National People's party and diverse *völkisch* parties, including the National Socialists. . . .

> After the German collapse [of 1918] the movement began anew from the point where it started forty years ago. The only difference being that the German Conservative party became the German National People's party; the anti-Semitic parties also loved to hang out new shingles. In general, nothing had changed at all. . . . The intellectual basis and the methods of implementation are today the same as those of thirty or forty years ago.[22]

Indeed, in the 1920's, the German National People's party—with a good deal more middle-class, non-Junker character—made the same cynical and opportunistic use of anti-Semitism as had the old Conservative party. In 1931, except for an emphasis on "Jewish sexuality" and greater use of the *Protocols of the Elders of Zion,* the content of Nazi anti-Semitism differed little from that of the old German Social party. And, in the early years, Nazi legislative proposals were also strikingly similar.[23] But the liberal defense organizations did not look beneath these superficial similarities. The spirit and the methods of agitation had become revolutionary, even murderous. The Nazis refused to be intimidated or put on the defensive by the "tried and true" measures of the past.

Thus, in a limited and indirect way, the conventional anti-Semites made their contribution to the destruction of European Jewish life attempted in the Third Reich. The defeat of the parliamentary anti-Semites in the imperial era inspired an unmerited confidence in the opponents of anti-Semitism during the Weimar Republic. Also, by exhausting the possibilities of, and thus discrediting, conventional anti-Semitism, the anti-Semitic parties of the empire cleared the way for the revolutionary brand practiced by the Nazis. It is significant in this respect that few latter-day anti-Semites found much to praise in the efforts of earlier anti-Semitic politicians. Böckel was lauded for awakening the "race consciousness" of the Hessian peasants, but his parliamentary activity is scarcely mentioned in Nazi histories. Stoecker and Liebermann, too, earned the grudging gratitude of the Nazis as "brave men." Their practical anti-Semitism, on the other hand, was scorned as hopelessly primitive and misguided, possibly doing more harm than good.[24]

Of all the revolutionary or conventional anti-Semites active in the German Empire, the Nazis most admired Theodor Fritsch, one of the very few "old fighters" to become an influential Nazi. His idea of the proper way to solve the Jewish question corresponded to their own.[25] Fritsch provided them with a living link to past errors, and, unlike them, he had directly experienced the shortcomings of conventional, parliamentary anti-Semitism. He, better than anyone else, knew that the road traveled by Liebermann and Böckel led not to the "Final Solution" but to a dead end.

Abbreviations

Abbreviations of frequently cited sources:

AJB   *Antisemitisches Jahrbuch* (Berlin)

AK   *Antisemitische-Korrespondenz* (Leipzig and Hamburg)

BYB   *Year Book of the Leo Baeck Institute of Jews from Germany* (London)

IDR   *Im Deutschen Reich* (Berlin)

MVA   *Mitteilungen aus dem Verein zur Abwehr des Antisemitismus* (Berlin)

RH   *Reichsherold* (Marburg and Berlin)

ZDSJ   *Zeitschrift für Demographie und Statistik der Juden* (Berlin)

Abbreviations of parliamentary proceedings:

VBLt   *Verhandlungen der Kammer der Abgeordneten des bayerischen Landtages im Jahre. . . .*

VHLt   *Verhandlungen der zweiten Kammer der Landstände des Grossherzogtums Hessen in den Jahren. . . .*

VPrLt   *Stenographische Berichte über die Verhandlungen des preussischen Abgeordnetenhauses in der Session. . . .*

VRt   *Stenographische Berichte über die Verhandlungen des Reichstages*

VSLt   *Mitteilungen über die Verhandlungen des ordentlichen Landtags im Königreiche Sachsen (Zweite Kammer)*

Notes

Chapter 1. Setting the Pattern

1. The most extensively used was Johann Andreas Eisenmenger, *Entdecktes Judentum, oder gründlicher und wahrhafter Bericht, welchergestalt die verstockten Juden die Hochheilige Dreieinigkeit, Gott Vater, Sohn, und Heiligen Geist, erschrecklicher Weise lästern und verunehren* (Königsberg, 1711). Also, two plagiarisms of Eisenmenger by August Rohling, *Der Talmudjude,* 6th ed. (Münster, 1877); and Elias Liborius Roblik, *Jüdische Augen-Gläser* (Brünn and Königgrätz, 1741–1743).

2. See Hartwig Hundt von Radowsky, *Judenspiegel. Ein Schand- und Sittengemälde alter und neuer Zeit* (Reutlingen, 1821). Also, his *Die Judenschule, oder gründliche Anleitung, in kurzer Zeit ein vollkommener schwarzer oder weisser Jude zu werden* (1822). For a discussion of related literature, see Eleonore Sterling, *Er ist wie du. Aus der Frühgeschichte des Antisemitismus in Deutschland, 1815–1850* (Munich, 1956). Also, Klaus Epstein, *The Genesis of German Conservatism* (Princeton, 1966), pp. 223–29.

3. For example, see the list of improvements suggested by C. L. Paalzow in H. D. Schmidt, "The Terms of Emancipation 1781–1812," *BYB* 1 (1956): 28–47. Also, Kurt Stillschweig, "Jewish Assimilation as an Object of Legislation," *Historia Judaica* 8 (1946): 8–12.

4. On the general problem of emancipation, see Reinhard Rürup, "Judenemanzipation und bürgerliche Gesellschaft in Deutschland," in Ernst Schulin, ed., *Gedenkschrift Martin Göhring* (Wiesbaden, 1968), pp. 174–99; Jacob Katz, *Out of the Ghetto. The Social Background of Jewish Emancipation, 1770–1870* (Cambridge, Mass., 1973).

5. See Ismar Elbogen, *Geschichte der Juden in Deutschland* (Berlin, 1935), pp. 262–64. Also, Stillschweig, "Jewish Assimilation," p. 9.

6. *Geschichte der Frankfurter Zeitung* (Frankfurt a. M., 1911), p. 51. Jacob Toury, *Die politischen Orientierungen der Juden in Deutschland. Von Jena bis Weimar* (Tübingen, 1966), p. 11.

7. Raabe's *Hungerpastor* (1864) and Freytag's *Soll und Haben* (1855) are discussed in Ernest K. Bramsted, *Aristocracy and the Middle Classes in Germany* (Chicago, 1964), pp. 132–209. See also George L. Mosse, "The Image of the Jew in German Popular Culture: Felix Dahn and Gustav Freytag," *BYB* 2 (1957): 218–27.

8. See Sterling, *Er ist wie du,* pp. 35, 132ff., 147–48.

9. Hans Rosenberg, *Grosse Depression und Bismarckzeit* (Berlin, 1967), pp. 51–117, probes the psychological effects of the crash of 1873.

10. See E. Kahn, "The Frankfurter Zeitung," *BYB* 2 (1957): 223–35.

11. See Hans Martin Klinkenberg, "Zwischen Liberalismus und Nationalismus im Zweiten Kaiserreich (1870–1918)," in *Monumenta Judaica. Beiträge zu einer*

Geschichte der Juden in Deutschland, 2nd ed. (Cologne, 1964), p. 314. Also, Raphael Strauss, *Die Juden in Wirtschaft und Gesellschaft* (Frankfurt a. M., 1964), p. 111.

12. Ernest Hamburger, *Die Juden im öffentlichen Leben Deutschlands. Regierungsmitglieder, Beamten und Parlamentarier in der monarchischen Zeit 1848–1918* (Tübingen, 1968), pp. 29–30.

13. Estimate from Toury, *Die politischen Orientierungen,* pp. 110–15.

14. On the spate of new companies, see Max Wirth, *Geschichte der Handelskrisen,* 2nd ed. (Frankfurt a. M., 1874), pp. 454, 551–52.

15. See VRt 27 (4 April 1873): 213–14.

16. See Kurt Wawrzinek, *Die Entstehung der deutschen Antisemitenparteien, 1873–1890* (Berlin, 1927), p. 9; Karl Buchheim, *Geschichte der christlichen Parteien in Deutschland* (Munich, 1953), p. 236.

17. See "Die Aera Bleichröder-Delbrück-Camphausen und die neudeutsche Wirtschaftspolitik," in the *Neue Preussische Zeitung (Kreuzzeitung),* 29 June–3 July 1875. For other anti-Semitic attacks on Bismarck, see Joachim Gehlsen, *Aus dem Reiche Bismarcks* (Berlin, 1894); Rudolf Meyer, *Politische Gründer und die Korruption in Deutschland* (Leipzig, 1877). On the 1870's in general, see Paul W. Massing, *Rehearsal for Destruction. A Study of Political Anti-Semitism in Imperial Germany* (New York, 1949), pp. 3–47.

18. See the obituary for Glagau by his disciple, Otto Böckel, in *RH,* 15 March 1892.

19. Otto Glagau, *Der Börsen- und Gründungsschwindel in Berlin* (Leipzig, 1876), pp. xxx–xxxi.

20. See Hans Schulz, *Deutsches Fremdwörterbuch* (Strassburg, 1913). Also, M. E. Aristide Astruc, *Origines et causes historiques de l'antisémitisme* (Versailles, 1884), pp. 6–7.

21. Wilhelm Marr, *Der Sieg des Judenthums über das Germanenthum. Vom nicht confessionellen Standpunkt aus betrachtet* (Bern, 1879), Foreword, pp. 39–42. The first edition of Marr's pamphlet appeared in 1879, not 1873, as most secondary sources maintain.

22. See Magdalene Zimmermann, *Die Gartenlaube als Dokument ihrer Zeit* (Munich, 1963), p. 11.

23. While I have found racist terminology widespread in the anti-Semitic literature of the 1870's, "racial thinking" was not as rigorously exclusive as it later became. Wilhelm Marr, for example, admitted "rare exceptions in the past eighteen hundred years" in which Jews had genuinely assimilated to Germandom. See his *Der Sieg des Judenthums,* pp. 21, 23, 49.

24. See de Gobineau, *Essai sur l'Inégalité des Races Humaines* (Paris, 1853–1855). Richard Wagner, *Das Judentum in der Musik* (Leipzig, 1869). For the influence of Wagner's Bayreuth festivals on the dissemination of Gobineau's ideas and as a meeting place for the later parliamentary anti-Semites, see Ludwig Schemann, *Lebensfahrten eines Deutschen* (Leipzig, 1925), pp. 71–78, 94; his *Fünfundzwanzig Jahre Gobineau Vereinigung* (Strassburg, 1919). Also, Winfried Schüler, *Der Bayreuther Kreis von seiner Entstehung bis zum Ausgang der wilhelminischen Ära. Wagnerkult und Kulturreform im Geiste völkischer Weltanschauung* (Münster, 1971), pp. 246–52.

25. On the application of Darwinism to social problems, see Hans Günter Zmarzlik, "Der Sozialdarwinismus in Deutschland als geschichtliches Problem," *Vierteljahrsheft für Zeitgeschichte* 11 (1963): 246–73; and Fritz Stern, *The Politics of Cultural Despair* (New York, 1965), pp. 344ff.

26. *Die Deutsche Wacht: Monatsschrift für nationale Entwicklung* (Berlin, 1880), pp. 4, 59–70. Marr edited the periodical from November 1879 to March 1880. See also, his *Wählet Keinen Juden! Der Weg zum Siege des Germanentums über das Judentum* (Berlin, 1879).

27. Hellmut von Gerlach, *Von Rechts nach Links* (Zurich, 1937), p. 102. See also Friedrich Naumann, "Was wir Stoecker verdanken," in *Werke* (Cologne, 1964), 5: 191–98. On his early years, Karl Kupisch, *Adolf Stoecker. Hofprediger und Volkstribun* (Berlin, 1970).

28. See Wanda Kampmann, "Adolf Stoecker und die Berliner Bewegung," *Geschichte in Wissenschaft und Unterricht* 13 (1962): 558–79. Also, Siegfried Kaehler, "Stoecker's Versuch, eine christlich-soziale Arbeiterpartei in Berlin zu begründen (1878)," in Paul Wentzcke, ed., *Deutscher Staat und deutsche Parteien* (Munich and Berlin, 1922), pp. 227–65.

29. See Franz Mehring, *Geschichte der deutschen Sozialdemokratie* (Berlin, 1960), 2: 486–91; Wawrzinek, *Antisemitenparteien*, p. 22 n. 16.

30. See a comparison of attendance figures for speeches on the Jewish question and those on other topics in Walter Frank, *Hofprediger Adolf Stoecker und die christlich-soziale Bewegung*, 2nd ed. (Hamburg, 1935), pp. 20–21, 126.

31. The peasantry and *Mittelstand* will be kept distinct in this study as they were by the anti-Semitic parties. For the best discussion of the problem of the *Mittelstand*, see Herman Lebovics, *Social Conservatism and the Middle Classes in Germany, 1914–1933* (Princeton, 1969), pp. 3–12. Also, Heinrich A. Winkler, *Mittelstand, Demokratie und Nationalsozialismus. Die politische Entwicklung von Handwerk und Kleinhandel in der Weimarer Republik* (Cologne, 1972), pp. 21–26.

32. Wilhelm Marr, *Das junge Deutschland in der Schweiz. Ein Beitrag zur Geschichte der geheimen Verbindungen unserer Tage* (Leipzig, 1846), p. 58; Erich Lüth, *Hamburgs Schicksal lag in ihrer Hand. Geschichte der Bürgerschaft* (Hamburg, 1966), pp. 66–67; Walter Gabe, *Hamburg in der Bewegung von 1848/49* (Heidelberg 1911) pp. 50–52, 125–27.

33. Reliable details about Marr are hard to come by. The above are supplied by him in *Die Deutsche Wacht*, pp. 2–3, 34, 74–75; his radical pamphlet, *Der Mensch und die Ehe vor dem Richterstuhle der Sittlichkeit* (Leipzig, 1848); and an anonymous work by one of Marr's colleagues in the Hamburg legislature, *Der arme Jude, wie ihn der grosse Demokrat Herr Wilhelm Marr besp . . . (richt). Von keinem Juden* (Hamburg, 1862). The latter writes off Marr's anti-Semitism as a product of thwarted political ambition. One myth concerning Marr can be laid to rest here, that of his supposed Jewish origins. He was the only son of the famous actor and director, Heinrich Marr. Both his parents came from old German Protestant families. See Paul A. Merbach, *Heinrich Marr 1797–1871: Ein Beitrag zur Geschichte des deutschen Theaters im 19. Jahrhundert* (Leipzig, 1926), pp. 5ff., 32, 38, 187–90. See also Wilhelm Marr, *Reise nach Central-Amerika* (Hamburg, 1863), 2: 264.

34. See Hellmut vom Gerlach, "Vom deutschen Antisemitismus," in *Patria! Jahrbuch der Hilfe*, 1904, p. 144.

35. See Wilhelm Oechelhaeuser, *Die wirtschaftliche Krisis* (Berlin, 1876), pp. 93–95.

36. See the full text and an explanation of the petition in *Schmeitzner's Internationale Monatsschrift: Zeitschrift für die Allgemeine Vereinigung zur Bekämpfung des Judentums* (Chemnitz and Dresden, 1883), pp. 314–16.

37. *Der Kulturkämpfer*, 1883, p. 194. On Förster and the petition, see Hans-Christian Gerlach, "Agitation und parlamentarische Wirksamkeit der deutschen Antisemitenparteien 1873–1895," (Ph.D. diss., University of Kiel, 1956), pp. 30–44.

38. On the history of the petition, see Wawrzinek, *Antisemitenparteien*, p. 38 n. 24; *Schmeitzners Monatsschrift*, p. 315.

39. See *AK*, 15 October 1888. Also, Marr in *Die Deutsche Wacht*, p. 75.

40. Otto Böckel, *Die Quintessenz der Judenfrage*, 5th ed. (Marburg, 1887), p. 3.

41. See, for example, the opinion of the popular philosopher, Eduard von Hartmann, *Das Judentum in Gegenwart und Zukunft*, 2nd ed. (Berlin, 1885), pp. 186–89.

42. Karl Massmann, *VDSter Fünfzig Jahre Arbeit für Volkstum und Staat* (Berlin, 1931), pp. 13–14; Hans Weber, *Geschichte des Vereins Deutscher Studenten zu Berlin, 1891–1906* (Berlin, 1912), pp. 3–5; Gerlach, *Von Rechts nach Links*, pp. 102–03, 111. Also, Theodor Heuss, *Friedrich Naumann* (Stuttgart and Berlin, 1937), pp. 39–43.

43. Heinrich von Treitschke, *Ein Wort über unser Judentum* (Berlin, 1880), p. 1, a reprint of the articles.

44. See an anthology of the polemics unleashed by Treitschke in Walter Boehlich, ed., *Der Berliner Antisemitismusstreit* (Frankfurt a. M., 1965). Also, Hans Liebeschütz, *Das Judentum im deutschen Geschichtsbild von Hegel bis Max Weber* (Tübingen, 1967), pp. 157–219.

45. See Christian Grotewold, *Die Parteien des Deutschen Reichstags* (Leipzig, 1908), p. 108.

46. See Ernst Henrici, *Was ist der Kern der Judenfrage?* (Berlin, 1881), the reprint of a speech delivered in Berlin on 13 January 1881.

47. Wawrzinek, *Antisemitenparteien*, pp. 38–39. An economic council was provided for in the constitution of the Weimar Republic.

48. See the full program in Max Liebermann von Sonnenberg, *Beiträge zur Geschichte der antisemitischen Bewegung vom Jahre 1880–1885* (Berlin, 1885), pp. 79–82.

49. See Max Liebermann von Sonnenberg, *Aus der Glückzeit meines Lebens* (Munich, 1911), pp. 1, 87–88, 176.

50. Liebermann von Sonnenberg, *Beiträge*, p. 106. *Reichstags-Handbuch. Zwölfte Legislaturperiode* (Berlin, 1907), pp. 314–15; Schemann, *Lebensfahrten*, p. 77.

51. Max Liebermann von Sonnenberg, *Gedichte* (Leipzig, 1891), p. 166.

52. On the influencing of elections by government officials, see Robert Nöll von der Nahmer, *Bismarcks Reptilienfonds* (Mainz, 1968), pp. 127–30.

53. See Kampmann, "Adolf Stoecker," pp. 563–64, 572–74.

54. Because of the vague nature of party membership in the *Kaiserreich*, Stoecker's dual party allegiance posed no special difficulties. See Thomas Nipperdey, *Die Organisation der deutschen Parteien vor 1918* (Düsseldorf, 1961), p. 18.

55. See Buchheim, *Geschichte der christlichen Parteien*, pp. 249–56. On Stoecker's equivocal position regarding the revocation of emancipation and the Anti-Semites' Petition, see Frank, *Hofprediger*, pp. 80–81; Massing, *Rehearsal*, pp. 52, 232 n. 3.

56. Buchheim, *Geschichte der christlichen Parteien*, p. 255.

57. Wawrzinek, *Antisemitenparteien*, pp. 37–39; Frank, *Hofprediger*, p. 83.

58. In Germany four synagogue desecrations were recorded between 1880 and 1914. Troops were sent to quell minor pogroms in 1881, 1891, and 1900. Anti-Semitic violence and vandalism in the Weimar Republic reached far greater levels with 178 synagogue and cemetery defilements. See Kurt Wilhelm, "The Jewish Community in the Post-Emancipation Period," *BYB* 2 (1957): 54; H. G. Adler, *Die Juden in Deutschland* (Munich, 1960), p. 150.

59. See *Die Verurteilung der antisemitischen Bewegung durch die Wahlmänner von Berlin, 12. Januar 1881* (Berlin, 1881), pp. 14–15, the speech of Eugen Richter.

60. Wawrzinek, *Antisemitenparteien*, p. 42 n. 50.

61. See ibid., p. 71 n. 8; *MVA*, 19 November 1893. Part of the difficulty faced by the *Bürgerverein* candidates was an electoral system weighted against the lower middle and working classes.

62. On the decline of the election meeting, see Nipperdey, *Organisation*, pp. 61–66.

63. On the function of the mass meeting in Wilhelminian politics, see Hans-Jürgen Puhle, *Agrarische Interessenpolitik und preussischer Konservatismus im wilhelminischen Reich, 1893–1914* (Hanover, 1966), pp. 118–19.

64. Hertzog purchased the *Neue Deutsche Volkszeitung* for Liebermann in 1882. After his death, the widow Hertzog carried on by providing bail and court costs for anti-Semites in trouble with the law. See *MVA*, 14 March 1900. Also, Nöll von der Nahmer, *Reptilienfonds*, pp. 126–30.

65. See Wawrzinek, *Antisemitenparteien*, p. 37, quoting Stoecker in the *Reichsbote*; Liebermann von Sonnenberg, *Beiträge*, pp. 202–04; Förster in *AK*, December 1888. Also, Willi Buch [Wilhelm Buchow], *50 Jahre antisemitische Bewegung* (Munich, 1937), p. 11.

66. See *MVA*, 13 August 1893; Buch, *50 Jahre*, p. 53. Also, *Deutsche Antisemiten-Chronik 1888 bis 1894* (Zurich, 1894), pp. 7, 30, 43–44.

67. See Wilhelm Giese, "Die deutschsoziale Reformpartei und die Reichstagswahlen des Jahres 1898," *AJB* (1899): 206, quoting Friedrich Lange.

68. These exponents of cultural pessimism are discussed by George L. Mosse, *The Crisis of German Ideology* (New York, 1964); Stern, *The Politics of Cultural Despair*; Harry Pross, *Die Zerstörung der deutschen Politik* (Frankfurt a. M., 1959); Ernst L. Ehrlich, "Judenfeindschaft in Deutschland," in Karl Thieme, ed., *Judenfeindschaft* (Frankfurt a. M., 1963), pp. 209–57.

69. See Bernhard Förster, *Deutsche Colonien in dem oberen Laplatagebiete* (Naumburg a. S., 1886). Also, *Der Kulturkämpfer*, 1888, pp. 267–71.

70. Quoted in *Der Kulturkämpfer*, 1883, pp. 197–98.

71. For well-documented allegations of fraud in the colony, see Julius Klingbeil, *Enthüllungen über die Dr. Bernhard Förster'sche Ansiedlung Neu-Germanien in Paraguay . . . Nach eigenen Erfahrungen mitgeteilt* (Leipzig, 1889). Also *Antisemiten-Chronik,* p. 23.

72. Quotations from a speech by Paul Förster in Liebermann von Sonnenberg, *Beiträge,* p. 261.

73. For examples, see Count Ernst zu Reventlow, *Judas Kampf und Niederlage in Deutschland* (Berlin, 1937); Buch, *50 Jahre;* Josef Müller, "Entwicklung des Rassenantisemitismus in den letzten Jahrzehnten des 19. Jahrhunderts," *Historische Studien* 372 (Berlin, 1940). Among the modern historians who arrange their studies on this basis, see Massing, *Rehearsal;* Ehrlich, "Judenfeindschaft in Deutschland"; Iring Fetscher, "Zur Entstehung des politischen Antisemitismus in Deutschland," in Hermann Huss, ed., *Antisemitismus. Zur Pathologie der bürgerlichen Gesellschaft* (Frankfurt a. M., 1965). An exception to this pattern is to be found in Armin Mohler, *Die konservative Revolution in Deutschland, 1918–1932* (Stuttgart, 1950), pp. 35–43. In his brief discussion of the *Kaiserreich,* Mohler employs virtually the same typology as outlined above, using the terms "reformist" and "conservative-revolutionary" where I have used "conventional" and "revolutionary." However, he confuses the situation by attempting to salvage the distinction between "racist" and "religious" anti-Semitism. Moreover, we disagree extensively when it comes to categorizing individual anti-Semites and anti-Semitic groups as revolutionary or conventional.

74. For example, see Gerlach, *Von Rechts nach Links,* p. 109.

75. For examples of the revolutionaries' attitudes regarding the anti-Semitic political parties, see Buch, *50 Jahre,* pp. 18, 52, citing Friedrich Lange and Theodor Fritsch. Also, Wawrzinek, *Antisemitenparteien,* p. 59; Schüler, *Bayreuther Kreis,* pp. 246–52.

76. *MVA,* 29 February 1892, quoting the *Reichsherold.* See *VHLt,* 26 March 1897, p. 122, a condemnation of Friedrich Lange by the Hessian anti-Semitic deputy, Philipp Köhler. See also a critique of the "noble but misguided" Eugen Dühring by Hellmut von Gerlach in *AK,* 15 September 1888.

77. See *Vorträge des Herrn Ivan v. Simonyi aus Pressburg und des Herrn M. Liebermann v. Sonnenberg aus Berlin über die Judenfrage gehalten am 5. Februar 1883 im deutschen Reformverein zu Chemnitz* (Chemnitz, 1883), pp. 11, 21–22.

78. Liebermann von Sonnenberg, *Beiträge,* pp. 107–13. By 1884 Liebermann had given up on the "ultramontane" Center. See *Beiträge,* pp. 248ff.

79. See Liebermann von Sonnenberg, *Beiträge,* p. 285.

80. For Bismarck's ideas about getting around a troublesome Reichstag, see Dirk Stegmann, *Die Erben Bismarcks. Parteien und Verbände in der Spätphase des Wilhelminischen Deutschlands. Sammlungspolitik 1897–1918* (Cologne and Berlin, 1970), pp. 113–28. Also Ralph H. Bowen, *German Theories of the Corporate State* (New York, 1947). Although Liebermann's by no means original version of a new *Ständestaat* appeared in the program of a later anti-Semitic party, he and his followers regarded it as a somewhat utopian ideal.

81. Quotations from Johannes Ziekursch, *Politische Geschichte des neuen deutschen*

Kaiserreiches (Frankfurt a. M., 1930), 3: 9. For a contrary opinion on the question of antiparliamentarianism, see Pulzer, *The Rise of Political Anti-Semitism,* pp. 41ff.

82. *MVA,* 8 December 1909.

83. See an indication of their success in the final product, *Manifest an die Regierungen und Völker der durch das Judentum gefährdeten Staaten, laut Beschlusses des Ersten Internationalen Antijüdischen Kongresses zu Dresden am 11. und 12. September 1882* (Chemnitz, 1883).

84. See Wawrzinek, *Antisemitenparteien,* pp. 50–53. According to police estimates, approximately two to four hundred rather than the three thousand delegates claimed by the anti-Semites actually attended. Moreover, the police comment only upon the presence of thirty Hungarian anti-Semites and make no mention of other non-Germans. See Hans Gerlach, "Agitation und parlamentarische Wirksamkeit," pp. 47–52.

85. On attendance at Chemnitz, see Wawrzinek, *Antisemitenparteien,* p. 54, quoting the *Deutsche Reform* (Dresden). Minutes of the proceedings are in *Schmeitzners Monatsschrift,* pp. 255–322, 764.

86. *Die Judenfrage als Rassen-, Sitten- und Kulturfrage. Mit einer weltgeschichtlichen Antwort* (Karlsruhe, 1880).

87. *Der Ersatz der Religion durch Vollkommeneres und die Ausscheidung alles Judentums durch den modernen Völkergeist* (Karlsruhe and Leipzig, 1883); *Schmeitzners Monatsschrift,* pp. 287–88. Also, Eugen Dühring, *Die Parteien in der Judenfrage* (Leipzig, n.d.), pp. 418–20.

88. See *AK,* 1 September 1888. Also, paragraph one of the *Deutscher Volksverein* program in Liebermann von Sonnenberg, *Beiträge,* p. 79.

89. *Schmeitzners Monatsschrift,* pp. 277–89. Also, Buch, *50 Jahre,* pp. 10–11.

90. *Schmeitzners Monatsschrift,* p. 272. Hannah Arendt has overemphasized the "internationalism" of the German anti-Semitic movement. See her *The Origins of Totalitarianism,* 2nd ed. (New York, 1958), pp. 39–40.

91. *Der Stürmer,* 16 September 1933.

92. Liebermann and Fritsch eventually broke with one another over this issue. See Müller, "Die Entwicklung des Rassenantisemitismus," pp. 42–43. Also, Theodor Fritsch, *20 Hammer-Aufsätze* (Leipzig, 1916).

93. Wawrzinek, *Antisemitenparteien,* p. 57.

94. *MVA,* 24 August 1904; *AK,* October 1885. Also, Buch, *50 Jahre,* pp. 50ff. Buch began his career as an anti-Semite working for Fritsch's *Hammer-Verlag.*

95. Fritsch's other pseudonyms were F. Roderich Stoltheim, Fritz Thor, and Theodor Kämpfer.

96. See *AK,* October and December 1885; January 1886.

97. *AK,* July 1886.

98. Otto Glagau's opinion of the Reichstag changed dramatically. In 1880 he had spoken contemptuously of the "worthlessness of modern parliamentarism." However, by 1888 he had come to appreciate the possibilities of parliamentary politics, although his acceptance of the Reichstag was reluctant and conditional upon the success of anti-Semitic plans. Compare *Der Kulturkämpfer,* 1880, pp. 341ff; 1888, pp. 225–27.

99. See *AK*, January 1886; Liebermann von Sonnenberg, *Beiträge*, p. 294.

100. See Ernst Deuerlein, *Der Reichstag* (Frankfurt a. M., 1963), p. 20.

101. For Böckel's views, see *VRt* 95 (5 May 1887): 436; *MVA*, 9 July 1893, quoting Böckel; Otto Böckel, *Die Juden, die Könige unserer Zeit*, 15th ed. (Marburg, 1887), p. 3. For similar views on the feasibility of the anti-Semitic program, see *AK*, 26 September 1895; *MVA*, 30 October 1892, quoting Liebermann; Wawrzinek, *Antisemitenparteien*, pp. 61–62, 69.

102. Liebermann von Sonnenberg, *Beiträge*, pp. 110–11, 286–308.

103. Wawrzinek, *Antisemitenparteien*, p. 57.

CHAPTER 2. The Outsiders

1. The term "Hessenland" was current in the nineteenth century and designated collectively the Grand Duchy of Hesse, Electoral Hesse *(Kurhessen)*, and the Duchy of Nassau. In September 1866, Prussia annexed the latter two sovereign states as *Provinz Hessen-Nassau*, which for the sake of convenience will be referred to hereafter as Prussian Hesse. The Grand Duchy of Hesse which sided against Prussia in the War of 1866 maintained diminished sovereignty upon payment of an indemnity, cession of a small piece of its territory, and partial inclusion in the North German Confederation. The present day *Land Hessen* corresponds with one exception to the areas under discussion. See Karl Demandt, *Geschichte des Landes Hessen* (Kassel and Basel, 1959), pp. 429, 450–51.

2. A trustworthy Böckel biography is probably beyond the reach of the historian. The details of his life are scanty, and the various accounts of his career have been distorted by political enemies or apologists. Two works by anti-Semites are of some usefulness: Ferdinand Werner's sketch in Ingeborg Schnack, ed., *Lebensbilder aus Kurhessen und Waldeck, 1830–1930* (Marburg, 1939); and Eugen Schmahl, *Entwicklung der völkischen Bewegung. Die antisemitische Bauernbewegung in Hessen von der Böckelzeit bis zum Nationalsozialismus* (Giessen, 1933). An objective attempt to deal with Böckel's career in Hessenland is Rüdiger Mack, "Otto Böckel und die antisemitische Bauernbewegung in Hessen 1887–1894," *Wetterauer Geschichtsblätter* 16 (1967): 113–47. Mack makes use of materials gathered by Böckel's daughter for a memorial celebration and a collection of his speeches and pamphlets intended as a Nazi primer for students. Böckel's so-called *Nachlass* contains none of his private papers.

3. Böckel, *Die Juden*, pp. 3–14. Böckel took the title of this work from *Les Juifs, Rois de l'Époque* (Paris, 1844), by the French anti-Semite of midcentury, Alphonse Toussenel. See also Böckel, *Quintessenz*, p. 17.

4. Otto Böckel, *Seelenland* (Michendorf, 1913), pp. 122–23.

5. Otto Böckel, *Handbuch des deutschen Volksliedes* (Marburg, 1908), pp. v–vi.

6. *"Völkisch"* is usually translated as "racist" in English, but its German meaning is not so precise and, moreover, has changed with time. In Böckel's day, *völkisch* already went beyond the geographical confines of the German state to embrace a racially conceived Germanic nationality. The *völkisch* vocabulary, at first largely

cultural and historical, had begun to add a layer of modish biological terminology which became increasingly popular in anti-Semitic circles.

7. For a discussion of Riehl's ideas and their influence on the *völkisch* movement, see Mosse, *The Crisis of German Ideology*, pp. 19–24.

8. Otto Böckel, *Psychologie der Volksdichtung* (Leipzig, 1906), p. iii.

9. Otto Böckel, *Die deutsche Volkssage*, 2nd ed. (Berlin, 1922), p. 120.

10. *RH*, 15 March 1892; Mack, "Otto Böckel," p. 127.

11. Karl Steinbrück, *Handbuch der gesamten Landwirtschaft*, 3rd ed. (Leipzig, 1921), 1: 44; Sarah R. Tirrell, *German Agrarian Politics after Bismarck's Fall: The Formation of the Farmers' League* (New York, 1951), p. 13.

12. Demandt, *Geschichte*, pp. 418, 433. For the effects of railroad construction upon life in Hessenland, see Erich Keyser, *Hessisches Städtebuch. 4. Südwestdeutschland* (Stuttgart, 1957), passim.

13. Steinbrück, *Handbuch*, 1: 45.

14. Keyser, *Hessisches Städtebuch*, pp. 325–26; Demandt, *Geschichte*, p. 431.

15. J. Rülf, *Entstehung und Bedeutung des Antisemitismus in Hessen* (Mainz, 1890), pp. 10–12.

16. See Demandt, *Geschichte*, pp. 429–36.

17. Tirrell, *German Agrarian Politics*, pp. 20–22; Steinbrück, *Handbuch*, 1: 45; Theodor von der Goltz, *Geschichte der deutschen Landwirtschaft* (Stuttgart, 1903), 2: 402–03, 405–06.

18. See *Die Landwirtschaft im Grossherzogtum Hessen. Bericht der Landwirtschaftskammer* (Darmstadt, 1912), Appendix 2, Table 3, pp. 175–76, 270; Tirrell, *German Agrarian Politics*, pp. 26, 29–30. Also, J. H. Clapham, *The Economic Development of France and Germany, 1815–1914*, 4th ed. (Cambridge, 1966), pp. 204–09.

19. See Böckel's elegy on the death of Bismarck in *Seelenland*, p. 136.

20. This much was granted by even his most dedicated enemies. See Gerlach, *Von Rechts nach Links*, pp. 171–72. Also, a perceptive series of articles beginning in *MVA*, 6 December 1891.

21. Buch, *50 Jahre*, p. 13.

22. Quotations from Wawrzinek, *Antisemitenparteien*, p. 65. On the unreliability of this survey, see Puhle, *Interessenpolitik*, p. 127 n. 79. Also, Rosenberg, *Grosse Depression*, p. 56.

23. See August Bebel, *Sozialdemokratie und Antisemitismus*, 2nd ed. (Berlin, 1906), p. 14; Gerlach, *Von Rechts nach Links*, p. 170; *MVA*, 6 March 1897, quoting Albrecht Weber. More recently, Mack, "Otto Böckel," pp. 118–22.

24. Munk's study is quoted in *MVA*, 28 January 1894. For examples of anti-Semitic statistical exposés of "Jewish criminality," see Egon Waldegg [Alexander Pinkert], *Die Judenfrage gegenüber dem deutschen Handel und Gewerbe* (Leipzig, 1880); F. Roderich Stoltheim [Theodor Fritsch], *Die Juden im Handel und das Geheimnis ihres Erfolges* (Leipzig, 1913); Wilhelm Giese, *Die Juden und die deutsche Kriminalität* (Leipzig, 1893). Distorted facts and manipulated figures lent an aura of scientific rationality to the charges of Jewish evil. On occasion, they provoked only somewhat less irresponsible answers from Jewish apologists. An honorable exception to this "lying with statistics" was provided by the *Zeitschrift für Demographie und*

Statistik der Juden, edited by Arthur Ruppin and Bruno Blau. The journal spent considerable time debunking anti-Semitic statistics but did so on the basis of official census figures and the highest professional standards. For example, Bruno Blau, "Die Kriminalität der Juden in Deutschland während der Jahre 1903–06," *ZDSJ* 5 (1909): 49–54; also, ibid. 1 (1905): 6–9.

25. "Verschiebungen in der örtlichen Verteilung der Juden in Deutschland," *ZDSJ* 1 (1905): 10–11.

26. Eleonore Sterling, "Anti-Jewish Riots in Germany in 1819," *Historia Judaica* 12 (1950): 129. P. H. Noyes, *Organization and Revolution: Working-Class Associations in the German Revolutions of 1848–1849* (Princeton, 1966), pp. 61–62.

27. Rülf, *Entstehung*, pp. 4–5; Mack, "Otto Böckel," pp. 113–19; Pulzer, *The Rise of Political Anti-Semitism*, p. 108 note.

28. "Die berufliche Gliederung der Juden in Hessen," *ZDSJ* 5 (1909): 50.

29. Bebel, *Sozialdemokratie und Antisemitismus*, p. 14; Clapham, *Economic Development*, pp. 222–23.

30. Rülf, *Entstehung*, pp. 10–12; "Verschiebungen," pp. 10–11.

31. Abraham Löb, *Die Rechtsverhältnisse der Juden im ehemaligen Königreiche und der jetzigen Provinz Hannover* (Frankfurt a. M., 1908), p. 52.

32. Toury, *Die politischen Orientierungen*, p. 138 n. 79.

33. Rülf, *Entstehung*, p. 19.

34. Demandt, *Geschichte*, p. 421.

35. Liebermann von Sonnenberg, *Beiträge*, p. 71. Also, Marr, in *Die Deutsche Wacht*, pp. 127–28, 177, 228.

36. Schnack, *Lebensbilder*, pp. 32–33; Mack, "Otto Böckel," pp. 126–27.

37. See the comments of Böckel's opponent in the Reichstag elections of 1898 and 1903 in Hellmut von Gerlach, *Das Parlament* (Frankfurt a. M., 1907), p. 25.

38. Wawrzinek, *Antisemitenparteien*, p. 66 n. 23.

39. Gerlach, "Vom deutschen Antisemitismus," p. 132; Mack, "Otto Böckel," p. 134.

40. Schmahl, *Entwicklung*, p. 24.

41. See a "history" of Böckel's entry into the Grand Duchy by his disciple, Philipp Köhler, in *VHLt*, 26 March 1897, p. 122.

42. See Philipp Scheidemann, *Memoiren eines Sozialdemokraten* (Dresden, 1928), 1: 62.

43. Demandt, *Geschichte*, pp. 428–29; Hans-Joachim Schoeps, *Preussen* (Berlin, 1966), p. 399.

44. On administrative changes occasioned by Oberhessen's forced entry into the North German Confederation, see Demandt, *Geschichte*, pp. 428–29, 443–46.

45. *VHLt*, 11 December 1897, p. 383.

46. Ibid., 12 February 1898, p. 569. See Clapham, *Economic Development*, p. 347; Tirrell, *German Agrarian Politics*, pp. 272–73.

47. See, for one example, Massing, *Rehearsal*, pp. 88–90.

48. See Adalbert Hess, *Die Landtags- und Reichstagswahlen im Grossherzogtum Hessen, 1865–1871* (Oberursel, 1964), pp. 36–37.

49. See *MVA*, 1 November 1891, quoting Böckel. For Böckel's influence on the retirement of Bamberger from political life, see Otto Hartwig, *Ludwig Bamberger*

(Marburg, 1900), p. 75. Also, Stanley Zucker, "Ludwig Bamberger and the Rise of Anti-Semitism in Germany, 1848–1893," *Central European History* 3 (December 1970): 350–52.

50. See *Marburg: Seine Universität und deren Institute* (Marburg, 1897), p. 21. Apparently, anti-Semitism entered the town of Marburg via the university. Rülf reports (*Entstehung,* pp. 17–18) that on a visit in 1882 his daughter was snubbed at the university because of her Jewishness while still accepted in the "best homes" of the town proper.

51. See Heinrich Class, *Wider den Strom. Vom Werden und Wachsen der nationalen Opposition im alten Reich* (Leipzig, 1932), p. 26.

52. See Chapter 4 below.

53. Quoted by Schmahl in *Entwicklung,* p. 65.

54. *RH,* 26 January 1892; 12 February 1892; 30 June 1892; Schmahl, *Entwicklung,* p. 67; Mack, "Otto Böckel," pp. 141–43.

55. Schmahl, *Entwicklung,* p. 66.

56. The government *Kreisberichte über den Antisemitismus,* destroyed during World War Two, are quoted extensively by Schmahl, *Entwicklung,* pp. 80–83. On Böckel's failure to penetrate Hessian cities, see Erwin Knauss, "Der politische Antisemitismus im Kaiserreich (1871–1900) unter besonderer Berücksichtigung des mittelhessischen Raumes," *Mitteilungen des Oberhessischen Geschichtsvereins* 53–54 (1969): 58–60.

57. See *Bericht der Landwirtschaftskammer,* pp. 244–45, for an account of the progressive agricultural legislation in the Grand Duchy. Also, Demandt, *Geschichte,* p. 411; Clapham, *Economic Development,* pp. 221–26.

58. See the detailed on-the-scene reports of Georg Winter in *MVA,* 3 January 1892; 10 January 1892; 31 January 1892; 8 May 1892; 7 July 1894. On Böckel's ignorance of the intricacies of peasant self-help organization and his consequent reliance upon outside experts, see Mack, "Otto Böckel," pp. 135–36, 141–42.

59. Steinbrück, *Handbuch,* 1: 44; Rülf, *Entstehung,* pp. 6–8; Gerlach, *Von Rechts nach Links,* p. 170; Gerlach, "Vom deutschen Antisemitismus," pp. 151–52.

60. See *RH,* 29 January 1892.

61. For variations in the depth of political apathy, see Hess, *Die Landtags- und Reichstagswahlen,* pp. 26–33. Also, *MVA,* 10 January 1892.

62. Compiled from the *Reichsherold.* See Wawrzinek, *Antisemitenparteien,* p. 80.

63. Compare Böckel's "refined" racism for Reichstag deputies in *VRt* 95 (5 May 1887): 435, with a more down-to-earth article in *RH,* 22 January 1892.

64. Quotation in *MVA,* 1 May 1892. Böckel unabashedly took the closing lines from a fiery appeal to German workers by Ferdinand Lassalle.

65. The customary distinction was between *schaffendes* and *raffendes* capital. The first was the result of honest industry and agriculture; the second was produced from "characteristically Jewish" speculations in the stock market, banking, and shady dealings in general. Such capital was morally stained as too easily gained, the fruit of a "mobile and ruthless intelligence" rather than good hard work. See Liebermann von Sonnenberg in *VRt* 133 (7 December 1893): 322–28. Massing, *Rehearsal,* p. 277, translates a portion of this speech.

66. Böckel, *Quintessenz,* p. 22.

67. See *RH*, 11 March 1887.

68. See letters to the editor in *AK*, 15 July 1888; 15 August 1888. Also, Wawrzinek, *Antisemitenparteien*, p. 68.

69. See *AK*, January 1886; March 1886; April 1887; November 1887.

70. See Wawrzinek, *Antisemitenparteien*, pp. 74–75.

71. Wohlfarth, "Bilder aus der antisemitischen Bewegung," *AJB* (1898): 42–43. *AK*, 23 June 1889, quotes the full text of the Bochum program. Also, *Antisemiten-Chronik*, p. 22.

72. Abwehr-Verein, *Antisemiten-Spiegel. Die Antisemiten im Lichte des Christenthums, des Rechtes und der Moral* (Danzig, 1892), p. 29. Max Schwarz, *MdR: Biographisches Handbuch der Reichstage* (Hanover, 1965).

73. *MVA*, 20 August 1893, quoting Paul Förster in the *Staatsbürger-Zeitung*, 15 August 1893.

CHAPTER 3. Anti-Semites and Conservatives

1. See Fritsch's speech extensively quoted in Reventlow, *Judas Kampf und Niederlage*, pp. 356, 359–60.

2. *AK*, 23 June 1889.

3. See Adolf Braun, *Die Parteien des deutschen Reichstags* (Stuttgart, 1893); Delbrück in *Preussischer Jahrbücher* 66 (1890): 634–37; 67 (1891): 685–86; 69 (1892): 707; 70 (1892): 793–94. Also, Gustav Schmoller, "Die heutige Judenfrage," in *Zwanzig Jahre deutscher Politik, 1897–1917* (Munich and Leipzig, 1920).

4. Schmahl, *Entwicklung*, pp. 69–71.

5. Buch, *50 Jahre*, pp. 41–42. Also, *MVA*, 11 May 1904, which lists ninety-six such hotels, spas, and resorts.

6. Buch, *50 Jahre*, p. 47; Hans Maier, *Die Antisemiten* (Munich, 1911), p. 6. On the liberal fronde within the *Verein Deutscher Studenten*, see Karl Friedrich Borée, *Semiten und Antisemiten* (Frankfurt a. M., 1960), p. 16.

7. J. Alden Nichols, *Germany after Bismarck: The Caprivi Era, 1890–1894* (Cambridge, Mass., 1958), pp. 88–90; Ziekursch, *Politische Geschichte*, 3: 13.

8. Erich Eyck, *Das persönliche Regiment Wilhelms II* (Zurich, 1948), p. 49. For the details of reform, see Nichols, *Caprivi Era*, pp. 88–97.

9. See *Schulthess' Europäischer Geschichtskalender*, 1892, p. 9.

10. Nichols, *Caprivi Era*, pp. 97–99, 160–91. Also, J. C. G. Röhl, *Germany without Bismarck* (London, 1967), pp. 79–85.

11. Quotations from *MVA*, 6 March 1892; *RH*, 9 February 1892.

12. On Stoecker's choice, see Buchheim, *Geschichte der christlichen Parteien*, pp. 280–81.

13. Buchheim, *Geschichte der christlichen Parteien*, p. 265; Nichols, *Caprivi Era*, p. 218; Puhle, *Interessenpolitik*, p. 119. On the agrarian and aristocratic character of the Conservative party, see Hans Booms, *Die Deutschkonservative Partei* (Düsseldorf, 1954), pp. 6–9.

14. See Ernst Engelberg, *Deutschland von 1871 bis 1897* (Berlin, 1965), pp. 326–27, quoting the Berlin *Vorwärts* of 11 January 1891 and 7 June 1891.

15. See Tirrell, *German Agrarian Politics*, pp. 52, 96; Engelberg, *Deutschland*, p. 327.

16. See Caprivi's explanation of the new commercial policy in *VRt* 118 (10 December 1891): 3303–04; Nichols, *Caprivi Era*, p. 144.

17. See Tirrell, *German Agrarian Politics*, pp. 136–37, 194. Also, Nichols, *Caprivi Era*, pp. 138–51.

18. Ziekursch, *Politische Geschichte*, 3: 60.

19. *VRt* 118 (18 December 1891): 3563–64.

20. Otto von Kiesenwetter, *Fünfundzwanzig Jahre wirtschaftspolitischen Kampfes* (Berlin, 1918), p. 39.

21. As early as 1887, Böckel spoke out in the Reichstag in favor of raising grain duties. See *VRt* 101 (2 December 1887): 107; 112 (7 December 1889): 753. Later the anti-Semites consistently backed the Kanitz motion, a measure designed to negate the effects of the commercial treaties by fixing grain prices and making the sale of grain a state monopoly. See Eyck, *Wilhelm II*, pp. 80–81.

22. *VRt* 101 (2 December 1887): 107–08; *RH*, 5 January 1892.

23. *VRt* 118 (11 December 1891): 3341.

24. Ibid. 127 (12 December 1892): 273.

25. Ibid. 95 (5 May 1887): 434–36.

26. Gerlach, *Das Parlament*, pp. 29–30; *AK*, March 1888.

27. *AK*, 1 October 1888, quoting the *Sächsische Landeszeitung*.

28. For examples, *AK*, 1 June 1888; 15 September 1888, quoting Helldorf's *Konservatives Wochenblatt*.

29. *Staatsbürger-Zeitung*, 18 May 1914.

30. *MVA*, 6 March 1892, citing a letter from Ahlwardt to the Berlin school board.

31. *MVA*, 19 November 1893.

32. For a romanticized version of Ahlwardt's early career, see *Politischer Bilderbogen* 7 (Dresden, 1893). For a perceptive psychological sketch of Ahlwardt, see Massing, *Rehearsal*, p. 92.

33. The whole work was published under the title, *Der Verzweiflungskampf der arischen Völker mit dem Judentum* (Berlin, 1890); *MVA*, 28 February 1892. For Ahlwardt's accusations against another prominent individual, Johannes Miquel, see Hans Herzfeld, *Johannes von Miquel* (Detmold, 1938), 1: 378–79; 2: 338.

34. *MVA*, 20 November 1892, citing the *Frankfurter Zeitung*. Also, *MVA*, 22 May 1892, quoting Helldorf in the *Konservatives Wochenblatt*.

35. See Hermann Ahlwardt, *Neue Enthüllungen. Judenflinten* (Dresden, 1892). Massing, *Rehearsal*, p. 93; *MVA*, 12 June 1892; 19 June 1892.

36. See Böckel and Liebermann's joint disavowal of Ahlwardt after his first libel conviction (28 November 1891), in Massing, *Rehearsal*, p. 240. Also, later and less decisive rejections of Ahlwardt by the Conservatives in *Kreuzzeitung*, 24 April 1892 (morning edition); 15 May 1892 (morning edition).

37. See Liebermann's cautious analysis of Ahlwardt in *AK*, 29 May 1892; and his strong denunciation after the arrest on 2 June in *AK*, 12 June 1892. On König and Förster, see *MVA*, 22 May 1892 and 17 April 1892.

38. On the pretext for Helldorf's ouster, see Friedrich Wilhelm von Limburg-Stirum, *Aus der konservativen Politik der Jahre 1890–1905* (Berlin, 1921), p. 6. Also, Booms, *Deutschkonservative*, p. 23.

39. After Ahlwardt's arrest in June 1892, the official organ of the Conservative party referred to "these numerous materials," which it was refraining from making public until the affair was cleared up. See *MVA*, 19 June 1892, quoting the *Konservative Korrespondenz*; *MVA*, 5 June 1892, quoting the *Frankfurter Zeitung*.

40. *Kreuzzeitung*, 1 May 1892 (morning edition); *MVA*, 8 May 1892.

41. *MVA*, 5 June 1892, quoting the *Frankfurter Zeitung*. Also, Nichols, *Caprivi Era*, p. 188.

42. Frank, *Hofprediger*, p. 232. Voting figures from *MVA*, 5 June 1892.

43. *AK*, 19 June 1892.

44. Frank, *Hofprediger*, p. 232; *MVA*, 19 June 1892.

45. Gerlach, *Von Rechts nach Links*, p. 114. Also, Franz Mehring, "Berliner Geschichten," *Neue Zeit* 10 (1891–1892): 229; *MVA*, 21 August 1892.

46. Robert Frank, *Der Brandenburger als Reichstagswähler 1867/71 bis 1912/14* (Berlin, 1934), Appendix, pp. 31, 34–36, 47, 131.

47. Julius Bachem, *Erinnerungen eines alten Publizisten und Politikers* (Cologne, 1913) p. 110.

48. *MVA*, 11 December 1892. Both Massing (*Rehearsal*, pp. 95–96) and Pulzer (*The Rise of Political Anti-Semitism*, p. 113) confuse Ahlwardt's own anti-Junker campaign of 1893 with this campaign of 1892, won largely with help from the Conservatives.

49. *MVA*, 11 December 1892, quoting the court sentence.

50. Nipperdey, *Organisation*, p. 255.

51. For the full text of paragraph one of the program as finally adopted, see *Konservatives Handbuch*, 3rd ed. (Berlin, 1898), p. 318.

52. Related by the eyewitness, Gerlach, "Vom deutschen Antisemitismus," p. 154; Nichols, *Caprivi Era*, p. 238.

53. Frank, *Hofprediger*, p. 234; Massing, *Rehearsal*, p. 66.

54. Quotation from Frank, *Hofprediger*, pp. 233–34. On the lack of democratic development within the party, see Nipperdey, *Organisation*, pp. 247–56. On Conservative attitudes toward political anti-Semitism, see Puhle, *Interessenpolitik*, pp. 119–20, 121, 133–35. Also, Kuno von Westarp, *Konservative Politik im letzten Jahrzehnt des Kaiserreiches* (Berlin, 1935), 1: 403.

55. Quotation from *MVA*, 18 December 1892; 12 June 1893.

56. Ziekursch, *Politische Geschichte*, 3: 68; Nichols, *Caprivi Era*, pp. 246–54; Eyck, *Wilhelm II*, pp. 70–71.

57. Maier, *Die Antisemiten*, p. 7.

58. Braun, *Die Parteien*, p. 27.

59. Ibid., p. 28.

60. Frank, *Hofprediger*, p. 236, quoting the resolution of the delegates' meeting of the Christian Social party, 1 June 1893.

61. Frank, *Hofprediger*, pp. 237–38. Stoecker retained his seat in the Prussian parliament representing Minden (Westphalia).

62. See Chairman Manteuffel's conclusions to this effect in *MVA*, 28 November 1896. Also, Westarp, *Konservative Politik*, 1: 21.

63. Tirrell, *German Agrarian Politics*, pp. 178–79, 182. Also, Puhle, *Interessenpolitik*, pp. 23–71, 295–97.

64. Nipperdey, *Organisation*, p. 249. Also, Puhle, *Interessenpolitik*, pp. 213–25; Stegmann, *Erben Bismarcks*, pp. 23–24, 38.

65. See Max Nitzsche, "Die Anfänge der agrarischen Bewegung in Deutschland," in *Patria! Jahrbuch der Hilfe*, 1905, pp. 187–211; Puhle, *Interessenpolitik*, pp. 125–40.

66. Abwehr-Verein, *Abwehr-ABC* (Berlin, 1920), p. 3. Also, *Schulthess' Europäischer Geschichtskalender*, 1893, pp. 162–65.

67. Quotation from *MVA*, 19 March 1893.

68. Puhle, *Interessenpolitik*, pp. 125–34.

69. Frank, *Hofprediger*, p. 240. Also, Max Maurenbrecher, "Caprivi und die politischen Parteien," in *Patria! Jahrbuch der Hilfe*, 1902, p. 113.

70. See *MVA*, 26 March 1892, quoting *Die Post* (Free-Conservative).

71. Gerlach, "Vom deutschen Antisemitismus," p. 154.

72. Schwarz, *MdR: Biographisches Handbuch*, pp. 806–07; Braun, *Die Parteien*, pp. 29–36. Theodor Fritsch estimated the "true strength of the anti-Semitic vote" at 400,000. See Massing, *Rehearsal*, pp. 229–30.

73. Duly noted and apologized for by Liebermann in *AK*, 6 July 1893, Beilage no. 27.

CHAPTER 4. A Fragile Unity

1. Böckel intervened personally against Stoecker in the Siegen district of Westphalia. See *MVA*, 13 August 1893; 20 August 1893; 9 July 1893; 16 July 1893.

2. See Böckel, *Quintessenz*, p. 24. Also, *RH*, 30 June 1892.

3. For an early formulation of this theory, see the program of the *Deutscher Volksverein* in Liebermann von Sonnenberg, *Beiträge*, p. 81.

4. Compiled from Schwarz, *MdR: Biographisches Handbuch*.

5. Giese, "Die deutschsoziale Reformpartei," p. 219.

6. See *Politisches Handbuch der nationalliberalen Partei* (Berlin, 1907), p. 44.

7. "Die Juden in Sachsen," *ZDSJ* 4 (1908): 109; Adler, *Die Juden*, p. 86.

8. See Salomon Adler-Rudel, *Ostjuden in Deutschland, 1880–1940* (Tübingen, 1959), pp. 2–4. On the strained relations between German and East European Jews, see Ahron Sandler, "The Struggle for Unification," *BYB* 2 (1957): 76–84; Wilhelm, "The Jewish Community," pp. 47–75.

9. Quoted in *MVA*, 11 March 1894.

10. Liebermann considered the possibility of "half anti-Semites" but felt certain that they would quickly become "full anti-Semites." See *AK*, 13 August 1893.

11. See *VSLt*, 9 February 1892, 1: 512–20. Also, *MVA*, 7 August 1892.

12. Lorenz Curtius, *Der politische Antisemitismus von 1907–1911* (Munich, 1911), p. 95. For other marks of official anti-Semitism, see Ismar Schorsch, *Jewish Reactions to German Anti-Semitism, 1870–1914* (New York, 1972), pp. 48–52.

13. Baron von Friesen, leader of the Saxon Conservatives, who strove for a "decent" anti-Semitism, referred to the German Reformers as "nauseating and loathsome." See *AK,* 19 June 1892. Nevertheless, an election alliance between Conservatives and anti-Semites gave them a majority in the Dresden city council for nearly twenty years.

14. *MVA,* 8 December 1894; Rudolf Kötzschke and Hellmut Kretzschmar, *Sächsische Geschichte* (Frankfurt a. M., 1965), pp. 373–74, 378. Small-scale industry fared somewhat better. See Donald Warren, *The Red Kingdom of Saxony* (The Hague, 1964), pp. 1–6. Also, Ludwig Holländer, *Die sozialen Voraussetzungen der antisemitischen Bewegung in Deutschland* (Berlin, 1907).

15. Warren, *Red Kingdom,* p. 12. Also, Ernst Heilmann, *Geschichte der Arbeiterbewegung in Chemnitz und Erzgebirge* (Chemnitz, n.d.), p. 267.

16. On the growth of the German Socials, see *Herr Liebermann v. Sonnenberg als Parteiführer und Gesinnungsgenosse. Von einigen Deutsch-Sozialen* (Leipzig, 1893), pp. 4, 6, 25. On anti-Semitic party activity in Saxony, see *AK,* 5 June 1892; 19 June 1892; 25 September 1892; 7 May 1893, Beilage no. 18; 21 May 1893, Beilage no. 20.

17. Statistics compiled from Braun, *Die Parteien,* p. 34.

18. Only one issue of the *Antisemitische-Korrespondenz* mentioned the presence of workers at a German Social meeting, and this was a clearly exceptional case. See *AK,* 5 June 1892. For the German Social interpretation of the election, see *AK,* 6 July 1893, Beilage no. 27. For the Social Democratic analysis which regretted anti-Semitic success with the *Mittelstand* vote, see "Die zweiten Wahlergebnisse," *Neue Zeit* 11 (1892–1893): 419–20.

19. It is again hypothesis rather than demonstrable fact that the *Mittelstand* votes gained by the Social Democrats in subsequent elections came from the Conservative and anti-Semitic parties. However, see Warren, *Red Kingdom,* p. 49; Kötzschke and Kretzschmar, *Sächsische Geschichte,* pp. 381–82. Also, Hans Delbrück's analysis of Saxon politics in *Preussischer Jahrbücher* 83 (1896): 593. The loss of anti-Semitic seats in Saxony was accompanied by a loss of votes too: 1898— 73,427; 1903—73,656; 1907—40,190; 1912—37,160.

20. See Chapter 6 below.

21. This provoked an angry response from the Reformer, Ludwig Werner, who complained that the "Conservatives treat us worse than the Jews." See *Staatsbürger-Zeitung,* 28 November 1893; also, *MVA,* 3 December 1893.

22. *Konservatives Handbuch,* 2nd ed. (Berlin, 1894), p. 14 note.

23. See Siegfried von Kardorff, *Wilhelm von Kardorff: Ein nationaler Parlamentarier im Zeitalter Bismarcks und Wilhelms II, 1828–1907* (Berlin, 1936), pp. 280–82. Kardorff was the foremost proponent of the government bill.

24. August Keim, *Erlebtes und Erstrebtes* (Hanover, 1925), pp. 66–67, 159–62; Nichols, *Caprivi Era,* p. 242.

25. Keim, *Erlebtes,* pp. 69–70. See also Prince Chlodwig zu Hohenlohe, *Denkwürdigkeiten des Fürsten Chlodwig zu Hohenlohe-Schillingsfürst* (Stuttgart and Leipzig, 1907), 2: 501–02.

26. Eyck, *Wilhelm II*, p. 74. The concession on financing was also meant to please the left liberals and part of the Center. Scheidemann's contention that Böckel's initial vote against the military bill stemmed from "democratic and antimilitaristic" causes ignores this reversal. See Philipp Scheidemann, "Wandlungen des Antisemitismus," *Neue Zeit* 24 (1905–1906): 635.

27. See Liebermann's analysis in *AK*, 6 July 1893; 17 August 1893.

28. *AK*, 6 December 1891.

29. See the most complete account of the meeting in *Kreuzzeitung*, 26 June 1892 (evening edition); also, *AK*, 19 June 1892; 14 September 1893, Beilage no. 37.

30. Giese, "Die deutschsoziale Reformpartei," p. 202, quoting the manifesto of the North German anti-Semite congress (26 June 1892).

31. *AK*, 17 August 1893; *MVA*, 23 October 1892.

32. *AK*, 27 December 1891. Also, *MVA*, 15 November 1891, citing the *Reichsherold*.

33. Schmahl, *Entwicklung*, pp. 24, 55; Mack, "Otto Böckel," pp. 135–43.

34. *MVA*, 4 September 1892.

35. Ibid., 11 September 1892; 30 June 1894, quoting Böckel.

36. Gerlach, *Von Rechts nach Links*, p. 171. Also, Curt Bürger, ed., *Antisemiten-Spiegel*, 3rd ed. (Berlin, 1911), p. 315. Bürger alludes to several bastards by a cook named Eva. For a sweeping denial of all charges, see Schmahl, *Entwicklung*, pp. 57, 87, 90.

37. *AK*, 4 October 1891, Beilage no. 91, quoting a statement by Philipp Köhler. On Pickenbach's shady past, see Schmahl, *Entwicklung*, p. 61.

38. *AK*, 17 August 1893; 6 July 1893, Beilage no. 27.

39. Ibid., 5 October 1893, Beilage no. 40. Böckel's letter was dated 19 September 1893.

40. *MVA*, 8 April 1894.

41. See *VRt* 125 (10 March 1894): 1734–37.

42. Admitted by Köhler after Böckel's fall in *AK*, 4 October 1894, Beilage no. 91. For earlier indications of treachery, see *MVA*, 8 April 1894; *AK*, 23 August 1894, Beilage no. 85.

43. *MVA*, 12 November 1893; 19 November 1893.

44. See Wohlfarth, "Bilder," pp. 45–47; *AK*, 21 June 1894, Beilage no. 76; *MVA*, 8 April 1894; 9 June 1894; and *MVA*, numbers for September 1894. Also, Theodor Fritsch, ed., *Handbuch der Judenfrage*, 48th ed. (Leipzig, 1943), p. 528.

45. *AK*, 16 August 1894, Beilage no. 84; 23 August 1894, Beilage no. 85; 30 August 1894, Beilage no. 86.

46. Ibid., 4 October 1894, Beilage no. 91.

47. Schmahl, *Entwicklung*, pp. 90–91.

48. Puhle, *Interessenpolitik*, p. 129 n. 97.

49. See Böckel's own admission in the *Deutsche Reform* of 10 February 1901, quoted in *MVA*, 6 March 1901.

50. Wohlfarth, "Bilder," p. 47; *AK*, 11 October 1894, Beilage no. 92.

51. *AK,* 11 October 1894, Beilage no. 92.

52. Ibid. Also, Wohlfarth, "Bilder," p. 49.

CHAPTER 5. Organization and Ideology

1. Nipperdey, *Organisation,* pp. 94–97.

2. *IDR,* May 1898; *MVA,* 17 November 1894.

3. Most of the following information comes from *AJB* (1898): 156–75, the German Social Reform party directory for 1896–1897. Also, *AK,* 7 November 1898.

4. See Nipperdey, *Organisation,* pp. 84–85. Also, Peter Molt, *Der Reichstag vor der improvisierten Revolution* (Cologne, 1963), p. 57.

5. See Wilhelm Giese, *Die Herren Raab und v. Liebermann in der Deutschsozialen Reformpartei* (Berlin, 1900), pp. 5, 15. See also Giese, "Die deutschsoziale Reformpartei," p. 202, discussing the criticism of Paul Förster concerning irregularities in procedure.

6. See *AJB* (1898): 156–58. Also, Wohlfarth, "Bilder," pp. 46–48.

7. See the account of the Halle congress in *AK,* 15 October 1896; the Nordhausen congress in ibid., 14 October 1897; *MVA,* 16 October 1897.

8. Giese, "Die deutschsoziale Reformpartei," p. 212.

9. The formula is quoted in *MVA,* 30 October 1892. There were double candidacies in Marburg (1898, 1907, 1912), Siegen (1893), Berlin VI (1893), Stettin (1898), Rinteln (1903), and Neustettin (1907).

10. *AK,* 20 August 1896; 3 September 1896; *MVA,* 27 March 1912. Also, Buch, *50 Jahre,* p. 30. The number of nonparty anti-Semitic newspapers was, of course, much greater. Individual papers with National Liberal, Centrist, Free-Conservative, and German Conservative affiliation frequently printed anti-Semitic articles. The organs of several *Mittelstand* groups and of the Agrarian League made fairly constant use of anti-Semitism. Altogether well over one hundred German newspapers could be classified as consistently or periodically anti-Semitic.

11. *AK,* 7 October 1897.

12. For example, Buch, *50 Jahre,* pp. 30, 51.

13. Buchheim, *Geschichte der christlichen Parteien,* p. 284; *MVA,* 17 April 1892; 27 March 1912; 15 September 1894; Schmahl, *Entwicklung,* p. 99.

14. *MVA,* 23 April 1898; 19 January 1895.

15. Willy Kremer, *Der soziale Aufbau der Parteien des deutschen Reichstages von 1871–1918* (Emsdetten, 1934), Table 59.

16. For examples of anti-Semitic complaints about their own press, see *AK,* October and December 1885; ibid., 7 October 1897; *MVA,* 26 February 1913.

17. Liebermann originated this scheme for payment of dues as a part of his "reasonable anti-Semitism" in 1883. See *Schmeitzners Monatsschrift,* p. 292. For criticism of the system, see *AK,* 8 December 1898.

18. Nipperdey, *Organisation,* p. 91.

19. *MVA,* 24 September 1893, quoting the *Staatsbürger-Zeitung.* Also, *MVA,* 21 January 1894, quoting a plea for contributions by the North German anti-Semites.

20. On the difficulty of estimating party strengths in this period, see Ludwig Bergsträsser, *Geschichte der politischen Parteien in Deutschland,* 10th ed. (Munich, 1960), p. 32. The ten percent formula gains some credibility when Friedrich Naumann's National Social Union, a later party resting on the same social base as the anti-Semites, is considered. In 1903, the National Socials had 3,000 members, or ten percent of those who voted for the party in that year. See Konstanze Wegner, *Theodor Barth und die Freisinnige Vereinigung* (Tübingen, 1968), pp. 92–93.

21. Evidence concerning *Reformvereine* dues is too scanty to make an exact calculation of the party's annual budget. Dues varied between one and eight marks. Taking four marks as an average, the approximate thirty thousand members of the party should have paid sixty thousand (one-half of one hundred twenty thousand) marks to the national treasury. However, in light of frequent complaints in the anti-Semitic press and at the annual congresses, dues collection appears to have been far from complete.

22. *MVA,* 2 July 1893. Also, *AK* numbers from June 1897 to June 1898 acknowledged a total of 4,320 marks for its special election fund.

23. See Nipperdey, *Organisation,* pp. 263–64, 241 n. 1, 153–55, 201. Also, Buch, *50 Jahre,* p. 47.

24. *MVA,* 16 February 1895.

25. Ibid., 15 June 1895.

26. See Molt, *Der Reichstag,* pp. 46–47. Also, on the financing of the Social Democratic party, see Scheidemann, *Memoiren,* 1: 159–61. On anti-Semitic absenteeism, see *Die Antisemiten im Reichstag* (Berlin, 1903), p. 11. On the anti-Semites as *"Diätenjäger"* (allowance hunters), see Abwehr-Verein, *Der politische Antisemitismus von 1903–1907* (Berlin, 1907), Foreword.

27. *AK,* 8 December 1898; *MVA,* 3 September 1898.

28. See Puhle, *Interessenpolitik,* pp. 43–71; Kiesenwetter, *Fünfundzwanzig Jahre,* p. 327. On the league's election campaigning, see *MVA,* 22 July 1899. Also, Jürgen Bertram, *Die Wahlen zum Deutschen Reichstag vom Jahre 1912* (Düsseldorf, 1964), p. 98.

29. See, for example, *MVA,* 10 April 1901.

30. Ibid., 4 August 1894. Also, Puhle, *Interessenpolitik,* p. 136, quoting the league newspaper, *Bund der Landwirte.* Puhle doubts that this division of labor ever became operative.

31. See Wohlfarth, "Bilder," pp. 49–50. Also, *MVA,* 26 October 1895; 9 October 1897, a survey of the German press. The complete text of the program may be found in Maier, *Die Antisemiten,* pp. 9–14.

32. Wohlfarth, "Bilder," p. 49.

33. For a similar statement by a left-liberal party, see Martin Wenck, "Die Geschichte der Nationalsozialen," in *Patria! Jahrbuch der Hilfe,* 1905, pp. 57–58.

34. *AK,* 31 October 1895.

35. For a translation of Böckel's program, see Pulzer, *The Rise of Political Anti-Semitism,* pp. 339–40. See the debates on the franchise question in *AK,* 31 October 1895. The Saxon anti-Semites later regretted their position when the Saxon franchise was altered in a way prejudicial to the anti-Semites as well as the Socialists. See ibid., 13 February 1896.

36. For typical complaints, see ibid., 28 June 1894; Giese, "Die deutschsoziale Reformpartei," pp. 217–18.

37. See Karl Saller, "Die biologisch motivierte Judenfeindschaft," in Thieme, ed., *Judenfeindschaft*, pp. 181–83.

38. See the criticism of earlier anti-Semitic "attempts to save capitalism" by August Bebel in *Protokoll über die Verhandlungen des Parteitages der Sozialdemokratischen Partei Deutschlands, abgehalten zu Köln* (Berlin, 1893), p. 236. Also, Bebel, *Sozialdemokratie und Antisemitismus*, p. 26.

39. For example, the speech of Center party leader Ernst Lieber in *VRt* 139 (6 March 1895): 1285–87. However, anti-Semitic deviations from the official policies of the Center party were frequent. See Chapter 7 below.

40. *MVA*, 11 May 1895; 5 December 1896.

41. On the divisiveness of the *Mittelstand*, see Stegmann, *Erben Bismarcks*, pp. 249–56; Curt Bürger, *Die politische Mittelstandsbewegung in Deutschland* (Berlin, 1912); Eva G. Reichmann, *Hostages of Civilization* (London, 1950); Winkler, *Mittelstand, Demokratie und Nationalsozialismus*, pp. 40–57.

42. Mildred S. Wertheimer, *The Pan-German League, 1890–1914* (New York, 1924), pp. 134–35. Wertheimer estimates that fifteen percent of the league's membership belonged to one of the anti-Semitic parties. Liebermann and Werner were founding members. See Alfred Kruck, *Geschichte des Alldeutschen Verbandes 1890–1939* (Wiesbaden, 1954), pp. 17–20.

43. See Mosse, *The Crisis of German Ideology*, pp. 218–25; Kruck, *Geschichte des Alldeutschen Verbandes*, pp. 130–31; Lothar Werner, "Der Alldeutsche Verband 1890–1918," *Historische Studien* 278 (Berlin, 1935), pp. 33, 85–86. On the neutrality of the organization regarding the Jewish question, see Uwe Lohalm, *Völkischer Radikalismus. Die Geschichte des Deutschvölkischen Schutz- und Trutz-Bundes 1918–1923* (Hamburg, 1970), pp. 45–46, 346 nn. 79–80.

44. Richard W. Tims, *Germanizing Prussian Poland* (New York, 1941), pp. 211, 72; Adam Galos, et al., *Die Hakatisten* (Berlin, 1966), pp. 61–62. Also a statement by one of the founders and leaders of the *Ostmarkverein*, Heinrich von Tiedemann, in *MVA*, 12 March 1898.

45. For one such case of anti-Semitic interference, see Westarp, *Konservative Politik*, 1: 21. Also, Toury, *Die politischen Orientierungen*, p. 257 n. 71.

46. *AK*, 13 January 1898; 8 September 1898; 13 October 1898.

CHAPTER 6. The Anti-Semites and Their Opponents

1. See Ernst R. Huber, *Deutsche Verfassungsgeschichte seit 1789* (Stuttgart, 1963), 3: 961–63. Also, Helmut Böhme, ed., *Probleme der Reichsgründungszeit 1848–1879* (Cologne, 1968), p. 349.

2. *VPrLt*, 20 November 1880, 1: 227ff.

3. See Wawrzinek, *Antisemitenparteien*, p. 38. Also, Friedrich Lorenzen, *Die Antisemiten* (Berlin, 1912), p. 10. Anti-Semites also reacted unfavorably to the government answer. See Fritsch, *Handbuch der Judenfrage* (1943), p. 525; and

Daniel Frymann [Heinrich Class], *Wenn ich der Kaiser wär'—Politische Wahrheiten und Notwendigkeiten,* 2nd ed. (Leipzig, 1913), p. 36.

4. Busch was author of the pamphlet, *Israel und die Gojim* (Leipzig, 1880). See also Wawrzinek, *Antisemitenparteien,* pp. 30–31.

5. Moritz Busch, *Tagebuchblätter* (Leipzig, 1899), 3 : 55. Also, Frank, *Hofprediger,* p. 92.

6. See Otto Jöhlinger, *Bismarck und die Juden* (Berlin, 1921), pp. 141–42. Also, Massing, *Rehearsal,* p. 38; Frank, *Hofprediger,* pp. 100–02.

7. See *MVA,* 17 May 1905, quoting Richter's speech to the Berlin election club of the *Fortschrittspartei* (6 April 1891). Also, Nöll von der Nahmer, *Reptilienfonds,* pp. 126–30; *Fürst Bismarck und der Antisemitismus* (Vienna, 1886), pp. 142–44; Gerlach, "Vom deutschen Antisemitismus," p. 149; Adler, *Die Juden,* p. 105.

8. Massing, *Rehearsal,* p. 38. Also, Fetscher, "Zur Entstehung des politischen Antisemitismus," p. 21.

9. Norman Rich and M. H. Fisher, ed., *The Holstein Papers. The Memoirs, Diaries, and Correspondence of Friedrich von Holstein* (Cambridge, 1955–1963), 2 : 228, the conversation between Bleichröder and Holstein, 5 August 1885. The *Reichsglocke* is mistakenly attributed to Otto Glagau. On the relationship between Bleichröder and Bismarck, see Fritz Stern, *The Failure of Illiberalism* (New York, 1972), pp. 55–73.

10. Frank, *Hofprediger,* p. 92.

11. Adolf Stoecker, *13 Jahre Hofprediger und Politiker* (Berlin, 1895), p. 28; Otto von Bismarck, *Gedanken und Erinnerungen* (Stuttgart and Berlin, 1919), 3 : 19. Also, Jöhlinger, *Bismarck und die Juden,* p. 157.

12. Jöhlinger, *Bismarck und die Juden,* pp. 183ff. Also, Busch, *Tagebuchblätter,* 2 : 33; 3 : 12–13.

13. Jöhlinger, *Bismarck und die Juden,* pp. 146–47, 184.

14. See Paul Förster's adulatory *Kaiser Wilhelms Deutsch-soziales Vermächtnis* (Leipzig, 1888). Also, Liebermann's elegy upon the death of Wilhelm, to the tune of "Deutschland über Alles," in *Gedichte,* p. 163.

15. See Massing, *Rehearsal,* pp. 44–46, 224–25 n. 24; Frank, *Hofprediger,* p. 92; Rich, *Holstein Papers,* 2 : 73; Kupisch, *Adolf Stoecker,* pp. 45–53.

16. Frank, *Hofprediger,* pp. 58, 64.

17. See *MVA,* 14 August 1901. Also, Karl M. Spamitz, "Tätigkeit der Deutsch-sozialreformerischen Abgeordneten in den Volksvertretungen während der Session 1897–1898," *AJB* (1899) : 180–81.

18. See Bismarck, *Gedanken und Erinnerungen,* 3 : 6–7.

19. See *AK,* 15 June 1888; 1 July 1888.

20. For examples of Wilhelm's personal feelings about Jews, see Michael Balfour, *The Kaiser and His Times* (London, 1964), pp. 216, 276–77, 402.

21. *MVA,* 1 September 1894.

22. Ibid., 2 June 1894.

23. Pulzer, *The Rise of Political Anti-Semitism,* p. 256.

24. Scheidemann, "Wandlungen des Antisemitismus," p. 633.

25. Quoted in the *MVA*, 24 April 1892.

26. *VRt* 133 (30 November 1893): 192–93.

27. Eyck, *Wilhelm II*, p. 98, quoting Philipp zu Eulenburg.

28. See Bürger, *Antisemiten-Spiegel* (1911), pp. 99, 130–31.

29. Schmahl, *Entwicklung*, pp. 55, 74–75.

30. *VHLt*, 26 March 1897, pp. 114–15, 121–22; 11 March 1902, pp. 2475–76.

31. *RH*, 22 April 1892; 12 February 1892.

32. *MVA*, 13 April 1892, quoting the *Mainzer Nachrichten*.

33. Abwehr-Verein, *Abwehr-ABC*, pp. 39–40. Also, *MVA*, 29 November 1891.

34. Frank, *Hofprediger*, p. 229.

35. *MVA*, 3 January 1892, quoting a letter to the *Verein zur Abwehr des Anti-semitismus* from the Cardinal of Cologne.

36. Adolf Lewin, *Geschichte der badischen Juden seit der Regierung Karl Friedrichs* (Karlsruhe, 1909), pp. 354–61. On Ellstätter's career as minister of finance, see Hamburger, *Juden im öffentlichen Leben*, pp. 31–32.

37. For examples of this attitude, see the views of Hans Delbrück, editor of the *Preussischer Jahrbücher*, in Annelise Thimme, *Hans Delbrück als Kritiker der Wilhelminischen Epoche* (Düsseldorf, 1955), pp. 24–26. The disdainful attitude was general in the Conservative party. See Westarp, *Konservative Politik*, 1: 21. Also, the views of an ex-anti-Semite, Hans Gustav Erdmannsdörfer, *Dem Abgrunde zu* (Berlin, 1898), p. 28; and the Jewish scholar Leopold Auerbach, *Wie ist die Judenhetze mit Erfolg zu bekämpfen?* (Berlin, 1893), pp. 6–7.

38. On this crucial development in German history, see the studies of Michael Stürmer, Hans Boldt, and Helmut Böhme in Michael Stürmer, ed., *Das kaiserliche Deutschland. Politik und Gesellschaft 1870–1918* (Düsseldorf, 1970). For the effect of the purge on Jews, see Hamburger, *Juden im öffentlichen Leben*, pp. 31–39.

39. See Liebermann von Sonnenberg, *Beiträge*, p. 119.

40. Hamburger, *Juden im öffentlichen Leben*, pp. 97, 398–99. Also, an article by Hugo Preuss in *Die Nation*, 8 April 1899.

41. For explicit demands of further exclusion of Jews from civil service jobs, see the programs of the German Social party (1905) and German Reform party (1906) in Karl Mahler, *Die Programme der politischen Parteien in Deutschland* (Leipzig, 1911), pp. 19–30. Also, *MVA*, 29 August 1906.

42. For a translation of the document, see Pulzer, *The Rise of Political Anti-Semitism*, pp. 337–38.

43. See the full text in *MVA*, 30 January 1901.

44. For a concise history of the organization, see Abwehr-Verein, *Abwehr-ABC*, pp. 115–16. Also, Schorsch, *Jewish Reactions*, pp. 79–101; Arnold Paucker, *Der jüdische Abwehrkampf gegen Antisemitismus und Nationalsozialismus in den letzten Jahren der Weimarer Republik* (Hamburg, 1966), p. 250 n. 46.

45. *RH*, 22 January 1892. For other unsuccessful direct encounters, see *MVA*, 15 November 1891; 10 January 1892.

46. See *MVA*, 7 February 1892; 25 June 1893. Also, Georg Winter's program in ibid., 13 December 1891; 27 December 1891.

47. Ibid., 30 January 1901; 31 January 1912. See also Egmont Zechlin, *Die deutsche Politik und die Juden im Ersten Weltkrieg* (Göttingen, 1969), p. 45. Zechlin

exaggerates the scope of intervention by resistance organizations in the elections of 1912. For typical accusations concerning financial sources, see Buch, *50 Jahre,* p. 49; *AK,* 2 August 1894, Beilage no. 82. Contributions from Jewish communities appear to have been considerable, although never as extensive as the anti-Semites claimed. See Schorsch, *Jewish Reactions,* pp. 93–94.

48. *MVA,* 21 September 1893; 21 September 1895; 24 October 1896; 2 July 1893.

49. The principle was first enunciated in ibid., 19 April 1904. It was reaffirmed by Barth in the issue of 6 March 1907. Albrecht Weber, a founding member of the *Verein,* never accepted the principle. See ibid., 6 March 1897; 6 March 1907. For Barth's struggle with his own party over this formula, see Wegner, *Theodor Barth,* pp. 111–21.

50. The *Antisemiten-Spiegel* appeared independently of the *Verein* in 1890, with four subsequent revisions and supplements under *Verein* auspices in 1892, 1900, 1903, and 1911. In 1920 it was retitled *Abwehr-ABC.*

51. *MVA,* 7 February 1892.

52. Renamed the *Abwehr-Blätter,* the newspaper appeared as a monthly from 1923 to 1933.

53. *MVA,* 6 March 1897. A word about the *MVA,* the major source for this study, is in order here. The paper's painstaking surveillance of the anti-Semites and their political organizations has made possible an accurate chronological reconstruction of their history. Detailed reports of anti-Semitic activity, the listing of court cases, and extensive, in-context quotations from the daily German press and from long-vanished anti-Semitic newspapers make the *MVA* the single most valuable historical source for the study of imperial anti-Semitism. Nearly as valuable as its factual data, however, are the *MVA*'s involuntary revelations about how a wide variety of contemporaries viewed the problem of anti-Semitism, a fine and a necessary corrective to our own vastly altered perspective. Although polemical in purpose, the *MVA* did not find it necessary to varnish the truth about anti-Semitism. The citation of sources of information and the known integrity of its sponsors speak to the reliability of this paper. Anti-Semitic counterattacks usually skirted the accusations of the *Verein.* Rarely did anti-Semites go to court to press for libel convictions. In a careful reading of twenty-four years of the *MVA,* I have come across only one retraction, the product of a successful (and trivial) libel suit instituted by an anti-Semite.

54. For examples, see *RH,* 22 January 1892; Schmahl, *Entwicklung,* pp. 70–72; Buch, *50 Jahre,* pp. 29, 49. Also, Puhle, *Interessenpolitik,* p. 149 n. 30, citing the Agrarian League handbook.

55. Quotation from *Geschichte der Frankfurter Zeitung,* p. 436.

56. *MVA,* 5 March 1893; 12 March 1893; quotation from the issue of 16 April 1893.

57. For details on Stoecker's "pyre letter" and the Hammerstein scandal, see Massing, *Rehearsal,* pp. 121–22. For typical reactions by the anti-Semites, see *RH,* 22 January 1892; *AK,* 13 July 1899.

58. *MVA,* 10 June 1903. For typically foul aspersions on their motives, see Fritsch, *Handbuch der Judenfrage* (1943), pp. 161–62.

59. On the initial efforts at collective self-defense, see Schorsch, *Jewish Reactions*, pp. 23–78.

60. Achim von Borries, ed., *Selbstzeugnisse des deutschen Judentums* (Frankfurt a. M., 1962), pp. 18–19. Also, Simon Dubnow, *Weltgeschichte des jüdischen Volkes*, trans. A. Steinberg (Berlin, 1923), 10: 27–28. On Bamberger's public reticence concerning parliamentary anti-Semitism, see Zucker, "Ludwig Bamberger and the Rise of Anti-Semitism," pp. 332–52.

61. See Schmidt, "The Terms of Emancipation," pp. 42–43. Also, Sterling, "Anti-Jewish Riots in Germany in 1819," p. 129.

62. Paul Rieger, *Ein Vierteljahrhundert im Kampf um das Recht und die Zukunft der deutschen Juden* (Berlin, 1918), p. 11.

63. See *MVA*, 12 June 1907, quoting a speech by Oskar Cassel to the *Liberaler Verein*. Also, Selmar Spier, "Jewish History as We See It," *BYB* 1 (1956): 14.

64. [Raphael Löwenfeld], *Schutzjuden oder Staatsbürger?* (Berlin, 1893), pp. 3, 19. Also, Alfred Hirschberg, "Ludwig Hollaender, Director of the C. V.," *BYB* 7 (1962): 40–41.

65. On the history, finances, and structural development of the organization, see Schorsch, *Jewish Reactions*, pp. 117–48; Rieger, *Ein Vierteljahrhundert*, pp. 24, 73–81. On the history and much-debated policies of the organization in the 1920's and 1930's, see Eva G. Reichmann, "Der Centralverein deutscher Staatsbürger jüdischen Glaubens," *Süddeutsche Monatshefte* 27 (September 1930): 818–27; a harsh critique by the Institute of Social Research, "Analysis of Central-Verein Policy in Germany," mimeographed (New York, 1945); the reply of Alfred Wiener, "The Centralverein Deutscher Staatsbuerger Juedischen Glaubens–Its Meaning and Activities," (Wiener Library, London, 1945); and the most balanced treatment by a participant, Julie Meyers, "Jewish Anti-Defamation Work in Pre-Hitler Germany," (New York, n.d.), available in the Bibliotheque Nationale, Paris.

66. The question of Jewish self-image is peripheral to this study. It is thoroughly, although unsympathetically, discussed in Schorsch, *Jewish Reactions*. The most intelligent and objective treatment is Ruth Pierson, "German Jewish Identity in the Weimar Republic," (Ph. D. diss., Yale University, 1970).

67. See *MVA*, 18 September 1897, quoting the *IDR*. Also, a similar position toward Zionism in *MVA*, 16 September 1903.

68. See, for example, ibid., 29 January 1893; Abwehr-Verein, *Abwehr-ABC*, p. 116; *MVA*, 4 February 1903, Theodor Barth's address to the *Centralverein* on itstenth anniversary.

69. See Rieger, *Ein Vierteljahrhundert*, p. 40; *IDR*, August 1903.

70. Eugen Fuchs, "Rechtsschutz und Rechtsfrieden," in *Um Deutschtum und Judentum* (Frankfurt a. M., 1919), pp. 4–5. Also, Paucker, *Der jüdische Abwehrkampf*, p. 74; Rieger, *Ein Vierteljahrhundert*, p. 27; Wiener, "Centralverein," p. 5.

71. On the tortuous legal path followed by the *Centralverein*, see Maximilian Parmod [Max Apt], *Antisemitismus und Strafrechtspflege* (Berlin, 1894), pp. 2–3, 5, 12, 44–45; Eugen Fuchs, "Rückblick auf die zehnjährige Tätigkeit (2. Februar 1903)," in *Um Deutschtum und Judentum*, p. 93. Also, Schorsch, *Jewish Reactions*, pp. 123–32.

72. Rieger, *Ein Vierteljahrhundert,* pp. 31–33.

73. For examples, see *MVA,* 11 September 1897; 18 June 1898; Fuchs, "Rechtsschutz," pp. 11–12.

74. Wiener, "Centralverein," p. 5.

75. Fuchs, "Rückblick," p. 94.

76. Buch, *50 Jahre,* p. 49.

77. Wiener "Centralverein," p. 5.

78. In compiling these statistics I have dismissed many cases that refer to individuals with very tenuous or highly questionable ties to anti-Semitism. These figures must be considered incomplete because neither the *MVA* nor the *IDR* claimed to be exhaustive in their coverage of trials.

79. See Wiener, "Centralverein," p. 3; Toury, *Die politischen Orientierungen,* pp. 203–07. For a contrary view, see Schorsch, *Jewish Reactions,* pp. 98–100, 134–35. I find Schorsch's denial of the essential similarity of outlook in the *Abwehr-Verein* and *Centralverein* generally unconvincing and particularly so in the matter of their common left-liberal politics.

80. Rieger, *Ein Vierteljahrhundert,* p. 38; Toury, *Die politischen Orientierungen,* p. 207 n. 21.

81. Fuchs, "Rückblick," pp. 84ff.; *IDR,* September 1898; Rieger, *Ein Vierteljahrhundert,* p. 40.

82. For the fullest discussion of the *"Jüdisches Zentrum,"* see Marjorie Lamberti, "The Attempt to Form a Jewish Bloc: Jewish Notables and Politics in Wilhelmian Germany," *Central European History* 3 (March-June 1970): 73–93. Also, Toury, *Die politischen Orientierungen,* pp. 276–94.

83. *Die Nation,* 8 April 1899, p. 36.

84. Fuchs, "Rückblick," p. 96.

85. *VHLt,* 30 December 1901, pp. 1798–1800.

86. *VPrLt,* 31 January 1901, 1: 926–36; Eyck, *Wilhelm II,* p. 103. See also *MVA,* 17 January 1906.

87. See Verband der Deutschen Juden, *Stenografischer Bericht über die zu Berlin am Montag, den 30. Oktober 1905 abgehalten erste Hauptversammlung* (Berlin, 1905). On the structure and other purposes of the *Verband,* see Schorsch, *Jewish Reactions,* pp. 150–62.

88. See *VSLt,* 7 November 1907, 1: 315.

89. *Korrespondenz-Blatt des Verbandes der Deutschen Juden,* May 1908.

90. Hamburger, *Juden im öffentlichen Leben,* pp. 53–63; Bürger, *Antisemiten-Spiegel* (1911), pp. 257–58. Also, Ernest Hamburger, "Jews in the Public Service under the German Monarchy," *BYB* 9 (1964): 232.

91. Hamburger, "Jews in Public Service," p. 230. Also, Klinkenberg, "Zwischen Liberalismus und Nationalismus," pp. 377–79. Quotation from Hirschberg, "Ludwig Hollaender," p. 42.

92. For the two exceptions, see Hamburger, *Juden im öffentlichen Leben,* pp. 44–47. Also, Toury, *Die politischen Orientierungen,* p. 197.

93. Hamburger, *Juden im öffentlichen Leben,* pp. 40–53.

94. *MVA,* 24 August 1910, using a study of the 1907 occupational census done by the *Kölnische Volkszeitung.*

95. See Karl Demeter, *Das deutsche Offizierkorps in Gesellschaft und Staat, 1650–1945,* 4th ed. (Frankfurt a. M., 1965), pp. 217–21.

96. The most penetrating study of this problem is Werner T. Angress, "Prussia's Army and the Jewish Reserve Officer Controversy before World War I," *BYB* 17 (1972): 19–41.

97. On the lack of Jewish active or reserve officers, promises and measures notwithstanding, see ibid., pp. 39–40; Klinkenberg, "Zwischen Liberalismus und Nationalismus," p. 375.

98. Hamburger, "Jews in Public Service," p. 227; *MVA,* 4 April 1906; 15 June 1910.

CHAPTER 7. The Parliamentary Solution is Tested

1. See the debate on the original motion in *VRt* 135 (10 March 1894): 1734, 1736–37. Also, Tirrell, *German Agrarian Politics,* p. 290.

2. *VRt* 139 (6 March 1895): 1304–06.

3. On Hasse's attitude, see Werner, "Der Alldeutsche Verband," pp. 83–84. On the groundlessness of Liebermann's fears, see *MVA,* 27 April 1895, quoting a study of naturalization figures in the *Berliner Korrespondenz.*

4. *VRt* 149 (2 April 1897): 5454–73. Also, Spamitz, "Tätigkeit," pp. 184–85; *IDR,* June 1897.

5. See *VRt* 167 (9 May 1899): 2113–14, for the speech of the left liberal, Karl Schrader; and ibid. 167 (25 April 1899): 1916–17, for Ernst Lieber's speech at the bill's first reading.

6. See *AK,* 15 October 1896; *Handbuch der nationalliberalen Partei,* p. 39.

7. *MVA,* 23 December 1899; *IDR,* May 1900.

8. On Heinrich Lieber's expulsion, see *AK,* 16 July 1896. For well-documented critiques of the anti-Semites' performance in the reform of the civil code, see *Handbuch der nationalliberalen Partei,* p. 40; and *MVA,* 17 April 1897; also, *Die Antisemiten im Reichstag,* pp. 9–11.

9. *MVA,* 9 June 1894; 10 July 1897; 17 July 1897; 21 May 1898.

10. See ibid., 6 May 1899, quoting the *Korrespondenz für Zentrumsblätter;* *Handbuch der nationalliberalen Partei,* pp. 38–41. Also, the bitter criticism of the anti-Semitic university students in Weber, *Geschichte des Vereins Deutscher Studenten,* p. 4.

11. See Karl Bachem, *Vorgeschichte, Geschichte und Politik der deutschen Zentrumspartei* (Cologne, 1929), 5: 397–98.

12. The starkest contrasts between the Nazis and the conventional anti-Semites of the empire are to be found in their attitudes toward parliament. See Wilhelm Frick, *Die Nationalsozialisten im deutschen Reichstag, 1924–1931* (Munich, 1932), p. 6. Also, a speech by Hitler which advocated making a shambles out of parliament in Walther Hofer, ed., *Der Nationalsozialismus* (Frankfurt a. M., 1957), p. 28.

13. See *Schulthess' Europäischer Geschichtskalender,* 1893, pp. 30–33.

14. See Dietrich von Oertzen, *Adolf Stoecker. Lebensbild und Zeitgeschichte* (Berlin, 1910), 2: 116–36.

15. Puhle, *Interessenpolitik*, pp. 120–21; Frank, *Hofprediger*, pp. 273–74.

16. See Puhle, *Interessenpolitik*, pp. 128–33, 301–02. See Chapter 9 below.

17. However, Hannah Arendt's puzzling assertion that the anti-Semites customarily voted with the Social Democrats was never at any time true. See Arendt, *The Origins of Totalitarianism*, p. 38.

18. *AK*, 13 October 1898; Abwehr-Verein, *Der politische Antisemitismus*, pp. 97–98.

19. See *RH*, 12 January 1892; 26 January 1892. Also, Braun, *Die Parteien*, p. 27; Scheidemann, *Memoiren*, 1: 71, 97–98.

20. For example, see the obituary for August Bebel in *Staatsbürger-Zeitung*, 4 September 1913. Also, Heinrich Pudor, *Deutschland für die Deutschen!* (Munich and Leipzig, 1912), p. 249.

21. See Karl Marx, "Zur Judenfrage," *Deutsch-französische Jahrbücher* (Paris, 1844), p. 211.

22. *VRt* 118 (12 January 1892): 3587.

23. Scheidemann, "Wandlungen des Antisemitismus," p. 636, emphasis in the original. Arguing from the same presuppositions, an anonymous analyst volunteered the inevitable "if the anti-Semites did not exist, they would have to be invented." See *Neue Zeit* 11 (1892–1893): 419–20.

24. *Protokoll über die Verhandlungen des Parteitages der Sozialdemokratischen Partei Deutschlands in Halle* (Berlin, 1890), pp. 270–72. A similar brushing aside of the problem took place at the Brussel's congress of the Second International in August 1891. See James Joll, *The Second International 1889–1914* (New York, 1966), pp. 68–69.

25. *Protokoll über die Verhandlungen des Parteitages der SPD (1893)*, pp. 224–40. Also, Bebel, *Sozialdemokratie und Antisemitismus*, pp. 1–27. Bebel concerned himself mainly with the political manifestations of anti-Semitism. In 1914 Karl Kautsky treated the problem in much broader and more theoretical terms than Bebel. See his *Rasse und Judentum*, 2nd ed. (Stuttgart, 1921).

26. See Bernstein in *Neue Zeit* 11 (1892–1893): 233–37. Bernstein vainly tried to get Friedrich Engels to take the problem more seriously in the 1880's. See Helmut Hirsch, ed., *Eduard Bernsteins Briefwechsel mit Friedrich Engels* (Assen, 1970), pp. 27–29, 33, 37, 257, 293, 299. Also, an early attack on Vollmar in *AK*, March 1888. On Scheidemann's struggle in Hessenland, see his *Memoiren*, 1: 62, 98; *Mitteldeutsche Sonntags-Zeitung* (Giessen), 24 September 1899. Scheidemann coedited this paper between 1895 and 1900. An orthodox Marxist who took anti-Semitism more seriously than most of his colleagues was Wilhelm Liebknecht. His *Über den Kölner Parteitag* (Bielefeld, 1893) was meant to reinforce Bebel's statement at the Cologne party congress.

27. For a view more critical of the Social Democrats, see George L. Mosse, "German Socialists and the Jewish Question in the Weimar Republic," *BYB* 16 (1971): 123–51. Mosse stresses those aspects of the socialist heritage which were compatible with anti-Jewish feeling. More sympathetic to the Socialists without ignoring the anti-Semitic incidents is Donald L. Niewyk, "German Social Democ-

racy and the Problem of Anti-Semitism, 1906–1914," (M.A. thesis, Tulane University, 1964), and his *Socialist, Anti-Semite, and Jew. German Social Democracy Confronts the Problem of Anti-Semitism 1918–1933* (Baton Rouge, 1971).

28. On the Social Democrats' success in keeping members clear of political anti-Semitism, see Robert Michels, "Die deutsche Sozialdemokratie, deren Parteimitgliedschaft und soziale Zusammensetzung," *Archiv für Sozialwissenschaft* 23 (1906): 519–21. Also, Hamburger, *Juden im öffentlichen Leben*, pp. 558–59; Massing, *Rehearsal*, p. 202.

29. See Edmund Silberner, "Austrian Social Democracy and the Jewish Problem," *Historia Judaica* 13 (1951): 121. For the anti-Semitic views of French socialists grouped around the periodical, *La Revue Socialiste*, see Z. Szajkowski, *Anti-Semitism in the French Labor Movement, 1845–1906.* Yiddish (New York, 1948), pp. 151–56.

30. For an early protest by the *Fortschrittspartei,* see *Die Verurteilung der antisemitischen Bewegung durch die Wahlmänner von Berlin* (Berlin, 1881).

31. See Adolf Rubinstein, *Die Deutsche-Freisinnige Partei bis zu ihrem Auseinanderbruch, 1884–1893* (Basel, 1935), pp. 22–23, 86; *MVA,* 26 February 1893; 5 March 1893; 12 March 1893.

32. Both figures include the seats of the left-liberal *Süddeutsche Volkspartei.* See Schwarz, *MdR: Biographisches Handbuch*, pp. 820–21.

33. Ziekursch, *Politische Geschichte,* 3: 67; Nichols, *Caprivi Era,* p. 255. Nichols attributes some of the loss to the Social Democrats as well.

34. See *MVA,* 18 September 1907, citing the resolution of the party congress.

35. See *Der zweite Parteitag der Fortschrittlichen Volkspartei, 5. –7. Oktober 1912* (Berlin, 1912), pp. 113–15.

36. See *VPrLt,* 30 January 1905, 6: 9198–233; 18 March 1905, 6: 892–904, for the speech of Oskar Cassel; see ibid., 31 January 1901, 1: 926–36, for the speeches of Martin Peltasohn and Barth.

37. Compiled from *VRt* 135–61 (1893–1898).

38. See Theodor Eschenburg, *Das Kaiserreich am Scheideweg. Bassermann, Bülow und der Block* (Berlin, 1929), pp. 39–63. Also Chapter 9 below.

39. See *Der zweite Parteitag der Fortschrittlichen Volkspartei,* p. 14.

40. See Liebermann's change of views in *Beiträge,* pp. 60–61, 293.

41. For example, see the unanimous resolution of the National Liberal club in Schleiz (Thuringia) in *MVA,* 1 April 1894.

42. Ibid., 10 October 1896; 24 October 1896. On Hessenland, see Philipp Köhler's speech in *VHLt,* 26 March 1897, p. 122; 11 March 1902, p. 2488. Also, Ludwig Bamberger's dispiriting experience with National Liberal anti-Semitism in Zucker, "Ludwig Bamberger and the Rise of Anti-Semitism," p. 349. In Baden, too, the National Liberals helped two anti-Semites to state parliament seats in order to fend off left-liberal competition. See *MVA,* 30 October 1897; 6 November 1897.

43. See *RH,* 15 January 1892; 26 January 1892; Curtius, *Der politische Antisemitismus,* pp. 40–41. On the crisis in the National Liberal party, see Klaus-Peter

Reiss, *Von Bassermann zu Stresemann: Die Sitzungen des nationalliberalen Zentralvorstandes, 1912–1917* (Düsseldorf, 1967), pp. 91, 161, 299.

44. Wawrzinek, *Antisemitenparteien*, pp. 11–12; *Historisch-politische Blätter für das katholische Deutschland*, 1873, p. 126; 1875, *Neujahrserinnerungen*. Also, Guenter Lewy, *The Catholic Church and Nazi Germany* (New York, 1964), pp. 270–71.

45. On the Rohling affair, see J. S. Bloch, *My Reminiscences* (Vienna and Berlin, 1923), pp. 64ff.

46. Compare Windthorst's speech with the more representative anti-Semitic views of the Centrist, Peter Reichensperger, in *VPrLt*, 20 November 1880, 1: 232–33, 248–50. Also, Ludwig Pastor, *August Reichensperger* (Freiburg, 1899), 2: 191.

47. See Buchheim, *Geschichte der christlichen Parteien*, p. 256.

48. The Prussian government expulsion of twenty thousand Catholic and ten thousand Jewish Poles in 1885–1886 produced a common outcry in the Jewish and Centrist press. See Helmut Neubach, *Die Ausweisungen von Polen und Juden aus Preussen 1885/1886* (Wiesbaden, 1967), p. 140. In north Germany where both Jews and Catholics were minorities, Catholic sympathies for the civil rights struggle of Jews were evident. However, such sympathy was not apparent in the South where Catholics were a majority. See Schorsch, *Jewish Reactions*, pp. 162–63.

49. *MVA*, 1 September 1895; Liebermann von Sonnenberg, *Beiträge*, pp. 110, 262.

50. See Zimmermann's accusations in *MVA*, 8 October 1898.

51. See K. Bachem, *Zentrumspartei*, 5: 397–98; Liebermann's attacks on the Center in *AK*, 7 June 1894, Beilage no. 74; *AK*, 27 September 1894, Beilage no. 98. For complaints about the lack of political help from the Center, see Giese, "Die deutschsoziale Reformpartei," pp. 205, 214.

52. *AK*, 22 August 1895.

53. See the speech of Center party leader Ernst Lieber in *VRt* 139 (6 March 1895): 1285–87.

54. See *AK*, 26 September 1895.

55. See *VRt* 160 (22 February 1898): 1197; 167 (25 April 1899): 1916–17; (9 May 1899): 2103–08; 179 (5 December 1900): 302–05. See also the favorable treatment of Lieber in *MVA*, 9 April 1902; 1 April 1894.

56. Both these questions have been raised by Massing, *Rehearsal*, pp. 216–17 n. 38; and Hamburger, *Juden im öffentlichen Leben*, pp. 48–51, 65–66, 345–46. Also, Hamburger, "Jews in Public Service," p. 236.

57. See *VBLt*, 28 November 1901, 7: 928–63. Evidence of the pernicious influence of Prussian discrimination against Jews in the civil service appeared in Heim's speech. When the Bavarian minister of justice cited the constitution as grounds for rejection of the motion, Heim confronted him with the example of the Prussian minister of justice, Schönstedt, who had defended the nonappointment of Jews to certain civil service posts on the grounds of popular feeling and maintenance of public peace (see Chapter 6 above). It should be noted that Heim's motion had no effect upon Bavaria's liberal policy with regard to Jewish appointments to the judiciary.

58. See *MVA*, 22 August 1896; 26 September 1900.

59. *Der politische Antisemitismus*, p. 11.

60. *MVA*, 15 February 1911, quoting an address by Bavarian parliament deputy Günther to a meeting of the *Centralverein*. Also, Abwehr-Verein, *Abwehr-ABC*, p. 122; Bürger, *Antisemiten-Spiegel* (1911), pp. 81–82. The most frequent anti-Semitic offenders among Center newspapers were the *Germania* and the *Schlessische Volkszeitung*. Anti-Semitic incidents in which Center party or Church dignitaries participated were reported by *MVA*, 2 May 1900; 19 September 1900; 27 October 1909; 3 January 1912; 17 January 1912.

61. See Toury, *Die politischen Orientierungen*, pp. 246–61, quoting from the *Jüdisches Volksblatt* (Breslau). Also, *Allgemeine Zeitung des Judentums* 76 (1912): 123, 135–36, 207, 219–20. (I am indebted to Werner T. Angress of the State University of New York, Stony Brook, for these citations.)

62. *MVA*, 25 January 1905.

63. On Erzberger's anti-Semitism, see Klaus Epstein, *Matthias Erzberger and the Dilemma of German Democracy* (Princeton, 1959), pp. 401–04; *MVA*, 3 January 1912. For his reversal, see *VRt* 290 (20 June 1913): 5655–56.

64. Giese, "Die deutschsoziale Reformpartei," pp. 199–200.

65. On Ahlwardt's American interlude, see the *New York Times*, 22 November–13 December 1895; 7–25 April 1896; 15 September 1896. Also, *MVA*, 4 April 1896; 13 November 1907.

66. *AK*, 13 October 1898, report of the Kassel congress, 8–10 October 1898. Also, Buch, *50 Jahre*, pp. 58–59, 83.

67. *AK*, 13 January 1898; *MVA*, 15 October 1898.

68. *AK*, 30 December 1897.

69. Frank, *Die Brandenburger als Reichstagswähler*, p. 45; Giese, "Die deutschsoziale Reformpartei," pp. 221–23, 228; *MVA*, 19 November 1898; *Die Antisemiten im Reichstag*, p. 40.

70. Gerlach, *Von Rechts nach Links*, p. 107. See also Oertzen, *Adolf Stoecker*, 2: 128–36.

71. The celebration was extensively covered in *MVA*, 8 January 1898.

72. Ibid., 19 November 1898.

73. Giese, "Die deutschsoziale Reformpartei," p. 228; *AK*, 13 October 1898; 30 June 1898.

CHAPTER 8. Breaking the Pattern

1. See the handbook commissioned by the *Verein Deutscher Studenten* and other right-wing groups, Alfred Geiser, ed., *Deutsches Reich und Volk*, 2nd ed. (Munich, 1910), 1: 157. On the *Deutscher Jugendbund* of Stuttgart, see Lohalm, *Völkischer Radikalismus*, pp. 57–58. Also, *IDR*, November 1899.

2. See Houston Stewart Chamberlain, *The Foundations of the Nineteenth Century*, trans. John Lees (London and New York, 1900), 1: 353. Also, the views of Chamberlain and Richard Wagner in Schüler, *Bayreuther Kreis*, pp. 246–47.

3. Weber, *Geschichte des Vereins deutscher Studenten*, p. 246; *AK*, 12 October 1899.

On the somewhat different path followed by the *Judgendbund* of Hamburg and its close connections to the anti-Semitic parties, see Iris Hamel, *Völkischer Verband und nationale Gewerkschaft. Der Deutschnationale Handlungsgehilfen-Verband 1893–1933* (Frankfurt a. M., 1967), pp. 72–82.

4. On Lange and the *Deutschbund*, see Lohalm, *Völkischer Radikalismus*, pp. 32–35; Class, *Wider den Strom*, pp. 31, 33; Buch, *50 Jahre*, p. 27.

5. To mention a few: the *Deutschvölkische Vereinigung* (1902, Stuttgart), which intended the total cleansing of Germanic life; the *Urda-Bund* (Munich), devoted to the spread of race-consciousness built upon study of the *Eddas;* the *Deutsche Vereinigung* (1907–1908, Bonn), "against ultramontanism, social democracy, and Jewry"; the *Vaterländischer Schriften-Verband* (1907, Berlin); the radically anti-Semitic youth group *Die Greifen* (the Griffins); and Theodor Fritsch's *Hammer-Gemeinden* (1902, discussed below in the Conclusion). See Geiser, *Reich und Volk*, 1: 187–209; Mosse, *The Crisis of German Ideology*, pp. 218–33; Pulzer, *The Rise of Political Anti-Semitism*, pp. 219–35.

6. *Die Antisemiten im Reichstag*, p. 7. Also, Pulzer, *The Rise of Political Anti-Semitism*, pp. 192–93. Pulzer mistakenly describes Böckel as a founder of the *Volksbund*.

7. See *MVA*, 25 April 1900, quoting Mosch in the *Deutsche Reform;* Geiser, *Reich und Volk*, 1: 206–07.

8. Buch, *50 Jahre*, p. 39; Curtius, *Der politische Antisemitismus*, p. 38.

9. For an early expression of concern regarding Mosch's radicalism, see *MVA*, 1 April 1894, quoting an article in the *Kreuzzeitung*. On kaiser and Reichstag, see Hans von Mosch, *Neue politische Gedichte, 1907–1913* (Berlin, n.d.), passim.

10. See Hans Arndt, *Herunter mit der Maske! Die Führer der deutschen Antisemiten im Lichte der Wahrheit* (Zurich, 1898).

11. See Wilhelm Giese, *Die Herren Raab und Liebermann*, pp. 5, 15, 107; *AK*, 14 September 1899. Quotation from *Die Antisemiten im Reichstag*, p. 19.

12. Lorenzen, *Die Antisemiten*, p. 19; *AK*, 30 June 1898; Puhle, *Interessenpolitik*, pp. 129–30 n. 98, 151 n. 44; *MVA*, 20 May 1899, quoting Wangenheim in the *Konservative Korrespondenz*.

13. See Liebermann von Sonnenberg, *Aus der Glückzeit*, pp. 27–28. On his appointment to the Pan-German League governing board, see *MVA*, 29 May 1901.

14. *AK*, 13 July 1899.

15. On the league's demand for greater discipline and unified leadership within the anti-Semitic party, see Puhle, *Interessenpolitik*, p. 130 n. 98, quoting *Korrespondenz des Bundes der Landwirte*, 5 Fanuary 1899.

16. *AK*, 5 October 1899; 8 February 1900.

17. See Giese, *Die Herren Raab und Liebermann*, pp. 23–27.

18. *AK*, 5 October 1899, report of the German Social Reform party's Hamburg congress, 10–11 September 1899.

19. Quotation in *AK*, 14 September 1899. Also, *MVA*, 16 September 1899.

20. *MVA*, 23 September 1899.

21. See Otto Böckler, "Die Konservativen im Wahlkampf," *AJB* (1899): 128–56.

22. See *AK*, 21 September 1899; 28 September 1899. For Giese's amended

theses, see *Schulthess' Europäischer Geschichtskalender,* 1899, p. 142. Also, Giese, "Die deutschsoziale Reformpartei," pp. 217–218.

23. Giese, *Die Herren Raab und Liebermann,* pp. 25–27; *MVA,* 30 January 1900; *AK,* 1 February 1900.

24. For accounts of Liebermann's many sins as party leader, see Buch, *50 Jahre,* pp. 20, 58; Arndt, *Herunter mit der Maske!,* passim; *Herr Liebermann v. Sonnenberg als Parteiführer,* pp. 1–2, 8, 10, 24–25. Also, *MVA,* 28 February 1900.

25. *AK,* 30 August 1900.

26. Ibid., 13 September 1900; *MVA,* 12 September 1900; 19 September 1900.

27. *AK,* 13 September 1900; *Die Antisemiten im Reichstag,* pp. 6–7.

28. See a survey of the press in *MVA,* 26 September 1900. The quotation is from the *Kölnische Volkszeitung.*

29. *MVA,* 26 September 1900, quoting the *Konservative Korrespondenz.*

30. *MVA,* 17 October 1896, citing a speech by Suchsland to the German Social Reform party's Halle congress.

31. See *MVA,* 1 January 1898; Abwehr-Verein, *Der politische Antisemitismus,* pp. 59–60.

32. *MVA,* 24 April 1901. Also, Liebermann's complaint in Puhle, *Interessenpolitik,* p. 137 n. 41.

33. See brief descriptions in *MVA,* 1 August 1900.

34. *AK,* 28 June 1900.

35. Ibid., 28 June 1900; 10 May 1900. Also, Abwehr-Verein, *Ergänzung zum Antisemiten-Spiegel* (Berlin, 1903), p. 24.

36. See the full manifesto in *MVA,* 9 May 1900. Compare the far more provocative pamphlet by Liebermann, *Der Blutmord in Konitz,* 7th ed. (Berlin, 1901).

37. Abwehr-Verein, *Antisemiten-Spiegel* (1903), pp. 22–23. Also, Massing, *Rehearsal,* p. 108.

38. *Die Antisemiten im Reichstag,* p. 25.

39. *MVA,* 15 October 1902; *Die Antisemiten im Reichstag,* p. 44; Abwehr-Verein, *Der politische Antisemitismus,* p. 63; Abwehr-Verein, *Antisemiten-Spiegel* (1903), p. 21.

40. Full text in *MVA,* 24 August 1901.

41. See *IDR,* February 1899, quoting an often repeated speech of Pückler. Also, the perceptive observation of the count's audience by Gerlach in *MVA,* 8 January 1902.

42. *MVA,* 7 December 1904.

43. *VRt* 171 (12 June 1900): 6038; *VPrLt,* 13 February 1903, 2: 1326–28, 1332.

44. For example, see *VRt* 160 (9 February 1898): 915–16; 161 (29 March 1898): 1875–76, Werner's speeches on the Zanzibar-Heligoland agreement (1890) and the treatment of Germans in Africa.

45. See *AK,* 16 November 1899; 28 September 1899. Also, Pauline Anderson, *The Background of Anti-English Feeling in Germany, 1890–1902* (Washington, D. C., 1939), p. 236.

46. Anderson, too, treats the anti-Semites and Pan-Germans as one group. See Anderson, *Anti-English Feeling,* pp. 298, 300, 353.

47. See *IDR,* October 1899. Also, *AK,* 25 January 1900; 19 October 1899.

48. Liebermann von Sonnenberg, *Beiträge*, p. 261, a speech by Förster.

49. Glagau's contention in *Der Kulturkämpfer*, 1888, p. 436.

50. *MVA*, 13 January 1900; 16 September 1899, quoting the *Deutsche Reform*; 28 November 1900, quoting a speech by Böckel in Erfurt.

51. *IDR*, November 1899; *AK*, 2 November 1899. Also, Wertheimer, *The Pan-German League*, pp. 42–43 n. 3.

52. See Rich, *The Holstein Papers*, 4: 236–37. Also, Anderson, *Anti-English Feeling*, p. 238. The phrase is Joseph Chamberlain's.

53. Schmahl, *Entwicklung*, pp. 116–17.

54. *MVA*, 30 January 1901.

55. *VRt* 171 (12 June 1900): 6038, 6042–44.

56. *Die Antisemiten im Reichstag*, p. 15.

57. See *MVA*, 19 December 1900, quoting from Zimmermann's *Deutsche Wacht*, the Magdeburg *Sachsenschau* (independent anti-Semitic), and the *Deutsche Zeitung* of Friedrich Lange.

58. Anderson, *Anti-English Feeling*, pp. 353–54, 332–33.

59. See Bernhard von Bülow, *Denkwürdigkeiten* (Berlin, 1930), 1: 552–55. Also, a more impartial account in Norman Rich, *Friedrich von Holstein. Politics and Diplomacy in the Era of Bismarck and Wilhelm II* (Cambridge, 1965), 2: 667–68.

60. *London Times*, 10 January 1902.

61. *VRt* 182 (10 January 1902): 3267–78.

62. *London Times*, 10 January 1902.

63. Ibid., 15 January 1902. Also, Anderson, *Anti-English Feeling*, p. 337. Concerning the setback to diplomatic cooperation between England and Germany, see Rich, *Friedrich von Holstein*, 2: 668–69.

64. For a large sampling of the press, see *MVA*, 15 January 1902.

65. Ibid., 5 November 1902; Buch, *50 Jahre*, p. 38. Also, Balfour, *The Kaiser*, p. 242.

66. See Liebermann's emphatic commitment to the Erfurt program's goals and methods in *MVA*, 24 August 1904; his speech at the German Social party's Hamburg congress, ibid., 21 October 1903. Also, Bindewald and Bruhn, ibid., 30 January 1901; Werner, ibid., 9 October 1901, a speech to the German Social Reform party congress.

67. Ibid., 5 December 1900; *Die Antisemiten im Reichstag*, pp. 10, 12–13.

68. *MVA*, 29 May 1901, report of the Brunswick congress of the German Social party. See also ibid., 8 October 1902.

69. Not to be confused with his more famous brother Count Ernst zu Reventlow-Altenhof, also an officer of the Agrarian League, Pan-German writer, and later member of the Nazi party. See Puhle, *Interessenpolitik*, p. 65 n. 147. Also, *MVA*, 12 June 1901.

70. *Reichstags-Handbuch. Zwölfte Legislaturperiode* (Berlin, 1907), p. 310.

71. Ibid., p. 354.

72. On the key role played by Raab, Zimmermann, and Schack and the relationship of the Shop Clerks' union to the anti-Semitic youth movement, see Hamel, *Völkischer Verband*, pp. 22–25, 44–68, 72–82.

73. Hamel, *Völkischer Verband,* pp. 44–55. Also, Hermann Schuon, *Der Deutsch-nationale Handlungsgehilfen-Verband zu Hamburg* (Jena, 1914), pp. 6–8, 16.

74. See *MVA,* 30 September 1899; Schuon, *Der DHV,* p. 17; *IDR,* February 1897.

75. On the growth of the union, see Hamel, *Völkischer Verband,* pp. 52–68, 110–22; Schuon, *Der DHV,* pp. 20, 241.

76. Giese, *Die Herren Raab und Liebermann,* p. 108; *MVA,* 10 February 1904.

77. Hamel, *Völkischer Verband,* pp. 111–13; Giese, *Die Herren Raab und Liebermann,* p. 108.

78. *VRt* 184 (4 June 1902): 5407–09; (11 June 1902): 5614–16.

79. See Liebermann's speeches in *VRt* 186 (28 November 1902): 6696–98; (11 December 1902): 7132–34. Also, Stegmann, *Erben Bismarcks,* pp. 140–43; Kiesenwetter, *Fünfundzwanzig Jahre,* p. 84; *MVA,* 12 October 1904.

80. Kiesenwetter, *Fünfundzwanzig Jahre,* p. 84.

81. See *MVA,* 7 January 1903.

82. See Erwin Knauss, "Die politische Kräfte und das Wählerverhalten im Landkreis Giessen während der letzten 60 Jahre," *Mitteilungen des Oberhessischen Geschichtsvereins* 45 (1961): 36–38. Also, Puhle, *Interessenpolitik,* p. 67.

83. *MVA,* 9 August 1905; 11 August 1909.

84. Abwehr-Verein, *Der politische Antisemitismus,* pp. 10–12; *MVA,* 1 July 1903.

85. *MVA,* 27 May 1903, quoting the *Deutsche Evangelische Korrespondenz.* Also, an analysis of Christian Social weakness in ibid., 14 January 1903.

86. Abwehr-Verein, *Der politische Antisemitismus,* pp. 10–12; *MVA,* 1 July 1903; 27 May 1903.

87. *MVA,* 1 July 1903.

88. Ibid., 24 June 1903; 1 July 1903.

89. Abwehr-Verein, *Der politische Antisemitismus,* pp. 36–37; *MVA,* 31 January 1906; 7 October 1903.

CHAPTER 9. Decline and Dissolution

1. *MVA,* 21 October 1903, report of the German Social Reform party congress in Berlin.

2. Quotation from Eschenburg, *Das Kaiserreich am Scheideweg,* p. 137. See also Kiesenwetter, *Fünfundzwanzig Jahre,* p. 359. On the lack of "anti-Semitic principles" in the Economic Union, see Buch, *50 Jahre,* p. 59; Grotewold, *Die Parteien,* pp. 64–66; Abwehr-Verein, *Der politische Antisemitismus,* pp. 50–51.

3. *MVA,* 18 November 1903.

4. Ibid., 13 October 1909; 11 September 1907.

5. Hamel, *Völkischer Verband,* pp. 112–13; Abwehr-Verein, *Der politische Anti-semitismus,* pp. 18–24. The German Socials reported going two thousand marks into debt because of the Eisenach contest.

6. Of some help in following the mergers, schisms, ideological conflicts, and changing political alliances of this loose coalition of organizations are Bürger, *Mittelstandsbewegung,* pp. 8–10, et passim; and Stegmann, *Erben Bismarcks,* pp. 44–46, 143–45, 182–83.

7. See Mahler, *Die Programme*, pp. 21–22, 28.

8. See Buch, *50 Jahre*, pp. 45–46; *MVA*, 31 October 1907.

9. Most specific is Bürger, *Mittelstandsbewegung*, pp. 12–16. Also, Leo Müffelmann, *Die wirtschaftlichen Verbände* (Leipzig, 1912), pp. 93–99.

10. Bürger, *Mittelstandsbewegung*, pp. 16, 27–29, 35, 38–40.

11. On the *Hansabund* and its courting of the *Mittelstand*, see Stegmann, *Erben Bismarcks*, pp. 176–94, 219–56.

12. Ziekursch, *Politische Geschichte*, 3: 116, 185. For an interpretation which credits Erzberger's sincerity, see Epstein, *Erzberger*, pp. 52–56.

13. George D. Crothers, *The German Elections of 1907* (New York, 1941), p. 105, quoting the *Norddeutsche Allgemeine Zeitung*.

14. Molt, *Der Reichstag*, p. 303 n. 53; Maier, *Die Antisemiten*, p. 8; *MVA*, 20 February 1907; 16 January 1907.

15. See Dieter Fricke, ed., *Die bürgerlichen Parteien in Deutschland. Handbuch der Geschichte der bürgerlichen Parteien und anderer bürgerlicher Interessenorganisationen vom Vormärz bis zum Jahre 1945* (Berlin, 1968), 2: 620–28; Stegmann, *Erben Bismarcks*, pp. 47–50. On the relationship between the league and the anti-Semitic parties, see Bürger, *Antisemiten-Spiegel* (1911), p. 104; Carl E. Schorske, *German Social Democracy, 1905–1917* (New York, 1965), pp. 61, 126.

16. *MVA*, 14 August 1907, quoting the *Antisemitische-Korrespondenz*. In 1909 the anti-Semites of Hesse also reversed their traditional stand in order to support an undemocratic reform of the franchise. See Schorske, *German Social Democracy*, p. 172.

17. Maier, *Die Antisemiten*, p. 17.

18. Quoted in Curtius, *Der politische Antisemitismus*, p. 107.

19. *MVA*, 16 January 1907; 20 February 1907; 6 March 1907. Also, Schorske, *German Social Democracy*, pp. 61–62; *IDR*, March 1907.

20. *MVA*, 20 February 1907; 30 January 1907.

21. Quotation from Abwehr-Verein, *Der politische Antisemitismus*, p. 32; Curtius, *Der politische Antisemitismus*, pp. 7, 44–45.

22. See Fricke, *Handbuch der bürgerlichen Parteien*, 1: 245–55.

23. Quotation from Massing, *Rehearsal*, p. 113.

24. Gerlach dated the end of anti-Semitism "as a political factor" in 1904. See his "Vom deutschen Antisemitismus," p. 156. Also, Grotewold, *Die Parteien*, p. 103.

25. Curtius, *Der politische Antisemitismus*, p. 49.

26. *VSLt*, 7 November 1907, 1: 317–18. See Curtius, *Der politische Antisemitismus*, p. 73. Mumm used the pseudonym of Monheim.

27. Quoted in *MVA*, 13 May 1908.

28. See an exposé of the budget debates of 1909 in Curtius, *Der politische Antisemitismus*, p. 74.

29. On Krösell and Mosch, see Abwehr-Verein, *Der politische Antisemitismus*, pp. 15–16; Curtius, *Der politische Antisemitismus*, p. 12; *MVA*, 31 March 1909. On Köhler, see Schmahl, *Entwicklung*, p. 117.

30. *RH*, September 1898; October 1898.

31. *MVA*, 12 March 1902; quotation from ibid., 28 January 1903.

32. See ibid., 11 February 1903; 23 February 1910.

33. For the domestic repercussions of the incident, see M. Schlegelmilch, *Die Stellung der Parteien des deutschen Reichstages zur sogenannten Daily-Telegraph-Affäre und ihre innerpolitische Nachwirkung* (Halle, 1936). Also, Wilhelm Schüssler, *Die Daily-Telegraph-Affaire* (Göttingen, 1952).

34. See *MVA*, 24 October 1906, quoting Zimmermann at the German Reform party congress in Kassel; Buch, *50 Jahre*, p. 38. On Ballin, see Curtius, *Der politische Antisemitismus*, p. 109, quoting Liebermann. For an attack on Ballin in the Reichstag, see Otto Böckler's speech in *VRt* 197 (14 January 1904): 275–77. Also, Lamar Cecil, *Albert Ballin: Business and Politics in Imperial Germany, 1888–1918* (Princeton, 1967), pp. 100–02, 109, 164. Bruhn's *Die Wahrheit* is quoted in *MVA*, 19 September 1906.

35. See Schlegelmilch, *Die Stellung der Parteien*, pp. 17–20, 26–29.

36. *VRt* 233 (10 November 1908): 5401–05.

37. Ibid. (11 November 1908): 5415–18. Also, Balfour, *The Kaiser*, pp. 274–77, 290–92.

38. *VRt* 233 (11 November 1908): 5415; Schlegelmilch, *Die Stellung der Parteien*, p. 12.

39. Schlegelmilch, *Die Stellung der Parteien*, pp. 29–34. See the address motion in *VRt* 249 (Aktenstück 1026): 5822.

40. For the reasons behind this failure of the Reichstag to act, see Schorske, *German Social Democracy*, pp. 149–52; Eyck, *Wilhelm II*, pp. 500–03; Epstein, *Erzberger*, pp. 86–88. Also, Eschenburg, *Das Kaiserreich am Scheideweg*, pp. 131–75.

41. *VSLt*, 7 November 1907, 1: 309–10.

42. See Peter C. Witt, *Die Finanzpolitik des Deutschen Reiches von 1903 bis 1913. Eine Studie zur Innenpolitik des Wilhelminischen Deutschland* (Lübeck, 1970), pp. 51f., 105ff.

43. See Curtius, *Der politische Antisemitismus*, pp. 57, 76–77. On the political maneuverings which led to the failure of financial reform, see Witt, *Finanzpolitik*, pp. 243ff., 303ff.; Puhle, *Interessenpolitik*, pp. 265–66.

44. See extensive quotations in Curtius, *Der politische Antisemitismus*, pp. 76ff.; Lorenzen, *Die Antisemiten*, pp. 44ff.; *MVA*, 29 September 1909; 6 October 1909.

45. See *MVA*, 6 October 1909.

46. *VRt* 237 (24 June 1909): 8832–34. Also, Lorenzen, *Die Antisemiten*, pp. 47–48.

47. Voting on the finance reform took three weeks (24 June–12 July 1909). For a handy guide to the complex voting with special attention to the record of the anti-Semites, see *MVA*, 6 October 1909. Voting on the third reading of the individual tax measures is in *VRt* 237 (9–10 July 1909): 9313–20, 9372–79. See also an historical comparison between programmatic commitments of the anti-Semites and their Reichstag voting record in Maier, *Die Antisemiten*, pp. 16–17.

48. Lorenzen, *Die Antisemiten*, p. 51; *MVA*, 29 September 1909; Curtius, *Der politische Antisemitismus*, p. 110.

49. See Curtius, *Der politische Antisemitismus*, pp. 25, 46–47; *MVA*, 20 March 1907; 15 July 1908; 13 January 1909; Buch, *50 Jahre*, p. 40.

50. See the speech of Fritz Bindewald in *VRt* 258 (21 January 1910): 748. Also, *MVA*, 1 December 1909.

51. *MVA*, 24 November 1910. Also, Abwehr-Verein, *Abwehr-ABC*, p. 41.

52. Curtius, *Der politische Antisemitismus*, pp. 104–06. On the *Triole* affair, see Hamel, *Völkischer Verband*, p. 117 n. 161.

53. *MVA*, 2 March 1910. Also, Fricke, *Handbuch der bürgerlichen Parteien*, 1: 756.

54. Cited in Curtius, *Der politische Antisemitismus*, p. 57.

55. For an early expression of this attitude, see Bernhard Förster in *Der Kulturkämpfer*, 1883, pp. 194–98. Also, *MVA*, 24 August 1904; 11 October 1911, quoting Fritsch. For an example from the Nazi period, see Robert Körber, ed., *Antisemitismus der Welt in Wort und Bild* (Dresden, 1935).

56. *MVA*, 24 April 1912.

57. This estimate is based on the last figures issued by the German Socials in 1910 and the Saxon branch of the Reformers in 1905, which account for about 13,500 members. See *MVA*, 19 October 1910; 23 October 1905. However, by 1912 membership in both parties had probably sunk much lower. See also Fricke, *Handbuch der bürgerlichen Parteien*, 1: 431, 754–56.

58. Maier, *Die Antisemiten*, p. 16.

59. Böckel, *Psychologie der Volksdichtung*, p. iv.

60. *MVA*, 30 November 1910; 17 January 1912; 13 March 1912.

61. *Staatsbürger-Zeitung*, 21 April 1914.

62. Abwehr-Verein, *Abwehr-ABC*, p. 7. Also, Schemann, *Lebensfahrten*, p. 75.

63. See Heuss, *Friedrich Naumann*, pp. 106–15, 144–46; Martin Wenck, "Die Entwicklung der jüngeren Christlichsozialen," in *Patria! Jahrbuch der Hilfe*, 1901, pp. 41–42. Also, Frank, *Hofprediger*, p. 238.

64. See, for example, Curtius, *Der politische Antisemitismus*, p. 64, quoting Burckhardt. Also, Fricke, *Handbuch der bürgerlichen Parteien*, 1: 253.

65. See Buchheim, *Geschichte der christlichen Parteien*, pp. 295, 314; Fricke, *Handbuch der bürgerlichen Parteien*, 1: 245–55. Also, *Statistisches Jahrbuch für das Deutsche Reich 1915*, pp. 433ff.

66. Massing, *Rehearsal*, pp. 118–21; Wenck, "Entwicklung der jüngeren Christlichsozialen," pp. 40–42.

67. See the program with commentary in Paul Laband, ed., *Handbuch der Politik* (Berlin and Leipzig, 1914), 2: 12–14. Also, Fricke, *Handbuch der bürgerlichen Parteien*, 1: 253.

68. *MVA*, 14 February 1912; 31 January 1912. The *Abwehr-Verein* estimate of Center votes is perhaps high. Yet it is difficult to see the increase in votes as a result of only Christian Social efforts. No spate of new organization had taken place; no particularly attractive candidates were running; and the campaign was not more vigorous than in past years. The Christian Socials' true strength, in my opinion, was still between twenty and forty thousand votes, where it had stood in the elections of 1898, 1903, and 1907. See Fricke, *Handbuch der bürgerlichen Parteien*, 1: 245–55; Maier, *Die Antisemiten*, p. 22; Curtius, *Der politische Antisemitismus*, p. 67.

69. *MVA*, 19 October 1910, report of the German Social party congress in Kassel, 9–10 October 1910.

70. *MVA*, 17 June 1908.

71. Carl Böhme, *Deutsche Bauernpolitik. Eine Auseinandersetzung mit dem Bund der Landwirte* (Würzburg, 1911), p. 94; Hermann Rehm, *Deutschlands politische Parteien* (Jena, 1912), p. 63.

72. See *MVA*, 3 July 1912; Massing, *Rehearsal*, pp. 107, 238 n. 11. See also Philipp Stauff, ed., *Semi-Kürschner oder literarisches Lexikon der Schriftsteller, Dichter, Bankier . . . Sozialdemokraten, usw., jüdische Rasse und Versippung die von 1813–1913 in Deutschland tätig oder bekannt waren* (Berlin, 1913). Stauff used the swastika as a symbol of Aryan blood; the *Antisemitische-Korrespondenz* printed his numerous retractions.

73. See *MVA*, 27 September 1911.

74. *Handbuch der Deutsch-Konservativen Partei*, 4th ed. (Berlin, 1911), pp. 8–9, 385. Also, *Kreuzzeitung*, 12 March 1912 (morning edition).

75. On the transformation of the Shop Clerks' union, see Hamel, *Völkischer Verband*, pp. 68–71, 110–22. On the key role played by Roth in the radical anti-Semitic politics of the Weimar era, see Werner Jochmann, "Die Ausbreitung des Antisemitismus," in Werner E. Mosse, ed., *Deutsches Judentum in Krieg und Revolution, 1916–1923* (Tübingen, 1971), pp. 427, 455–63; Lohalm, *Völkischer Radikalismus*, pp. 56–66. On the difficult but largely successful struggle to win back the Shop Clerks' union to active right radical politics in the Weimar Republic, see Albert Krebs, *Tendenzen und Gestalten der NSDAP: Erinnerungen an die Frühzeit der Partei* (Stuttgart, 1959).

76. Schmahl, *Entwicklung*, pp. 121–22.

77. See *MVA*, 19 October 1910.

78. "Juden im preussischen Abgeordnetenhause," *ZDSJ 2* (1906): 94.

79. On the "democratization" of the National Liberal party and its very modest achievements, see Nipperdey, *Organisation*, pp. 95–102; Stegmann, *Erben Bismarcks*, pp. 28, 306–11, 441–46. Also, Toury, *Die politischen Orientierungen*, p. 261; Angress, "The Jewish Reserve Officer Controversy," p. 38.

80. *MVA*, 6 April 1910; 22 December 1909; 10 February 1904; 17 February 1904.

81. Ibid., 25 October 1905, report of the Saxon Reform party congress in Dresden; 15 January 1908; Curtius, *Der politische Antisemitismus*, pp. 88–89. Also, Warren, *Red Kingdom*, pp. 63–82.

82. Curtius, *Der politische Antisemitismus*, p. 56; *MVA*, 24 November 1909; 7 June 1911.

83. On the election alliances, see Schorske, *German Social Democracy*, pp. 226–35. On the election results, see Schwarz, *MdR: Biographisches Handbuch*, pp. 820–21.

84. *MVA*, 14 February 1912.

85. Compiled from Giese, "Die deutschsoziale Reformpartei," pp. 219–23; Bertram, *Die Wahlen zum Deutschen Reichstag*, pp. 200–07; Braun, *Die Parteien*, pp. 29–36; *MVA*, 14 February 1912; 24 June 1903; Abwehr-Verein, *Der politische Antisemitismus*, pp. 10–12. The statistics refer to the German Social party, German

Reform party, German Social Reform party, and *Deutscher Volksbund.*

86. *MVA,* 14 February 1912.

87. *AK,* 25 March 1914; *MVA,* 25 March 1914; 26 February 1916. Lohalm, *Völkischer Radikalismus,* pp. 69–84, maintains that unification strengthened the membership and organization of the party. I have found no evidence to support this contention. In fact, the membership figure Lohalm cites for 1919 (9,000) indicates a loss of at least 4,500 members since 1912. No new *Reformvereine* were established between 1912 and 1918.

88. On the insignificance of parliamentary anti-Semites in the German National People's party, see Lewis Hertzman, *DNVP: Right-Wing Opposition in the Weimar Republic* (Lincoln, Neb., 1963), pp. 124–27; Werner Liebe, *Die Deutschnationale Volkspartei 1918–1924* (Düsseldorf, 1956), pp. 7–9, 24–25; Zechlin, *Die deutsche Politik und die Juden,* pp. 562–63; Fritsch, *Handbuch der Judenfrage* (1943), p. 533. A *Deutschvölkischer Bund* did try to keep alive a separate identity for the parliamentary anti-Semites even after the merger with the German National People's party. But it, too, soon disappeared (October 1919) into the *Deutschvölkischer Schutz- und Trutz-Bund* along with several other groups. Of the former parliamentary anti-Semites, only the latecomers Ferdinand Werner and Alfred Roth played significant roles in the Weimar period. See Lohalm, *Völkischer Radikalismus,* pp. 70–84.

CONCLUSION

1. See *MVA,* 1 March 1911; 6 November 1912, the speech of Georg Gothein to the general assembly of the *Abwehr-Verein. IDR,* March 1912. Also, Curt Bürger, *Deutschtum und Judentum* (Berlin, 1913), p. 9.

2. On Spahn's article, see Zechlin, *Die deutsche Politik und die Juden,* pp. 45–46. On the Conservative reactions, see *Kreuzzeitung,* 14 January 1912 (morning edition); *MVA,* 31 January 1912, quoting Count Julius von Mirbach; ibid., 28 February 1912, quoting Wangenheim.

3. Schröter's directive is quoted in *MVA,* 26 March 1913. Departures from it were alluded to in ibid., 4 June 1913, and 7 May 1913. Anti-Semites were especially angered when the *Kreuzzeitung* of 31 January 1913 gave strongly favorable support to a new book which espoused assimilation as a solution to the Jewish problem. See Pudor, *Deutschland für die Deutschen!* pp. 17–18. Also, other anti-Semitic condemnations of the Conservative "defection" in *MVA,* 23 April 1913.

4. For a contrary view, see Puhle, *Interessenpolitik,* pp. 137–40, 274. Puhle's contention about the transformation of the Conservative party into a "sincerely" anti-Semitic part of the *völkisch* movement comes from what I consider a one-sided and exaggerated emphasis on the influence of the Agrarian League's use of anti-Semitism. Further, Puhle does not pursue developments in the Conservative party beyond the 1912 elections.

5. See anti-Semitic complaints that Fritsch was merely exploiting party personnel to distribute his propaganda in *MVA,* 20 December 1911; 14 February 1912. Also, Bertram, *Die Wahlen zum deutschen Reichstag,* pp. 173–78.

6. See Nipperdey, *Organisation,* pp. 41ff., 66, 87–89, 246–48.

7. See the text of the German Social program in G. W. B. Stille, *Der Kampf gegen das Judentum* (Hamburg, 1913), pp. 189–211; *MVA*, 26 February 1913, the report of the Saxon Reformers' congress.

8. For examples, see Hans-Günter Zmarzlik, "Der Antisemitismus im Zweiten Reich," *Geschichte in Wissenschaft und Unterricht* 14 (May 1963): 280. Also, Pulzer, *The Rise of Political Anti-Semitism,* pp. 299–300.

9. See Hamburger, *Juden im öffentlichen Leben,* pp. 558–62; Angress, "Jewish Reserve Officer Controversy," pp. 25–26.

10. This is not a view shared by Hamburger, who stresses the decline of middle-class Jewish deputies. Anti-Semites, of course, did not care that the affiliation of Jewish members had switched from liberal to Socialist. See Hamburger, *Juden im öffentlichen Leben,* pp. 254, 558–59.

11. See Puhle, *Interessenpolitik,* pp. 125–37, 200; Massing, *Rehearsal,* p. 109.

12. Quotations from *MVA*, 27 March 1912; 4 June 1913. For the *Reichshammerbund* and its direct links to the Nazis, see Lohalm, *Völkischer Radikalismus,* pp. 56–66; Reginald Phelps, "Theodor Fritsch und der Antisemitismus," *Deutsche Rundschau* 87 (May 1969): 446–48.

13. See Daniel Frymann [Heinrich Class], *Wenn ich der Kaiser wär'—Politische Wahrheiten und Notwendigkeiten,* 2nd ed. (Leipzig, 1913), pp. 30–38, 74–78. He called for the closing of borders to Jewish immigration, expulsion of unnaturalized *Ostjuden,* revocation of emancipation, and rigorous enforcement of an aliens law. On Class's development, particularly his rejection of conventional anti-Semitism, see his *Wider den Strom,* pp. 29–33. Also, Lohalm, *Völkischer Radikalismus,* pp. 32–40.

14. Essentially similar ideas were put forth in a *Denkschrift* submitted to two hundred "leading personalities" by Class's friend and associate, Konstantin von Gebsattel. See Hartmut Pogge von Strandmann and Imanuel Geiss, *Die Erforderlichkeit des Unmöglichen. Deutschland am Vorabend des ersten Weltkrieges* (Frankfurt a. M., 1965).

15. The phrase is from Zechlin, *Die deutsche Politik und die Juden,* p. 47. The view is also advocated by Lohalm, *Völkischer Radikalismus,* pp. 27–32.

16. Lohalm, *Völkischer Radikalismus,* pp. 61–62.

17. See *MVA*, 9 April 1913, quoting the *Hammer* of 1 April 1913, which contains Fritsch's admission that the "anti-Semitic medicine" had failed to cure the ills of the German Empire. Also, Reginald Phelps, "Before Hitler Came. Thule Society and Germanen Orden," *Journal of Modern History* 35 (1963): 245–61; Phelps, "Theodor Fritsch," p. 445.

18. On the reception accorded the anti-Semitic portions of the *Kaiserbuch* and Gebsattel *Denkschrift,* see Stegmann, *Erben Bismarcks,* pp. 295–304; Pogge von Strandmann, *Erforderlichkeit der Unmöglichen,* pp. 20–26, 30–39, the response of Bethmann Hollweg and Wilhelm II.

19. On the caution of the Reich League, see Zechlin, *Die deutsche Politik und die Juden,* p. 49. On the *Ostmarkverein,* see Bürger, *Antisemiten-Spiegel* (1911), pp. 100–03. Class took great pains to keep his identity as author of the *Kaiserbuch* a secret even from members of the Pan-German League. He consistently refused to go

along with Gebsattel's suggestions to have the league end its official neutrality on the Jewish question. It was not until 18 June 1917 that the league declared open war on "*Alljudentum*." See Lohalm, *Völkischer Radikalismus*, pp. 45–49, 346 n. 79; Fricke, *Handbuch der bürgerlichen Parteien*, 1: 774–77.

20. In 1918 for the first time, anti-Semitism provided the integrating force for a viable organization that contained both "sincere" and "demagogic" anti-Semites, that is, *Mittelständler* and representatives of the propertied and educated elite. The *Deutschvölkischer Schutz- und Trutz-Bund*, composed of ten *Mittelstand* organizations, including Fritsch's *Reichshammerbund* and the remaining parliamentary anti-Semites, was brought together by Class's Pan-German League. With funds and guidance from the Pan-Germans, the *Bund* used Fritsch's methods to conduct propaganda more massive and revolutionary than ever dreamt of by the conventional anti-Semites of the imperial era. See Lohalm, *Völkischer Radikalismus*, pp. 19–107; Jochmann, "Die Ausbreitung des Antisemitismus," pp. 433–37, 459–62.

21. On the *Centralverein* collaboration in *Alarm*, a militant antifascist newspaper meant to speak the Nazi's own language, see Paucker, *Der jüdische Abwehrkampf*, pp. 110–28. Also, Meyers, "Jewish Anti-Defamation Work," pp. 12, 21. Greater cooperation between the *Centralverein* and the Social Democrats took place in the Weimar era, but the Socialists' view of anti-Semitism also remained rooted in the imperial period. See Mosse, "German Socialists and the Jewish Question," pp. 123, 130.

22. *Abwehr-Blätter*, March 1931, speech of Georg Gothein.

23. See Hertzman, *DNVP: Right-Wing Opposition*, pp. 19–23, 124–64; Frick, *Die Nationalsozialisten im deutschen Reichstag*, p. 10.

24. See Müller, "Die Entwicklung des Rassenantisemitismus," pp. 9–11, 37; Reventlow, *Judas Kampf und Niederlage*, pp. 352–53, 360ff.; Buch, *50 Jahre*, p. 8; Körber, *Antisemitismus der Welt*, p. 189; Schmahl, *Entwicklung*, introduction by Jakob Sprenger, the Nazi *Gauleiter* of Hesse.

25. See *Der Stürmer*, 16 September 1933; 9 September 1943. Also, Phelps, "Theodor Fritsch," pp. 442–43; 448, quoting the fulsome praise of Hitler and Streicher. Also, Müller, "Die Entwicklung des Rassenantisemitismus," passim; Buch, *50 Jahre*, p. 51; Reventlow, *Judas Kampf und Niederlage*, p. 360.

Selected Bibliography

1. Primary Sources and Contemporary Interpretations

Ahlwardt, Hermann. *Die Processe Manché.* Berlin, 1891.

—————. *Der Verzweiflungskampf der arischen Völker mit dem Judentum.* Berlin, 1890.

—————. *Neue Enthüllungen. Judenflinten.* Dresden, 1892.

Die Antisemiten im Reichstag. Berlin, 1903.

Der arme Jude, wie ihn der grosse Demokrat Herr Wilhelm Marr besp . . . (richt). Von keinem Juden. Hamburg, 1862.

Arndt, Hans. *Herunter mit der Maske! Die Führer der deutschen Antisemiten im Lichte der Wahrheit.* Zurich, 1898.

Auerbach, Leopold. *Wie ist die Judenhetze mit Erfolg zu bekämpfen?* Berlin, 1893.

Bankberger, Hilarius. *Die sogenannte deutsche "Reichsbank," eine privilegierte Aktien-Gesellschaft von und für Juden.* Berlin, 1877.

[Bauer, Erwin]. *Der Untergang der antisemitischen Parteien. Von einem alten Antisemiten.* Leipzig, 1895.

Bebel, August. *Sozialdemokratie und Antisemitismus.* 2nd ed. Berlin, 1906.

Bismarck, Otto von. *Gedanken und Erinnerungen.* 3 vols. Stuttgart and Berlin, 1919.

Bloch, J. S. *My Reminiscences.* Vienna and Berlin, 1923.

Böckel, Otto. *Die deutsche Volkssage.* 2nd ed. Berlin, 1922.

—————. *Die europäischer Juden-Gefahr.* Berlin, 1886.

—————. *Handbuch des deutschen Volksliedes.* Marburg, 1908.

—————. *Die Juden, die Könige unserer Zeit.* 15th ed. Marburg, 1887.

—————. *Die Napoleoner von 1812.* 2nd ed. Michendorf, 1912.

—————. *Nochmals: "Die Juden—die Könige unserer Zeit"!* Berlin, 1901.

—————. *Psychologie der Volksdichtung.* Leipzig, 1906.

—————. *Die Quintessenz der Judenfrage.* 5th ed. Marburg, 1887.

—————. *Seelenland. Bilder aus deutscher Heldenzeit.* Michendorf, 1913.

Böckler, Otto. "Die Konservativen im Wahlkampf." *AJB* (1899):128–56.

Boehlich, Walter, ed. *Der Berliner Antisemitismusstreit.* Frankfurt a. M., 1965.

Böhme, Carl. *Deutsche Bauernpolitik. Eine Auseinandersetzung mit dem Bund der Landwirte.* Würzburg, 1911.

Borries, Achim von, ed. *Selbstzeugnisse des deutschen Judentums.* Frankfurt a. M., 1962.

Braun, Adolf. *Die Parteien des deutschen Reichstags.* Stuttgart, 1893.

Buch, Willi [Wilhelm Buchow]. *50 Jahre antisemitische Bewegung.* Munich, 1937.

Bürger, Curt. *Deutschtum und Judentum.* Berlin, 1913.

————. *Die politische Mittelstandsbewegung in Deutschland.* Berlin, 1912.

Busch, Moritz. *Israel und die Gojim.* Leipzig, 1880.

————. *Tagebuchblätter.* 3 vols. Leipzig, 1899.

Chamberlain, Houston S. *The Foundations of the Nineteenth Century.* Translated by John Lees. 2 vols. London and New York, 1900.

Class, Heinrich. *Wider den Strom. Vom Werden und Wachsen der nationalen Opposition im alten Reich.* Leipzig, 1932.

Comite zur Abwehr antisemitischer Angriffe in Berlin. *Die Juden in Deutschland. 1) Die Kriminalität der Juden in Deutschland. 2) Die Juden als Soldaten.* Berlin, 1896.

Curtius, Lorenz. *Der politische Antisemitismus von 1907–1911.* Munich, 1911.

Deutsche Antisemiten-Chronik 1888 bis 1894. Zurich, 1894.

Deutschkonservative Partei. *Konservatives Handbuch.* 2nd ed. Berlin, 1894.

————. *Konservatives Handbuch.* 3rd ed. Berlin, 1898.

————. *Handbuch der Deutsch-Konservativen Partei.* 4th ed. Berlin, 1911.

Die Deutsche Wacht: Monatsschrift für nationale Entwicklung. Berlin, 1880.

Dühring, Eugen. *Der Ersatz der Religion durch Vollkommeneres und die Ausscheidung alles Judentums durch den modernen Völkergeist.* Karlsruhe, 1883.

————. *Die Judenfrage als Rassen-, Sitten- und Kulturfrage. Mit einer weltgeschichtlichen Antwort.* Karlsruhe, 1880.

————. *Die Parteien in der Judenfrage.* Leipzig, n.d.

————. *Sache, Leben und Feinde.* 2nd ed. Leipzig, 1902.

Eisenmenger, Johann A. *Entdecktes Judentum.* Königsberg, 1711.

Erdmannsdörfer, Hans G. *Dem Abgrunde zu.* Berlin, 1898.

Der erste preussische Vereinigte Landtag. Vollständiger Abdruck der auf den Landtag bezüglichen Gesetze, Verordnungen u.s.w., sowie der Verhandlungen seiner Kurien. Berlin, 1847.

Förster, Bernhard. *Deutsche Colonien in dem oberen Laplatagebiete.* Naumburg a. S., 1886.

————. *Parsifal-Nachklänge.* Berlin, 1884.

————. *Das Verhältnis des modernen Judentums zur deutschen Kunst.* Berlin, 1881.

Förster, Paul. *Deutsch-Sozial.* Berlin, 1890.

————. *Kaiser Wilhelm's Deutsch-soziales Vermächtnis.* Leipzig, 1888.

————. *Der Kampf des deutschen Volkes um sein Dasein.* Leipzig, 1889.

Frantz, Konstantin. *Der Nationalliberalismus und die Judenherrschaft.* Munich, 1874.

Frick, Wilhelm. *Die Nationalsozialisten im deutschen Reichstag, 1924–31.* Munich, 1932.

Fritsch, Theodor. *Antisemiten-Katechismus.* 8th ed. Leipzig, 1888.

————. *Geistige Unterjochung.* 5th ed. Leipzig, 1913.

————. *Hammer-Blätter für deutschen Sinn.* Leipzig, 1901–1926.

————. *Handbuch der Judenfrage.* 27th ed. Hamburg, 1910.

————. *Handbuch der Judenfrage.* 48th ed. Leipzig, 1943.

————. *Zur Bekämpfung zweitausendjähriger Irrthümer.* Leipzig, 1886.

————. *20 Hammer-Aufsätze.* Leipzig, 1916.

Frymann, Daniel [Heinrich Class]. *Wenn ich der Kaiser wär'—Politische Wahrheiten und Notwendigkeiten.* 2nd ed. Leipzig, 1913.

Fuchs, Eugen. *Um Deutschtum und Judentum.* Frankfurt a. M., 1919.

Fürst Bismarck und der Antisemitismus. Vienna, 1886.

Gehlsen, Joachim. *Aus dem Reiche Bismarcks.* Berlin, 1894.

Geiser, Alfred, ed. *Deutsches Reich und Volk,* 2 vols. 2nd ed. Munich, 1910.

Gerlach, Hellmut von. "Vom deutschen Antisemitismus." In *Patria! Jahrbuch der Hilfe,* 1904, pp. 141–56.

————. *Von Rechts nach Links.* Zurich, 1937.

Geschichte der Frankfurter Zeitung. Frankfurt a. M., 1911.

Giese, Wilhelm. "Die deutschsoziale Reformpartei und die Reichstagswahlen des Jahres 1898." *AJB* (1899): 199–234.

————. *Die Herren Raab und v. Liebermann in der Deutsch-Sozialen Reformpartei.* Berlin, 1900.

————. *Die Juden und die deutsche Kriminalität.* Leipzig, 1893.

————. *Die Judenfrage am Ende des 19. Jahrhunderts.* Berlin, 1899.

Glagau, Otto. *Der Börsen- und Gründungs-Schwindel in Berlin.* 4th ed. Berlin, 1876.

————. *Der Börsen- und Gründungs-Schwindel in Deutschland.* Leipzig, 1877.

————. *Des Reiches Noth und der neue Culturkampf.* 3rd ed. Osnabrück, 1880.

Gobineau, Joseph Arthur de. *Essai sur l'Inégalité des Races.* Paris, 1853–1855.

Hartmann, Eduard von. *Das Judentum in Gegenwart und Zukunft.* 2nd ed. Berlin, 1885.

Henrici, Ernst. *Der Neustettiner Synagogenbrand vor Gericht.* Berlin, 1883.

————. *Was ist der Kern der Judenfrage?* Berlin, 1881.

Hundt von Radowsky, Hartwig. *Judenspiegel. Ein Schand- und Sittengemälde alter und neuer Zeit.* Reutlingen, 1821.

Holländer, Ludwig. *Die sozialen Voraussetzungen der antisemitischen Bewegung in Deutschland.* Berlin, 1907.

The Jewish Encyclopedia. 12 vols. New York and London, 1907.

Der Judenspiegel: Ein Monatsschrift. Berlin, 1901.

Keim, August. *Erlebtes und Erstrebtes.* Hanover, 1925.

Kiesenwetter, Otto von. *Fünfundzwanzig Jahre wirtschaftspolitischen Kampfes. Geschichtliche Darstellung des Bundes der Landwirte.* Berlin, 1918.

Kobler, Franz, ed. *Juden und Judentum in deutschen Briefen aus drei Jahrhunderten.* Vienna, 1935.

König, Adolf. *Ein Bubenstück, ersonnen, um eines Mannes Ehre zu vernichten.* Hagen i. W., 1888.

Der Kulturkämpfer: Zeitschrift für öffentliche Angelegenheiten. Berlin, 1880–1889.

Die Landwirtschaft im Grossherzogtum Hessen. Bericht der Landwirtschaftskammer. Darmstadt, 1912.

Lange, Friedrich. *Reines Deutschtum.* 4th ed. Berlin, 1904.

Lattmann, Wilhelm. *Die Wahrheit über die Reichsfinanzreform 1909.* Leipzig, 1909.

Herr Liebermann v. Sonnenberg als Parteiführer und Gesinnungsgenosse. Von einigen Deutsch-Sozialen. Leipzig, 1893.

Liebermann von Sonnenberg, Max Hugo. *Aus der Glückzeit meines Lebens. Erinnerungen aus dem grossen deutschen Krieg 1870/71.* Munich, 1911.

―――. *Beiträge zur Geschichte der antisemitischen Bewegung vom Jahre 1880–1885.* Berlin, 1885.

―――. *Der Blutmord in Konitz.* 7th ed. Berlin, 1901.

―――. *Gedichte.* Leipzig, 1891.

―――. *Vorträge des Herrn Ivan v. Simonyi aus Pressburg und des Herrn M. Liebermann v. Sonnenberg aus Berlin über die Judenfrage gehalten am 5. Februar 1883 im deutschen Reformverein zu Chemnitz.* Chemnitz, 1883.

Liebknecht, Wilhelm. *Über den Kölner Parteitag.* Bielefeld, 1893.

[Löwenfeld, Raphael]. *Schutzjuden oder Staatsbürger?* Berlin, 1893.

Lorenzen, Friedrich. *Die Antisemiten.* Berlin, 1912.

Mahler, Karl. *Die Programme der politischen Parteien in Deutschland.* Leipzig, 1911.

Maier, Hans. *Die Antisemiten (Wirtschaftliche Vereinigung).* Munich, 1911.

Manifest an die Regierungen und Völker der durch das Judentum gefährdeten Staaten, laut Beschlusses des Ersten Internationalen Antijüdischen Kongresses zu Dresden am 11. und 12. September 1882. Chemnitz, 1883.

Marr, Wilhelm. *Goldene Ratten und rothe Mäuse.* Chemnitz, 1880.

―――. *Der Judenspiegel.* Hamburg, 1862.

―――. *Vom jüdischen Kriegsschauplatz.* Bern, 1879.

―――. *Das junge Deutschland in der Schweiz. Ein Beitrag zur Geschichte der geheimen Verbindungen unserer Tage.* Leipzig, 1846.

————. *Der Mensch und die Ehe vor dem Richterstuhle der Sittlichkeit.* Leipzig, 1848.

————. *Öffnet die Augen! Ihr deutschen Zeitungsleser.* Chemnitz, 1880.

————. *Reise nach Central-Amerika.* 2 vols. Hamburg, 1863.

————. *Der Sieg des Judenthums über das Germanenthum. Vom nicht confessionellen Standpunkt aus betrachtet.* Bern, 1879.

————. *Wählet Keinen Juden! Der Weg zum Siege des Germanenthum über das Judenthum.* Berlin, 1879.

————. *Lessing contra Sem.* 2nd ed. Berlin, 1885.

Marx, Karl. "Zur Judenfrage." *Deutsch-französische Jahrbücher.* Paris, 1844.

Massow, Wilhelm von. *Die deutsche innere Politik unter Kaiser Wilhelm II.* Stuttgart and Berlin, 1913.

Meyer, Rudolf. *Politische Gründer und die Korruption in Deutschland.* Leipzig, 1877.

Mommsen, Wilhelm. *Deutsche Parteiprogramme.* 2nd ed. Munich, 1964.

Mosch, Hans von. *Neue politische Gedichte, 1907–1913.* Berlin, n.d.

Müffelmann, Leo. *Die wirtschaftliche Verbände.* Leipzig, 1912.

Politischer Bilderbogen. Dresden, 1893–1894.

Politisches Handbuch der Nationalliberalen Partei. Berlin, 1907.

Naudh, H. [Heinrich Nordmann]. *Israel im Heere.* Berlin, 1879.

————. *Die Juden und der deutsche Staat.* Berlin, 1861.

————. *Die Verjudung des christlichen Staates.* Leipzig, 1865.

Neue Preussische Zeitung (Kreuzzeitung). Berlin.

Oertzen, Dietrich von. *Adolf Stoecker. Lebensbild und Zeitgeschichte.* 2 vols. Berlin, 1910.

Paasch, Karl. *Eine jüdisch-deutsche Gesandtschaft und ihre Helfer . . . Nebenregierungen und jüdische Weltherrschaft.* 2 vols. Leipzig, 1891.

Parmod, Maximilian [Max Apt]. *Antisemitismus und Strafrechtspflege.* Berlin, 1894.

Protokoll über die Verhandlungen des Parteitages der Sozialdemokratischen Partei Deutschlands, Halle 1890 bis Jena 1913. Berlin.

Pudor, Heinrich. *Deutschland für die Deutschen!* Munich and Leipzig, 1912.

Rehm, Hermann. *Deutschlands politische Parteien.* Jena, 1912.

Reichstags-Handbuch 1890. Achte Legislaturperiode 1890/95. Berlin, 1890.

Reichstags-Handbuch. Zwölfte Legislaturperiode. Berlin, 1907.

Reichstags-Handbuch. 13. Legislaturperiode. Berlin, 1912.

Reiss, Klaus-Peter. *Von Bassermann zu Stresemann: Die Sitzungen des nationalliberalen Zentralvorstandes, 1912–1917.* Düsseldorf, 1967.

Reventlow, Ernst zu. *Judas Kampf und Niederlage in Deutschland.* Berlin, 1937.

Rich, Norman, and Fisher, M. H., ed. *The Holstein Papers. The Memoirs,*

Diaries, and Correspondence of Friedrich von Holstein. 4 vols. Cambridge, 1955–1963.

Rohling, August. *Der Talmudjude.* 6th ed. Münster, 1877.

Rülf, J., *Entstehung und Bedeutung des Antisemitismus in Hessen.* Mainz, 1890.

Ruppin, Arthur. *The Jews of Today.* Translated by Margery Bentwich. New York, 1913.

Scheidemann, Philipp. *Memoiren eines Sozialdemokraten.* 2 vols. Dresden, 1928.

————. "Wandlungen des Antisemitismus." *Neue Zeit* 24 (1905–1906): 632–36.

Schemann, Ludwig. *Fünfundzwanzig Jahre Gobineau Vereinigung: Ein Rückblick.* Strassburg, 1919.

————. *Lebensfahrten eines Deutschen.* Leipzig, 1925.

Schmeitzner's Internationale Monatsschrift: Zeitschrift für die Allgemeine Vereinigung zur Bekämpfung des Judentums 1883. Chemnitz, 1883.

Schmoller, Gustav. "Die heutige Judenfrage." In *Zwanzig Jahre deutscher Politik, 1897–1917.* Munich and Leipzig, 1920.

Schulthess' Europäischer Geschichtskalender. Munich, 1861 *et seq.*

Schuon, Hermann. *Der Deutschnationale Handlungsgehilfen-Verband zu Hamburg.* Jena, 1914.

Schwarz, Max. *MdR: Biographisches Handbuch der Reichstage.* Hanover, 1965.

Spamitz, Karl M. "Tätigkeit der Deutschsozialreformerischen Abgeordneten in den Volksvertretungen während der Session 1897–98." *AJB* (1899): 176–98.

Staatsbürger-Zeitung. Berlin.

Stauff, Philipp, ed. *Semi-Kürschner oder literarisches Lexikon der Schriftsteller, Dichter, Bankier . . . Sozialdemokraten usw., jüdischer Rasse und Versippung die von 1813–1913 in Deutschland tätig oder bekannt waren.* Berlin, 1913.

Stenographische Berichte über die Verhandlungen des Preussischen Herrenhauses in der Session 1907/08. Berlin.

Stille, G. W. B. *Der Kampf gegen das Judentum.* Hamburg, 1913.

Stoecker, Adolf. *Christlich-Sozial. Reden und Aufsätze.* Bielefeld and Leipzig, 1885.

————. *13 Jahre Hofprediger und Politiker.* Berlin, 1895.

Stoltheim, F. Roderich [Theodor Fritsch]. *Die Juden im Handel und das Geheimnis ihres Erfolges.* Leipzig, 1913.

Der Stürmer. Nuremberg.

Toussenel, Alphonse. *Les Juifs Rois de l'Époque: Histoire de la Féodalité Financière.* 2 vols. 3rd ed. Paris, 1886.

Treitschke, Heinrich von. *Ein Wort über unser Judentum.* Berlin, 1880.

Verband der Deutschen Juden. *Korrespondenz-Blatt des Verbandes der Deutschen Juden.* Berlin, 1907–1912.

————. *Stenografischer Bericht über die zu Berlin am Montag, den 30. Oktober 1905 abgehaltene erste Hauptversammlung.* Berlin, 1905.

Verein zur Abwehr des Antisemitismus. *Abwehr-ABC.* Berlin, 1920.

————. *Antisemiten-Spiegel. Die Antisemiten im Lichte des Christenthums, des Rechtes und der Moral.* Danzig, 1892.

————. *Antisemiten-Spiegel. Die Antisemiten im Lichte des Christenthums, des Rechtes und der Wissenschaft.* 2nd ed. Danzig, 1900.

————. *Antisemiten-Spiegel. Die Antisemiten im Lichte des Christenthums, des Rechtes und der Wissenschaft.* ed. Curt Bürger. 3rd ed. Berlin and Frankfurt a. M., 1911.

————. *Ergänzung zum Antisemiten-Spiegel. Die Antisemiten im Lichte des Christenthums, des Rechtes und der Wissenschaft.* 2nd ed. Berlin, 1903.

————. *Die Juden im Heere.* Berlin, n.d.

————. *Der politische Antisemitismus von 1903–1907.* Berlin, 1907.

Die Verurteilung der antisemitischen Bewegung durch die Wahlmänner von Berlin: Bericht über die Allgemeine Versammlung der Wahlmänner aus den vier Berliner Landtags-Wahlkreisen am 12. Januar 1881 in oberen Saale der Reichshallen. Berlin, 1881.

Wagner, Richard. *Das Judentum in der Musik.* Leipzig, 1869.

Wahrmund, Adolf. *Der Culturkampf zwischen Asien und Europa.* Berlin, 1887.

————. *Das Gesetz des Nomadentums und die heutige Judenherrschaft.* 2nd ed. Munich, 1919.

Waldegg, Egon [Alexander Pinkert]. *Die Judenfrage gegenüber dem deutschen Handel und Gewerbe.* Leipzig, 1880.

Werner, Ferdinand. *Ein öffentliches Heinedenkmal auf deutschem Boden?* Leipzig, 1913.

————. *Der Wahrheit eine Gasse.* Munich, 1919.

Wilberg, J. *Weshalb ich zum Deutschen Volksbund ging.* Berlin, 1901.

Wilmanns, C. *Die "Goldene" Internationale und die Notwendigkeit einer sozialen Reformpartei.* Berlin, 1876.

Winter, Georg. *Der Antisemitismus in Deutschland.* Magdeburg, 1896.

Wohlfarth. "Bilder aus der antisemitischen Bewegung." *AJB* (1898): 41–76.

Zimmermann, Oswald. *Die Wonne des Leids.* 2nd ed. Leipzig, 1885.

Der zweite Parteitag der Fortschrittlichen Volkspartei zu Mannheim, 5. -7. Oktober 1912. Berlin, 1912.

2. Secondary Sources

Adler, H. G. *Die Juden in Deutschland.* Munich, 1960.

Adler-Rudel, Salomon. *Ostjuden in Deutschland, 1880–1940.* Tübingen, 1959.

Anderson, Pauline. *The Background of Anti-English Feeling in Germany, 1890–1902*. Washington, D. C., 1939.

Angress, Werner T. "Prussia's Army and the Jewish Reserve Officer Controversy before World War I." *BYB* 17 (1972): 19–42.

Arendt, Hannah. *The Origins of Totalitarianism*. 2nd ed. New York, 1958.

Bachem, Karl. *Vorgeschichte, Geschichte, und Politik der deutschen Zentrumspartei*. 9 vols. Cologne, 1929–1932.

Balfour, Michael. *The Kaiser and His Times*. London, 1964.

Barth, Theodor. "Der Politiker Heinrich Rickert." In *Patria! Jahrbuch der Hilfe*, 1905, pp. 1–16.

Bein, Alexander. "The Jewish Parasite—Notes on the Semantics of the Jewish Problem, with special reference to Germany." *BYB* 9 (1964): 3–41.

Bergman, Hugo. "Eduard von Hartmann und die Judenfrage in Deutschland." *BYB* 5 (1960): 177–97.

Bergsträsser, Ludwig. *Geschichte der politischen Parteien in Deutschland*. 10th ed. Munich, 1960.

Bertram, Jürgen. *Die Wahlen zum Deutschen Reichstag vom Jahre 1912*. Düsseldorf, 1964.

Bienenfeld, F. R. *The Germans and the Jews*. Translated by H. Pender. London, 1939.

Blau, Bruno. "Sociology and Statistics of the Jews." *Historia Judaica* 11 (1949): 145–62.

Böhme, Helmut, ed. *Probleme der Reichsgründungszeit 1848–1879*. Cologne, 1968.

Boom, Wilhelm ten. *Die Entstehung des modernen Rassenantisemitismus (besonders in Deutschland)*. Leipzig, 1928.

Booms, Hans. *Die Deutschkonservative Partei. Preussische Charakter, Reichsauffassung, Nationalbegriff*. Düsseldorf, 1954.

Borée, Karl Friedrich. *Semiten und Antisemiten*. Frankfurt a. M., 1960.

Bramsted, Ernest K. *Aristocracy and the Middle-Classes in Germany*. Chicago, 1964.

Broszat, Martin. "Die antisemitische Bewegung im Wilhelminischen Deutschland." Ph. D. dissertation, University of Cologne, 1952.

Buchheim, Karl. *Geschichte der christlichen Parteien in Deutschland*. Munich, 1953.

Cecil, Lamar. *Albert Ballin: Business and Politics in Imperial Germany, 1888–1918*. Princeton, 1967.

Crothers, George D. *The German Elections of 1907*. New York, 1941.

Demandt, Karl. *Geschichte des Landes Hessen*. Kassel and Basel, 1959.

Demeter, Karl. *Das deutsche Offizierkorps in Gesellschaft und Staat, 1650–1945*. 4th ed. Frankfurt a. M., 1965.

Deuerlein, Ernst. *Der Reichstag.* Frankfurt a. M., 1963.

Dubnow, Simon. *Die neueste Geschichte des jüdischen Volkes: Das Zeitalter der zweiten Reaktion, 1880–1914.* Vol. 10 of *Weltgeschichte des jüdischen Volkes.* Translated by A. Steinberg. Berlin, 1929.

Edelheim-Muehsam, Margaret T. "The Jewish Press in Germany." *BYB* 1 (1956): 163–76.

Ehrlich, Ernst L. "Judenfeindschaft in Deutschland," In *Judenfeindschaft,* edited by Karl Thieme. Frankfurt a.M., 1963.

Elbogen, Ismar. *Geschichte der Juden in Deutschland.* Berlin, 1935.

Engelberg, Ernst. *Deutschland von 1871 bis 1897: Deutschland in der Übergangsperiode zum Imperialismus.* Berlin, 1965.

Epstein, Klaus. *The Genesis of German Conservatism.* Princeton, 1966.

———. *Matthias Erzberger and the Dilemma of German Democracy.* Princeton, 1959.

Eschenburg, Theodor. *Das Kaiserreich am Scheideweg. Bassermann, Bülow und der Block.* Berlin, 1929.

Eyck, Erich. *Das persönliche Regiment Wilhelms II. Politische Geschichte des Deutschen Kaiserreiches von 1890 bis 1914.* Zurich, 1948.

Fetscher, Iring. "Zur Entstehung des politischen Antisemitismus in Deutschland." In *Antisemitismus. Zur Pathologie der bürgerlichen Gesellschaft,* edited by H. Huss and A. Schröder. Frankfurt a. M., 1965.

Frank, Robert. *Der Brandenburger als Reichstagswähler 1867/71 bis 1912/14.* Berlin, 1934.

Frank, Walter. *Hofprediger Adolf Stoecker und die christlichsoziale Bewegung.* 2nd ed. Hamburg, 1935.

Fricke, Dieter, ed. *Die bürgerlichen Parteien in Deutschland. Handbuch der Geschichte der bürgerlichen Parteien und anderer bürgerlicher Interessenorganisationen vom Vormärz bis zum Jahre 1945.* 2 vols. Berlin, 1968–1970.

Galos, Adam, et al. *Die Hakatisten.* Berlin, 1966.

Gerlach, Hans-Christian. "Agitation und parlamentarische Wirksamkeit der deutschen Antisemitenparteien 1873–1895." Ph.D. dissertation, University of Kiel, 1956.

Gerlach, Hellmut von. *Das Parlament.* Frankfurt a. M., 1907.

Goltz, T. von der. *Geschichte der deutschen Landwirtschaft.* 2 vols. Stuttgart, 1903.

Hamburger, Ernest. *Juden im öffentlichen Leben Deutschlands. Regierungsmitglieder, Beamten und Parlamentarier in der monarchischen Zeit, 1848–1918.* Tübingen, 1968.

———. "Jews in Public Service under the German Monarchy." *BYB* 9 (1964): 206–38.

Hamel, Iris. *Völkischer Verband und nationale Gewerkschaft. Der Deutschnationale Handlungsgehilfen-Verband 1893–1933.* Frankfurt a. M., 1967.

Harmelin, Wilhelm. "Jews in the Leipzig Fur Industry." *BYB* 9 (1964): 239–61.

Hartwig, Otto. *Ludwig Bamberger.* Marburg, 1900.

Heilmann, Ernst. *Geschichte der Arbeiterbewegung in Chemnitz und Erzgebirge.* Chemnitz, n.d.

Herre, Paul. *Kronprinz Wilhelm, seine Rolle in der deutschen Politik.* Munich, 1954.

Hertzman, Lewis. *DNVP: Right-Wing Opposition in the Weimar Republic.* Lincoln, Neb., 1963.

Herzfeld, Hans. *Johannes von Miquel.* 2 vols. Detmold, 1938.

Hess, Adalbert. *Die Landtags- und Reichstagswahlen im Grossherzogtum Hessen, 1865–1871.* Oberursel, 1964.

Heuss, Theodor. *Friedrich Naumann.* Stuttgart and Berlin, 1937.

Hirschberg, Alfred. "Ludwig Hollaender, Director of the C. V." *BYB* 7 (1962): 39–74.

Hofer, Walther, ed. *Der Nationalsozialismus.* Frankfurt a. M., 1957.

Holborn, Hajo. *A History of Modern Germany.* 3 vols. New York, 1959–1969.

Huber, Ernst R. *Deutsche Verfassungsgeschichte seit 1789.* 4 vols. Stuttgart, 1957–1963.

Institute of Social Research. "Analysis of Central-Verein Policy in Germany." New York, 1945. Mimeographed.

Jochmann, Werner. "Die Ausbreitung des Antisemitismus." In *Deutsches Judentum in Krieg und Revolution, 1916–1923,* edited by Werner Mosse. Tübingen, 1971.

Jöhlinger, Otto. *Bismarck und die Juden.* Berlin, 1921.

Kaehler, Siegfried. "Stöcker's Versuch, eine christlich-soziale Arbeiterpartei in Berlin zu begründen (1878)." In *Deutscher Staat und deutsche Parteien,* edited by Paul Wentzcke. Munich and Berlin, 1922.

Kahn, E. "The Frankfurter Zeitung." *BYB* 2 (1957): 228–35.

Kampmann, Wanda. "Adolf Stoecker und die Berliner Bewegung." *Geschichte in Wissenschaft und Unterricht* 13 (1962): 528–79.

———. *Deutsche und Juden. Studien zur Geschichte des deutschen Judentums.* Heidelberg, 1963.

Kardorff, Siegfried von. *Wilhelm von Kardorff: Ein nationaler Parlamentarier im Zeitalter Bismarcks und Wilhelms II, 1828–1907.* Berlin, 1936.

Katz, Jacob. *Out of the Ghetto. The Social Background of Jewish Emancipation, 1770–1870.* Cambridge, Mass., 1973.

Keyser, Erich. *Hessisches Städtebuch. 4. Südwestdeutschland.* Stuttgart, 1957.

Klinkenberg, Hans Martin. "Zwischen Liberalismus und Nationalismus im Zweiten Kaiserreich, 1870–1918." *Monumenta Judaica. Beiträge zu einer Geschichte der Juden in Deutschland.* 2nd ed. Cologne, 1964.

Körber, Robert, ed. *Antisemitismus der Welt in Wort und Bild*. Dresden, 1935.

Kötzschke, Rudolf, and Kretzschmar, Hellmut. *Sächsische Geschichte*. Frankfurt a. M., 1965.

Krebs, Albert. *Tendenzen und Gestalten der NSDAP: Erinnerungen an die Frühzeit der Partei*. Stuttgart, 1959.

Kremer, Willy. *Der soziale Aufbau der Parteien des deutschen Reichstages von 1871–1918*. Emsdetten, 1934.

Kruck, Alfred. *Geschichte des Alldeutschen Verbandes 1890–1939*. Wiesbaden, 1954.

Kupisch, Karl. *Adolf Stoecker. Hofprediger und Volkstribun*. Berlin, 1970.

Laband, Paul, ed. *Handbuch der Politik*. 3 vols. 2nd ed. Berlin, 1914.

Lamberti, Marjorie. "The Attempt to Form a Jewish Bloc: Jewish Notables and Politics in Wilhelmian Germany." *Central European History* 3 (March–June 1970): 73–93.

Laqueur, Walter. "The German Youth Movement and the 'Jewish Question'." *BYB* 6 (1961): 193–205.

Lazare, Bernard. *L'Antisemitisme. Son histoire et ses causes*. Paris, 1934.

Lebovics, Herman. *Social Conservatism and the Middle Classes in Germany, 1914–1933*. Princeton, 1969.

Leon, A. *The Jewish Question: A Marxist Interpretation*. Mexico City, 1950.

Leschnitzer, Adolf. *Saul und David: Die Problematik der deutsch-jüdischen Lebensgemeinschaft*. Heidelberg, 1954.

Lewin, Adolf. *Geschichte der badischen Juden seit der Regierung Karl Friedrichs*. Karlsruhe, 1909.

Lewy, Guenter. *The Catholic Church and Nazi Germany*. New York, 1964.

Liebe, Werner. *Die Deutschnationale Volkspartei 1918–1924*. Düsseldorf, 1956.

Liebeschütz, Hans. *Das Judentum im deutschen Geschichtsbild von Hegel bis Max Weber*. Tübingen, 1967.

Limburg-Stirum, Friedrich Wilhelm von. *Aus der konservativen Politik der Jahre 1890/1905*. Berlin, 1921.

Löb, Abraham. *Die Rechtsverhältnisse der Juden im ehemaligen Königreiche und der jetzigen Provinz Hannover*. Frankfurt a. M., 1908.

Lohalm, Uwe. *Völkischer Radikalismus. Die Geschichte des Deutschvölkischen Schutz- und Trutz-Bundes 1919–1923*. Hamburg, 1970.

Mack, Rüdiger. "Otto Böckel und die antisemitische Bauernbewegung in Hessen 1887–1894." *Wetterauer Geschichtsblätter* 16 (1967): 113–47.

Massmann, Karl. *VDSter Fünfzig Jahre Arbeit für Volkstum und Staat*. Berlin, 1931.

Maurenbrecher, Max. "Caprivi und die politischen Parteien." In *Patria!*

Jahrbuch der Hilfe, 1902, pp. 98–116.

Mehring, Franz. *Geschichte der deutschen Sozialdemokratie.* 2 vols. Berlin, 1960.

Meyer, Michael. "Great Debate on Anti-Semitism—Jewish Reaction to New Hostility in Germany 1879–1881." *BYB* 11 (1966): 137–70.

Meyers, Julie. "Jewish Anti-Defamation Work in Pre-Hitler Germany." New York, n.d. Mimeographed.

Michels, Robert. "Die deutsche Sozialdemokratie, deren Parteimitgliedschaft und soziale Zusammensetzung." *Archiv für Sozialwissenschaft* 23 (1906): 471–556.

Mohler, Armin. *Die konservative Revolution in Deutschland, 1918–1932. Grundriss ihrer Weltanschauungen.* Stuttgart, 1950.

Mosse, George L. *The Crisis of German Ideology.* New York, 1964.

———. "German Socialists and the Jewish Question in the Weimar Republic." *BYB* 16 (1971): 123–51.

———. "The Image of the Jew in German Popular Culture: Felix Dahn and Gustav Freytag." *BYB* 2 (1957): 218–27.

Müller, Josef. "Die Entwicklung des Rassenantisemitismus in den letzten Jahrzehnten des 19. Jahrhunderts." *Historische Studien* 372. Berlin, 1940.

Neubach, Helmut. *Die Ausweisungen von Polen und Juden aus Preussen 1885/1886.* Wiesbaden, 1967.

Nichols, J. Alden. *Germany after Bismarck: The Caprivi Era, 1890–1894.* Cambridge, Mass., 1958.

Niewyk, Donald L. "German Social Democracy and the Problem of Anti-Semitism, 1906–1914." M.A. thesis, Tulane University, 1964.

———. *Socialist, Anti-Semite, and Jew. German Social Democracy Confronts the Problem of Anti-Semitism 1918–1933.* Baton Rouge, 1971.

Nitzsche, Max. "Die Anfänge der agrarischen Bewegung in Deutschland." In *Patria! Jahrbuch der Hilfe,* 1905, pp. 187–211.

Nipperdey, Thomas. *Die Organisation der deutschen Parteien vor 1918.* Düsseldorf, 1961.

Nöll von der Nahmer, Robert. *Bismarcks Reptilienfonds.* Mainz, 1968.

Parkes, James. *The Emergence of the Jewish Problem 1878–1939.* London, 1946.

Pastor, Ludwig. *August Reichensperger.* 2 vols. Freiburg, 1899.

Paucker, Arnold. *Der jüdische Abwehrkampf gegen Antisemitismus und Nationalsozialismus in den letzten Jahren der Weimarer Republik.* Hamburg, 1966.

Phelps, Reginald. "Before Hitler Came. Thule Society and Germanen Orden." *Journal of Modern History* 35 (1963): 245–61.

———. "Theodor Fritsch und der Antisemitismus." *Deutsche Rundschau* 87 (May 1961): 442–49.

Pierson, Ruth. "German Jewish Identity in the Weimar Republic." Ph. D. dissertation, Yale University, 1970.

Pogge von Strandmann, Hartmut, and Geiss, Imanuel. *Die Erforderlichkeit des Unmöglichen. Deutschland am Vorabend des ersten Weltkrieges.* Frankfurt a. M., 1965.

Pross, Harry. *Die Zerstörung der deutschen Politik.* Frankfurt a. M., 1959.

Puhle, Hans-Jürgen. *Agrarische Interessenpolitik und preussischer Konservatismus im wilhelminischen Reich, 1893–1914.* Hanover, 1966.

Pulzer, Peter G. J. *The Rise of Political Anti-Semitism in Germany and Austria.* New York, 1964.

Reichmann, Eva G. "Der Centralverein deutscher Staatsbürger jüdischen Glaubens." *Süddeutsche Monatshefte* 27 (September 1930): 818–27.

———. *Hostages of Civilization.* London, 1950.

Rich, Norman. *Friedrich von Holstein: Politics and Diplomacy in the Era of Bismarck and Wilhelm II.* 2 vols. Cambridge, 1965.

Rieger, Paul. *Ein Vierteljahrhundert im Kampf um das Recht und die Zukunft der deutschen Juden.* Berlin, 1918.

Röhl, J. C. G. *Germany without Bismarck: The Crisis of Government in the Second Reich, 1890–1900.* Berkeley, 1967.

Rosenbaum, Eduard. "Some Reflections on the Jewish Participation in German Economic Life." *BYB* 1 (1956): 307–14.

Rosenberg, Hans. *Grosse Depression und Bismarckzeit.* Berlin, 1967.

Rubinstein, Adolf. *Die Deutsche-Freisinnige Partei bis zu ihrem Auseinanderbruch, 1884–1893.* Berlin, 1935.

Rürup, Reinhard. "Judenemanzipation und bürgerliche Gesellschaft in Deutschland." In *Gedenkschrift Martin Göhring,* edited by Ernst Schulin. Wiesbaden, 1968.

Saller, Karl. "Die biologisch motivierte Judenfeindschaft." In *Judenfeindschaft,* edited by Karl Thieme. Frankfurt a. M., 1963.

Sandler, Ahron. "The Struggle for Unification." *BYB* 2 (1957): 76–84.

Schleier, H., and Seeber, G. "Zur Entwicklung und Rolle des Antisemitismus in Deutschland von 1871–1914." *Zeitschrift für Geschichtswissenschaft* 9 (1961): 1592–97.

Schlegelmilch, M. *Die Stellung der Parteien des deutschen Reichstages zur sogenannten Daily-Telegraph-Affäre und ihre innerpolitische Nachkwirkung.* Halle, 1936.

Schmahl, Eugen. *Entwicklung der völkischen Bewegung. Die antisemitische Bauernbewegung in Hessen von der Böckelzeit bis zum Nationalsozialismus.* Giessen, 1933.

Schmidt, H. D. "The Terms of Emancipation 1781–1812." *BYB* 1 (1956): 28–47.

Schnack, Ingeborg, ed. *Lebensbilder aus Kurhessen und Waldeck, 1830–1930.* Marburg, 1939.

Schorsch, Ismar. *Jewish Reactions to German Anti-Semitism, 1870–1914.* Philadelphia and New York, 1972.

Schorske, Carl E., *German Social Democracy, 1905–1917.* New York, 1965.

Schüler, Winfried. *Der Bayreuther Kreis von seiner Entstehung bis zum Ausgang der wilhelminischen Ära. Wagnerkult und Kulturreform im Geiste völkischer Weltanschauung.* Münster, 1971.

Schüssler, Wilhelm. *Die Daily-Telegraph-Affaire.* Göttingen, 1952.

Silberner, Edmund. "Austrian Social Democracy and the Jewish Problem." *Historia Judaica* 13 (1951): 121–40.

———. "German Social Democracy and the Jewish Problem prior to World War I." *Historia Judaica* 15 (1953): 3–48.

Spier, Selmar. "Jewish History as We See It." *BYB* 1 (1956): 3–14.

Stegmann, Dirk. *Die Erben Bismarcks. Parteien und Verbände in der Spätphase des Wilhelminischen Deutschlands.* Cologne and Berlin, 1970.

Sterling, Eleonore O. *Er ist wie du. Aus der Frühgeschichte des Antisemitismus in Deutschland, 1815–1850.* Munich, 1956.

———. "Anti-Jewish Riots in Germany in 1819." *Historia Judaica* 12 (1950): 105–42.

———. "Jewish Reaction to Jew-Hatred in the First Half of the 19th Century." *BYB* 3 (1958): 103–21.

Stern, Fritz. *The Politics of Cultural Despair.* New York, 1965.

———. *The Failure of Illiberalism.* New York, 1972.

Stern, Selma. *Der preussische Staat und die Juden.* Tübingen, 1962.

Stillschweig, Kurt. "Jewish Assimilation as an Object of Legislation." *Historia Judaica* 8 (1946): 8–12.

Strack, Hermann. *Der Blutaberglaube bei Christen und Juden.* Munich, 1891.

Strauss, Raphael. *Die Juden in Wirtschaft und Gesellschaft.* Frankfurt a. M., 1964.

Szajkowski, Z. *Anti-Semitism in the French Labor Movement, 1845–1906.* Yiddish. New York, 1948.

Tal, Uriel. "Liberal Protestantism and the Jews in the Second Reich 1870–1914." *Jewish Social Studies* 26 (1964): 23–41.

Thimme, Annelise. *Hans Delbrück als Kritiker der Wilhelminischen Epoche.* Düsseldorf, 1955.

Tims, Richard W. *Germanizing Prussian Poland.* New York, 1941.

Tirrell, Sarah R. *German Agrarian Politics after Bismarck's Fall: The Formation of the Farmers' League.* New York, 1951.

Toury, Jacob. *Die politisichen Orientierungen der Juden in Deutschland. Von Jena bis Weimar.* Tübingen, 1966.

Warren, Donald. *The Red Kingdom of Saxony: Lobbying Grounds for Gustav Stresemann, 1901–1909.* The Hague, 1964.

Wawrzinek, Kurt. *Die Entstehung der deutschen Antisemitenparteien, 1873–1890.* Berlin, 1927.

Weber, Hans. *Geschichte des Vereins Deutscher Studenten zu Berlin, 1891–1906.* Berlin, 1912.

Wegner, Konstanze. *Theodor Barth und die Freisinnige Vereinigung.* Tübingen, 1968.

Wenck, Martin. "Die Entwicklung der jüngeren Christlichsozialen." In *Patria! Jahrbuch der Hilfe,* 1901, pp. 34–67.

———. "Die Geschichte der Nationalsozialen." In *Patria! Jahrbuch der Hilfe,* 1905, pp. 37–136.

Werner, Lothar. "Der Alldeutsche Verband 1890–1918." *Historische Studien* 278. Berlin, 1936.

Wertheimer, Mildred S. *The Pan-German League, 1890–1914.* New York, 1924.

Westarp, Kuno von. *Konservative Politik im letzten Jahrzehnt des Kaiserreiches.* 2 vols. Berlin, 1935.

Wiener, Alfred. "The Centralverein Deutscher Staatsbuerger Juedischen Glaubens—Its Meaning and Activities." London, Wiener Library.

The Wiener Library. *German Jewry: Its History, Life and Culture. Catalogue Series no. 3.* London, 1945.

Wilhelm, Kurt. "The Jewish Community in the Post-Emancipation Period." *BYB* 2 (1957): 47–75.

Winkler, Heinrich A. *Mittelstand, Demokratie und Nationalsozialismus. Die politische Entwicklung von Handwerk und Kleinhandel in der Weimarer Republik.* Cologne, 1972.

Witt, Peter C. *Die Finanzpolitik des Deutschen Reiches von 1903 bis 1913. Eine Studie zur Innenpolitik des Wilhelminischen Deutschland.* Lübeck, 1970.

Zechlin, Egmont. *Die deutsche Politik und die Juden im Ersten Weltkrieg.* Göttingen, 1969.

Ziekursch, Johannes. *Politische Geschichte des neuen deutschen Kaiserreiches.* 3 vols. Frankfurt a. M., 1930.

Zmarzlik, Hans-Günter. "Der Antisemitismus im Zweiten Reich." *Geschichte in Wissenschaft und Unterricht* 14 (May 1963): 273–86.

———. "Der Sozialdarwinismus in Deutschland als geschichtliches Problem." *Vierteljahrsheft für Zeitgeschichte* 11 (1963): 246–73.

Zucker, Stanley. "Ludwig Bamberger and the Rise of Anti-Semitism in Germany, 1848–1893." *Central European History* 3 (December 1970): 332–52.

Index

325